Washington and the World
2001-2005

Llewellyn King

Copyright © 2006 by
University Press of America,® Inc.
4501 Forbes Boulevard
Suite 200
Lanham, Maryland 20706
UPA Acquisitions Department (301) 459-3366

PO Box 317
Oxford
OX2 9RU, UK

Library of Congress Control Number: 2006926772
ISBN-13: 978-0-7618-3490-8 (paperback : alk. paper)
ISBN-10: 0-7618-3490-7 (paperback : alk. paper)

Contents

Foreword

The years 2001-2005 have been among the most momentous of any in the modern history of the United States. Millions of words have been written and spoken about them. But no one has covered the events of these years more intently or interpreted them more incisively than syndicated columnist Llewellyn King, White House correspondent, host of the nationally televised talk show, "White House Chronicle," and for more than three decades one of the leading journalists of the nation's capital.

In this enlightening and entertaining volume of his columns and commentaries, King offers us a living history of the times we have so recently lived through, helping us to understand the motives and missteps of the key players and the consequences of their actions. He traces the evolution of the Bush presidency, the impact of the 9/11 tragedy, the wars and nation-building in Afghanistan and Iraq, the divided loyalties of Europe, and the articulate stoicism of America's closest ally, Tony Blair.

Though based in Washington, King succeeds in bringing the outside world of this period into our living rooms and lets us in on some of its secrets. He introduces us to some of its most colorful heroes as well as its basest villains. Born in Bulawayo in what is now Zimbabwe, where he began his reporting career for Time magazine, King makes no secret of his love for Africa and its people, and is withering in his depiction of the murderous dictator Robert Mugabe, the Saddam Hussein of Africa, and the hell-on-earth he has created for the gentle, once prosperous and productive people of Zimbabwe, whose idyllic climate and rich soil made their country the breadbasket of Africa, but whose economy now lies in ruins while its people starve.

As the reader quickly discovers, King remains first and foremost a sharp-eyed reporter with a unique ability to place developments in a broader perspective. He was the first, for example, to report on Russia's emerging policy of using its vast natural gas reserves as a new diplomatic weapon to increase its control over neighboring countries—a development noticed only many months later by the world's mainstream media and ultimately confirmed as official policy by Vladimir Putin's top economic adviser, Andrei Illarionov, who resigned in protest as the year 2005 was drawing to a close. King was also the first American journalist to reveal the close ties between the then Iraqi exile leader Ahmed Chalabi and the revolutionary leaders of Iran.

These essays also take us to Ireland, another land close to King's heart, where in contrast to the politically correct reporting on the wonders of Ireland's economic miracle, he divines the underlying unhappiness of many Irish over what rampant economic development and Europeanization is doing to their country, their countryside and their cherished way of life. You will also find here some surprising insights on the frequently ignored human side of people like Kenneth Lay, the much vilified former chief executive of Enron, whom King knew well.

Whether he is accompanying the President on a trip abroad or traveling alone to a place of interest, King has a reporter's eye for the detail that reveals the whole, a romantic's excitement on the discovery of unexpected treasures, a humanitarian's concern for the poor and marginalized, and an instinctive disdain for the political grandstanding and deceptions so often found in the corridors of power, whether in Washington or London, Brussels or Harare.

King guides us through these often painful years with a sure-footed understanding and a delightful eye for the absurd that makes "Washington and the World" not only a reassuring trove of wisdom and fascinating insights, but a true pleasure simply to read. It is written with an élan often missing in today's reporting. You will find yourself coming back to savor it again and again.

A. JOHN ADAMS

2001

BUSH CABINET IS A TRIUMPH—IF IT BEHAVES

If the Cabinet were a dinner party, George W. Bush would have a winner on his hands. So diverse. So accomplished. So skillfully balanced.

All that would remain for the president-elect would be the seating plan. Would he, for example, sit Colin Powell next to Linda Chavez, or might that be risking it? How about Christie Todd Whitman as a dinner companion for John Ashcroft? Would he tactfully suggest to the guests that affirmative action, religion, and abortion are not subjects to discuss?

Nonetheless, President-elect Bush or Vice President-elect Dick Cheney have performed a political miracle in assembling a Cabinet that has silenced the Democrats and left the civil rights movement, the trade unions, and the women's groups gasping for air. It is a stunning first step, albeit that some feel Donald Rumsfeld is generationally out of touch with the Pentagon, that John Ashcroft is quite the wrong man for attorney general, and that Condoleezza Rice does not know enough of the world outside of Russia and Eastern Europe.

One trade unionist said to me: "Wow. The Democrats have given us Terry McAuliffe, while the Republicans have come up with Colin Powell. We're outclassed."

Certainly, the permanent opposition in Washington to the Republicans has been unable to land a glove on the new Cabinet—beyond pounding at Ashcroft. The question now is how will this eclectic group work together, and to what extent will they be directed by the White House, and by whom?

Bush has made a point of being a delegator—a strong hint that the new administration will aim for Cabinet government rather than central direction by the commander in chief. Historically, this has not been very effective, as each Cabinet secretary is wont to make his or her own policy and to act as a bunch of unruly barons in feudal England.

Republican circles are talking of corporate governance, with the president as chairman of the board and the members of the Cabinet acting as vice presidents. This would leave Bush free to be, well, Bush.

More likely, it will lead to trouble to Bush close to home. Cheney is not a delegator and knows the pitfalls of giving the Cabinet a loose rein—that this leads to fiefdoms and internecine war.

Then there is the matter of Andrew Card, the designated chief of staff. Will he be overwhelmed by the tough customers in the Cabinet such as Ashcroft, Powell and Chavez?

And the biggest question of all: How will Card interface with Cheney? Bill Clinton gave Al Gore the largest role any vice president has ever had. But Cheney is coming to office with the largest role that any vice president-elect has ever had. Nearly all of the Cabinet would appear to be Cheney picks and to owe their new stature to the vice president rather than to the president.

Then there is the matter of political incest. Many of the Cabinet had served together, or for each other, in earlier administrations. Only two of the new Cabinet members are certifiably Bush loyalists: Rod Paige and Don Evans. Sometimes it is not who you know, but when you knew them.

In his shining new Cabinet, the president is the outsider. To effectively control the Cabinet, Bush will need to get to know them. He will also need to lay down ground rules to overcome the clash of doctrines. It will be a wobbly administration if Powell is practicing affirmative action at the State Department, while Chavez is stamping it out at Labor. Or if Whitman is publicly supporting a woman's right to choose, while Ashcroft is preparing a brief to overturn late-term abortion.

And, of course, there is the ever delicate relationship between the national security adviser and the secretary of state. Bush is comfortable with Rice and Powell is very comfortable with himself. He is, after all, a retired four-star general—and four-star generals have a bad history of taking advice from less-accomplished civilians.

Having delegated—and made a point of delegating—Bush, within six months, will have to surreptitiously redefine delegation and tell the Cabinet that there is a team and that they are on it. He may also want to back off the corporate analogy. After all, the one thing he has promised is a reduction in the government's revenue stream—a very uncorporate thing to do.

January 2, 2001

WORLD AFFAIRS CROWDING IN ON BUSH'S AGENDA

The honeymoon of George W. Bush as president ended last week. It was a wake up week. After a more or less successful visit with Mexican President Vicente Fox the previous week, less affable foreign leaders began to crowd in on Bush's space.

Although Bush was happy touring the country pushing education, the aftermath of escalated bombing in Iraq took its toll.

Specifically, a range of countries told the administration that they were not amused. These were all, in a sense, allies or near friends and included France, Saudi Arabia and Russia.

Clearly, the administration has increased the stakes for itself in the Middle East—and it may have done so without a clear idea of what is to come.

It is not being helped by its belligerent friends in the Washington think tanks. They are urging the president, and advising the public, that it is time to get tough with Saddam Hussein in a way that former President Clinton and his administration failed to do. The fact is that there is no strategy on what to do about Saddam without annoying critical allies—and even if we were prepared to pay this price, there is still no guarantee that he can be removed from office. Or if he is removed from office, that he will be replaced by a friendly regime.

It is easy to make noises in a think tank and more difficult, and dangerous, to do so in the White House. But Bush has made noises and now has to devise a strategy that placates his friends in the Middle East and his doubters in Europe, while appeasing the extremes in his administration and Republican zealots outside of it. Welcome to realpolitik, Mr. President.

However, the new administration's foreign woes are not confined to Iraq. Bush, for example, failed to get a commitment from British Prime Minister Tony Blair to support his national missile defense plan, and the administration is facing a real crisis in the collapse of the Turkish lira.

Bush and his advisers have been adamant in their opposition to "bailouts," but they may yet have to do something dramatic to save Turkey. Turkey, a Muslim country and a key member of NATO, is of critical importance to the maintenance of what stability there is in that region and to the economic well-being of its neighbors. It is one thing when campaigning for office to take a hard line on countries that get into economic difficulties. It is another, when you are in power, to see such a country implode and take down other countries with it. If the new treasury secretary, Paul O'Neill, does not understand the stakes, he should be reminded of how dramatically Thailand took down all of Asia, with serious consequences for the global economy.

As Secretary of State Colin Powell trudges around the Middle East, he will hear clearly that the fear of Saddam, which prevailed 10 years ago, has metamorphosed into a fear that the United States will push its friends in the region too far.

The wisdom in Washington is that Saudi Arabia lives in fear of Saddam. The Saudis live in fear but at present that fear is not of the Iraqi leader, but of Muslim fundamentalists who have designs on the Saudi kingdom. To bolster its Muslim standing, Saudi Arabia is likely to take a hard line on oil pricing and even to curtail its oil production. The Saudi royal family may be well-disposed toward the United States, but its loyalties are to itself and its survival, which is always precarious.

No wonder Powell looked ashen when he left Washington for an unenviable tour of the Middle East.

Tough talk in Washington can play badly abroad. Because of the dependence on Middle East oil, Powell will be at lengths to mollify the Saudis even as the president, goaded by his friends in and out of the administration, antagonizes them.

The Arab World is in an ugly mood since the election of Ariel Sharon in Israel and the collapse of the peace process. The Arabs feel that the United States is once again playing favorites with Israel and has turned away from their cause. This intensifies their sense of betrayal, their admiration for Saddam, and their desire to be associated with the *intifada* in some way.

Europe is especially sensitive to this deteriorating situation. But outside of the State Department, the new world fragility is not being recognized in Washington. Friends of the administration are still euphoric about having a Republican in the White House and are oblivious to the spreading anti-Americanism in the Middle East and much of Europe. The failure of Blair and Bush to come to some positive accords, and of Bush to understand European anxiety, has not played well across the globe.

To be fair, Europeans were predisposed to expect to worst of Bush. However, the first weeks of his administration have done nothing to reassure them.

At home, the new president is about to discover just how self-interested Congress can be. His own party will be analyzing his budget proposals with an eye to how they will play in the election of 2002. If Congress feels that popular local programs are to be starved of funds to pay for a tax-cut, beef up the military, supplement education, and create a missile-defense system, they make take up arms against their president.

These are the first difficult weeks of this administration, and Bush will have to do more than spread around nicknames and belabor the charm offensive. Congress, like many overseas, will enjoy the charm only when they are getting their way.

As is so often the case, international affairs are intruding on a president when he wants to marshal all of his resources to achieve a domestic objective.

February 27, 2001

IT IS THE WINTER OF DEMOCRATIC DISCONTENT

The Democrats are having a terrible time of it. Worse than they should be having, considering their strength in Congress and their popularity in the nation.

The first cause of their discomfort is the seeming leadership vacuum—seeming because public attention is on the wrong players in the party. There is Bill Clinton preoccupying the media; Hillary Clinton getting undue attention; and by association Terry McAuliffe, at the Democratic National Committee, is radioactive, too.

Tom Daschle, the minority leader in the Senate, is robbed of his authority by these distractions. Daschle is ready to lead a charge and to rally the Democrats, but he cannot be heard, and therefore there is no sense among the Democrats that they have a leader in the Senate.

This is absurd, as Democrats control half the seats in a body that is less ideological than the House. Daschle's Democrats should be able to extract from the administration concessions across the board, but they are so dispirited they forget how really strong they are.

House Minority Leader Dick Gephardt is, compared to Daschle, in worse shape. This is partly because the House is not a consensual body, partly because House Republicans are more doctrinaire, and partly because Gephardt himself is the face of yesterday's party. He has wanted to be speaker, he has wanted to be president, he has championed unpopular causes. And now there is something tired about his political voice. The Democrats might want to think of finding a new leader in the House: an untrammeled person who can take the battle to the Republicans.

Then there is the sheer skill with which the Republicans and the new administration have demolished many sound Democratic arguments. They have succeeded in dismissing the media as "liberal," the Democrats as spendthrifts, and they have painted the Democrats as exponents of class warfare.

Additionally, for good measure, the Republicans like to suggest that the all the Democrats in Congress are hopeless Clinton acolytes.

Of course, Republicans are standing truth on its head with some of these charges, but they cannot be faulted for political savvy. Take two of the Republican positions:

1. They push the tax cut in part on the flimsy logic that if it is not enacted, the Democrats will spend the money. In the last Congress, Republicans worked cheek-by-jowl with Democrats in the pork barrel. You could not tell party affiliation from the hind ends of the guzzling porkers.

2. Class warfare may well be going on, but not in the way the Republicans characterize it. A party of rich men and women, represented by a Cabinet of millionaires, is indeed waging war against labor, social programs, the environment, and other causes. Yet the Republicans have finessed the argument to cast the Democrats as the aggressors.

The political skill which the Bush administration and its allies in Congress have exhibited is awesome. Leaving alone the merits or otherwise of the tax-cut, the daring strategy of trying to pass the tax-cut before the budget is breathtaking. In New York, they call it chutzpah. It is a case of cutting the cloth before the customer has been measured for the suit. If it does not fit, the customer will have to lose weight.

However, the Bush administration cannot be hated for doing what it said it would do and seizing on the Democratic disorder to drive for victory. That is what politics is about, and that is how the game is played.

In the fiercely Republican magazine, *Insight*, a writer takes the Republican tactic of hanging the Democrats with their own petards a step further. Jennifer Hickey states: "With an eye toward 2002, Democrats suddenly turned their backs on bipartisan civility and returned to their vituperous strategies of racial and class warfare." Wow.

That after the House Ways and Means Committee reported out enabling legislation for the $1.6 trillion tax cut with very little discussion and no consultation with the Democrats. You see how the Republicans are doing it—and getting away with it.

And get away with it they will, until such time as the Democrats can find and articulate, passionate spokesperson who can turn Republican arguments back on Republicans with the same mastery that Republicans are turning Democratic arguments back on Democrats.

The approach of 2002 should embolden the Democrats and they should implore their former president to go abroad, possibly to India, or some country where communications are poor, and do good works there.

The Bush administration has started well, has a good Cabinet, and is enjoying the momentum of newness coupled with the organizational skill that has marked its first days in office. It is to be expected. But politics is not a static undertaking and there are chinks in the Republican armor, not the least of which is the limitations of the president himself. With the first crisis, the Democrats will be heard from again.

And next year, who knows, the Democrats may have their day again. That is, if they can unite and go from their reactive stance to a proactive one.

Meanwhile, one might ponder why the Republicans are doing so well at landing blows on the Democrats, while the Democrats have not laid a glove on the new administration and Republicans in Congress.

The new politics is the politics of kleptomania: Find out what is working for your opponents and steal it. British Prime Minister Tony Blair did it to the Conservative Party and Bill Clinton did it to the Republicans. Come to think of it, boxing is not the right analogy for politics. The martial arts of the East, where you leverage your opponent's strength, are more fitting.

March 6, 2001

ENERGY CRISIS AGAIN REARS ITS UGLY HEAD

While we are preoccupied with tax-cutting, campaign finance reform and education restructuring, the United States is heading into a dire emergency this summer: An emergency that will afflict the economy and negate present attempts to resuscitate it.

This summer we will be into the largest energy crisis since the 1970s, and there is no quick fix. At a conference convened by the U.S. Chamber of Commerce in Washington this week, speakers from across the country, and across the energy industries, described the coming crisis in stark tones. There were no maybes. There will be shortages of gas, refined petroleum products, and electricity. In California, New York, and possibly elsewhere, blackouts will be a regular occurrence if temperatures are not exceptionally cool.

What makes the situation particularly bleak is that there are no quick fixes in sight. Refineries are operating at near capacity, and gas pipelines and electric lines will also be fully charged. The temptation to blame OPEC, or electric deregulation, will be strong, but the problem has been decades in the making and it will take years to restore the energy supply to normal.

As Vice President Cheney and his advisers seek to hammer out a national energy policy, they will be confronted with an immediate crisis which they can tweak but cannot resolve. The villain, for once, is not OPEC but the cumulative effect of public resistence to new refineries, new power plants, new transmission lines, and new pipelines.

The national energy supply has been so dependable, so efficient, so pervasive that the public has come to believe in its infinite elasticity. The crisis in California this winter was the first domino of many which may fall across the nation this summer. We got here by increasing the demand for all energy sources without increasing supply. What is more, the markets with the coercion of the government, have shielded consumers from price signals which would have stimulated conservation and warned off an impending crisis.

Nearly 10 years of economic boom, the switch in new electric generating from coal and nuclear to natural gas and special gasoline formulations have all played a role. If there is anything that should worry the administration, it is this impending energy shortfall.

We know from the 1970s that high prices for oil and gas affect not only their direct use, but indirectly thousands of products which rely on natural gas and oil as a feedstock.

Fertilizers, pharmaceuticals, chemicals, and rubber are in difficulty already because of high feedstock costs. There is fear in these industries that manufacturing will go offshore, where feedstocks are available and more reasonably priced. This is especially true of industries dependent on natural gas.

The Cheney team can, with little effort, produce a long-term energy policy. Immediate crisis management will be more difficult. There are already signals that the administration understands the implicit dangers in moving too much electricity generation to natural gas. And it can endeavor to reverse this trend by extending its patronage to coal—but with an environmental price.

Electricity now becomes a villain because it is sucking up more and more natural gas while coal languishes, and the power source that hardly dare speak its name—nuclear—is frozen out.

In the short term, the administration has to come up with a crisis management package to ease the nation through the coming summer. In the long term, it has to divert utilities from the onward rush to natural gas and back to coal and nuclear. The burning of more coal is an environmental tradeoff and semantics like "clean-coal technology" will not hide the difficulties of burning coal, even with state-of-the-art pollution controls.

Nuclear is another matter. The nuclear problem is entirely one of public acceptance and the arguments against nuclear power are so asymmetrical as to be illogical.

Nuclear aircraft carriers circle the globe, and nuclear submarines lurk in all the oceans. Nuclear disarmament goes forth apace. These activities produce nuclear waste, which will have to be contained and stored, but there is no public outcry. The very mention of a nuclear power plant and nuclear waste is on every activist's lips.

Yet the case for nuclear gets stronger, not weaker. There are no greenhouse gases whatsoever from nuclear power. And the 103 reactors now producing power in this country are doing so cheaply, safely and reliably.

We have much to be grateful to the environmental movement for, but its blind spot has been the benign benefits of nuclear as opposed to the environmental aggravation caused by all fossil fuels, even natural gas. This aggravation varies from fossil fuel to fossil fuel, but it is there always.

Nuclear waste from power plants disturbs the conscience because it is long-lived. But there is no logic in not sending it to the same disposal facilities where the military waste will have to end up. Compared to all other means of generating electricity, nuclear electricity is the greenest. Hydrodams disturb habitat and change watersheds. Windmills deface the countryside, are a liability to birds and produce, when all is said and done, very little electricity. Direct solar power is inherently limited by the vagaries of the sun and is, at best, supplemental. There is no way that any solar technology can be regarded as a primary source of electricity.

For this summer, the Bush administration will have to seek emergency powers to abrogate a number of environmental rules to allow all power plants and refineries to operate at their highest efficiency—with an environmental price.

In general, there are no simple solutions to complex problems—until, that is, the problems have become so intractable that they are amenable only to simple solutions. Of course in this extreme, a lot of niceties are trodden under foot. The Cheney team will want to look at wide-open throttles in the short term and sensible, proven technologies, nuclear in particular, in the long term. We cannot put the entire burden of electric production on natural gas.

Finally, the administration is going to have to push for something else that is not popular: additional refineries. For good measure, it will have to cloak its actions in the rhetoric of conservation and solar power. Higher prices will give us conservation. And solar power will become a serious contributor if and when we learn to store electricity.

March 20, 2001

THE CHINA CRISIS AND HOW WE SET OURSELVES UP

If the Bush administration had approached its plans for an anti-ballistic missile defense shield with less fanfare, if it had not renounced the Kyoto climate change talks out of hand, if its senior officials had not been as intemperate in their remarks about China, and if it had not expelled 50 Russian diplomats on spying charges, it is just possible that it would not be embroiled in its first international crisis.

But the administration is in a crisis over our surveillance aircraft now sitting on Hainan island in the South China Sea. Of course, nobody knows whether the Chinese would have chosen to blow up this incident. But there is a possibility that if the Bush administration had declared itself through its actions to be a good international citizen rather than a tough one, then the matter would have been resolved with apologies all around.

The problem is that the administration has talked globalization while thinking isolation. It has fallen into the trap of antagonizing its friends and predetermining its foes, before there is a need for that finding. It has long been a Republican belief that the world takes unfair advantage of the United States, and that all that has been required was a "tough" Republican president to redress the situation. In reality, the world is complex and dangerous. And it is unwise to antagonize on principle, or to believe that you can go it alone.

The administration has shown no interest in diplomacy, and has restricted the room for maneuver of Secretary of State Colin Powell.

Apart from anti-ballistic missile defense, Kyoto, remarks about China, and Russian spies, the administration has also come down on the Europeans for their plans for a rapid-reaction force, upset them over our Balkan commitment; shut the door on any possibility of an evolutionary change in Cuba; undone the progress made in reforming North Korea; and withdrawn our forceful moral participation in the Middle East and Northern Ireland. Yet, it talks about globalization.

All of this has caused much of the world to think that there is a bully in the White House: a spoiled child of a president who will only play the game according to his own rules. This works to a limited extent, but unravels when you need friends and allies and diplomatic initiatives. It is not so much that what the fledgling Bush administration has sought is wrong, but that it has done so by intemperate means.

It has, in effect, scorned diplomacy and protocol in favor of fiat and dictum. Now comes a genuine diplomatic crisis, and the administration is hoist on its own petard.

It is time for Powell to speak up in the councils of the administration to protect our diplomatic influence; to urge the soft words which should go with carrying a big stick; and to persuade his president that the feelings of other nations need to be respected—even when we disagree with those nations.

At this time, the United States is headed for a kind of isolation when it is still spread around the world. It is using the language of campaigns in the pursuit of international objectives. A bad move.

That the United States is rich and powerful and pervasive is a given around the globe. And because of that, there is no gain in giving the world the back of its hand. We are dependent on foreign sources of oil, overseas markets, and an abiding cooperation with Europe. To wage an ideological war with our friends and to cast China in the role of the former Soviet Union achieves nothing. It can only serve to paint us as a pariah in the world and to further convince China that we wish it harm.

It is possible that in 25 years, China will be a competing global power with the United States—and a belligerent one, at that. Much depends on our ability to manipulate Chinese aspirations, not assault them.

The Bush administration had hoped that it would come to power and, through simplistic virtue, establish the United States' dominance in the world. Instead, it may only establish the United States' isolation in the world through simplistic misunderstanding of the world. The smaller, globalized world is Hegelian in nature, as bound together diplomatically as it is economically.

After the resolution of the current crisis, the administration needs to do some deep thinking on how to influence the world without deriding its institutions, hectoring its recalcitrants, and being preoccupied with the old shibboleths of isolationist Republicanism.

The administration needs to resist the temptation is to cast nations we disagree with into the outer darkness though sanctions, isolation, and technological starvation. What we do not need is another Iraq or Afghanistan. Nations cast into the outer darkness get up to no good in the dark, and do not capitulate to our desires.

April 3, 2001

THE FIRST 100 DAYS: SLIPS BUT NO DISASTERS

One hundred-day fever is raging in Washington. Franklin D. Roosevelt gave us the tradition of measuring the first 100 days of a presidency. And although everyone denounces this as arbitrary, everyone does it.

The Bush administration will probably welcome it—not just because they are great believers in testing, but because President George W. Bush will come through his first 100 days beating expectations. As former White House press secretary Joe Lockhart pointed out recently, low expectations have been a godsend to the new administration.

They also have been helped by the implosion of the Democratic Party—a party which has lost faith in what it stands for and has found no new belief, according to Robert Reich, the most coherent voice of liberalism writing and broadcasting today.

Despite these important gifts in Bush's first 100 days, there are signs that the administration is running into trouble and that the president is leading from behind his advisers. This would probably be all right, except that these advisers are clearly going in different directions, confusing our allies and, at times, Bush appointees.

During the campaign, stalwart Republicans said it did not matter that Bush was not a man for all seasons, that good advisers would compensate in foreign policy, the environment, and the military. Well, it seems as though the advisers are as divided as the Senate.

There will, no doubt, be a special place in the history books for those who prevailed upon Bush to abandon the Kyoto process and, in so doing, to needlessly upset the rest of the world. It was not exactly a threat to our way of life: The Senate had already rejected the treaty—it was only a framework for talking. But those who saw it as the work of the previous administration prevailed upon Bush to offend our friends, annoy our enemies, and help the fund-raising of environmental groups.

In the China crisis, the cooler heads, presumably led by Secretary of State Colin Powell, overcame those who will never forget Munich, nor probably learn from it. It is an historic reference wholly outside of context, and yet very popular in right-wing circles. The problem for the administration with China begins now: It did not end with the return of our surveillance crew.

The choices faced by Bush are to get tough now and hope for rapprochement later, or to continue the hated Clinton policy of "constructive engagement." Neither is clearly a winning strategy. But they are strategies.

Because of the divisions in the administration, we are likely to see a little of each—and neither strategy will work if it is adulterated. Yet there are signs Bush will, when the pressure mounts, seek a middle course even though that is a poor reaction to an international crisis.

Bush has been paddling wildly to the middle, after his disastrous beginnings in environmental policy. Although the larger of the errors may be over carbon emissions and the Kyoto protocol, the one which has sent him fleeing to midstream is arsenic in drinking water. This was handled ineptly and the trap sprung by the outgoing Clinton administration snapped shut on the Bush administration. That the Clinton standards were unachievable and excessively severe does not matter. It is a political disaster to tell people that a little arsenic is good for them. Arsenic is, after all, the one poison that every man, woman and child has heard of.

In trying to repair the damage, the Bush administration has signed the toxic chemical treaty. But this action is not enough to ameliorate the damage that has been done to his presidency: In the first 100 days, Bush has established himself as uncaring about the environment. No matter what actions he takes from now on, the perception is there. And the environmental movement will do everything it can to keep that perception alive. Environmental organizations have always done better when they have Republicans to attack than when they have Democrats to defend.

Then there are Bush's problems of his own creation with the military. He believes, or he says he believes, that morale in the military is very low. In the campaign, he blamed this on lack of spending, poor wages and living conditions, and a lack of funds for readiness.

Now that he has decided against a supplementary budget request for the military, he has shifted the blame for the real or imagined crisis in morale to our foreign commitments. He was at it again over the weekend, saying morale is low because the military is stretched with too many commitments abroad. This is probably only true of National Guard units which have been called up for long periods. But—a dirty little secret—the regular forces like to serve abroad. That is what they see their job as and that is what they were recruited to do.

Then there is the messy business of the tax-cut. This may be the one part of the Bush agenda that owes nothing to advisers. It is, by all accounts, his own—the

centerpiece to what George W. Bush really believes America needs. It is something that his party wants to give to him simply because he wants it, not because
they believe in it or that it will help get us out of recession. Republican lawmakers are just as fond of taxing and spending as their Democratic counterparts—it is
just that they want to spend on different things, including the military.

There is a third bonus that Bush is enjoying along with lowered expectations
and Democratic demoralization: The working press at the White House likes
George W. Bush. His hokey, chummy way goes down well with reporters. They
also have fallen in love with Laura Bush because she is not like Hillary Clinton
and because they have wives, mothers, and sisters at home who are very like her.
Hillary Clinton made good copy, but she was not liked.

In all, the Bush administration has gotten off to a halfway decent start, but
it may yet founder on the divisions within it. The no-news, button-down,
hermetically-sealed strategy that has worked through the first 100 days will come
unstuck with the first defections from the administration. The first staffers who
bail out will tell tales of how decisions were made, who were at each others'
throats, and who had the president's ear and for how long.

If you think that the loyal insiders are not keeping diaries, noting down times
and conversations, then you do not understand political life in the age of the book
deal.

April 24, 2001

BIG BILL GATES DISPENSES WISDOM, WIT AND DOLLARS

He has the demeanor of a retired British Army officer: tall and straight. His charm
has been honed in the practice of law in the provinces, where the style of the
lawyer is as important as the niceties of the law. At 6 feet 7 inches, he has the platform to dispense avuncular wisdom and good humor—and he uses it to effect.

This Western lawman came to Washington last week to dispense patriotism, humanity, and to argue for the retention of the estate tax. You might think that he and
his family had nothing to pass on to future generations. But you would be wrong.
This distinguished proselytizer, aged 75, is none other than Bill Gates Sr., father
of the richest man in the nation, nay, the world on some days.

Gates sees paying the estate tax—known to Republicans, who are seeking its repeal, as the "death tax"—as the patriotic duty of those fortunate enough to be born
in the United States and to accumulate wealth in part due to that initial good luck
in life. To him, it is an act of thanks for the opportunities afforded by the United
States and the contributions made to great fortunes by the conditions which prevail here.

Gates said: "To me, clearly, as you think about people's wealth . . . the principal reason for their success, for this accumulation, is not just a function of their
brains, or of their luck, or of their effort. It's a function of having been born in this

place, where schools are subsidized; a place where there is an orderly market; a place where research is subsidized; a place where the ingredients of one's success are largely to be attributed to others through taxes."

Gates heads the Bill and Melinda Gates Foundation, the largest in the world, with assets of $23 billion. Dick Ryan, president of the National Press Club, where Gates spoke last week, told the audience that by law, Gates had to give away $3 million a day. And Gates told his audience that he was "having a good time" doing it.

Not only does Gates think it is wrong to repeal the estate tax—he advocates some minor modifications—but he claims to have developed a liking for the tax over many years. "I practiced law for 40 years in the course of which, I developed some affection for this tax. I saw its impact on people, close and personal."

However, Gates said: "The proponents of repeal of the estate tax have really done a wonderful job of creating this illusion of the tax which is a burden to everyone. It is certainly not a burden to everyone. Some argue that the estate-tax system is a major gift to society, and that 98 percent of people don't pay it at all. . . . It's a progressive tax. My sense is that the argument about the validity of progressive taxation is over. I think that the people of this country believe in progressive taxation, and this tax is the purest example of good, progressive taxation."

Among his other points, Gates stressed the importance of society as a whole, where opportunity is equal and where the progeny of the wealthy do not get an undeserved head start. "Part of the argument about the estate tax, ever since it was imposed, is the issue of attempting to create a society in which there is not an aristocracy of wealth . . . I think that most of you would appreciate the inevitable multiplication of large estates in this country of ours if they are not interrupted by a significant transfer tax."

Gates said these estates would grow and grow, increasing the opportunity "for excessive power in the hands of a limited number," and presenting a significant danger for our society. "I don't think we would like to have a country in which there are many, many families able to hoard billions of dollars," he said.

In the question period Gates, as a foundation head, revealed himself to be a globalist and a liberal, in the classic sense of that abused word. When a questioner asked why the foundation gave money for vaccines and nutrition in the Third World, while seemingly ignoring domestic problems, Gates responded: "When my daughter-in-law, Melinda, talks about what we are doing with the foundation money, she always asks the question: 'Does it matter where a child dies?' We don't think so. The problem is enormous, and the disparity is unconscionable. Three million kids die every year from diseases for which vaccines already exist."

"Come on, what's wrong with spending money to change those numbers?" he asked. " I mean, in this country, we have the National Institutes of Health; we have got philanthropy all over the place dealing with local issues. Do we demean that? No, we do not. . . . If there is a serious problem in the world, it is the incredible disparity in the health of kids: kids who had nothing to do with where they ended up. They live beside a river that is full of guinea worms, or they live in a country that cannot figure out what to do with the AIDS problem. And now they are orphans. I am pretty ready to defend that set of decisions."

God made Gates Sr. tall and gracious, but it is his son who has made him famous and into one of the great paymasters of charity in the world. So the questions about the founder of Microsoft are always present. And daddy is ready to answer them. The de rigeur question last week was how did Gates and his wife feel about their son dropping out of Harvard University? "It was very troublesome to his mother. I was more accepting of it. But we were concerned about it and, you know, still in his [Bill Gates Jr.] office, he has a plaque there. All of us have our law degrees or whatever, and he has got his high school diploma."

It is widely accepted in Washington that Bill Gates Jr. mishandled the Justice Department's lawsuit against Microsoft, and that he did not enhance his cause in personal appearances. He should have sent in dad: Microsoft-sized a charmer.

May 15, 2001

THE ENERGY PLAN: THAT OLD FEELING AGAIN

Two cheers, please, for President Bush's national energy plan. One cheer because it is finally out, and one cheer because of its assessment of the dilemma. A third cheer has to be withheld because there is no new idea in the document released Thursday. And there is no cohesive plan of action that could be the basis for policy.

The report, which looks as though it was prepared by people whose regular work is putting together corporate annual reports, replete with emotive pictures, elegant charts and simple maps, says nice things about every source of energy, and is even generous to conservation. However, it is short on goals, targets and mechanisms. And Bush, in recent days, has sounded like a man who has discovered the size of the problem and is praying for the discovery of a technological solution.

The progression of administration thinking, now revealed in the report of the National Energy Policy Development Group, shows logical transformation as the facts about energy supply have emerged from the study. It is as though its authors studied the sky for four months and returned to announce: "The sun rises in the East and sets in the West."

Clearly, there was an incipient belief when the administration came to town that if the yoke of regulation were lifted from energy producers, the stuff would flow in abundance. Instead, they have found that the politics of energy are brutal and that the prospects of increasing supply are limited.

It has long been part of the Texas view of the world that there is plenty of oil and gas in the ground, which goes untapped because of government interference and environmental intransigence. The National Energy Policy Development Group, chaired by Vice President Dick Cheney, with Andrew Lundquist as staff director, seems to have found this not to be so. Mind, it does not say so in so many words. But the smorgasbord of proposals—105 in all—is testimony in itself to the size of the problem and the fallacy that regulation created it.

Overall, Lundquist and his team have clearly labored hard and have been open-minded in most of their treatment of inputs. Left to their own devices, they might not have been as enthusiastic about renewable energy and conservation. But given the administration's predisposition towards fossil fuels and nuclear energy, it is a fair document and its assessments seek to be honest.

There is nothing new in it because the energy picture changes slowly. Many of its passages could have been written for earlier studies; some of it is the language of the Carter administration; the conclusions are the conclusions of the Ford and Nixon administrations, with changes that reflect modest alternations in reality over the years. For example, electricity transmission is a new crisis, but gas transmission is not. Emphasis on coal and nuclear energy were favored both in the Ford and Nixon administrations. And conservation and renewable energy were darlings of Jimmy Carter. The largest change, in reality, is the new dependence on natural gas for electric generation.

All presidents since Nixon have hoped that there would be technological breakthroughs that would change the energy equation. There have been breakthroughs, but they have not altered the equation by as much as previous presidents had hoped.

The Bush administration is spiritually close to the Reagan administration. But that administration left energy policy to the market and had the good luck to face no energy crisis. President Clinton was even luckier. For almost all of his eight years in office, energy prices were historically low and he was able to indulge in energy whimsy for the first six years of his administration. He was able to cold-shoulder nuclear and to promote solar because there was some equilibrium in the markets. It is no coincidence that the new report sounds like those of the 1970s, and the emphasis on new supply and new science reprises that decade.

My impression is that this is a document of some anguish; that it was put together by an administration that believed that there were relatively simple solutions to what are enormously difficult political and supply problems. In its infancy, the administration relied heavily on the concept of "policy," as if this alone will repair the degraded energy infrastructure.

I think that the emphasis in the report on energy efficiency is timely and has been reached in view of the facts—not as an offering to the environmentalists. I am more suspicious about the administration's position on renewable energy. This appears to be a political add-on to the central thrusts of its policies. And I think the administration has reason itself to be suspicious of diffuse sources of power, whose principle virtue is that they are culturally appealing, particularly to Democrats.

It is an odd document, in some ways, to issue from an administration that believes as a modus operandi in "focus." Odd, too, that it relies on tax incentives, where overall these have not been effective in incubating major new power sources. Subsidies are the way of the government diverting the market surreptitiously.

I would rather that the president and his task force had had the moral courage to say: Energy is a national security issue, therefore the government is prepared to directly assert itself to achieve reliable supply. It could do this by indemnifying utilities against the risk of building new nuclear power plants. It could mandate and, if necessary, finance electric transmission lines. And it could force improved fuel-efficiency standards, particularly for automobiles.

The document released Thursday is at odds with the ways that Bush has been governing. It seeks to fix too many extraneous things, and in so doing will aggravate too many constituencies. It is interesting that Texaco and Enron are both moving into the liquefied natural gas business in a big way. This is a clear message that two large and smart companies do not believe that additional drilling will make much difference to the supply of gas domestically, and that coal may not overcome its environmental hurdles. The smart money has spoken.

Focus, Mr. President, focus.

May 22, 2001

BUSH NEEDS TO MASTER THE BULLY PULPIT

The end of Scene I, Act I of the presidency of George W. Bush is drawing to a close, and it is desperate for one thing: a ringing peroration. Bush is doing better than Washington thinks, probably better than the White House believes. And what he needs now is to find his way into the bully pulpit.

Since the days of the ancient Greeks, politicians have been defined by their speech-making. This gives the natural orators an unfair advantage, but the playing field has been more or less leveled by the introduction of professional speech-writers and the TelePrompTer. Bush has no reason to fear the public platform: He should embrace it.

Too many of Bush's speeches are trite, repetitive, cautious and empty. They read as though they were written by a committee and vetted by a focus group. This will never do.

A single speech can transform political stature, correct past mistakes, and inspire loyalty and following. The right speech from the president can intimidate Congress, awake the media, and give ordinary Americans a sense that they have the right man in the White House: a leader.

Clearly, though, Bush has been awed by the task of selling his program articulately himself. His father was ridiculed for his bad syntax, and Bush has been reviled for the same propensity. He should not worry. He reads well in public — a talent not shared by everyone. For example, Tim Russert, the best interviewer on television, stumbles over the shortest script on a TelePrompTer.

Bush should find a subject that lends itself to a great, transcendental speech, hire a speechwriter who can execute it, and go forth and deliver it.

Not only do great speeches nowadays carry global audiences, they are a lot easier to deliver than they were in the Roman Forum, or even the House of Commons until the introduction of amplification.

Because a speech now can be so produced, there really is no excuse for Bush not to sell his programs with more conviction than we have seen.

He may be down in the polls, but Bush can count some real victories. He has mollified the Europeans and, increasingly, he is getting respect in Europe. Particularly, European leaders are glad that he has again endorsed nuclear power. High French, German and Japanese officials have told me that this has been for them the most important aspect of the Bush presidency so far for them. These countries desperately need to come on with new electric generation, and they fear that without American leadership they will be stymied by their own Green parties. Ergo, they are prepared to shrug off their initial annoyance at the U.S.'s abandonment of the Kyoto treaty and are increasingly less worried about the United States building a missile shield—they think it will take decades, anyway.

On his recent European trip, Bush's major foreign policy speech may have been buried by bad timing, and his remarks about Vladimir Putin may have been sophomoric, but they were surprisingly comforting to our allies. The Europeans are now more sure of their ability to talk to Bush—and that he is not a crazy gunslinger from Texas.

Yes, Bush is doing a great job of talking to Aznar, Blair, Chirac, Schroeder, Putin and Koizumi. But he is really falling down on the job of talking to us. If he does not speak up soon, the Republican leadership in the Senate will continue to grouse and grumble, and the Republicans in the House will forget that they are part of the Bush team and concentrate on re-election next year.

Bush does not need to take any more trips, go to any more schools, or give one more photo opportunity. He needs to take his opportunity to make a really good speech to remind his own party, the Democrats, and ourselves that he is the president. After that, he can take his vacation in Texas, and we can go to the beach with the feeling that things are all right. If he does not reverse his fortunes in the only way known in politics, the sense that is already infecting Washington, that Bush is too small for the job, will spread. There is no evidence for that indictment yet. He can stop this decay of his position in 35 minutes of old-fashioned stem-winding.

July 10, 2001

A CONSUMER GUIDE TO POLITICAL CULT CRUISING

I have been aware for years that the *National Review*, the conservative journal founded by William F. Buckley Jr., sponsors an annual cruise on which right-minded people lecture each other on the right things.

What I did not know is that Victor Navasky, publisher of *The Nation*, also sponsors cruises, where the unashamedly liberal can rail against the kinds of people who are on Mr. Buckley's cruise.

I wonder what it is like, this political cult cruising? Do the Buckley people affirm Alger Hiss's guilt? Do the Navasky people assert his innocence?

What is it like to be confined with people of such strong opinions? If you agree with all those present, why go? It must be the quality of the company: and there are certainly some amusing people on both the left and the right. But there are also some prigs. I wonder, for example, does Bill Bennett go on the *National Review* cruise to check on the morality of his companions? Or, if you go on *The Nation* cruise, will there be some awful church lady frowning when you try to knock back a few stiff ones with Christopher Hitchens?

It would seem that the wine and the attire would be better on the MV Buckley than it would be on the MV Navasky. I imagine that there is a dress code—black tie for dinner with the *National Review* boys, and sandals and native costume for *Nation* people; beads, too.

Of course, prayer might be obligatory on the Buckley cruise. But you should be able to get by with a mantra on the Navasky cruise.

You could go very wrong these days in trying to guess at the pastimes of the politically committed. I tend to prefer right-wing meetings because there is plenty to drink and there are cigars. But there is a kind of purity on the left, or I imagine there to be, which I suspect favors beer and a sitar player. I have generally found it hard to get a belt among the extreme liberals, who have a dangerous tendency toward health food and bottled water.

I do not know where the next Buckley cruise is headed, but the Navasky cruise is sailing down the west coast of Mexico. I would hope that the MV Buckley cruises in the Mediterranean and the Black Sea, where there are sophisticated restaurants to which the men of the right can wear their English-tailored clothes. I bet you not one suit with a center vent is seen in Mr. Buckley's company.

The Navasky commune is really rather letting down the side by sailing on the west coast of Mexico. Surely they would be happier in the Caribbean, where the ship could put in at Haiti, Cuba, Venezuela, with a side trip to Nicaragua, every man wearing a *quallavera*.

I should, as a journalist, go on these cruises, but I do not have the temerity. A week of all-right-all-the-time or a week of all-left-all-the-time is more than your correspondent could endure. Hiding in a lifeboat for a week is not fun.

Now if *Vanity Fair* ever puts on a cruise, I might consider it. Better still, I would like to go cruising with the readers of the British magazine, *The Oldie*, who talk about the good times before World War II, the mistake of letting India go, and who can reminisce about taking the mail boat up the Irrawaddy. Instead of talking about Alger Hiss, I know they will be debating the abdication.

August 14, 2001

GET US BACK IN THE AIR, PLEASE, MR. BUSH

The eyes are drying now. But the heart heals slowly, if ever. So America stumbles around in mourning, rage, and longing for vengeance. If President George W. Bush feels these emotions as we do, he would be well advised to keep them in check. As our leader it is his duty to assuage our grief, but also to look out for our larger well-being.

In short, the administration should be seeking vengeance with its left hand not its right. Vengeance will come, those responsible will be rooted out, and we will be more vigilant about terrorism.

However, terrorism—that ultimate bellow of rage from the fanatically obsessed—will never be wholly defeated. Individual zealots without regard for the value of their own lives will always be able to wreak havoc. The British know this in Northern Ireland, the Spanish know this in the Basque country, the Sri Lankans know this in the Tamil-controlled northern sector of the island, and the Turks know it in their struggle with the Kurds.

So the president's first responsibility is not in defeating terrorism but in containing it. His second and overriding responsibility is to restore the nation to normalcy. To do this he needs to get the air traffic flowing again, and quickly. Successive administrations have favored air transportation over surface transportation, and now it is our primary system.

Much of what is going on in airline security today is cosmetic, and probably ineffective against a calculating enemy. Throwing in a federal police force to screen luggage may improve the quality of those inspections, but it will not yield 100 percent security. For that, we have to wait for technology to catch up, so that luggage can be screened effectively and quickly without the human factor.

The president should declare the airlines safe to fly today and to demonstrate it, he should send his close associates visibly on commercial flights. The economy will not recover in a state of immobility. And Bush must get the economy moving, or the terrorists will have won another round.

To get the public back into the skies, the president has to move quickly to moderate the four-hour wait for baggage screening, and to return to making air transport convenient. The price that he and the nation will pay if the airlines remain wounded will be high indeed.

In addition he must mandate the security of cockpits, and the arming of one cabin crew member with stun guns. Ballistic weapons are lethal in the air for everyone.

He must also reopen Washington's Reagan National Airport, maybe with restrictions on private aircraft.

The idea floated by Secretary of Transportation Norman Mineta that flights from Reagan National should land from the south and take off to the south only is nonsense. It would probably reduce the traffic at that airport to one-quarter of its previous level. The prevailing winds in Washington are from the northwest, which means that in any serious wind condition, no flights would operate at Reagan National. As a concession and reasonable precaution, runway 15, for example, should not be used except in extreme weather conditions, as this runway is directly aligned with the Pentagon.

The whole apparatus of flight training and flight certification needs a look, too: something equivalent to a security clearance may now be necessary for anyone who flies. I say this with a heavy heart because I have been a pilot for nearly 30 years, and it is the freedom of the skies that attracts us to aviation—the last frontier where we can take our lives in our own hands. But civilian aircraft, which have always been lethal if mishandled, have now become lethal weapons in the hands of fanatics.

The president must work on making the skies safer, but he must not make them safe by keeping them empty or the country will go from recession into depression. And the hijackers will have won another victory. That cannot stand.

September 18, 2001

IT IS THE END OF THE BEGINNING

Hello, from Vacuum City U.S.A., aka Washington D.C. Like 7,000 other journalists here, I do not know what is going on. We are all writing and regurgitating speculation and scenarios from former generals, CIA personnel and FBI agents.

Anyone who has had anything to do with security or can speculate about potential future attacks by terrorists is in demand to be interviewed, to fill up the op-ed pages and to try to satisfy the public's desire to know and journalism's inability to tell.

James Woolsey, a former director of the CIA, told me that he had 99 requests for interviews from news organizations, plus numerous requests for op-ed pieces.

From academia, think tanks, and federal retirement lists come the experts. They do not know anything either, but they have enough historical knowledge to make their speculation sound informed.

An Irish editor asked me to write a piece. When I told him I did not know anything, he said: "But would you send me 1,200 words?" I sent them and they were published.

Such is the dearth of news in this period of hiatus. Shock, pain, grief, dispossession and anger are ever so gradually giving way to a huge uncertainty.

The Bush administration is sending us no guidance. On the one hand, the president urges us to get back to normal; to take an airplane, to go shopping and go to restaurants. On the other hand, Reagan National Airport remains shuttered, troops have been called up, police forces are on overtime, highways are closed, and helicopters whirr overhead. Even traffic-spotting planes are grounded, as though the government knows of some clear and present danger that it cannot communicate to us.

It is a dreadful situation.

In this issue, my colleague Bill Sammon reports on the agony of the media: to ask is to seem unpatriotic, and not to ask is a dereliction of your duty.

Meanwhile, around Washington, there are signs of serious economic impact—people are being laid off, hotels are empty, some restaurants have failed, and apprehension is in the air.

This week, next week, or the week after, the administration will have to level with us on the size of the threat and what its strategy for the war on terrorism is. The state of vacuum can only produce economic implosion and wear thin the enormous patriotism that has sustained the country in the days since Sept. 11.

Crisis is not a license to keep people perpetually in the dark. We are a free people, prepared to make huge sacrifices to defend freedom. But because of that, we are not a people who trust the dark or believe that things are done better in secret.

There is tremendous sympathy for the burdens on the president and the whole of the nation's security and war apparatus. But the time is coming when we need to be told what is going on and what to expect. If the administration does not open up to the media, and through the media to the people, rumor and disinformation will begin to undermine the national confidence.

Even in the dark days of World War II, Churchill understood the need for a flow of information, even when things were going against Britain. He used the newspaper proprietors to disseminate information. There was propaganda, for sure, but there were also facts. Had the situation in which Britain found itself not been made explicitly clear, had an information vacuum existed, Churchill's great rallying speeches would have had no effect. Had he told the British people that they would have to fight on the beaches and in the streets, this would have sounded very strange if they had not known how dire their situation was.

Churchill was many things—a soldier, a statesman, a politician, a historian. But he was also a journalist. He made his early name with a scoop on the siege of Mafeking in South Africa. Churchill believed in high purpose in government, but he knew it could not be achieved without letting the people in on your plans. As he did not like leaks, he preempted them himself: He briefed the proprietors and top editors of the day, before corrosive rumors and speculation spread. This annoyed his commanders, but kept loyalty high on the home front.

If the administration is to prosecute a war, it must come to terms with the role of information in war; it must take up arms against disinformation and speculation, and the fear that goes with them. The best way to do that is through unrelenting candor.

October 2, 2001

WHAT HAPPENS IF SAUDI ARABIA AND PAKISTAN FALL

Saudi Arabia has been running with the hares and hunting with the hounds since 1973. The fragile kingdom, sitting on top of the largest proven oil reserves on earth, has sought to survive by appeasing its patrons in the West, most notably the United States, while supporting Islamic charities all over the world, including fundamentalists in Pakistan and Afghanistan, as well as funding PLO activities.

The Saudi strategy of being a loyal ally and the banker of Islam moved into a new and dangerous era during the Gulf War. Fearing Iraq's Saddam Hussein, it aligned itself with the United States and allowed U.S. military bases on Saudi soil for the first time. It was a dangerous calculation that has now become the proximate cause of fundamental Islamic rage, because Saudi Arabia is home to the two holiest sites of Islam: Mecca and Medina.

To fundamentalist Muslims, the presence of the U.S. forces defiles their holy land. Many of these fundamentalists have been inculcated with extreme fervor in Islamic schools paid for by the Saudis, in a classical peace of Middle Eastern irony.

Now Middle Eastern scholars in the United States and Europe believe that the days of the Saudi kingdom are numbered. They believe that the kingdom has reached the end of the line in its strategy of pleasing its customers and protectors in the West while financing what have become its detractors in the Middle East.

Students of the region had believed that Saudi Arabia, with its brutal penal code, repression of women and official joylessness, would fall to a liberal revolution. The thinking, until a few years ago, was the modern communications—telephones, faxes and the Internet—would force a liberal evolution in Saudi Arabia. Instead, quite the reverse has occurred. Those very communications links with the outside world have become instead a conduit for fundamentalists' conservative Islamic opinion. And this opinion finds the kingdom wanting in Islamic rigor.

The fundamentalists see the entire Saudi royal family as betraying Islam, corrupt, venal and a puppet of the United States. The royal family's policy of doling out money to Islamic institutions while courting the protection of the United States has inflamed strict Muslim opinion against Saudi Arabia. Its covert protection of some terrorists and financial support have not been enough to keep it from becoming the target of those who see it as hopelessly corrupt, two-faced and out of touch with Islam. They see it as embodying the worst of the West, despite its attempts to buy favor with Islam.

For the United States, and the rest of the world, which depends on Saudi oil production, the growing hostility to the Saudi kingdom may be one of two great crises ahead. The second, but not the least of these looming crises, is the tenuous hold on power of the government of Pakistan and its dictator, Pervez Musharraf. Pakistan is now a nuclear-weapon state with its estimated 45 weapons.

The headaches are these:

1. If there is a revolution in Saudi Arabia, the world's largest reserves of oil would fall into fundamentalist Islamic hands, endangering the economies of the world.
2. If Musharraf is overthrown, for the first time sworn enemies of Israel would have nuclear weapons, changing the balance of power in the region, and threatening any country perceived as anti-Islamic.

Students of the region, who are loath to speak out in public but who are talking with high agitation in private, see some of the greatest foreign-policy challenges of the last 50 years facing the Bush administration in the near future. According to sources, Secretary of State Colin Powell is especially aware of the looming dangers and this understanding has cast him among the more bellicose in the administration as a dove.

Scholars believe that much will depend on Islam's holy month of Ramadan, when Saudi Arabia will host millions of devout Muslims making their pilgrimage to Mecca. Should the pilgrims become inflamed, there is little that the Saudi regime can do to control them. If it were to fire on the pilgrims, all Muslims — fundamentalist and moderate alike — would be in uproar.

It is against this gathering storm that President George W. Bush is prosecuting his war against terrorism. Experts do not believe that he has any alternative, but they do wonder whether the administration understands how extraordinarily fragile the world has become, economically and militarily.

Both a revolution in Saudi Arabia and the overthrow of Musharraf would require Western intervention on a scale not yet contemplated — a seizure of the oil wells in Saudi Arabia and the elimination of Pakistan's nuclear capacity.

The people in the think tanks and universities who are so agitated about the future have two little jokes they repeat grimly: of Musharraf, they say, "dead man walking," and of the Saudi royal family, they say, "dead men walking."

October 16, 2001

THE LAST FRONTIER FOR HUNTERS AND GATHERERS: OIL

At the end of World War II, North Atlantic cod was so plentiful that it was used to make fish meal for fertilizer. The shoals were so large that fishermen said you could walk on them. Every year since, the cod supply has declined and the price has increased. In ocean fishing, as in other things, the days of the hunter-gatherer are numbered.

This is largely recognized and fish, trees and other once abundant natural products are farmed and husbanded.

When it comes to oil and gas, though, hunting and gathering is still the only game. In the United States in 1945, the hunting and gathering took place in Texas and Louisiana. And there was plenty to go around. Today it takes place in climates natural and political that are hostile and dangerous; the Arabian Gulf, the Caspian Sea, Nigeria and Angola. Leaving aside the political problems, these geographic locations alone point to the increasing demand and declining availability of oil and gas in friendly climates.

Add the political dimension and it is clear that the hunter-gatherers of oil and gas are now fishing far from home in deep waters — the only places where the shoals are still something like abundant.

As the world demand for oil continues to increase with its economic development, it is clear that any perturbation could upset the hunters and gatherers of oil and gas and their tenuous trading routes. Even in the world that is friendly and stable, there is the possibility of extinction for most of the supplies in 50 years. In the world we have, interruption can come as suddenly and viciously as the attacks on the World Trade Center and the Pentagon. Of particular concern is the stability of Saudi Arabia, and the integrity of pipelines and tankers bringing the catch of oil from the Caspian Sea to Europe and the United States.

This is a real threat to Western civilization and industrial economies.

And yet, both the Bush administration and Congress seem to believe that with enough financial incentive, the hunter-gatherers of the oil and gas industries can bring home an ever-increasing catch.

If we knew that we were in danger of terrorist attacks before Sept. 11, as many experts and studies predicted, we should be aware today that there will be interruptions in our oil supplies from overseas. We are also just beginning to import liquified natural gas, and in a small way establishing a new vulnerability.

The Bush administration, in its early days, clearly identified the problem. But, to use the fish analogy, its solution was not to husband the resource and to discourage its wasteful use. No, the administration, in the matter of oil and gas, called for more fishermen and encouraged them to catch every last sprat.

The energy bill passed by the House of Representatives (H.R. 4) has as its simple prescription: find more, burn more. Of course, it has other things wrong with it, particularly its lavish generosity to the energy companies.

But it is the bill's fundamental conception that needs to be reexamined. The Senate, if we are to have a bill this year, has an opportunity to redress the excesses of the House version and to change, by a few degrees, the course that the nation has been on in energy consumption. However, Senate Democrats cannot do it by force. They need to do it the old-fashioned political way: They need to cut a deal.

Hard as it will be for Democratic senators such as Jeff Bingaman, chairman of the Senate Energy Committee, and John Kerry to swallow, they need to offer up drilling in the Arctic National Wildlife Refuge as a quid pro quo for really tough conservation rules. In tandem, these actions would tell oil exporters, particularly in the Muslim world, that we have the fortitude to do something about our own predicament.

A bill largely written by lobbyists, as was H.R. 4, will not achieve the national security goal. The Senate needs to buckle down and write its own bill itself. It should not be guided by commercial interests but by those of national security.

October 30, 2001

HARD TIMES FOR WASHINGTON'S SELF-IMPORTANT

Washington is a deflated place these days. The denizens of the capital have been robbed by the crisis of their dearest possession: self-importance.

This is, of course, not true of the people who work in the Pentagon, the White House, and some committees of Congress. But the majority of those who scurry about Washington—lobbyists, lawyers, consultants, journalists, and sundry influence-peddlers—have lost their ebullience.

The old game of hinting that you know people in high places, fraternize with the powerful, and intimate that the president hangs on your words, is shut down.

A new team of insiders has stolen the limelight. They are obscure professors of Middle Eastern studies, diffident Arabists, retired military officers, and old Pakistani and Afghan hands. Even the syndicated columnists, with such a reverence for their own opinions on all matters, great and small, are diminished. They are trying to project yesterday's knowledge in today's crisis, often with a vacuous effect, and sometimes no more than a boring repetition of what one of the new experts has told them.

Maureen Dowd's acidity, George Will's loftiness, and Charles Krauthammer's bellicosity all seem quite irrelevant. The only journalist who can hold up his head is writing for a weekly magazine in New York. Yes, the redoubtable Seymour Hersh is back in business. His previous excesses are forgotten, and he has developed a new statesmanlike TV style. God, is he despised. The profane, loud-mouthed hero of yesterday is actually getting scoops, and has something to say that is based on the here and now, not on analysis.

Worse, Hersh is breaking news not in *The New York Times* or *The Washington Post* but in the grayest of gray magazines: *The New Yorker.*

Washington, which so loves process and so loves to chew up thousands of hours debating whether a particular bill will move or come to the floor on the Hill, is quite simply speechless. The Washington professionals, whose stock-in-trade is to divine the will of Congress and to try to influence it, have nothing to do and less to talk about. Terrorism, so to speak, has got their tongues.

Most journalists are not much better off than the lobbyists, lawyers and consultants. They are reduced to constructing what happened before Sept. 11 and to analyzing the events which led up to that catastrophe. Despite the large number of journalists encamped in Islamabad, and the brave souls actually inside Afghanistan, no one has broken any news, except the aforementioned Hersh.

What is particularly galling for journalists is that they now know that Hersh will break more stories because people with a tale to tell will contact him, now that he is established as the premier war correspondent many thousands of miles from the front.

But if you have a tear to shed for the journalists, you must weep copiously for the influence-peddlers. They can no longer convincingly tell you that their contact in the White House is "working the problem." It is patently obvious that the White House is very busy and is not working on any problem except the national one.

The last refuge for the influence lobby is the House of Representatives, where patriots like Majority Leader Dick Armey and Majority Whip Tom DeLay are still stuffing bills with goodies for corporations, maybe in the belief that they can please their donors and be saved from their folly by the Senate. But there is a weakness in this for the I-know-everyone-who-counts gang, because no one really wants to admit being close to Armey or DeLay.

One lobbyist I know bustled into a meeting with a little bit of the old esprit. He announced that he had been playing tennis with high-ranking members of Congress. This may keep you alive in the lobbying game, but it doesn't count in the new normalcy. Had he been able to say, "I've been batting a few balls about with Tom Ridge," or that he had been having breakfast with Gen. Tommy Franks, we would know that he is still a very important person.

And what about all those wonderful people who went to school with George W. Bush? Well, I learned that they are not getting in to see him. The president is in war mode and does not want to reminisce about Yale. More self-importance punctured.

The chiefs of the big trade associations have always prided themselves on their access and their ability to ingratiate themselves with Cabinet secretaries, White House staff, and congressional committee chairmen. But if you cannot drop names, influence legislation, get your clients into the White House, and pretend to be at the very center of things now, what is the point?

How, you might wonder, can one man in a cave in Afghanistan eviscerate so many in their cavernous offices on K Street and elsewhere? They are the unsung victims of terrorism, too.

November 6, 2001

WAR AND CRISIS: BUSH GROWS AS BUSINESS REELS

Our assumptions have been most brutally shaken up this year. Of course, they have received the most violence from the events of Sept. 11 and its aftermath, but assumptions were under attack before that. Probably, it began with the collapse of the dot.com boom. It was a bubble which bewitched the world. But like other economic bubbles, it had to burst.

However during the dot.com era, a new kind of economic philosophy, defiant of all previous economic history, emerged. It said that since we were now the most powerful country on earth, and that because we had mastered the business cycle, an endless prosperity was at hand. People wrote books about how the Dow would advance 40-fold and more, and about how free markets would deliver the American bounty to the globe.

There were new companies, driven by new incentive schemes for their employees and a sense of limitless horizons. The greatest of these — and still is — was Microsoft. But mentioned in the same breath was the energy giant, Enron. It was a corporation with an amazing growth record and with super-talented managers, who believed in the new economy and in themselves.

Enron, without the advantage of a unique product like Microsoft, believed that the things that had worked in transforming it from a small pipeline company to an energy behemoth would work for it in every endeavor it undertook. It believed it could operate as a financial house, a trading house, an electric utility, as well as a gas and oil company. It also believed that it could bring its magic to the water industry. In short, it began to believe that it was not the product but the Enron way of doing business that made for its success.

Now, it has imploded in one of the most dramatic business failures in history. It made a mistake which is common to successful business: It did not differentiate between where it had been lucky and where it had been skillful.

It is a mistake which oil companies made when they have attempted to diversify, that Philip Morris made in its early diversification, and that most companies make when they allow their hubris to overwhelm their judgement; when they believe that the vendor is bigger than the product, and that management is what the customer buys rather than the product.

Not many months ago, Ken Lay, the gifted chairman of Enron, was talking about growing the company 10-fold and more. The assumptions were wrong.

Politically, assumptions are frequently wrong because they, too, are based on ideology and not on reality.

The deteriorating economy was not dreamed of by the right wing when it campaigned for George W. Bush. Equally, the left wing had a set of assumptions that were hugely negative about Bush. They assumed that presented with a foreign-policy crisis, President Bush would implode and hand the conduct of the crisis over to Vice President Cheney.

In reality, Bush has outperformed even the expectations of his supporters. He may not be a great orator, nor have a profound knowledge of history, but he has an excellent memory and it has been serving him well as he deals with foreign leaders, doubting allies, and a skeptical media.

It is way too early to say that Bush will make a great president. But he has been a good president in the current crisis, using what he has just learned to good effect. He has also shown fortitude in balancing the views of the hawks and the doves within his own administration.

Bush has also used his skill with people to send away heads of state, who expected very little of him, happy and reassured. His principal problem is that his charm has a small radius: It is more intense the closer you are to him, but it does not carry over on television or on radio. If you attend a Bush event in person, you are likely to be impressed. But to watch the same event on television is to be underwhelmed.

Yet, Bush is the president that most Americans—the polls confirm it—seem to want in this crisis. It is, in a sense, a crisis made for him: a crisis in which his black-and-white view of the world is justified; a crisis in which Bush's sense of American exceptionalism sits well with the public, and has not been as offensive to the more liberal publics of our allies.

Nobody's assumptions about Bush, good or ill, are proved out yet. But there is considerable evidence that the assumption that he would collapse in crisis is clearly wrong. And as for Cheney running the country, hell, he cannot be found.

Crisis and war are great levelers: business is reeling, has lost faith in its managerial skills; and George W. Bush is growing in stature and growing on us. Crisis and war are also great liberators, giving opportunity to new voices and destroying old hierarchies everywhere—in the media, in business, and in politics.

November 13, 2001

CUT THE HYSTERIA, LET'S GET BACK INTO THE AIRPLANES

While we have been worrying and debating about who should check our dirty laundry at the airport, a giant leap forward in airport security is taking place: Cockpit doors have been fortified against intruding passengers.

This is the most palpable guarantee that the events of Sept. 11 will not be replicated. The shocking and tragic truth is that cockpit doors should have been made invulnerable after the first hijacking decades ago. Why pilots were not protected in the same way as homeowners, convenience stores, gas stations, and the bridges on ships, is a disgrace. It is a tale of lethargy and penny-pinching which never should have been allowed to develop.

The airlines, aircraft manufacturers and flight crews knew about the vulnerability of cockpits. But they did nothing because the airlines did not want to spend the money to make the cockpits impenetrable. The airlines, of course, won because their political friends saw it their way, and the FAA saw it the way the airlines' political friends saw it.

Now that it is being accomplished, airplanes are immeasurably safer from hijacking than they were heretofore. That does not mean that they do not have vulnerabilities—to explosives and to attack from the ground. But they are much safer.

The proximate cause of the public's shunning air travel is the fear of a repeat of the 9/11 events. They should be told that safety is already better and that they should return to flying. Somebody with some credibility should tell them: President Bush or, at the least, the director of homeland defense, Tom Ridge. Ridge would seem to be the ideal person to start the campaign because he has not been allowed to direct homeland defense, as Attorney General John Ashcroft regards it as part of his portfolio and his modus operandi has been to instill fear, not confidence.

As the Taliban crumbles and Al Qaida shrivels, the big job of the administration is to get America back to normal so that the economy will recover. The economy will recover not because of the asymmetrical largesse in the Republican plan on the Hill, but because people feel secure enough to unleash their pent up demand. In the short run, the most effective way of boosting the economy and the national sense of well-being is by getting the only real public transportation system we have, the airlines, back to normal.

The rest of the airline security challenge will take years to accomplish. X-ray machines hooked to computers will have to examine all airline baggage. Technology has to come galloping to the rescue because there is no way that the tired eyes of dispirited people staring at X-ray machines will identify all lethal objects. No matter who pays them, no one can be expected to examine hundreds of bags a day without their eyes glazing over. The fact that they will become federal employees will improve their living standards, but that is all. Heck, there are enough dispirited people in the bureaucracy with glazed-over eyes as it is.

The second thing, which will do much to reassure the public, is apparently not yet at hand. That is an arrest or, at least, an explanation of the anthrax letters. Here, Ashcroft needs to step forward and tell us what are the lines of investigation. He need not give out information which will impede the investigation or alert the suspects, but he should tell us something. So far, we have had nothing but silence from him on any issue which might reassure the public. Instead he has warned us of "credible" threats.

Bush has been strong, clear and reassuring that the threat abroad will be vanquished. But at home, there has been no such reassurance, only alarm.

Nothing will jog the economy back to life faster than getting people moving again. This requires an assurance that aircrafts are secure and that passengers can board aircraft at a reasonable time. Nobody is going to fly anywhere if they have to check in three hours before a one-hour flight, or if any small incident will cause the airport to close down, as happened last week in Atlanta. This is not security. It is hysteria. The last thing we need is more hysteria, whether it is generated by airport officials or by the attorney general and the vice president themselves.

November 20, 2001

TWO LIVES: TWO DIFFERENT VISIONS AND FAILURES

This is a tale of two men who reached for the brass ring, grabbed it, and then saw it slip away; two dissimilar men, sharing only lofty vision and seeing it destroyed by circumstance.

The first man is Milton Shaw, who died this weekend at the age of 80. He sought to save the nation from a bleak energy future through advanced nuclear power. The second man is Kenneth Lay, the embattled chairman of Enron.

Shaw came out of Adm. Hyman Rickover's nuclear reactor program. In the late 1960s and early 1970s, Shaw was one of the most powerful technocrats in the federal government. As the head of reactor development at the Atomic Energy Commission (AEC), Shaw was the commanding figure of nuclear power. He was committed to the widespread deployment of light water reactors and to the introduction of the liquid metal fast breeder reactor, which he believed was the key to the United States' future energy security.

Like his mentor Rickover, Shaw was autocratic, passionate and a slave to his vision. In the early days of his civilian career, he was unassailable. He was to nuclear power development what Robert Moses was to road construction in New York. He was the man, and people quaked in his presence. Shaw held sway over the General Electric Company and Westinghouse Electric, and coerced the national laboratories. There is, I think, in today's bureaucracy no technocrat of such drive, power and vision and authority.

In the first years of Shaw's civilian life, he was supported by admiring friends in Congress in the Joint Committee on Atomic Energy, which gave him disproportionate authority to go up against the commissioners who were his legal supervisors. The Joint Committee on Atomic Energy—the only joint committee of Congress that was ever empowered to introduce legislation—was a secretive fiefdom of true believers in the atom.

The joint committee's power emanated from its unique status and from the stature of its House and Senate members. These included: Reps. Chet Holifield (D-Calif.) and Craig Hosmer (R-Calif.), and Sens. Albert Gore, Sr. (D-Tenn.), George Aiken (R-Vt.) and John O. Pastore (D-R.I.). From the mid-1950s to the early 1970s, these men fostered nuclear power; saw that the commissioners were sympathetic to their point of view; and used staff men, such as Shaw, to implement what was in effect an industrial policy for nuclear.

By 1968, there were signs that they could no longer operate their nuclear policy without the rest of Congress and the growing environmental movement having a say. Also, the technology was proving more difficult than they were willing to admit. There were questions about the emergency core cooling systems on light water reactors, and their chosen repository for nuclear waste in the salt mines of Lyons, Kan., turned out to be a disaster—water leaked in and out of the mines.

Through all of this, Shaw soldiered on, single-minded, energetic, hardworking and out of touch with the changing world around him. Finally in 1973, he was fired by the last chairman (her word) of the AEC, Dixy Lee Ray. The compact was broken and the nuclear industrial policy was in tatters.

Remembering him, the penultimate chairman of the AEC, James Schlesinger, said: "Milt was the finest of public servants. He was not only focused and dedicated to the task, but also enthusiastic and committed to his mission."

Ken Lay, who built Enron from a sleepy gas pipeline into the most commanding of energy companies, shared with Shaw a great vision. It, too, apparently is not to be, as Enron spirals down in one of the most extraordinary business catastrophes that we have seen. There will be business books, business school case studies, court cases, and years of recriminations.

Lay's dream was of building an enormous company driven by market forces, breaking up energy fiefdoms, and driving down the cost of energy to the consumer. And yet, as Lay's wealth and prestige climbed, he remained the most human of titans—never forgetting old friends, dropping names, playing the celebrity card, nor moving with a phalanx of aides. He has always enjoyed the company of less successful men and women, and I have never seen him in a chauffeured car: Lay likes to rent odd vehicles—jeeps and convertibles—and drive himself to events.

How Enron spiraled out of control with so many of its executives freelancing and self-dealing without Lay curbing them, is something that we have yet to learn. And Lay will be answering questions for a decade.

For the rest of his life, Shaw mourned the abandonment of the high purposes that the nuclear establishment had espoused and spent his time teaching at various universities, but always, always, patriotically advancing the nuclear cause. During this long period, he was a lion in winter, with little regard for his personal career.

The aspirations of Shaw and Lay were very different, and yet very American. Maybe in the end, the greatest commonality between these disparate men is the light that failed.

November 27, 2001

THE YEAR THAT WAS: WHAT A YEAR IT WAS

In the good old days of journalism, they developed a practice of substituting annual reviews around Christmastime for news and analysis. This was, I believe, a defense against a prevalent malady of the time: party-induced amnesia.

Of course, journalists are much more enlightened now and sip only fizzy water at parties. But back then, the men and women of the Fourth Estate often forgot all the reporting they had just done as they went hither and thither to celebrate Christmas, Hanukkah, New Year's, and their own surviving in employment for another year. To make up for the lack of any news they had discovered or any ability to concentrate, they developed the practice of writing long, silly pieces about the year that was ending. This was a lot easier than original work, because all you had to do was flip through copies of the newspaper to be reminded of what had happened.

For the sake of old times, here is an example:

George W. Bush became president with a shaky mandate and an expectation among many that he would unravel in office. Instead he had a shaky start, but everything changed with the tragedy on Sept. 11. Now his popularity is astronomical, and even the media is prepared to applaud his handling of the crisis.

In fact, everything has changed. And it has changed on Bush's watch. If you want to be mean about it, deficits are back and the economy is in the tank. Yet, Russia is now our best friend; China is now a member of the World Trade Organization and the major source of American flags; and it has been revealed to be a strange, two-wheeled scooter which will be hailed by orthopedic surgeons as a boon to their practice.

On the other hand, there were losers. Big losers. Enron, the company most admired in the casino decade of the 1990s, imploded, taking a lot of investors with it. It was a company so clever that ordinary analysts couldn't fathom it, so they recommended the stock to be on the winning side. Now it is a metaphor for hubris.

Afghanistan, which the British couldn't conquer, which defeated the Soviet Union, fell to the rag-tag Northern Alliance and American bombs.

The celebrity famous for celebrity, Madonna, is fading fast. She has no more clothes to take off and no new heresies to commit. What is a girl to do?

In the Department of Just Fancy That, Rush Limbaugh began to go deaf, Pat Robertson quit the Christian Coalition, the Senate flipped with the defection of one senator, Casual Friday wore thin, and Geraldo Rivera quit being a liberal talk show host to be a war correspondent for a conservative TV network. Bill Clinton lost his headline appeal, his wife became a serious senator, and even The Weekly Standard got tired of Clinton-bashing. The magazine's editors turned their vengeance on Colin Powell instead. But it is hard to get outraged about him.

It was a terrible year for the journals of political opinion. The soaring popularity of Bush neutered the left, while the absence of any liberal initiatives defanged the right. But there was recent fun when Bob Barr, Bill Safire and Ollie North all attacked John Ashcroft's plans for military tribunals. To hear Ralph Nader praising Barr and Safire, as he did on TV, was at least exquisite.

The year was, of course, defined by its last three months, when Americans were told to prepare for more terrorist attacks and to go on living their lives as usual. How this was to be done was not explained: Should you go to dinner in a flak jacket and jog in a gas mask?

For next year, these things are in: formal attire, patriotism, Tim Russert, George Stephanopolous, Bill O'Reilly, Fox News, domestic bottled water, and owning a family cave. Out are: Sam Donaldson, Cokie Roberts, the liberal agenda, environmentalism, and the peace process in the Middle East and elsewhere.

And incidentally, if you bought Texas gear when the Bush's came to town, hold a yard sale. The president gets less Texan every minute.

There are other things that have been turned on their heads, but I shall not get into them because I have a plethora of receptions to attend: my homage to the journalists of yesteryear.

December 11, 2001

2002

THE EXTRAORDINARY BIRTH
OF EUROPE'S LATEST INVENTION

BORDEAUX, France—In the 12 countries of the 15-member European Union that welcomed a new currency this new year, there has been a nonstop party. Gin-ever, grappa, Cognac, beer, and all of the hundreds of European liquors in be-tween, are being raised to thirsty lips to celebrate the end of the old and the be-ginning of the new.

Now if you are an economist you might think that the wild European celebra-tion of their new currency, the euro, is misplaced, even illogical. But do not try to tell that to the people on the streets here, or anywhere else in the new Euroland.

Only Denmark and Sweden, who voted to stay out of the euro, are feeling a lit-tle bereft. And Britain is positively hostile, especially its principal newspapers. The Danes and Swedes feel that they may have made a mistake, while the British, especially conservative opinion, feel they have saved their sovereignty.

The principal currencies of Europe, many of them with distinguished histories, like the French franc, the Italian lira, the German mark, and the Greek drachma, are now museum pieces. The people celebrating believe that they are on the verge of some new, remarkable European renaissance; that they are part of the creation of a great, new and noble near-country called Europe; that they are celebrating the end of 2,000 years of internecine war on the continent; and that some glorious though ill-defined future is at hand.

It is stirring to feel the passion for this future in which a disparate heritage will become a common history. Suddenly Michelangelo, Beethoven, Pasteur, Picasso and Sibelius are everybody's ancestors. All are now great Europeans, not national figures. The step dance, flamenco, and the waltz are part of the single European culture. Historical diversity has been collected in a new fabric and this tapestry is everyone's.

That is what the joy is about.

The economics are something quite different. The principal argument against the euro, the one used by American economists and British objectionists, is that it will not work; that Europe is anything but one place; and that you cannot manage a single currency to deal with recession in Portugal and inflation in Ireland.

Americans, in particular, have pointed out that Europe has very little labor mobility, and that our diverse land can function with a single currency because labor mobility is both a reality and a possibility. A worker from New England can fit in easily in California, but a worker from Portugal faces cultural and linguistic barriers if he or she wants to move to Finland. Culture and language make a mockery of the free movement of labor.

In its first three years of existence, the European Central Bank has been timid, with one eye on Washington and the other on its political creators. It has not promulgated an economic philosophy for Europe, nor shown how it can manage so diverse an economy. Major European financial transactions have been taking place in euros for three years, during which time the euro has lost some 20 percent of its initial value against the U.S. dollar. That, say its defenders, is because it opened too high. That, say its detractors, is because you cannot have a one-size-fits-all-currency with so diverse a group of countries, and that additional devaluation will follow the admission to the European Union and its monetary system of countries in eastern Europe.

What is undeniable is that at a time when the world is dissembling, there is something enormously hopeful, uplifting and imaginative about the European project. What has historically been the most creative continent is suddenly pulling itself together, seeking cohesion and peace. It is a grand ambition, subjugating national rivalries to the concept of a larger common good.

To the people here in Bordeaux, and across the other 11 euro states, it is the birth of something vast, something inspired, something like 1776 in America. It is an ambition that has been two bloody millennia in gestation. Can you blame people for celebrating?

I hope this currency works because it is inspired by exquisite purpose. Meanwhile, they make the finest wine in the world around here and I must go out and join the celebration, and do my part to burp the euro.

January 2, 2002

GEORGE W. BUSH AND THE GOP: A DILEMMA

Partisan politics, *The Washington Post* informs me, has returned to Washington. Oh, boy. I didn't know it had gone away, although it has been pretty subdued since Sept. 11.

The party in the White House likes to talk about bipartisanship as though it was some virtue: an intent of the Founding Fathers. How absurd. Partisanship is the basis of two-party democracy. And I venture to submit that when the two parties agree over too many issues for too long, something bad is afoot.

Although it's the fashion for Democrats and Republicans to seek the middle ground at present, there are really very few commonalities between them. And that's how it should be. Democrats are more liberal and do represent a more liberal constituency, while Republicans are unashamedly on the side of business and the monied.

In my book, that's how it should be. And the loyal opposition should draw as much blood as it can as it battles to represent the people who sent it to Capitol Hill.

What's more, this is going to be a bitterly partisan year as both parties struggle to gain seats in the House and the Senate. President George W. Bush has understandably wrapped himself in the war on terrorism and implies that those who don't enact his agenda are somehow letting the side down. Right now, that's an effective strategy. But it's unlikely to hold up if the economy doesn't recover.

Bush, in the election that brought him to the White House, had no demonstrated coattails, and he had developed none for the gubernatorial elections of last year. He has to hope that the war on terrorism has changed this, and that he can have a Republican House returned and wrest the Senate away from the Democrats. If this doesn't happen, his second two years in office will be bitter and frustrating, and will not leave him in a good position to run for a second term.

And with the highest poll ratings of any president, one would think that Bush has nothing to worry about. But then, there's the coattail issue.

Americans, it would seem, have separated in their minds the commander in chief from the political leader. Politics at this time are separate from the White House, and Americans want to give the president the fealty they would give a monarch. Lacking, as we do, any titular leader in the country except for the president, we confer our patriotism on the office and its incumbent.

Bush is a very appropriate president for the moment — no nonsense, no intellectual sophistry, and an appealing simplicity of style and vision. He's enhanced by the qualities he lacks. He doesn't have the intellectual depth of Wilson, the scope of FDR, the duplicity of Johnson, or the articulation of Reagan. And all this sits just fine with people.

But there's no evidence that Bush's popularity extends to his party, hence the Democrats will fight the GOP on legislative issues, seeking to leave the presidency out of the battle as much as they can.

It'll be a year of bitter, partisan fisticuffs without the knockout punch of any big idea. The battle will be borne within known parameters over issues that have been well-aired already. This is unfortunate, and it represents a failure of vision from the Democrats. If the Democrats had succeeded in throwing some grand, compelling idea into the ring, the Republicans and the president would be off-balance and vulnerable.

At this point, the Democrats don't have a big idea and the Republicans have only one idea: cut taxes. This isn't a disadvantage to the Republicans, but it's a disadvantage to the Democrats. They are defending not augmenting their agenda.

Somehow the Democrats have failed so far to drive home the issue of the economy and the trusted issues of health care and Social Security. Worse, they are jockeying among themselves for a candidate to run against Bush in 2004, and they find themselves defined by the meagerness of their own potential candidates. Deep down Democrats know that barring a disaster in the presidency, their chances of taking the White House in '04 are not great. Therefore, the Democrats have to fight hard in the Senate and the House to convince voters that they are credible legislators.

Bush will get into the fray, but voters will still see him as above it.

Unemployment and insecurity will help the Democrats, but if the economy should turn around, as some believe it will, in the middle of the year, they'll have to find something more to offer the public than a Capitol Hill slugfest.

If, however, the economy, as others believe, will be mired in recession until next year, then the Republicans have to play the patriotic card, and Bush has to deliver palpable victories against terrorism for the Republicans to take back the Senate and hold onto their slim majority in the House.

The partisan balance is also a challenge to Bush: Should he tangle with the Democrats at every chance or maintain his lofty separation as the president of all the people?

It's a matter of strategy, and it's one that's already beginning to keep the political strategists in the White House, led by Karl Rove, awake at night.

January 8, 2002

IT WAS THE YEAR OF BUSH THE UNKNOWABLE

Who is George W. Bush? Nearly a year after he was sworn in as president, we still do not really know him. We know that he rose to the occasion of combating terrorism; that when the conditions are right, he is warm and friendly and personable. We know what he eats, drinks, and when he jogs. But we do not know him in the ways that we have come to know public figures in this media age.

We know that Bush has faith in his own star; that he is not riddled with doubt or self-analysis; and that he can walk away from some unachievable policy issues, such as school vouchers.

We know that he had very little interest in the world outside the United States, and that now he seems more comfortable on foreign-policy issues than he does on domestic ones.

There is flexibility and inflexibility. Those things on which Bush seems to be most inflexible are close to his core beliefs, or what we know of them. Take cutting taxes. This is clearly a core Bush belief: a strong conviction that Americans are overtaxed and pay a price for their overtaxation in big government and economic sluggishness.

Yet it is the tax part that Bush clearly believes more than his stated horror of big government. The evidence is that neither growing government nor increasing deficits alarm Bush.

He seems to be a man formed by a small number of deep beliefs, leaving the rest to political accommodation.

Amazingly, of all of those who have claimed to know Bush over the years, none can recall a particular conversation, or tell you about the gleam in his eye when he was in college or running an oil company.

We do not know what the president and his wife talk about over dinner, or whether he expresses opinions about the books that his political adviser, Karl Rove, has been giving him to read. He and Rove both claim to be great admirers of Winston Churchill, but we do not know how they react to Churchill. Do they discuss the contradictions in Churchill?

If they do, what do they make of Churchill's lifelong claim to be a liberal, despite twice leading the Conservative Party? What does Bush make of Churchill's leniency to condemned prisoners when he was home secretary: he commuted about half the cases that came before him. What does Bush make of Churchill's support of a nationalized health service in the United Kingdom?

In short, it would be nice to know if the president has any deliberative conversations. Or is he a man who comes to decisions based exclusively on those few core beliefs?

He brushed off a question from my colleague, Bill Sammon, on whether he had changed since he has been president. Bush said that he did not look in the mirror except to comb his hair. It was either a flip remark or a revelation of the real Bush—a man of action, not of contemplation.

Even so, the world has changed enormously in the year that Bush has been president, with terrorism, a failing economy and new relationships with Russia, Pakistan, India and Europe. The next phase in the war against terrorism cannot be taken without some vision of its outcome: What happens if we invade Iraq, send troops into Somalia, and ground forces into the Philippines and Indonesia? Bush has shone at leading the war against terrorism, but it is a war of reaction. Its next stage will be proactive, putting in play a whole new set of forces.

Oddly, the one event that may have most unnerved Bush is the collapse of Enron. It does not fit with what we know of the core beliefs. This is not about evil-doers in faraway places. This is the failure of a beloved company, headed by a man who was Bush's friend and not dissimilar from Bush himself. Kenneth Lay, chairman of Enron, I suspect was more than a friend and campaign contributor to Bush. I think he was a role model and an exemplar of the core Bush beliefs. He was everything that Texas stands for; everything that God-fearing, family-loving, hardworking, patriotic American business is about. Everything that George W. Bush is about.

Lay, like Bush, is a man who believed that there were rewards for the righteous, and that business is good for the individual and good for America. Now Lay, whom I have known for nearly 30 years, is a fallen idol. His company is in bankruptcy and his own reputation is indelibly sullied. It must pain Bush in a way that deficits, recession and war do not.

So much as we can tell, Enron was the kind of commercial success that Bush admired and believed in as a fulfilled American destiny.

One year into his presidency, we know that Bush is a convincing commander-in-chief, has lost most of his domestic agenda, and is hugely popular with the public. The real Bush we may never know and when we look back on him in years out, we will only be able to surmise; to guess at what he saw as his triumphs, failures and, for that matter, to guess at what he thinks about the world leaders with whom he moves so easily, but from whom he is so far apart.

It is a year in which Bush has performed better than his critics anticipated and, more importantly, better than his supporters dared hope. Act I, Scene II will begin with his State of the Union address, but we will not know more about him then than we do now.

January 15, 2002

HOW TO ENJOY DAVOS IN NEW YORK

Dear Jean-Michel,

I was delighted to learn that you have risen so much in your organization that you'll be attending the World Economic Forum in New York. I think that it was nice of the organizers to move it from Davos, Switzerland, to show solidarity with the victims of the Sept. 11 attacks.

First, collect as many Enron jokes that you can because we're getting tired of the ones we've heard. Enron jokes are a great currency at the moment and if you have five or six European ones, you'll be a hit wherever you go. Arthur Andersen jokes are good, but euro jokes aren't—we haven't quite understood yet that the euro is now a large and legitimate currency.

I advise you to rent a limousine because all taxis in America are awful, dirty and dangerous. They are driven, for the most part, by people our attorney general would like to interview, and few of them have grasped even the elemental geography of the cities in which they ply their trade. What passes for a limousine is probably not much better than the average taxi in Paris, but at least they'll be clean and some of the drivers know where they're going.

You can now walk the major streets in New York in safety. But make sure you visit the men's room before you leave the hotel because New York, like other American cities, has no public toilets. The trick is to walk purposefully into a restaurant or bar. If you're well-dressed, you'll get away with this. Otherwise, you'll have to order a drink. We have no toilets because of a bizarre interpretation of an otherwise excellent law: the Americans with Disabilities Act. You see, those neat little outdoor-kiosk toilets that clean themselves after each use apparently can't accommodate wheelchairs, so we all must endure.

Compared with Davos, you'll find prices quite reasonable in New York. And you may eat as well as you would in Switzerland. New York hosts the greatest profusion of restaurants of all kinds on earth, and at present they're really keen to get your business.

Almost everyone in the service industries that you deal with will exhort you to "have a nice day." Smile and say, "You, too." This is a very annoying practice because they don't care what kind of day you have, but it has entered into our language as an empty phrase, sometimes issued with a snarl. It's not just people who will tell you to have a nice day. Cell phones, exercise equipment and the atrocious, automated telephone directory recordings also urge you to have a nice day.

Getting back to the euro, don't expect to find a bureau de change on every street corner. Our entrepreneurs haven't worked out that one, and you have to change your money in the hotel or get U.S. dollars from an ATM. Not every bank will change your money either. We're very suspicious of any money other than our own.

I wonder what will go on at the conference, given the world situation. At Davos, they used to love to talk about globalization, but we haven't heard that word since Sept. 11. Worse, Enron was our poster boy for a globalized company and we're rethinking that bit of post-colonial colonialism. I expect that there will be a lot of talk about the North-South divide and the need for investment in the Third World. But I doubt whether there will be any American companies stepping forward to invest in Congo, Sierra Leone or Zimbabwe. Come to think of it, I doubt that European corporations want to pony up in the trouble spots, although the European Union itself likes to talk about reconstruction and investment.

American corporations that had the global itch in the 1990s and threw their money around in Argentina, Brazil, Indonesia and Pakistan are now talking about their "core businesses" in the United States, and dumping overseas assets rather than investing there.

But my dear Jean-Michel, don't let all of this get you down. New York remains the most exciting city in the world, with incredible energy, lethal traffic, and a sense of possibility that can be found nowhere else on earth.

Remember, of course, that the World Economic Forum is a place to be seen, not a place to get things done. So you may as well enjoy the city: its great galleries; wonderful boutiques; a great opera house; and really exceptional drinking dives, which stay open until 4 a.m., in case the labors of solving the world's economic problems have kept you awake.

If you find you have a taste for these world economic forums, with their noble agendas and high purpose, I can recommend a bunch of them. There's the Renaissance Weekend in Hilton Head, S.C., favored by former President Clinton; the Business Council annual meeting, favored by people with private jets. And last but not least, the Aspen Institute, until this year, favored by the chairman of Enron. These grand conclaves are something like meetings of the old Soviet Politburo. If you have fallen by the way in business, you just disappear; you're metaphorically air brushed out of the picture.

Enjoy, but don't take any of this nonsense too seriously.

Sincerely,
Your Friend Who Hasn't Been Invited

January 29, 2002

THE DIFFICULTY OF NICKNAMING THE PRESIDENT

There is a little problem here in Washington that I have been trying to address, but I have to admit that I have come up empty-handed. President Bush gives everyone a nickname, but he himself really does not have one.

Bush has names for nearly everyone. "Kenny Boy" for the chairman of Enron, "Stretch" for a tall reporter, and "Super Stretch" for an even taller one. He mints them instantly and they stick. But the president himself has no handle.

Yes, yes, Molly Ivins and others in Texas did call him "Dubya." But that was before the present crisis, and before he achieved astrophysical popularity in the polls. Now it is over, as dead as his carousing days of yore.

Dubya just does not do it. He needs something grander. The trouble is the name George. It is a very difficult name to do anything with, as it does not lend itself to alliteration and does not rhyme with serious words. That is why the British like to call so many of their kings George, particularly as the quality of their monarchs has declined steadily since Elizabeth I. You could not refer to "George the Lion-hearted" or "George the Conqueror."

Another George, George Bernard Shaw, knew all about the problems with the name, which he affected to dislike. To make his point, and because he had funny ideas about spelling, he said that it should be spelled "Jawj." In this way, he said, people would see what an ugly name it was. Of course, it is not an ugly name at all, it is just incorruptible. It has no short form. And the diminutive is actually longer than the name George itself: Georgie.

Now try to get some alliteration out of the name yourself. See just how bad these can get: Good George, Grand George, Gracious George, Gorgeous George, Godly George, or Gifted George. It just does not work. It is hard to get a rise out of the name George.

Nursery rhymes have had the devil of a job with George because only silly words rhyme with it. The only rhyme that comes to mind is "Georgie Porgie," and that does not fit George W.

Then there is the problem that the president is pretty regular in his appearance. There is no baldness to lampoon, or big ears or other physical characteristics that one can catch on to. He is short, but not too short. The name-maker has the same trouble as the cartoonists. Some critics had predicted that if elected, he would always look like a deer caught in headlights. It has not happened, so "Deer George" does not make it.

If there were a scandal, Bush would be for it. The scribes would not be able to resist "Bushgate" or "Georgegate" or, heaven forefend, "Dubyagate." But there is no scandal, and the joy of naming is denied the scribes. Even as the president continues to give them nicknames.

Bush's history is not helpful either. He has had no exceptional hobbies, nor remarkable military service. So it cannot be "Rough Rider George," "Trooper Bush" or "Flyboy George."

You try for yourself, but it is not easy. It is hard to imagine, no matter what the president's success is, that he will be remembered in history by the Victorian expression "Great George," or "St. George the Dragonslayer."

A Mexican friend has a partial solution, she refers to the commander-in-chief as "Gringo Uno." You can use that one if you take a holiday south of the border.

February 5, 2002

PLEASE TELL US WHAT IS NEXT, MR. PRESIDENT

At this time of year, one waits for the first thrusting shoots of spring. They are a few weeks off, but something else is happening. The monolithic support that President George W. Bush has enjoyed for five months is beginning to wilt.

The shoots of dissent are growing quite slowly in the liberal garden. But they are showing through more clearly in the stonier ground of the conservative flower patch.

On Sunday morning television, Senate minority leader Trent Lott seemed to find it difficult to say that the economy is being hurt by the death of the president's stimulus package on Capitol Hill. In fact, tears for the package are few and far apart as conservative lawmakers hear from the folks back home. Conservatives have always railed against deficits and even in a time of crisis, there is no enthusiasm for them.

A correspondent to the staunchest of conservative magazines, *Insight*, lumped deficit spending with the collapse of Enron. Inference: one day the United States would implode like the energy trading giant.

Likewise, the pettiness of some of the security measures is beginning to rankle. Leaving aside the intellectual arguments about the erosion of freedoms, ordinary people are getting fed up with make-believe security at airports, sporting events and other gatherings.

The press corps is furious at their pointless exclusion from Andrews Air Force Base, when nearly all of them have so-called White House hard passes, issued by the Secret Service after vetting by the FBI. It seems rank officiousness. In fact, the security madness has led to an outpouring of officiousness at nearly every level where the government deals with the public.

These and other dissatisfactions have not yet eroded the president's high approval ratings. But can slippage be far behind? The administration is full of piety about its war against terrorism, but the public wants to know what is coming next. Susan Eisenhower, president of the Eisenhower Institute, this week advised the president to unleash the nation's scientists to quantify the kinds of threats we are facing so that the life of the public can return to something like normal.

The change in opinion about the president's State of the Union address is symptomatic of the nascent unease with the administration. The day after its delivery, the speech was lauded in all quarters. But since then it has been dissected, analyzed, leading to a general uncertainty about what is to come. People have pored over the speech and found that it contains almost everything except reassurance.

Abroad, the speech has been received badly—almost around the globe. It has been read as a declaration of unilateralism; of might-is-right and of the president's insensitivity to the real concerns of our real allies.

While many Americans can still find comfort in it, our allies find bellicosity, arrogance and fear in it. The president needs to define his intentions and to reassure the world that we are not in for the kind of military adventures favored by the colonial powers in the 19th century.

The first conservative analyst to take after the speech was Arnaud de Borchgrave, whose conservative credentials are beyond reproach. He was, after all, the first editor of *The Washington Times*, and has been a lifelong crusader against communism and its fellow travelers. But de Borchgrave was appalled at the linkage of North Korea, Iraq and Iran as an evil axis. He thought it was a monstrous misreading of geopolitical reality.

From now on, patriotic phrases may not carry Bush forward or maintain his image as the strong leader he has unquestionably been since Sept. 11. What is next, is a reasonable question. Does Bush know, is a loaded question. But it is one to which he will have to have an answer as the spring advances.

February 12, 2002

"GREED IS GOOD" PHILOSOPHY HIT BY ENRONITIS

Margaret Thatcher approved of greed when she was British prime minister. It was the underlying ethos of the wild 1980s, when Britain cast off many of its restrictions on business and did enter a long period of sustained growth. Whether this was the result of greed posing as virtue or of better governance is debatable.

Thatcher's predecessor—a less successful prime minister, it must be said—Edward Heath ran into untrammeled greed in the person of Tiny Roland, the chairman of a raw materials company called Lonrho. Heath found Roland's unbelievably lavish lifestyle, subsidized by tax deductions, to be "the unacceptable face of capitalism." A traditionalist, Heath found the new capitalists to be repulsive, tasteless and exploitative.

Now, courtesy of Enron, a quiet reexamination of greed as an ethic is going on in the United States. The proponents of greed, and there are many in the think tanks and on the right wing of journalism, see it as the great motivator, unleashing the positive forces of capitalism. Maybe.

The weakness in the greed argument is the unexamined assumption that those craving more will put forth greater effort than those satisfied with their rewards. Enron shows us that the greedy-minded will put forth stupendous effort in quite the wrong ways, as did Michael Milken and Ivan Boesky before them.

The argument about the role of greed in enterprise is not new, but it has been dressed up in recent times with an intellectualized veneer. If you believe in the motivating power of greed, you endanger excellence, craftsmanship and stability.

John Kenneth Galbraith, the liberal Harvard economist, in his book on the history of economics assigned greed as the motivation for most chicanery and for the European empires of the 18th and 19th centuries. Intellectually honest, Galbraith confessed he ran out of thesis when he studied the British civil service in India. He said he could not explain why so many dedicated people worked so hard to perfect administration without any personal gain beyond their salaries.

Most of us work very hard for our salaries, and have little expectation of windfall profit for our endeavors. The military performs with valor and takes casualties for extremely modest salaries. Now, we have rediscovered the stalwarts of the fire and police departments who do not fit into the greed-motivates mold. Service also motivates.

It must be galling to the millions who toil on farms and in factories, shops and government to learn of the gross looting of public companies by their managers, consultants and law firms.

Speaking of law firms, there was a nifty little law firm here in Washington, D.C., employing about 80 professionals, all of whom were earning in the region of $500,000 per year. Not too shabby, you say. Well, some of them thought it was really shabby, and literally tore the firm apart in the belief that their income should double. The solid workhorses of the firm liked things the way they were, but those highly motivated by—yes, greed—wanted to change it from a regulatory practice to something much more lucrative. The firm was sold off, and the craftsmen separated from the money-obsessed. This was at a time when lawyers were more interested in remuneration of their colleagues than their own very adequate take-home pay.

The damage from the greed at Enron is still being counted, and may never fully be accounted for: First, there is the damage to the employees; second, there is the damage to the stockholders; and then there is the damage that unmitigated greed has done to the energy industries and the stock market in general. Financial swashbuckling serves the purpose of some executives, titillates when these same executives are treated as celebrities, and can do enormous collateral damage.

Ambition and greed are not the same things. Greed is ambition stripped of its nobility, of any higher purpose, and entirely without the recognition that it is the quietly toiling millions that make it possible for the few to count human achievement by the tens of millions of dollars. In later life, Andrew Carnegie was haunted by the terrible things he had done to make himself the richest man in the world, and told his former compatriot in greed, Henry Clay Frick, that they both deserved to roast in hell. For a man who knew something about greed, it was not looking so good.

February 19, 2002

R.I.P. ZIMBABWE, GOLDEN HOPE OF AFRICA

You cannot inter a country, throw earth in its grave, and mourn it over a bottle of booze. Countries are full of people and although all civil order, reason and humanity may die, the people live on.

I write this because I am trying to mourn the death of Zimbabwe. But as I was born there, and lived there for the first 20 years of my life, I cannot erase the memories of its gentleness, its nobility and its innate kindness. Nor can I consign it wholly to the past in my mind, because I cannot forget the people — the wonder of the children and the tolerance of the adults. The children are still there, but the tolerance has failed.

Today, as they do every day, hundreds of thousands of Zimbabweans, mostly women, will be trying to plant a little corn with a primitive hoe called a "budza" because famine, an old enemy, will be back this year. Zimbabweans have always tried to grow some of their own corn, even if they live in the city, but they have relied on the big mechanized farms for the bulk of their staple diet. This year will be different, and many years to come will be different. The farms are stilled and despair is creeping across the country.

It does not matter who wins the coming election because the electoral process was destroyed, like the farms. And Robert Mugabe, the country's president since its formal independence from Britain in 1980, and his cronies will continue to run and pillage the country.

The breadbasket of southern Africa is well on its way to becoming the basket case of the region.

The misery will not stop with hunger. The country is ravaged with AIDS, and there are no medical services to treat the sick or to comfort the dying. The same Mugabe, who has lain waste the infrastructure of the country, led it into a ruinous war in Congo, has campaigned against the use of condoms. Real men, according to him, do not wear those things.

Countries, like people, are fragile. And the African countries are especially so. But Zimbabwe was supposed to escape the horrors of Angola, Congo, and Mozambique. Zimbabwe was born with a silver spoon in its mouth. After its war of independence, a bitter conflict, Zimbabwe pulled itself together — blacks and whites got along amicably, international investment resumed, and Mugabe and his new government became the showplace of Africa.

It was a net exporter of grain, gold, chromium, citrus, tea, coffee, and meat. Whites and blacks in the capital city of Harare (the Salisbury of my youth) talked happily of its future.

Unfortunately, people who were not affected turned a blind eye to the warning signs that Mugabe was bent on dictatorship at any price to anyone. The principal daily newspapers came under government control. And Mugabe dispatched his North Korean-trained Fifth Brigade to practice genocide in Matabeleland against the minority there, who had been traditional enemies of his Shona majority.

Still, to many, Mugabe was the West's best hope of a new kind of African leader. The West hoped mightily, and Zimbabwe's tiny white minority also hoped.

The commercial farmers, nearly all white, hoped too, and hid their fears in the love of the land.

In Zimbabwe, the sun shines as steadily and benignly as it does in San Diego, and it is easy to count your blessings and hard to innumerate your fears. So people ignored the growing megalomania of the president and his steady erosion of their civil liberties. People in Zimbabwe are always saying, "All will come right." It is a kind of national mantra.

All has now gone hideously, horrendously, and possibly irrevocably wrong. Millions will die needlessly, and millions will live lives of little worth.

Of course, Mugabe is not immortal—he is 78. And he will be succeeded by someone from his own party or from the opposition. But it will take a Solomon to put back what he has destroyed: a viable economy, a sophisticated stock market, a heretofore incorruptible police force, an impeccable school system, and a good system of roads and railroads. To say nothing of a tolerance among the mixed peoples of Zimbabwe.

So what was it like in colonial and post-colonial central Africa? I can tell you that it was hopeful, peaceful, tolerant and safe. In the first days of Mugabe rule, Zimbabwe had become a Camelot, with all of the virtues of its earlier time, minus the racism.

February 26, 2002

SORRY, THAT'S ENTERTAINMENT, TED

A nasty spat between some very rich people with very large egos is providing the counterpoint to the grim news of war. I refer, of course, to The Walt Disney Company's desire to replace Ted Koppel's "Nightline" with the "Late Show with David Letterman." At face value, Disney Chairman Michael Eisner is trying to unseat one aging talking head with another aging wisecracking head.

The New York Times believed that this was so momentous that it broke the story on Page One. The news has inflamed Sam Donaldson—himself probably at the end of his network career—and other television news savants. Those who feel that they have a few years left on the box have been remarkably quiet, notably Barbara Walters and Diane Sawyer. Presumably, they would like to swing on their gilded perches a little longer.

Now I do not think that "Nightline" should be cancelled, because it is one of the few broadcast news shows of any consequence, and because it has a healthy audience of over 5 million viewers. With numbers like that, this is not a fight about money. It is a cultural clash between ABC and its parent, Disney.

Eisner and Disney are pure entertainment players; it probably galls Eisner to watch his network at night and hear about the U.S. strategy in Afghanistan or the politics of redistricting. News in Hollywood is not what news is elsewhere. The big questions are not whether the Senate will pass an energy bill, but who will win the Oscars, what is Michael Ovitz doing, and what will be the next powerplay from Barry Diller. Out in Hollywood, those are real news stories. And showbusiness is life.

Of course, these people do not have a reverence for news programming; it is alien to them. And they find journalists, particularly TV journalists, to be annoying, arrogant and given to standing on principle about issues which seem self-evidently ridiculous to showbusiness people.

Probably, Eisner thinks Koppel should call him and thank him for 22 years on the air—11 years longer than the longest-running sitcom, which was "M*A*S*H."

The culture of showbusiness is one of in-with-the-new-and-out-with-the-old. It is summed up in a bitter expression that runs around television networks. It goes like this: There are only two kinds of people in television; those who have been cancelled and those who are going to be cancelled. To people in this milieu, the news programs with their long-lived personalities must be both a curiosity and an annoyance.

The quick excuse from the suits of Hollywood for shortchanging news and dumbing down their programming is that there is news aplenty on cable and the public can vote with their remote controls. This is not quite true. Cable has made very little incursion into the core audience of broadcasting, and the 5 million-plus viewers of "Nightline" will not automatically go to cable or to public broadcasting. Specific viewers, like specific newspaper readers, tend to disappear when the medium of their fancy itself disappears.

There will be a loss to the nation if "Nightline" is replaced by anything other than a news program. But let us not get totally carried away with sympathy for television news. Most of it is generated from newspapers, and very little of it has any serious effect on public policy or perceptions. Newspapers are still the primary channel for floating ideas, alerting the public, and providing an enormous range of information.

When Crown Prince Abdullah of Saudi Arabia wanted to float a new peace initiative he carefully chose *The New York Times* as the most effective way of grabbing the attention of the world. He would not have done it on "Nightline" or "This Week with Sam and Cokie" or "Meet the Press."

Television amplifies the news, but it is still the print reporter who breaks the news. Koppel and his colleagues play an endless game of catch up. Their news sources are the front pages of the newspapers, and their contribution is only to put pictures and opinions behind the news.

This is not because there are no good journalists in television; rather it is because television itself is a very inefficient news medium. There is no immediate record and the speed at which television transfers information is painfully slow. All the information in a big 13-minute segment on "60 Minutes" or one of the other newsmagazines contains no more information than about 10 paragraphs in a newspaper. Worse, the television viewer is a passive captive of every word and every image, whereas the newspaper reader is proactive, working over a smorgasbord of information options from detailed accounts overseas to health news at home.

Television only comes into its own with breaking news; otherwise it is a slow, though captivating, rehash of what is already known.

There are those who think that if we had nothing but the best of broadcasting, serious documentaries, inspired talk shows, immediate news, and good historical programs that we would be a better-educated people. Maybe. Television is too in-efficient, too segmented, and too superficial to educate anyone. Books, magazines and newspapers are the only source of real information, and that may never change. They have it all over television because of what I will call "information density."

Television is an entity complete unto itself, with some of the same attributes as drinking: it suspends time, dampens insecurity, and comforts the lonely and the alienated. But it is a poor way to get information.

I will be sorry to see Koppel go. And so, after awhile, will ABC itself. In the fi-nal irony of this spat, the international situation which created "Nightline" is re-playing itself, and an awful lot of people, maybe more than 5 million, will want a wrap-up of hostilities around the globe at 11:35 p.m. They will get, instead, a clown.

March 5, 2002

FROM IRELAND WITH LOVE—AND A HINT OF CRITICISM

The arrival of the Irish prime minister at the White House, just before St. Patrick's Day, has become as predictable as the stocking of bars with green beer across the United States.

The current Irish prime minister, Bertie Ahern, will, like his predecessors, hope that pictures of him and President Bush play prominently in the Irish media. It is good for Irish prime ministers to be seen exiting the Oval Office, all smiles and handshakes.

It is also good for the incumbent president to be seen warmly receiving the Irish prime minister and to be photographed leaving the Oval Office in the company of Ireland's leader. More smiles and handshakes.

American presidents have all courted the Irish vote, and as more than 40 mil-lion Americans claim Irish ancestry, it is a serious courtship.

In Ireland, pacifistic and neutral, American presidents do not always play so well. John Kennedy was the most loved because he was the real thing, his family the most recent to leave the old sod. It wasn't Lyndon Johnson territory, and it wasn't Richard Nixon territory. But Ronald Reagan tried manfully to establish his Irish credentials. The Irish were less than enthusiastic about him. They preferred the more general European view that Reagan was a dangerous cowboy, not a "wise old Irish-American."

Bill Clinton was their man. And was nearly as revered in Ireland as was Kennedy. Also he threw himself and his administration into seeking peace in Northern Ireland with some success. Clinton, Kennedy—they were sons you could be proud of.

Bush has had no opportunity to solicit the favor of the Irish. In Ireland, he is re-garded much as Reagan was: bellicose, unsympathetic, and maybe a dangerous man.

But none of this will cloud Ahern's meeting with Bush. First, the news from Ireland is fairly good. In the north, a brittle peace has been operating, and there has been some reduction in tension since the IRA began decommissioning its weapons. For the moment, Ireland's peace process has matured beyond "process" to "peace." Yet the peace is very fragile and the arrangements enshrined in the Clinton-backed Good Friday Agreement could implode. But they have not.

So Bush can look forward to an amiable exchange with Ahern, unlike many visitors of recent times. Ahern does not have to be cajoled into standing with the United States against terrorism, although he may have doubts about the prosecution of the U.S. war against terrorism. It is unlikely, for example, that Ahern will urge Bush to go into Iraq. He may feel, after many years of terrorism in Northern Ireland, that he has some insights into controlling urban violence.

And, in particular, he may be quite keen to tell Bush where the British got it wrong: how detention without trial became a nightmare for the British, and how the British had to concede many points of principle to bring about the fragile peace. These included releasing convicted terrorists, including murderers, and allowing members of the IRA's political party, Sinn Fein, to sit in the House of Commons in London without swearing fealty to the Queen.

Ahern just might tell Bush that after a war comes politics, and that politics can involve some very unpleasant retreats by the victor. He also may share some information on how terrorists launder money and buy arms. These are things understood on both sides of the border in Ireland.

Years ago, Irish prime ministers came to Washington to be seen, to criticize British intransigence and to raise money. None of that will be on Ahern's agenda this time. Ireland is the most prosperous member of the European Union, having gone from being one of the most pathetically poor countries in Europe with intractable unemployment to one of its richest. In the 1990s, Ireland has had an annual growth rate that edged over 15 percent. And even in weaker economic times, it looks like it will top out this year at more than 5 percent.

If Bush asks Ahern how this was achieved, he should tell him: "We learned to export by wire and wireless, instead of by ship and airplane."

"Mr. President," Ahern should say, "we were able to use our high literacy rate to secure a commanding position in the world Internet market. Every day we attract more Internet companies, not because we lead the world in science and math education, but because we lead it in literacy."

The Irish revolution has been one of the most astounding, and I have watched it up close for a decade. Every year I journey to the Humbert Summer School, a think tank in the west of Ireland. In the early 1990s, Irish politicians would come and address our sessions and confess that they did not believe that structural unemployment in the Emerald Isle would ever fall below 22 percent. In recent times, the Irish have been short of labor and there have been determined efforts to attract the Irish who were living abroad to come home, and take the jobs that were begging.

The New Ireland, as it is called, has all the problems of other advanced countries: traffic, drugs, immigration, high housing costs and threatened natural resources. But it is a far cry from the Old Ireland with its poverty, drunkenness and despair.

The Humbert Summer School is one of 40 or so summer schools that come to life every summer in Ireland. They started with literary and music schools, and spread to politics and world affairs. The Humbert Summer School is named for French Gen. Jean Humbert, who landed in the northwest of Ireland to help the 1798 Irish uprising against the English. Through the Humbert School, I have met nearly every major player in Ireland on both sides of the border, including former President Mary Robinson, Sinn Fein leaders Gerry Adams and Martin McGuinness and, yes, Bertie Ahern.

Bush will again find Ahern an affable, easy guest, who nonetheless will press on the president the European view of him as an isolationist, a unilateralist, but a friend of Ireland all the same. It is, of course, very Irish to hold two disparate views simultaneously and to give them equal weight in argument. Bernard Shaw, an Irishman, did it on the stage, and Irish politicians do it all the time. It is part of the charm of Ireland and of the Irish mind. I have learned my lessons well at summer school.

March 12, 2002

THE BLAND LEADING THE BLAND:
THE CONFIRMATION TRAP

You cannot quantify its ravages, calibrate its destruction, or ever know what might have been, but it takes a terrible toll. It is purity: Washington purity. It is the insidious disease, which keeps the most gifted people out of government service and off the courts.

It has just reared its ugly head in the case of Judge Charles W. Pickering, who President Bush nominated to the 5th U.S. Circuit Court of Appeals. It is of no matter that the judge has not been confirmed. But it is a grave matter that the advise-and-consent role of the Senate has become so bitter that no self-respecting man or woman of talent would want to subject themselves to the awful scrutiny which awaits people who are ready to serve their country.

An equally virulent strain of the disease awaits those who seek public office. It is the public dissection of a life: ruthless, cruel and pointless. Over the past 30 years, both the electoral process and the presidential appointments process has become so ugly that one of the questions which should be asked of candidates and nominees is: What is wrong with you that you would subject yourself to this?

Any man or woman who has led a full life or, worse, has mused in print, at whatever age, will be put in the stocks and pounded in the search for the truly pure candidate. The result is that we get the truly pure: people like Rudyard Kipling's Tomlinson, the man who did not have the courage to take a stand on anything and was fit for neither heaven nor hell.

Gray is the word. We are getting a government of gray men and women, who have lived modestly because they have much to be modest about and whose principle feature is that their lives have been so without contrarian thought, controversial action, or outrage that they can slide smoothly through the confirmation process into the high offices of the land. It is not their fault, but it is one of the unintended consequences of today's political life.

It was bad 30 years ago, when good people first started turning down the very suggestion that they become a deputy or assistant secretary in some critical department, and things have gone south since then. Ditto, of course, if you want to run for political office. Many fine talents have weighed the process against the damage to their families and careers and have elected to remain in the private sector. They are probably people who were willing to take a substantial cut in pay to serve their country, but not to have their families humiliated.

. The fault is not with the Democrats or the Republicans. They share it.

So ugly has confirmation process become that Judge Robert Bork had his record of movie rentals exposed and Judge Pickering had to face interrogation about his youthful opinions of decades ago. That is what is in store for the merely intellectually active. God help them if they were active in some more earthy way, like making money, falling in love, or taking a drink. All will be laid bare in as hurtful a manner as possible. The Senate has become a Star Chamber, prosecuting thought, conduct and indulgence.

There are occasions when it is truly appropriate for the Senate to withhold its consent, but they are few. And if the process had not become so hugely charged with political venom, the president, any president, might seek the advice of the Senate before that body is put in a position of withholding its consent.

Only Supreme Court justices, because of the huge philosophical issues at stake, should deserve heavy scrutiny. If we proceed as we are, we will have in every critical post in government men and women who are proven nonentities—no thoughts in their heads and no fire in their bellies. The bland leading the bland. What a prospect.

The media is not without fault in propagating this debilitating disease. But it takes its cue from the politicians and pressure groups, which see every minor appointment as an opportunity to try the sitting president on the very issues he was elected on.

The talent deficit in Washington grows with each administration, as the confirmation process worsens and the caliber of high government officers declines. Just one of the unintended consequences of this state of affairs is the increasing number of retired military who are popping up in jobs they are not particularly qualified for. Alone, former military officers have detailed personnel records. And, besides, the Senate is loath to pass judgment on their battlefield skills—at least until now.

Incidentally, I do not believe that either Judge Bork or Judge Pickering should have been nominated. But that is by the by.

March 19, 2002

HOW AGEISM IS DUMBING DOWN MEDIA

There is something of an industry studying media. There are think tanks, there are charities, there are university departments, to say nothing of journalism reviews produced by several universities and some private organizations.

Alas, these earnest analysts are probably looking at the wrong institution. They almost certainly should be looking at the advertising industry and its impact on all media, but most especially on television. The matter of whither-the- news comes to mind because of a new book by Leonard Downie and Robert Kaiser of *The Washington Post,* as well as Ted Koppel's brush with death at ABC, and Louis Rukheyser's summary fall at Maryland Public Television.

Those who analyze the news worry too much about its content, whether it is politically left or right, or whether news organizations prosecute controversial stories with sufficient zeal.

It is not the appetite for news that is changing the nature of the news media, but the appetite for young readers and viewers. You may be loaded with disposable cash, which many oldsters are, but in advertising mythology, you are not worth the chase.

The advertising agencies control what we watch on television and, more important, what we will be seeing in their frantic pursuit of their ideal market: 18- to 45-year-olds. They are the people either who have very low incomes, because they are young, or very high expenses, because they are starting families and worrying about school fees.

Yet in the mythology of Madison Avenue, they are the young gods. This reflects partially on the youth of creative people in advertising agencies, and on an unproven theory that if hooked young, they will stay with a brand for life. But the agencies will admit that their target audience mainly spends its money on beer, soft drinks, movies and apparel. Big-ticket items, such as luxury cars, cruises, fine jewelry and lifestyle items, are bought in middle age and later, when the financial burdens of homemaking and childrearing have been lifted. There is something wrong here.

Wrong it may be, but it is affecting what we watch on television, what we read in glossy magazines and, to a lesser extent, newspapers. Self-respecting news organizations adamantly reject the notion that they allow advertisers to influence content-and by and large they do not, story for story. But in the larger sense, they are totally captive to the advertising industry and its group-think.

The advertising industry has also affected the newpaper industry by assiduously following a policy of winner-take-all. That means that a newspaper with 10 percent more circulation than its rival will get 50 percent and more of the available advertising. Ergo, many good second newspapers have gone to the wall, even though they offered respectable readerships and more than competitive rates.

National advertisers go to the largest circulation in a given market and stop there. They are also looking for those young readers, but the pressure is less overt. The exception was *USA Today,* when the new newspaper achieved desirable circulation but could not point to enough of those young gods with an endless appetite for beer, soft drinks, movies and clothes.

Vanity Fair is so fat with advertising that you need a wheelbarrow to get it home. But its competitor, *Talk*, founded by Tina Brown, who made *Vanity Fair* what it is today, and which achieved a respectable circulation, died for want of advertising. Magazines that are getting all the advertising are known by Madison Avenue and by advertising agencies all over the country as "hot books." Those in the trade will explain to you that when a book is hot, you want to place your client's advertisements in it not because it will sell more goods, but because it is a showcase for advertising agencies putting their best feet forward.

So what we read, what we watch and what we listen to is determined not by consumer demand for news, but by advertisers' probably mistaken belief that only the youth market is worth pursuing.

There is huge consumer spending among people who watch thoughtful programming, read quality newspapers, and listen to mature radio programs. Unfortunately, a small number of advertising executives decide in the long term what will be offered.

Some of those many institutions that are forever analyzing media, carping about media standards and looking for political bias, might take a few of their researchers and look into the blatant ageism which dominates the advertising industry and affects the content of the media more profoundly than the politics of the companies that own the media, or the opinions of editors.

There are culprits in the dumbing down of media: those who are in hot pursuit of the young gods.

March 26, 2002

THE UNHAPPY LOT OF THE PEACEKEEPER

A policeman's lot is not a happy one, goes an old English song. Indeed.

In the 19th century, British politicians were constantly declaring, "We will not be the world's policemen." But Britain was the world's policeman. Those who felt endangered were always calling on Britain, the strongest power, to intervene.

As time went on the British developed various sophisticated mechanisms for doing this, and almost inadvertently increased the size of their empire. The British found that one of the easiest ways to be a policeman was also to be a proprietor. Some colonies were taken by the sword. But others became protectorates, or were taken under the British wing by extending the monarch's "suzerainty."

Of course, the British were not without self-interest and divided up their possessions into those they considered fit for British habitation, such as Kenya and Southern Rhodesia (Zimbabwe), and those that they administered and policed without a clear concept of their future. Exit strategies were not discussed in the 18th or 19th centuries.

With the various gradations of administration and policing, the British were able to limit the incursions of their European rivals, and at times to protect the indigenous inhabitants from local marauders. A case in point was the extension of British protectorate status to Bechuanaland (Botswana), which otherwise would have part of South Africa after the Boer War.

Depending on how you read history, the British police actions were either an act of genius or the subtle extension of colonialism. More recently, the British have had a different experience with police actions-particularly in Northern Ireland, where the British intervened to protect the Catholic minority and quickly became the object of its hatred.

It would seem that the price of superpower status is policing—and down the road from policing, nation-building. All the colonial powers found that they had to police first and build nations second, even if those nations eventually evicted them. Ask the British, the Dutch, the French, and any other nation that wandered far from its own shores.

Now the pressure is on for the United States to police the world. And, yes, re-build shattered nations. By default this process is underway in Afghanistan, Bosnia and Kosovo. Yet we are the most reluctant of policemen, and the most skittish of nation-builders. It is not written in our history or our experience, outside of the Philippines, to police, govern and build. Had we had the confidence of the 19th century, we would surely have pressed on to Baghdad in the Gulf War an established an administration there, with a preparedness to administer the country until such time as a viable local leader emerged.

Now Palestine, in its agony, cries out for some American presence to restore and keep the peace. The Bush Doctrine of leaving local belligerents to their own devices is under serious threat. Worse, the awful crisis of today has been worsened by what seems to be the careless use of words by President George W. Bush.

In last month's press conference, the president said it was "not helpful" when Israel made its first incursion into Ramallah. Now his press secretary, Ari Fleischer, says that the Palestinians' suicide bombings have changed everything; that the Israelis have a right to defend themselves. Ergo, Israeli Prime Minister Ariel Sharon got a yellow light from Bush in March, which has now turned to green.

The worst crisis since the Israeli-Egyptian war of 1973 is now upon the Middle East. And the Arab street is inflamed as never before.

In Washington this week, people are asking how long Saudi Arabia can keep supplying the world with oil before it provokes the same wrath now directed at the United States. The administration needs to act with strength and coherence; to lay out a doctrine of how much we will tolerate from our friends as well as their enemies; and to establish in its own mind when a belligerent is a terrorist and when he or she is a freedom-fighter.

Debates over who did what to whom and when exacerbated the long wars of attrition, leading to the end of European imperialism. Again and again, terrorists became statesmen. And the price of peace was the inclusion of old adversaries.

But history has its processes and they are not to be speeded up. Right now, the administration needs a plan to stop the killing in Israel and in the occupied territories. And this may include a commitment on the ground.

Winston Churchill said a decision not made is nonetheless a decision. So far, the administration's decisions in the Middle East have been decisions of omission. If the administration fails, not only will there be greater bloodshed, but the long-term survival of Israel itself will come into question.

These are desperate times. And like a good policeman, Bush must lay down the law.

April 2, 2002

SADDAM HUSSEIN MAKES HIS MOVE

The frustration in the White House can only be guessed at as President George W. Bush and his closest advisers sample the frustrations of superpowerdom. Our ally Israel defies us; our staunchest friend, Britain, takes a cautious line; and our enemy, Saddam Hussein, becomes the de facto leader of the Arab street by declaring that Iraq—alone or in company—will restrict the amount of oil it sells into the world market.

None of the options open to Bush clearly meets the present crisis. Military action against Saddam will so inflame Arab populations across the region that it is almost inevitable that they will join some form of oil stoppage.

Even Saudi Arabia, the region's great equivocator, might be so afraid of the reaction of its own people to an American attack on Iraq, that they would restrict their oil production.

The oil weapon has always been the most threatening in the Arab armory. A world oil stoppage would harden European and Asian opinion against the United States as their economies begin to contract.

Saddam's move is fiendish in its timing, its malice and its thrust. In a decade, it transforms the Iraqi dictator from the feared villain of the region to the status of its leader—and the leader of many non-Arab Muslims.

Libya, even Iran, have already said that they will follow Iraq's lead if other oil producers join in. The small states of the Gulf, including Kuwait, are suddenly showing courtesies to Iraq, which it has been denied since the Gulf War.

It is a region, as travelers there are often told, which is always looking for a new prophet, a new Saladin; a leader who will redress the humiliation that the Arabs feel they have suffered for centuries at the hands of the West. Saddam has applied for the job and may get it, despite his bloody resume and notorious past as the bully of the region.

Suddenly, Arabs feel that they are all of the same stock; and whether it is true or not, victims of the same forces.

Saddam, a student of Stalin, has seized the moment to project himself as the voice of the Arabs, the man prepared to stand up to the United States; and in so doing secure for himself an heroic position in Arab and Muslim history.

The calculation in the White House has to be whether the world, with enough of its oil supply in jeopardy, will stand still for a unilateral American invasion of Iraq. France and Japan will be apoplectic; Russia will be unhappy; and across the globe, there will be a surge of anti-Americanism as rising oil prices crimp economies and inflation takes hold.

The inflationary spiral triggered by the oil embargo of 1973-74 caused 23 heads of state to lose their jobs. No government can be sanguine about any diminution of the flow of oil out of the Middle East-oil is a fungible commodity and the most globalized of commodities. Thus, any loss of oil affects all consumers of oil, unless they are domestically self-sufficient. The United States might be the least affected because of its proximity to Canada and Venezuela. But the rest of the world, including the poorest nations, could be devastated and set back economically for a decade or longer.

But the president may have to take some action. It is unlikely that the visit of Secretary of State Colin Powell to the Middle East will produce anything like peace, and probably not even a cease-fire, leaving the greatest power on earth looking surprisingly impotent.

The next several weeks will be critical. If Saddam becomes the hero of the Arab street, then a major change of alignment in the Arab world would have taken place. And it is one that the United States can probably not afford to let stand.

For Bush, the frustrations must be enormous. He has done the right things, the moral things, the correct things. Yet anti-American feeling is rising around the world, and his powers of persuasion are palpably impaired. The tools that we use in foreign policy—trade, sanctions, financial support, persuasion and leadership—are not the appropriate to calm the crisis.

Some big, bold action with high cost may now be inevitable, unless anarchy is to engulf the whole of the Middle East and Saddam is to triumph.

April 9, 2002

MEASURING MAN'S INHUMANITY ANIMAL BY ANIMAL

How do you measure horror? Is there a scale that quantifies it, hidden in some academic institution? Is it linear, like most scales or it is geometric, like the Richter scale?

Or do we measure it from a small sample because we cannot contemplate big numbers when it comes to death, mutilation and the violation of all things civilized?

Are we more affected by visiting Auschwitz with its mass cruelty or by the diary of one Jewish girl, Anne Frank?

I raise these questions because I am the recipient of the most terrible e-mails from the country of my birth, Zimbabwe. Some of these e-mails are complete with photographs of the victims of the murderous gangs, which are operating with more ferocity since the Zimbabwe election.

There is no containment, no reason, no justice, no logic to the youths that the insane barbarian, President Robert Mugabe, has indoctrinated to terrorize and murder the last of the valiant farmers of European descent and their African partners. People who are being murdered, beaten and dispossessed are my peers-men and women I went to school with, their children and their grandchildren. People who never thought to leave Africa for easier lives elsewhere, but stayed to make something of the new and once hopeful country.

They are men and women who thought their duty and their allegiance to Africa was primary; who knew that a new country needed their skills, energy and commitment. They put behind them their days as British colonialists and agreed to be tiny minority in a very different place. For a while, their faith seemed justified and more than any other country that has suffered a civil war that I know of, hope flourished as the memory of Rhodesia faded.

But then Mugabe ceased to be the poster boy of African progressives— outshone by South Africa's Nelson Mandela, who also married the woman Mugabe hoped to marry. Mugabe then turned into the evil, vengeful potentate who is dragging his people towards the abyss of social disintegration, economic ruin and famine.

Among the murder and the beatings of anyone of any color suspected of opposing Mugabe politically, maybe the terrible story is best told through the suffering of farm animals, which are being mutilated across the country. Now some of those who are left with their health and the will to fight have launched a movement to try to end some of the suffering by going into the dangerous areas of the abandoned farms to rescue or to put down the animals. For this they need money as well as courage to buy their safety from the gangs that now occupy the farms and for fuel, medicine, cartridges, pet food and veterinary bills.

One of my correspondents writes: "Dogs are being hanged alive on hooks from farm gates. And children's ponies are having one hoof chopped off to serve as a proof of what would happen to the farmers themselves, if they endeavor to return."

Recently, in an English newspaper, one farmer wrote: "I am leaving now and I have a terrible choice to make. My trailer only takes one horse and I have two. And I have to decide which one to shoot."

A fund has been set up in South Africa to help in the humane disposition of the animals. The organizers say: "We avoid, at all costs, any political stand, as this would jeopardize our project. So all we can do is ask the media to help publicize what we do in the hope that the community can support us in our endeavor. Please, please, consider doing an article on the project.

"We also have horrifying photographs and reports from the rescuers themselves that we can pass on. We would appreciate any help of any kind."

The Zimbabwe Pet Rescue Project can be reached by e-mail at sjcwalt@global .co.za.

The animals remain on the farms because the farmers are evicted with less than an hour of notice. And thousands of animals—cattle, horses, dogs, cats, ostriches and sometimes tamed wildlife, such as zebras—are being abandoned to the cruelty of the gangs, and the complicity of the police.

How then do you measure horror—by farm laborers beaten to death by thugs while the police watch, or the abandonment of any serious treatment of AIDS by the government? There is a word for the thugs that Mugabe has sent forth: terrorists.

I cannot deal with the whole picture of the suffering of my homeland. I can only just get my thoughts around the suffering of the animals. It is my starting point on the scale of horror.

April 16, 2002

GEORGE W. BUSH, OUR SARTORIAL SAVIOR

We, the denizens of Washington, got it all wrong. When George W. Bush came to Washington, we were prepared to go Texan; to wear Stetsons, string ties, lizard Western boots, and to forsake the cocktail circuit for the backyard barbecue.

But Texas has not annexed Washington. Indeed in style, the East Coast has won handily over Texas.

Start with the president himself. He dresses conservatively, with a hint of the preppy he used to be. He favors mostly white shirts, pastel ties and dark suits—no chalk stripes, fancy English cuts, or any other ostentation.

There are no barn dancers at the White House, pickup trucks in the driveway, or flashy oilmen trooping in and out. It is subdued conservativism, in sharp contrast to the Clinton days. Members of Congress still speak in horror about going to visit Clinton in the Oval Office and finding him in shorts, sipping diet soda from the can.

No longer is the White House overrun with young staffers dressed any way they feel like. Bush said he would set a tone and he has—sartorially.

Washington has responded quickly by eradicating Casual Friday across the city. In fact, Casual Fridays had spread into Casual Weeks, even in Washington's big-bucks law firms.

No one is sorry to see the casualness go. One law firm that thought it was being progressive ended up with a lot of unhappy people. Middle-aged male lawyers who had dressed out of Brooks Brothers since they passed the bar exams felt silly in golf shirts and khaki pants—and often looked worse. Casual clothes, after all, tend to be kinder to the young than those who are wearing their success around their middles.

And casual mania was disastrous for female lawyers. When you made it through law school and managed to get into a top law firm, and dreamed of getting out of jeans and into a designer suit, who wants to be told you have to go on wearing what you wore in college? Not Washington's female lawyers. Some wondered whether this was a different manifestation of the glass ceiling: you can make partner, but you can't dress the part.

The president may not have solved the problems of the world, moved his domestic agenda, or brought Ariel Sharon to heel, but he has solved the dress crisis in Washington.

For small things be thankful. We are thankful that we can go back to wearing proper clothes, that we do not have to dress like characters out of "Gunsmoke," and that White House staffers look as though they have shown up for work, not to play softball.

Of course, the Bush administration has only restored the status quo ante. It has not taken us on a cultural flight. It has not taken us into the world of haute cuisine and couture, the symphony and the ballet. It is not Camelot. But it is not Midland, Texas, either. It is deeply comforting to Washingtonians, who think of themselves as culturally adventurous if they eat Thai food once a month and sophisticated if they get tickets to the hugely popular show "Mamma Mia!," based on the music of Abba.

Washington is, after all, Middle America East. And George W. Bush and his administration are a comfort to the permanent residents of the nation's capital.

Consider: While Washington feels it leads the world and is a power city, it nonetheless does not boast a world-class restaurant, nor a hotel to rival those of New York, Los Angeles and Europe. If Washington did not make laws, it feels as though it would make rope or steel or something useful. It is self-confident about the things it does—even arrogant about them. But it would not dream of challenging New York for art, Houston for money, or Los Angeles for style.

Yes, it is a very George W. Bush kind of place.

April 23, 2002

DOES GEORGE W. BUSH HAVE A HYBRID CAR IN HIS FUTURE? HE SHOULD

When the energy bill finally emerges from its House-Senate conference, if it is signed by President Bush, it will join a stack of other energy bills passed with sound and fury but signifying nothing.

The problem with Bush's energy proposal was that it owed more to the energy thinking of the 1970s than it did to the realities of the 2000s. It was a proposal designed to increase production and to reward the producers. Its foes in the Senate had hoped that they would be able to add aggressive conservation measures, but by and large they failed.

All in all, it does not matter what is in the energy bill that finally makes its way to the president's desk. What matters is that technology is appearing which can alter the energy equation more profoundly than mandatory conservation or heroic efforts to increase production. Even those of us who believe that the Arctic National Wildlife Refuge could be safely drilled are not heartbroken that the Senate rejected the president's proposal. There isn't enough oil there to affect U.S. imports very much.

But something much more important and exciting is underway: hybrid cars.

Hybrid cars are now available in the showrooms of Honda and Toyota. Next year, most significantly, Ford will introduce a hybrid sport utility vehicle.

While hybrids will not make a huge difference in energy consumption in many years, they break with the past in a revolutionary way. Laymen know that hybrid vehicles have a gasoline engine, extensive batteries, and that they generate power previously wasted in braking. But the real significance of the hybrids is more profound. They are electric platforms with sophisticated computers and electronics just waiting for the gasoline engine to be replaced by something else; maybe a compressed natural gas engine, maybe a fuel cell running on hydrogen, maybe a fuel cell making hydrogen from natural gas. Or just possibly, a battery so efficient that it can offer range in the hundreds of miles instead of the current 60 miles for electric vehicles.

So far, the market penetration of hybrid cars has been so small as to barely register as a statistic. Of the 17 million new vehicles sold last year in the United States, only 20,000 were hybrids.

A great deal will rest on next year's introduction of the Ford hybrid SUV. If it catches the public imagination, it will represent the largest major innovation in automotive technology in history.

Today's hybrid vehicles use less gas than their conventional counterparts. Their significance lies not so much in that saving but in the introduction of a car that is fundamentally ready for a fuel cell, or for a long-lived battery.

The electric platform opens the possibility, in a time of oil crisis, for the manufacturers to move quickly to a vehicle that does not require any oil. That is a possibility as dramatic as Henry Ford introducing the moving production line.

Nobody is going to suggest that the tentative beginnings offered by hybrid vehicles is any kind of panacea, or that it will get Venezuela and Saudi Arabia into line. But they do offer a direction for the future—a future where oil will be important but less critical, while we wait for a hydrogen or a compressed natural gas economy, or a purely electric one.

In the early days of trying to replace oil with electricity in automobiles, designers ran into two obstacles. The first was that electricity, as it cannot be stored, has to be regenerated from very powerful batteries, and they do not exist. The second is today's automobile itself. With millions of people-years of development, they are quite fabulous. And every time an alternative vehicle has been tried, it has been in asymmetric competition with the wonders of the car as we know it.

The genius of hybrids is that they incorporate what we have and build on the past to reach the future.

If the president can be persuaded next year to tool around his ranch in a hybrid SUV, instead of the gas-guzzler he favors at the moment, then a respectable market share for the new vehicles will be assured. President Kennedy took his hat off and changed the dress of men for probably all time. Now, it is Bush's chance to put his foot down in a different kind of vehicle and to change the way automobiles are designed for all time.

April 30, 2002

SMALL BUSINESS GETS KIND WORDS FROM BUSH

President Bush has issued a proclamation to recognize Small Business Week. Bravo. Now if only he really meant it or, rather, if he and his administration had any visceral feeling for small business.

This is an administration of people who know and understand big business, listen to big business, fraternize with big business, and talk a good game about small business.

That they wish it well, I have no doubt. But they simply do not know it, nor understand the imperatives that drive small business people or the problems that confront them.

Here, then, is a primer on small business. To start one, you need to have a small business gene in your makeup. You need to believe, at a very basic level, that it is better to own your own modest enterprise than it is to prosper in a large company. It is a very primal thing, where the driving force is not profit but independence; a self-definition by being self-employed and free. Of course, nobody who operates a small business is free, and by definition they are not rich: if they were rich, they would no longer operate a small business but a medium-sized or large one.

I have the small business gene, my father had it, and so did my grandfather. Ergo, although I have worked for some very large newspapers, it never really occurred to me that being employed was a serious way to conduct your life.

It also never occurred to me that the government would have any role in my business. Most people who operate small businesses are not looking for any collaboration with the government. But they do wish that government, at all levels, would treat them even-handedly—with the same generosity it exhibits to big business.

They would like, for example, to be allowed the same deductions for the taxes as are handed out to big public companies. They would like the Internal Revenue Service to treat them as the serious contributors to society that the president says they are.

I quote from Bush's May 6 proclamation: "To help businesses recover from September 11, my administration has made more than $520 million in disaster loans available to business owners nationwide. I also remain committed to a domestic policy that stimulates economic growth, boosts consumer purchasing power, and creates a level playing field."

I do not know anybody who owns a small business who is much interested in the loans, but I do know a lot of people who would like to see that level playing field. Where, pray, is it located?

Here in Washington, we know perfectly well that if you do not have the money to sign on a lobbyist, the playing field is going to rise up in front of you. The situation is probably worse at the local level. When a county or a state lures a big company with tax incentives, it tilts the playing field away from the new arrival and, as often as not, up against existing small businesses.

The romance of small business, talked about by the president and many politicians, is a fiction. Their real friends are Wal-Mart, Home Depot, McDonald's, H&R Block, Safeway, and the Pep Boys. And when any one of these chain store companies come into an area, they cause the failure of many small businesses. In one area of Virginia, by my count, about a dozen hardware stores failed on the arrival of Home Depot. Those are small businesses that are gone forever.

Back to Bush's proclamation: "America's small business owners represent more than 99 percent of all employers and their businesses employ more than half of the private work force. These entrepreneurs, who create more than 66 percent of the jobs nationwide and generate more than 50 percent of the nation's gross domestic product growth, are critical to our country's prosperity and well-being of our communities."

Indeed. Why then is official Washington so preoccupied with the needs of that final 1 percent (the president's figure), and not at all concerned with the garage owner, the grocer, the haberdasher, or the service station owner?

Now that we know that the president really cares about the mom-and-pop operations of the nation, maybe he will send the person who wrote the proclamation around to find out what is happening on Main Street—those parts that are not yet boarded up.

May 7, 2002

TECHNOLOGY, NOT POLITICS, IS IN DRIVER'S SEAT

By and large, more lives will be changed in the decades ahead by technology than they will be by war or politics. That is the conclusion that stares at us from the last century. Savage wars came and went, and four great political ideas contended. But it was technology that changed things.

Only one of the political ideas—liberal democracy—has survived intact and the others have perished. The losers were socialism, communism and fascism. Clearly, technology felt most comfortable with liberal democracy-because at its best, it allows things to happen.

Benign authoritarianism comes right behind liberal democracy as an environment in which technology can grow: witness Hong Kong and Singapore. But it is in the liberal democracies of Europe and the United States that technology continued to change the human prospect: a change that was initiated in the Industrial Revolution and has continued with little abatement.

Democracy works for technology and other things when it is supported by strong, independent institutions, which control and modify its political excess. Plurality may be enough, as in the benign, authoritarian countries, to keep technological evolution alive, but they are unlikely to be sufficiently enlightened to sustain permanent technological evolution. And democracy without countervailing institutions is a hollow thing—as capable of undoing the good in a society as it is at advancing it. Take the failed democracies of Africa and Latin America.

So long as technology has an incubator—in the 20th century, it was the United States and in the 19th century, Great Britain—its benefits will grow despite political and religious opposition.

And what changes have been wrought? It is easy to get carried away by the Internet and telecommunications. But more lives have been enhanced and social changes brought about by a range of relatively simple technologies than those technological poster-children.

Some of the most revolutionary technologies have been found in the home. Air-conditioning, now far from glamorous, has changed the demographics of the world and especially of the United States. The great migration from north to south was initiated by air-conditioning. Millions of people would simply not want to live in cities like Houston, Miami, New Orleans, Phoenix and Washington without it.

And then, there are the labor-saving devices in the home. Without them, there would have been no women's revolution and without the women's revolution, the industrialized countries of the world would not have doubled their talent pool. The doubling of the talent pool gave those counties that do not repress women a great advantage over those which traditionally do. The simple washing machine, vacuum cleaner and dishwasher can claim a revolutionary status alongside many more dramatic inventions.

The trouble with invention is that it is uneven and that politicians will, if they can, try to regulate shape and suppress new inventions before they are deployed. If the air conditioner had had to be authorized by Congress, it would never have been deployed with the speed or the impact that was the case. If we had known about highway fatalities, would automobiles have come rolling off the production lines?

Old technologies clearly find it harder to evolve than new, uninhibited ones, such as the Internet-particularly energy and transportation technologies are lagging behind in innovation. We are hunters and gatherers of our basic fuel, oil, and we make electricity the same way it was made 100 years ago. We also move electricity on the same kind of power lines.

Public transportation is past its heyday. The automobile has improved incrementally, but there has been no revolution.

Along comes a new way of moving people: Dean Kamen's Segway. And along comes a bunch of politicians trying to prohibit it on sidewalks and streets before it has been tested in general use. Yet, it is the first revolutionary idea on how to move people in more than a century. The Segway may not be the answer to urban traffic congestion, but its gyroscopic technology offers a wonderful future with less pollution, greater mobility and the movement of less unwanted mass, which we have in automobiles.

It is good that a free, democratic society has provided the conditions to incubate this technology. Now we have to try to dissuade petty politicians from messing with the eggs.

May 14, 2002

BUSH SHOULD SAVE INDUSTRY FROM ITSELF

The Bush administration's basic philosophy towards business seems to be: find out what they want and give it to them.

Unfortunately, what business thinks it wants is not very good for it. It thinks it wants freedom from regulation, ease of merger, lax accounting standards, and subtle forms of protectionism.

Yet business will be hurt if it gets everything it wants, or even most of what it wants. The reason is simple: it will stagnate. Most large corporations have given up on the idea that they can grow their companies by expanding their product lines, and instead are hell-bent on expanding their market share by merger and acquisition.

The history of mergers is not a happy one. Bigger is clumsier, slower to change, more opaque, and more inclined to monopolistic practices.

Yet it is now a common boardroom ambition to turn any company into an 800-pound gorilla, in the belief that there will be security and comfort in corporate enormity. Setting aside the sad story of AOL and Time Warner, the urge to merge is strong in many boardrooms, and investment bankers and lawyers have an interest in urging their clients to "grow the company." But everywhere there is evidence that it is the small, the lean, and the new that produce the goods and services that change things for the better.

Very big corporations look less to the markets for prosperity and increasingly to the government to ease their passage in everything, from accounting standards to environmental rules to taxes. The Washington office and its lobbyists are now an important part of any corporation. They are aided in their lobbying by umbrella groups, such as the National Association of Manufacturers and the U.S. Chamber of Commerce. All of them peddle the same myth—the myth that business is constrained only by regulation and by public policy. This is music to the Bush administration's ears, and business gets a very favorable hearing. It also gets a very favorable hearing on Capitol Hill, where it has financed both parties, but especially the Republicans.

The trouble with this is that business is not as constrained as it likes to think it is, and that it is throwing too much energy and talent at changing the laws instead of bringing innovative new products to market. Alone among major industries, the pharmaceutical industry spends lavishly on the next generation of products. Much of the rest of industry spends little or nothing, and hopes for a long life for the products it has in the marketplace today.

That is why most of the truly revolutionary products that have changed life for the better have come out of military research—yes, research done by the government. These blockbuster discoveries include the Internet, global-positioning satellites, the aeroderivative turbine, and a plethora of new materials that have revolutionized everything from automobiles to inline skates.

American business has much to be proud of, but it needs to take a hard look at itself and its future. This not least because the current generation of government military research is less likely to yield the civilian bonanzas it has produced in the past. There is broad agreement among experts that what is on the drawing boards today is less subject to what is known as "crossover." Anti-terrorist technologies, antidotes to biological agents, and surveillance devices are not likely to find their way into the civilian market. And the government has no intention that they should.

The great technological advances that have so helped business will not emerge when business is devoting too many of its resources and too much of its talent to growing by acquisition, and trying to get the government to help it by frustrating public policy.

The next great business success, the next Microsoft, if you will, will be another Microsoft, a company that grew because it seized the moment, innovated and provided product that customers wanted. It will not be because of mergers and the lack of government oversight. Enron already showed us that route.

In its inner councils, the administration should question whether it is helping corporations or helping them grow lazy and stagnant.

May 21, 2002

BUSH DIPLOMACY: MAKE 'EM LAUGH

PARIS—When George W. Bush likes someone, he really likes him or her. He is a man with a passion for those he likes, and foreign leaders wishing to incur the favor of the United States should hope that they meet Bush's passion standard.

On his tour of Europe, his man of the hour, his friend, even his idol was Vladimir Putin, the enigmatic Russian president. Bush almost fell over himself with praise of Putin—he declared over and over how close they were and how they shared the same values, particularly when it came to their families and their daughters. Putin, a former KGB official, seems to like Bush. But whether he likes the American president with the same unalloyed enthusiasm will only be known when various contentious Russian undertakings play out, such as the consolidation of Russian power in the former Soviet republics in Central Asia, and Russia's determination to sell nuclear reactors to Iran.

French President Jacques Chirac is another Bush favorite, but he is not in the same league as Putin. Whereas Bush and Putin do a marvelous public performance as equals, the show is a little different with Chirac. Chirac seems to be amused by Bush, but in an avuncular way, as though he is the son of a friend rather than the friend himself.

Bush, in one of his more unfortunate remarks, caused bemusement to Chirac when he could not remember a reporter's question and blamed it on jet lag and being 55 years old. Chirac, who is 69, stared at Bush in puzzlement. To be fair, Bush was tired—the night before, his good friend Vladimir Putin had kept him up way past his bedtime. In fact, Putin, who has visited the Bush ranch in Crawford, Texas, seemed keen to impress on Bush the glittering wonders of St. Petersburg, the jewel of a city founded by Peter the Great and expanded by Catherine the Great. The sights and wonders that were laid for Bush in Germany, Russia and France must have dazzled the president, indeed. The Europeans and the Russians know how to put on a great show, and they have the sets to do it.

It is less certain how well Bush gets on with the German chancellor, Gerhard Schroeder. Their joint appearance after their talks had less warmth than the Putin-Bush fest or the Chirac-Bush performance. Bush appeared to be discomforted by having no notes or cue cards, while Schroeder thrives on extemporaneous appearances.

But all in all, Bush has one asset that is always available: his humor. It is an integral part of him—spontaneous, disarming and redeeming. And it is hard for Bush's European critics, who like to think of him as a warmonger, executioner and unilateralist to overcome his quick and ubiquitous humor.

Bush's other asset is his passion for specific people. It is engaging and persuasive.

Whether these unusual qualities work as statecraft is more doubtful. The Europeans are madder than ever about the United States' abandonment of the Kyoto agreement, about the farm bill, about capital punishment, and the United States' intentions in Iraq. When the going gets tough and the jokes and declarations of friendship do not rise to the occasion, Bush resorts to what are now a series of clichés about values, the deity and civilization. So far, there is no indication that the formula has modified Russian conduct or mollified western Europe. Nor is there any indication that it has moved Russia or western Europe to have Bush's same sense of high purpose about the war on terrorism.

Part of Bush's insouciance may derive from what his advisers have told him: Europe has no options, nowhere to go and can only rail against the United States. Militarily it is insignificant and economically it has to take what the United States dishes out. Besides, the real concerns of Europe do not involve the United States. They are its high crime rate, its declining indigenous birth rate, the prospect of conquest through immigration, and its expanding union. Europe might as well enjoy Bush, embrace his friendship and tolerate his unilateralism: Their only counter is rhetorical. So Bush can make jokes, form friendships and play the celebrity president—he is dealing from strength. One day his friends in Russia may be able to challenge him. But by that day, there will be another president in office and China will probably have changed the equation.

Meanwhile, there is something endearing about Bush diplomacy, even if he sometimes sounds like the warm-up act for the real president, who never comes on.

May 28, 2002

WHEN DEATH COMES TO VISIT CLOSE TO HOME

When, pray God, will the killing stop? I write not about the great bestialities of Afghanistan, Kashmir, the Middle East, Zimbabwe or Colombia, but about young people in America killing each other.

Death has touched my small office twice in as many weeks. First, the young nephew of a colleague was shot dead in a carjacking. And then the longtime boyfriend of a stellar young woman who works with me was killed in a drive-by shooting.

"Murder most foul," wrote Shakespeare. But he had no experience of the sense-less bloodshed, which is a daily occurrence on our urban streets: a way of life and death that defies comprehension. What automobile, pair of sneakers, leather jacket or disrespect can so arouse a generation that it will kill for one of these trivia?

There is something especially horrific about the deaths of teenagers and young adults, whether it is by their own hand or that of someone else. They have just mastered childhood and are setting out on life's great adventure: untrammeled, ex-pectant and redolent with promise.

My first experience with young death was when the leading lady in our chil-dren's theater company-our star, the one we thought would make it in show busi-ness with her warmth and her Judy Garland voice-took her own life because she had been jilted by her 17-year-old boyfriend. Could anyone love that much at that age for the ultimate remedy? Her name was Jennifer Wood, and somehow I expect to hear that she is a star on Broadway or in London's West End. It has been decades, but I cannot believe that she is dead because these deaths of young peo-ple are so terribly out of context.

There is no national mourning to help salve the grief. It is as though the young die in secret without drama; part of no great legacy, just a casual forgotten end. A young widow of just such a death once said to me: "If only he could have died in war." She meant if only the death of her husband, who was accidentally electro-cuted, had been part of some larger identifiable purpose not just a wretched, lonely accident.

So it is with the deaths that have visited this precinct. They are tragic, horrific, purposeless, rendering their brief lives starkly inconsequential. Only those who love them will remember them—and remember them in anger because there was no reason for them to die.

If we are not as a nation willing to do something about the availability of hand-guns, as apparently we are not, then maybe we should, in a sense, embrace them by teaching young people just how deadly they are and how irrevocable one squeeze of the trigger can be. Maybe, like driver's education, knowing that a large number of urban youths will procure firearms, we should pack whole classes off to the firing range to learn that guns speak a deadly language for all of their tac-tile seductiveness. It is my understanding that most guns used in urban homicides have never been fired by their owners. There is no place to go target-shooting on city streets. Maybe their owners do not really comprehend the compact lethality of even a .22-caliber pistol.

Young people have a poorly developed sense of cause-and-effect, negating the deterrence of life sentences and capital punishment. Not understanding consequences is part of being young and the violence on urban streets tells its own terrible story of consequences not understood and of cause not being related to effect.

If the tools of death are to be freely available in the cities, legally or illegally, then it behooves us to teach young people exactly what it is they have stuck in a waistband or deep in a pocket. Teach them that it gives a false sense of manliness, of control over the situation. Teach them that guns, for all of their appeal, effectively end the life of the perpetrator as well as the victim.

There is something about guns that is well nigh irresistible: the weight, the craftsmanship, the balance, and the sense of superiority that they imply. I grew up with guns and I cannot deny their allure. But I also survived, as many urban youths will not. If we can find the resources to preach against cigarette smoking, possibly we can find the resources to explain guns.

We have an arrogant disinterest in what happens outside of our social class until death comes to visit close at home: the worst kind of death—the pointless death of young people.

June 4, 2002

INDIA, WHERE THE TIGER HAS SLEPT

India is a country you want to take by the shoulders and shake. Yes, that sprawling country with 100 languages and eight major religions, needs shaking.

India, with a population almost as large as that of China, is back in the news. And, as usual, it is in the news for the wrong reasons. It is in the news because of the delicate situation with Pakistan over Kashmir.

It should be in the news because it has some of the most inventive people in the world—great engineers and some of the finest writers in the English language. It should be in the news for the reasons that China is in the news: It should have a burgeoning economy and a competitive, global entrepreneurial class. And it should be able to throw moral weight about.

But India always seems to take the wrong turn. After it gained independence from Britain in 1947, it came out of the box and veered left. And its leaning towards socialism without being socialist has cost it dearly over the decades. India's first prime minister, Jawaharlal Nehru, wanted to be an instant world figure, and he championed what was then known as the "unaligned movement." This meant he got some pretty unsavory bedfellows from the socialist bloc and turned the United States against India.

Nehru had dreams—maybe inherited from the British—that somehow he could divide the world and rule it. But the world was divided between the West and the Soviet Union, and there was no room for a third grouping. So India was seen as a friend of the soviets rather than as a member of the world family of democracies. It was a strategic error of India's own making.

Other factors intervened in later years to conspire against India. Notably Pakistan, its rival and enemy, became important to the United States in fighting the Soviet Union in Afghanistan, and now in fighting the war against terrorism. By any measure, Pakistan is a reprehensible country compared to India. But the United States has had to work with Pakistan, and in so doing has snubbed India.

Another wrong turn India made has been its inability to liberalize its economy. Had it done so decades ago, it might be a world force to reckon with today. Instead, it has protected its internal markets and the small coterie of families who control much of Indian commerce. They grew rich while mother India stayed poor. Contrast these protected few with the Indian businessmen who migrated to England, and who have been enormously successful in a much freer economy.

There are two other factors that have held back India: its vicious class system and its awesome bureaucracy. The Indian bureaucracy owes much to the days of British rule. The British in India were famous for their administrative skill, and after independence the Indian bureaucracy made administration a goal in itself, without regard to its stifling impact on initiative. India also suffers from a state system in which too much authority resides in the states and not the central government.

And yet, India has not broken up as some had predicted, and bit by bit has been freeing its economy. Today, it boasts a 175-million-strong middle class. Indian computer engineers write more software, primarily around Bangalore, than is written anywhere else in the world.

The current crisis over Kashmir is forcing the Bush administration to take another look at India and it ought, overall, to like what it sees. If you are going to have an ally in South Asia, it ought to be one which is not predominantly Muslim, which is a democracy, and which is edging towards a free market.

An alliance of mutual values, not dissimilar from the one that we enjoy with Britain, is possible with India. There are also about 3 million Indians living in the United States, and their impact on the computer and electric industries as engineers is palpable. It may not be within our diplomatic reach to influence the tug-of-war over Kashmir, but there are innumerable other areas where we can strengthen our ties to India. Particularly, we can nudge India towards liberalizing its economy, speeding up its judicial process, and taming the bureaucracy.

India has yet to put forth a leader with the courage to tackle these internal weaknesses. The country is ready for its own version of Margaret Thatcher or Ronald Reagan. Absent such a leader, it behooves us to pressure India to help itself and in so doing, provide a counterweight in Asia to China.

India is an annoying, difficult country. But it is in our interest to forge a far better relationship with India: a country which has huge wealth in its people and a fundamental appreciation of freedom.

June 11, 2002

HOW WE ELECTROCUTED OUR UTILITY INDUSTRY

Back in The Roaring Twenties, the youthful electricity industry roared as loudly as any.

Think dot-coms, and you will have a picture of electricity in its early years. It was the great new technology that spread at amazing speed. It also attracted some of the greatest stock manipulators and speculators in Wall Street's history. Stock certificates were printed like newspapers, and a new economy had arrived.

Then with the Stock Market Crash of 1929, the electric business deflated, fortunes were lost, and it became apparent that so vital a commodity requiring such an inflexible infrastructure had to be regulated. By 1935, the go-go days were over for electric promoters. In that year, the Electric Utility Holding Company Act was passed and electricity became a severely regulated commodity.

Intrastate regulation was handled by state utility commissions. And interstate transactions were overseen by the Federal Power Commission, now the Federal Energy Regulatory Commission (FERC).

By and large, it was a system that worked very well with some notable distortions—in particular the costs were passed on to consumers almost willy-nilly, and managerial mistakes were buried in the "rate base."

In the 1980s, a new religion was abroad in the land: deregulation. Airlines, trucking, oil, natural gas and telephones all were freed from the oversight of regulators, but with mixed results for consumers. Innovation arrived arm in arm with price volatility, dubious marketing, and a sense of invincibility in the deregulated companies. They did not all fare well, and most sought to grow not by increasing market share but through a raft of takeovers and mergers. Expectations were high and a casino atmosphere prevailed.

The last major regulated industry to feel the winds of change of deregulation was electricity. But electricity is different from any other industry; it operates in real time, its product cannot be stored, and has to be manufactured in tandem with demand. Regulation had bred in the electric industry a culture that professed allegiance to the free market but had never been exposed to it.

The legislators, the utility commissions and the companies had no idea what a deregulated market would look like, but an irregular army of consultants, economists and lawyers was very sure. They descended on state capitals, utility commissions and the companies with varying deregulation schemes. Many companies sold off their generating plant and new generators entered the market. Every possible vision of the future of the electric industry was advanced.

But one thing did not happen: Nobody built any new power lines to move electricity in the new deregulated and semi-regulated world. Interstate power lines are regulated by the FERC and are hard to build because of local opposition. The amount of generation went up and the amount of transmission remained constant, except that electricity was now flowing from new destinations to old markets.

Enter the energy trader. This new breed, unknown in the world of electricity, destroyed the old sense of service that had dominated since the 1930s and replaced it with the trader's values of buy-low-sell-high and God-bless-a-shortage. The chief trader was Enron, a maverick company that set a bad example for its competitors.

Today deregulation, to quote one of the wiser leaders of the electric industry, John Rowe, chairman and chief executive officer of Exelon Corporation, "is a mess."

With a dozen states deregulated or in the process of deregulation, there is no big idea of what to do. The utilities in most regulated states, especially in the South, want to keep regulation, while trading electricity through unregulated subsidiaries. Companies that have already been deregulated want a level playing field and the ability to sell into other states.

No large idea on how to address the confused deregulation or how to build new power lines is on the horizon. Congress is torn by differing constituencies without regard to party. The FERC is still trying to find out what happened in California and to find a way of getting more power lines built.

Patrick Wood, chairman of the FERC, says that electric supply will be fine for this summer and the immediate future, but not because of anything that is happening in the industry. He credits lack of economic activity.

Until Congress gets a clear idea of what to do, more trading scandals are likely and transmission congestion will continue. Adverse weather and renewed economic activity can bring about more electric blackouts and brownouts. It all has the feeling of something that was not broken has been fixed.

                                                                      June 18, 2002

ALL ABOARD FOR A BUMPY RIDE ON AMTRAK

Amtrak, that great invalid of public service, struggles under two shadows: right-wing hostility and the 19th century.

Conservatives, somewhere along the line, took vehemently against public transport—unless it is by airline or highway—and especially against trains. Possibly, this is because liberals tend to favor public transport and have a sentimental attachment to trains.

Yet trains are a very satisfactory way to move large numbers of people between adjacent cities and into cities from far-flung suburbs. Boston, Chicago, New York, Washington, D.C., Philadelphia and the big cities of Europe and Asia could not function without trains. They would seize up.

The principal argument advanced against trains is that they do not make money; that they have to be subsidized at about 50 percent a seat mile. This, the anti-rail forces claim, is evidence that they should be banished in favor of the automobile and the airplane. The trouble is that automobiles and airplanes are also subsidized, often in very complex ways—for example, our military involvement in the oil-producing regions of the world, to say nothing of air traffic control and the impact, environmentally and socially, of cars.

No, no. I am not suggesting that trains can substitute for the family car, or that we should be dragged off airplanes and forced to ride Amtrak between nearby cities. I do believe, though, that trains are a great way to move people from where they live to where they work and to link cities which are within, say, 500 miles of each other. But the trains need to be up-to-date, fast, plentiful and the experience effortless.

Amtrak trains do not meet these criteria. Instead they are dirty, slow and inconvenient. The nation's commuter trains, many of which are run by Amtrak, are less than the state-of-the-art, but congestion makes them competitive with driving.

Our intercity trains suffer from underinvestment and from their genesis in the 19th century. Railroads are now diesel or electric, but they have their roots in the 19th century. Much of the thinking about them also belongs back in those halcyon days of rail travel, when the track was laid down in a vast, empty land and the same rights of way dominate today.

For really fast intercity travel, some of these old corridors need to be realigned and new technologies deployed. A little of the technology of the 20th century has been glommed on today's railroads in switching, tracking cars, centralized command. And yet, they are still lumbering monsters from the past, even if they do not belch smoke and steam as they once did.

When the French built their high-speed rail service, they found it necessary to build new track, design new engines and electrify the whole system from their nuclear power stations. Today's inter-country European express trains, with speeds of up to 200 mph, are the backbone of European business travel, competing and beating out short-haul airlines.

Of course, there is a subsidy at work. But there are also huge benefits: less congestion, less pollution, less aircraft noise and very convenient travel. Even the recalcitrant British boast that they can be in Paris in three hours from London (and the going in Britain is slower than it is in France). Brussels is an hour and 20 minutes from Paris, and London is two hours and 30 minutes from Brussels. And that, as they say, is downtown to downtown. It may cost some money, but think what it saves.

The Japanese, likewise, have discovered the only way to move very large numbers of people cleanly and efficiently is by modern train. Yet the United States, the world's technological leader, has trains that have not much improved—and may have deteriorated—over decades.

The paradigm is Europe—with large areas, congestion, pollution and impressive technology. We will get none of this while the funding of passenger service is parsimonious. And there is a philosophical bent among many politicians against trains.

To fix passenger service, Amtrak needs more than money. It needs a grander sense of itself and its purpose, and a persuasive argument for surface transportation. That, of course, means an attempt at a cohesive transportation policy, which we have never had and which is not even talked about anymore.

All aboard for a long, bumpy ride on Amtrak.

June 25, 2002

FOR PRESIDENT BUSH, THE GOING GETS ROUGH, CONFUSED

If President George W. Bush were a contemplative man, which he is not, he would wonder why his presidency has lost so much altitude in the last two months.

He would wonder why we are at odds with Europe—with whose people we share the values that he cherishes and promotes. He would wonder why the Israeli-Palestinian conflict is further from settlement than it has been in decades and under any other president.

He would wonder, too, why his administration has abandoned two critical ideological positions: a balanced budget and free trade.

And finally, he would wonder why America's largest companies, which he has so admired, have been looted by their executives and have been seeking to hide their mismanagement in accounting fraud.

But the president is not given to contemplation. Instead, he offers his principles—a catechism of American good—and seems angered that opponents at home and abroad are not drawn to his beacon.

George W. Bush's world is clearly a simple place where virtue—American Republican virtue—ought to be admired and replicated. But more Americans are seeing Bush as so pragmatic that he tips into the opportunistic, ordered around by the politicial imperatives of small constituencies.

After Sept. 11, Bush gathered the country and the world to him. Now they are slipping away, worried about his long-term vision and his capacity to promote and adhere to long-term policies. He has changed course on Israel, trade, peacekeeping and foreign aid. And he has accepted debilitating compromises on education, campaign finance reform and the farm bill.

Even the war against terrorism is looking a little ragged. He has not told us what he plans for Iraq, suggesting he does not have a plan. He has kicked up a constitutional storm over the rights of detainees and citizens caught up in the war against terrorism. Civil libertarians fear that the war against terrorism, which presumably will go on forever, is also an excuse for authoritarianism and an erosion of constitutional protections for all Americans.

Bush is reorganizing the government to create a massive new Department of Homeland Security, which prima facie will not function any better than its component parts have in the past. President Jimmy Carter created the Department of Education and the Department of Energy because he could not fix the education system or solve the energy crisis. So there is reason to wonder why a Department of Homeland Security will mitigate terrorism.

The president has his environmental problems, undercutting his own Environmental Protection Agency and antagonizing the world, especially Europe.

Some of Bush's problems are problems of style, particularly in dealing with our allies on the environment and trade. And some of them reflect his naivete in dealing with the world.

At heart, he is a fundamentalist: a good man who sees issues in terms of good and evil and who seems to have no understanding or comprehension of the roots of conflict.

Of all the president's disagreements beyond our shores, the escalating differences with Europe are the most significant. What, in the end, are trivialities are dividing the great Western house, which has shaped our civilization for centuries and is the greatest alignment the world has ever known.

As Bush relaxes this summer, he may want to ask himself why things are going wrong and why he is dividing, not uniting, the Western world. The division has no purpose: it will not make American industry more competitive, it will not save the environment, and it will not lift up Africa.

After 18 months in office, the president needs to do some deep thinking and make a course correction. Newt Gingrich, the former speaker of the House, hailed Bush's election as the onset of a "transformational presidency." Indeed. But a transformation to what?

July 2, 2002

CIAO, EUROPE—WE ARE GOING DIFFERENT WAYS

DUBLIN—Scads of well-intentioned people are running around the capitals of Europe and Washington, D.C. lamenting the deteriorating relationship between Europe and America. The Europeans are quick to blame President George W. Bush for the estrangement. And the Americans wish that their European colleagues had a better understanding of the imperatives of the American presidency.

But, in fact, relations between Europe and America have been decaying since well before Bush's election, and although he has taken his sledgehammer to the wedge separating the Atlantic partners, cracks were visible throughout the Clinton years and growing all the time.

Europeans and Americans—so close for so long—are simply in different places. Europe is in what has been described as a post-modernist phase, committed to diplomacy, internationalism, collaboration, and a decline in nationalism. They also feel themselves to be in a post-military world where the use of force has little validity. Hence, European defense budgets keep shrinking and budgets for the tools of diplomacy, such as foreign aid, are rising.

Conservative American intellectuals such as Irving Kristol and his son, Bill, and Richard Perle have been pouring scorn on Europe since the mid-1990s, and have convinced the conservative faithful that Europe is somehow wet, rotten and without moral compass. Religion is not a force in Europe, and Europe persists in a social agenda, which is an anathema to conservatives and centrists in America.

From the European point of view, America is harsh, uncaring, reactionary and bellicose. Europeans will not spend on defense and Americans feel that the burden of European defense has long been shouldered by the United States.

What is more, the metaphorical Arab street now runs through Europe, where Muslim migrants make up a substantial minority. Even the British Prime Minister Tony Blair, keen to be seen as the strong right hand of the American president, is aware that if he is too supportive of the war against terrorism and of a possible invasion of Iraq, riots will engulf some of his cities. French President Jacques Chirac, with a bigger Muslim minority, has to tread even more carefully than Blair—likewise for many other European leaders, from Germany to Spain.

Even as the makeup of America is changing, so, too, is the makeup of Europe. We share a common liberal democratic heritage, but it is strained by the new realities.

The cracks might have been papered over for longer if it had not been for the advent of Bush. Europeans have always been wary of American conservatives—they were of Ronald Reagan, despite the fall of the Soviet Union—and they see their worst suspicions confirmed in Bush.

They see him as a callous hick, favoring military action over diplomacy, force majeure over reconciliation, and blindly led by religious conservatives. Religion in Europe has become a museum piece, not an integral part of policy. They are as shocked by Bush's frequent references to God as we are by their endless humanistic deliberations.

Bush may have thrown down the gauntlet with his dismissal of the Kyoto treaty, his abandonment of the ABM treaty, and repudiation of the International Criminal Court, but the schisms were already there. The drift was already underway.

The great American achievements in Europe, including the participation in two world wars, the Marshall Plan, the Berlin Airlift, and the containment of the Soviet Union, are nearly forgotten now. Even in Ireland, with its special relationship with America—a relationship even more special than the one between Britain and America—the memory is fading. The fact that the United States gave new life to millions of Irish immigrants is less in people's minds than it once was. With the collapse of the moral authority of the Catholic Church in Ireland and the United States, yet another bond has been loosened.

In Ireland, as everywhere else in Europe, people are distressed by the use of the death penalty in America, the severity of our penal system, and what they see as our unbridled arrogance in international affairs.

Although Europeans are treated to an enormous amount of American music and television, the cultures and the replacement immigrant population are very different, widening the Atlantic.

In light of this sorry state of affairs, it is ironic that the new television hit is Europe is "The West Wing"—but then they like that liberal, humanitarian TV president better than the real thing.

July 9, 2002

HOMELAND DEPT.: OLD SUSPECTS IN NEW CLOTHES

When you cannot fix something, create a Cabinet-level department. At least that is what Jimmy Carter did. Frustrated with the schools, he created the Department of Education, and the schools have gotten no better. When Carter was panicked about energy supply, he created the Department of Energy. And it, too, has failed to deliver.

In fact, the Energy Department might be a case study for the problems ahead for the proposed Department of Homeland Security. The Energy Department was cobbled together from disparate entities, often only linked semantically. After two decades, it is still an archipelago of independent fiefdoms, programs and missions, defying managerial cohesion.

The Energy Department is charged with facilitating the supply of energy, making nuclear weapons, running the national laboratory complex, doing research on nuclear safety, disposing of nuclear wastes, cleaning up nuclear sites, and pushing renewable energy. Understandably, no secretary of energy has got his or her arms around the whole complex, with the possible exception of its first secretary, James Schlesinger, who was in at the creation.

Subsequent secretaries of energy have applied their attention to aspects of the department, leaving much of it to be run by middle managers and transient political appointees. It would probably have been broken up long since if anyone had had a good idea about where to put the pieces. There is simply no relationship between the Strategic Petroleum Reserve, the nuclear waste on the Hanford reservation, drilling the Arctic National Wildlife Refuge, and simulating nuclear tests. This behemoth is beyond management.

Now, we are to be treated to a Department of Homeland Security where disparate parts of the government, including the Department of State's consular activities, the Coast Guard, the Immigration and Naturalization Service (INS), the Customs Service, the Animal and Plant Health Inspection Service, and the Transportation Security Administration are to be swept under the umbrella of homeland security.

The mistakes of the Energy Department are about to be repeated. First, there will be years of cultural realignment, turf battles and frustration before the new department functions in anything close to cohesion. Then there is the problem of personnel. The very people who issued visas willy-nilly will still be issuing them. The same INS inspectors who sent visas to dead terrorists will be plying their trade at the new department. The overworked and very competent Coast Guard will find itself with strange bedfellows. The Customs Service will wonder what it is looking for: drugs, contraband or terrorists. Its historic mission will be distorted.

All this will do very little to make the United States more secure. Security against terrorism depends on intelligence, from the CIA abroad and the FBI and the NSA at home. These engines of security are being exempted from the Homeland Security Department. If these agencies cannot now communicate with each other, what will impel them to share their secrets with the new department? Most of the parts of the new agency have no experience with classified information and are unlikely to get the cooperation from the security agencies that the department would need in order to be effective.

I would bet money that in no time the monstrous new entity will decide that it needs its own intelligence service. What is more, the one thing we can rely on it to do is to try to operate in the dark. Nearly 200,000 bureaucrats will be able to avoid scrutiny by the press and even Congress on "national security" grounds. It is a horrendous prospect.

As we have seen with the Energy Department, once these super-entities have been created, it is almost impossible to dismantle them. Congress would be ill-advised to push through the legislation, so that it can be signed on Sept. 11, 2002. That would be neat and tidy and foolish.

President Bush's point man pushing the new department is Tom Ridge. According to Ridge, and others in the administration, the creation of the Homeland Security Department is the greatest restructuring of government in 50 years. Ridge misspeaks himself. It is the greatest reshuffling of government in half a century, which may create more problems than it solves, if the smaller Energy Department is anything to go by. Cabinet departments are not more efficient than small, dedicated agencies. We already have too many bloated Cabinet departments, such as Agriculture and Health and Human Services, where the secretary does not know all the programs within the department. Big is not so beautiful.

July 16, 2002

OOPS! I LEARNED I'M PAST MY SELL-BY DATE

Sunday, July 21, was a seminal day. Not in the way of Sept. 11, 2001, or any other marker day in history. But it was an enormous day for me.

It was the day that I got my first senior-citizen discount. Mind you, I did not seek it and I did not want it. But it was given to me. And I have a feeling that as with all seminal days, nothing will be quite the same again.

I alighted from my small boat at the landing dock at Mount Vernon, George Washington's Virginia home. The nice man who works for the Mount Vernon Ladies' Association said it would be $9 for each person and $8.50 for me, because I would get the senior-citizen discount. He did not ask for proof of my age, so I do not know at what age the discount begins. But, clearly, he could see that I had passed that meridian.

My first reaction was to tell him that he had made a mistake. And my second was to remonstrate at why the discount was so small—a shade over 5 percent. If I had joined a class, I wanted class action. I wanted to tell him that it was shameful that the discount was so small. Didn't he know we old people have to struggle?

In 30 seconds I went, in my own mind, from being youthful to taking an interest in the privileges of age. I also was a little shattered that someone might think that my life's work is behind me and I need special treatment in my dotage. Off I went into my memory to see what great things senior citizens had accomplished. I recall that George Bernard Shaw wrote his greatest plays after he was 65; that Winston Churchill became prime minister of Britain when he was 65; and that Konrad Adenauer was antique before he pulled Germany together after World War II.

I was comforted to recall all the senior executives that were being brought out of retirement across America to clean up the mess made by their younger cohorts. I was never that fond of Ronald Reagan, but I am feeling quite warm about him now that I realize that I am of an age where I can make mistakes and blame it on forgetfulness.

Actually, we are rather awful to old people in America. And I don't mean locking them up in nursing homes. I mean a more subtle kind of abandonment: treating them as though they are no longer a part of the mainstream; treating them as non-combatants in life's daily wars. Placing them, if you will, under glass.

It is the little insults we throw at the elderly that hurt. We treat them as if they were beyond life's pleasures; neutered specimens in a laboratory—heirs to privation but not to pleasure. The greatest of the little hurts is the generational incuriosity about anything that happened to earlier generations. When I was a young newspaperman, we wanted to know about the greats in journalism who had preceded us. Now, it seems to me, young journalists are more interested in how they can get a great job than in how an earlier generation shaped the craft. Only in sports is there a healthy curiosity about the giants of yesteryear.

Of course, I am not talking about the big problems that affect the elderly, like health care, housing and mobility. Those have their seeds in the little exclusions that begin right after middle age.

Publications aimed at—oh, ghastly euphemism-people in their golden years, add insult, not comfort. They emphasize mortality, disease, impotence and financial implosion. Only one I know is joyous. It is called *The Oldie* and it is published monthly in London. And it emphasizes that unique pleasure that only older people can enjoy: reminiscence.

Anyway, having discovered on a hot Sunday afternoon in Mount Vernon that I am of a certain age (62, actually), I am off to reap some of the benefits of my newly learned status. I hear I can get a 10-percent discount on Amtrak, from certain taxi companies, and from select vendors. Also, I can remind my political friends that I now belong to the one class in society that votes rain or shine. Yes, I am a gray panther and I want them to know it.

July 23, 2002

AGONY AND ROMANCE UNDERGROUND

Briefly, the near disaster and ultimate triumph at the Black Wolf coal mine in Somerset, Pa., lifted a small corner of the veil on deep mining. Although it is now much safer than it has been historically, deep mining is still a tough, dangerous way to earn a living.

Yet men and women still go down the mines and take enormous pride in this, the hardest of jobs.

For all the safety procedures, the earth is treacherous, the air is uncertain, and severe injury or death is as present a part of a miner's day as the lamp on his helmet. Especially coal mines.

Hard rock mines, as they are called, are intrinsically a little safer than coal mines. The rock, in which gold, copper, uranium and other minerals are found, is more predictable than the uncertain geology of coal mines. Yet these, too, can be subject to collapse, flood and poisonous air. Mineral mines follow seams in rock. Coal mines follow the coal seam under every kind of overburden: rock, treacherous earth, aquifers and springs.

For a coal mine to operate economically, a large amount of coal has to be removed. Great areas of the mining holes have to be shored as the miners press forward into the seam. Technology has made a difference, but it has not made mines safe places. It has made them somewhat safer.

Three decades ago, about 250 coal miners a year were killed in direct mine fatalities. Now it is about 50, to say nothing of those who die later of lung disease. This, too, is improving with modern respirators, but a deep mine is not a place you would go for your health.

But miners love to mine. They are caught up in the manliness of it, the romance of it, and the permanence of working underground. In recent years, there has been a shortage of new recruits to mining, and those whose fathers and fathers before them had gone down the mines are at premium: men like the brave souls who clung together in the Black Wolf.

The dying trades of fishing, steelmaking and mining have about them an aura of big men doing big work in extreme conditions. Big John is not a mining myth for nothing. Mines are full of Big Johns, nine of them in the Black Wolf.

There is something about people who work with their whole bodies in dangerous places. Something that modern society has not been able to replace. A man—and in some cases a woman—who descends into the earth every day to wrest from it the things that surface-dwellers want is, in the world of work, fully defined. The miner does not need awards, degrees or citations to know who he or she is.

So the last of the miners are the last of the great laborers, hiring out their muscles and the prime years of their lives to the mine owners. It is not the profession that middle-class families dream of for their children. Less and less is it the undertaking that miners themselves wish on their children. But the hereditary call of the pits remains, particularly in small towns.

Mining today, as opposed to the bad days of the 19th century and the first decades of the last century, is fairly decent employment, not subject to the vagaries of weather and because of the demand for coal, fairly immune to layoffs. In the mining towns of the East, a way of life, small-town life goes on, even as it is disappearing elsewhere. Coal miners are a legacy of another time, often with the values and community of another time.

Mining is a communal business. The mines that provide community, income, security and tragedy, exert a mystic force on their workers. They are both God and the Devil. And sometimes, just sometimes, the heroism and skill of the miners defeats the Devil, as in Somerset.

When things do wrong down the mine, there is terrible anguish as families wait and pray for their loved ones to be brought to the surface. When mine disasters were more common, reporters regarded them as the worst of stories to cover, much more so than fires and other accidents. It is especially terrible when there has been a large loss of life and after days, and sometimes weeks, it becomes apparent to the families that their loved ones are not coming out of the cruel earth alive.

Those of us who have been around mines and their tragedies were lifted in spirit beyond imagining by the triumph in Somerset.

July 30, 2002

HOW POLLING POLLUTES THE POLITICAL DEBATE

Political players of all stripes believe they know what is going on by following the polls. But it is exactly because of the polls that most politicians are on the other side of the river from those who elected them.

The polls have become the news and the agenda. Ergo if you want to put something on the national agenda, commission a poll.

It seems that the questions posed in national polls are tired, old and concentrate too much on abstract issues that someone—the pollster or the organization commissioning the poll—thinks is relevant. Yet in daily conversation, the issues that people talk about are not the issues raised by each new round of polling.

Now that Congress is in recess, members have gone home to their constituencies and will hear something very different than the issues raised in polls. They will hear, in general, that Americans are concerned about great issues like Iraq. But specifically, they will hear about peoples' concerns about their quality of life. If people are financially secure, the quality-of-life issues that concern them are probably pollution, traffic and delays at the airport. If they are old, health care, retirement benefits and prescription drugs are high on the list.

And for the middle class, the overriding issue is education. Not education in general—the way President Bush talks about it—but the education of their children and the burden of sending them through college. It is a dominant theme in middle-class preoccupations across the country. Some restrict the number of children they have because they fear the educational burden. Others live far from where they work because the schools there are reportedly better.

Members of Congress who are listening will get an earful about traffic congestion, high-density development and the inadequacy of public transport, where it exists. Nothing so affects the quality of life of the average American as traffic congestion. It lengthens the workday, it intrudes into leisure time, and it deducts years of useful time from their lives. People love their cars, but in the vicinity of cities and on some interstate highways, driving them has become a hazardous torture. It can take hours to traverse San Francisco, and Washington, D.C., is second only to Los Angeles in car congestion. Interstate 95 is backed up almost from Boston to Miami.

The members of the legislative branch will hear little about some of the great issues that they have been wrestling with, like the creation of Department of Homeland Security, the faith-based initiative, anti-cloning legislation, or the impending hostilities with Iraq. Cleaner air and water are abstractions that people want but unclear about how they should be brought about. Members of Congress will hear anger from their constituents about corporate shenanigans, but they are unlikely to be pressed for further tax cuts, or to be thanked for those that have been enacted. The American public is inured to taxes, but they want the rich to cough up their fair share.

Thoughtful members of Congress listening in their districts might begin to realize that Americans are not interested in many of the issues that consume Washington—issues which are generated by polls and interest groups, and which have little bearing in daily lives. If politicians are serious about re-engaging with the public, they need to find better mechanisms for testing public expectations, otherwise they will continue to be regarded as an elite, as separate from ordinary people—as are those who summer in the Hamptons. Frustrated with national debates that do not seem to involve them, constituents can only judge their representatives and senators on how much pork-barrel spending is directed their way.

Things get tougher for politicians as ideology fades and in the public mind, left and right coalesces into a remote "them."

Polls seem unable to penetrate this apathy or to redirect political thought towards voters. Polls have an intrinsic flaw in that they pick up what people think but not what they dream. And they do not penetrate the soul of the electorate. Although scientifically accurate, people do not see themselves in polling results. They do not feel that these are their answers, even though the science of polling says that if they were asked the same question they would give the same answers.

Worse, people feel so sidelined by polling that they feel no compunction to vote.

August 6, 2002

BUSH TEAM OVERDUE FOR PERFORMANCE EVALUATION

Loyalty is one of the greatest of human qualities, but it can become a liability. And it is becoming one for President Bush. His loyalty to his own lieutenants and his Cabinet is becoming one of his weaknesses.

For a man who prides himself on his ability to take hard decisions, it is a strange paradox that he will not examine the performance of his own management team. The president came to Washington determined to run the government with corporate efficiency and himself as chairman of the board and chief executive officer.

But one of the things that good CEOs do is to constantly evaluate the performance of their team, and to shed weak members without tears. The Bush team is overdue for a performance evaluation. But those close to the president say there is no chance that he will shuffle the Cabinet or throw any poor performers out of the inner circle.

Yet as he struggles to boost confidence, to right the economy, and to help Republicans this November, one of the fixes at his command is off the table. In Washington and elsewhere, the Cabinet is regarded as uneven and, in two instances, as an embarrassment to the president.

Treasury Secretary Paul O'Neill is a likeable fellow; eccentric, loose, and a liability. Neither Wall Street nor the international financial community has any faith in O'Neill. They see him as a man in the wrong job, lacking in diplomatic skills and economic know-how. What made him a very successful executive in the aluminum industry has not transferred to the Treasury. A word from the president and this honorable man would slip away quietly, indeed enhanced in stature.

Then there is Attorney General John Ashcroft; a very different kind of man, and one with a substantial following on the right wing of the Republican Party. He is not plagued with self-doubt. Nor does he revere the office of chief law enforcement officer. Ashcroft is an activist, vigorously in favor of the right-wing agenda. He might not have become an embarrassment to the president if he had not thrown himself so wholeheartedly into the war against terrorism and, in the process, shown a totalitarian infatuation with the suspension of established civil rights.

The damage Ashcroft does to the administration is twofold: He frightens centrists, who are broadly supportive of the president, and negates years of U.S. preachments about human rights abroad. The next American detained without charges or legal representation abroad cannot expect a convincing argument on legal grounds from the United States. Our chief law enforcement officer has cut the moral high ground out from under us.

Observers say that because Ashcroft is so revered in conservative circles, Bush cannot reassign him or remove him. This is typical Washington mythology. The president can reassign him or reason with him, pointing out the damage his presence will do to the centrist vote in the fall elections. Ashcroft has gotten enough bad press for grandstanding and headline-grabbing from conservative commentators that Bush could press home his point.

Of course, there would be a bellow of rage from the right wing. But standing up to the extreme wings of one's own party is one of the essential but less delectable requirements of a democratic leader. The tougher the firing, the clearer the indication that the CEO is in charge.

Michael Milken destroyed Drexel Burnham because his bosses would not stand up to him. And Enron was perverted because no one would stand up to Jeffrey Skilling and Douglas Fastow.

A Cabinet shuffle would enhance the president's stature, increase Wall Street's confidence, and pacify swing voters in the fall.

There are other members of the Cabinet who are not stellar performers, but they are not doing palpable damage to the administration. They are good, solid people of low-profile, who have not made names for themselves pushing the president's agenda. In fact, only three names in the Cabinet come readily to mind: Defense Secretary Donald Rumsfeld, Secretary of State Colin Powell, and Ashcroft.

The president said in the buildup to his economic forum that the answer to the nation's economic woes is not in Washington. This was a little old campaign rhetoric and an inadvertent admission that big ideas are not being manufactured in the Cabinet. That he can fix.

August 13, 2002

JAW-JAW ABOUT WAR-WAR, BUT WHAT ABOUT OIL?

The jaw-jaw in Washington is about war-war. These discussions are oddly juxtaposed with anecdotes about summer vacations. Washington generally shuts down in August, and this year is no exception. President Bush is in Texas and Congress is in recess. But there are still enough people around to keep the war talk going.

Most seem to think, as did a former secretary of defense I talked to, that Bush has so talked up an attack on Iraq that he now has no option but to follow through. Yet, as there is precious little information about the president's war deliberations, there is massive speculation.

It is not known whether it would be a go-it-alone attack or whether there would be reluctant help from our traditional allies. But history has one certain lesson: If there is war in Iraq, the price of oil will bound up whether there is an actual interruption in supply or not.

The threat of war or the commencement of hostilities in the Middle East always puts pressure on the price of oil. And if the president goes to Congress with a plan for war, the price of oil will begin to rise inexorably. Bush has asked Secretary of Energy Spencer Abraham to speed up filling the Strategic Petroleum Reserve (SPR): an ominous though sage precaution.

The advocates of war are dismissing the oil threat, either because they do not remember what happened in 1973 and 1974, in 1978 and 1979, or in 1991, or they are deliberately glossing over the problem. Oil markets are jittery and nothing spooks them more than the hostilities in the Middle East. The war lobby in Washington is discounting the negative oil effect, citing Russian production, the SPR, and Saudi Arabian assurances that oil will not be used to signal its displeasure.

Their arguments misstate the oil supply situation. Oil is the most globalized commodity and the most indispensable. To understand the world oil market, it should be seen as a whole, not as a series of bilateral deals between producers and consumers. Oil, as economists like to say, is fungible. Tankers on the high sea, we have learned, do not respect nationality and like to offload at the nearest port paying the highest price.

Countries can only rely on their domestic production reaching their own refineries. Ergo, world panic or world shortage affects all importers. And the United States is a massive importer, buying about 60 of our oil requirements from global producers, including Iraq.

Non-Persian Gulf producers will stretch their production willingly to profit from the shortage. But that does not guarantee that they can produce enough to make up for any serious Persian Gulf production interruption.

The first casualty would be, presumably, Iraq, from which the world buys nearly 3 million barrels a day. Saudi Arabia can boost its production from an average of 7 million barrels a day to over 10 million barrels a day, if it is so inclined.

Russia would have difficulty in squeezing out another million barrels a day above its current production of 6 million barrels a day due to transportation and technical limitations. Iran, which produces about 4 million barrels a day, probably does not have a lot of spare capacity and its intentions are not known.

Venezula can produce more than it is now selling on the world market, but not by a dramatic amount. Mexico and Canada cannot make a big difference in the short term.

So the balance still lies in the Middle East and every tanker coming out of that region has to pass between the narrow Straits of Hormuz, traditionally a nightmare for strategic planners. If these straits were blocked even for a few days, world oil supplies would be curtailed.

Additionally, oil varies enormously in its cost of production, called the "lifting price." The lifting price in Saudi Arabia is about $2 a barrel—the cheapest in the world. In Russia, this cost is $6 to $8, as it is in Mexico, Venezuela and the United States. So even if non-Arab producers can make up the slack that might result from a war, there would be tremendous underlying price pressure.

The president's planners have to think about guarding the oil fields of the Gulf, even if their proprietors do not want our help.

August 20, 2002

IF AFRICA HAS A FUTURE, IT IS ITS WOMEN

What a charnel house is Africa. It is consumed by disease, tribalism, and poverty so oppressive that it turns human beings into foraging animals. And saddest of all, Africa is consumed by the half-baked, self-destructive concepts it has imported from elsewhere.

Even as the World Summit on Sustainable Development lumbers on in Johannesburg, many delegates must wonder whether Africa has a sustainable future. A continent of once kind and hospitable people has lost its head.

In northern Nigeria, a young woman faces death by stoning for adultery; in Zambia, people die of starvation because the government will not distribute American grain, having bought the pernicious view of European environmentalists that it is a health hazard; and in South Africa, President Thabo Mbeki has convinced himself—again an imported idea—that HIV is not the precursor to AIDS.

Africa is short on law; short on coherence; still clinging to dictatorial socialism, as in Zimbabwe; and awash in weapons. The situation is so bad that Max Hastings, the British journalist and editor, has called for the world to essentially abandon Africa—no more to have its treasures stolen and its humanity wasted.

Even the most aggressive critics of what is seen as the West's parsimonious aid to Africa wonder whether it has ever done any good or whether the continent can be helped; whether AIDS and tropical disease will simply depopulate the continent, its people dying of the most terrible privation.

Well, there is some hope in Africa. It rests with the continent's indomitable women of Africa, who bear the brunt of its failure and the hope that there will be morning there.

Although African societies treat women appallingly through general polygamy, female circumcision in the North and the West, and now routine rape, particularly in South Africa, it is the women who hold together what is left to hold together.

It is the women who do much of the labor, hoard the precious food, suffer the hunger of their children, preserve the cultures, and keep tribal heritage and language intact. It is the women who stand between possibility and hopelessness.

And yet, because of the dominance of men, the world has had little to do with the women of Africa; its contacts always are with men. In Zimbabwe, in the 1950s and 1960s, white and black idealists planned for the future of that now-troubled place without ever considering its women.

Today, in the cities of Africa, women keep things running: Men have the titles and women do the work. Old Africa hands know that if you have a problem and you have to deal with a governmental agency or a commercial establishment, you should try to find a woman in charge.

Gordon Brown, the British chancellor of the exchequer, has proposed a $50 billion Marshall Plan for Africa. Unfortunately, if it were to come about, it would fail. The nature of the Marshall Plan was that it returned Europe to the status quo ante. In Europe, there was a base and a memory. But in Africa, there is no base and no memory, save for the hated colonialism.

So Brown's plan cannot but repeat the mistakes of the past-massive corruption, misallocation and theft.

A whole new scheme is needed for Africa: a scheme that circumvents the nominal leaders and their culture of Mercedes-Benzes, AK-47s and Swiss bank accounts, and delivers aid directly into the hands of the people who hold African society together as best they can: the women.

If ever there were a great cause for the feminists of the world, it is Africa. And it is the delivery of non-economic aid to the women of the villages. This aid needs to be simple education about hygiene, reproduction and the tools of survival; hoes, water jars, household medicines, and home economics.

You cannot till the soil without an implement, store water without a receptacle, or save the life of a child who has trod on a thorn without disinfectant. And you cannot save Africa without its women.

September 3, 2002

NOBILITY IN THE FACE OF BARBARITY

"Why? Why?" a school friend of mine asked in his tears when his father died suddenly. Such is grief. It poses questions that the human heart can only repeat and the human mind cannot answer.

Grief seems to be of a whole, related even when it is disconnected. The grief that results from violence would seem to be the most terrible of all. At its core, it has discontinuity: broken lives, shattered families, and confidence in the order of things terminated.

As we grieve for the victims of Sept. 11, 2001, we grieve for all irrational killing. And we question the malignity of the perpetrators, the planners, and the kind of exultant hate that can see justice in the slaughter of innocents.

One wonders about the perpetrators, how their indoctrination in faraway places led to unflinching purpose in a land they understood, among people whom they had come to know. People who had shown them an alternative vision of life: open, free and rewarding.

One wonders about their vision of their God as a superintendent of death. A barbarous, vengeful view of God, robbed of grace, compassion and love.

We have to wonder at the hate so consuming and a faith so perverted that it can see no value in other lives and endeavors.

Finally, we must wonder at the known grand futility of the exercise: vengeance without purpose, slaughter without victory, and sure and terrible retribution after the deeds. With what manner of fluid had their religious supervisors so washed their brains that they would kill and unleash more killing? Would their deeds promote their faith, proselytize those of other faiths, or restore the dignity that their faith enjoyed in the 16th century?

When, one wonders, and by what route did the extremes of Islam abandon its tradition of tolerance exemplified by Saladin's forbearance in Jerusalem centuries ago? Islam is a monotheistic religion entwined with Judaism and Christianity. The Prophet did not preach hatred in the service of God. Yet all across the Islamic world today, there are imams, some living in the West, whose love of God is a love of hate, and who find their redemption in urging their acolytes to commit fiendish crimes of violence.

In this contorted world of diabolical passion, 9/11 was a masterpiece: bloody, brutal, pointless, murder most foul without mitigation.

Even as the crimes were born in hate and executed in lunacy, they brought out our own great humanity. For some, the wounds can never heal.

But for the nation, there is healing. And there is a sense of our quiet worthwhile commonality. The days after 9/11 were days of rare civility, of recognition that all of us take the human pilgrimage and can use a hand along the way.

Bleeding, broken New York became instantly inspiring and invincible. It joined cities that found their strength and their soul in adversity; London during the blitz, Stalingrad during the siege, and Dresden under bombardment. That intense concentration of talent and energy, that cutting-edge of innovation and possibility has now reached out to the rest of America even as we try to reach out to it.

The hijackers conferred honor when they intended only destruction. The Pentagon is no longer just a great gray building on the banks of the Potomac, but is now a symbol of the best of human beings in adversity.

And what heart cannot melt at the spirit and courage of those the bravest of souls on United Flight 93, who found their untimely end in a Pennsylvania field, having frustrated the hijackers in their attempt to drive the aircraft into another target? As their own lives were clearly circumscribed, they made the supreme effort and, minutes from their own deaths, saved unknown lives.

Slowly, oh, so slowly, after this the first anniversary of the abomination, we must let it go. Woe is the nation that cannot forget its grief. But there is a time to mourn and a time to look forward. Those nations that cannot move on suffer reprise after reprise—such as the Balkans and Northern Ireland.

It is not, I think, the American way. I think we need to shed our tears and then dry them.

September 10, 2002

THE ARMS DILEMMA:
INVENTING AGAINST OUR INVENTIONS

The arms race is back, with a new twist. We are now engaged in a race to develop new weapons and systems against ourselves. It works like this: We develop new technologies and they are replicated quickly in hostile countries or among small terrorist-minded groups.

Norman Augustine, the legendary former chairman and chief executive officer of Lockheed Martin, recently said on the Washington television show "White House Chronicle" that he saw no end in sight in the race to develop smarter and smarter weapons. He implied that it will go on forever.

According to Augustine, the latest twist is civilian technologies that have a military application. He said that whereas many civilian technologies owed their genesis to "crossing over" from the military to the civil realm, now civil technologies are being utilized in weapons development abroad.

Examples of off-the-shelf technologies that can be of use, particularly to terrorists, include the cellular phone, global positioning system (GPS) and ordinary computers. The military may have developed GPS, but it is now so widely available, and gives such detailed information, that it becomes a threat to the United States. Likewise, the innocent cell phone is being used to detonate terrorist bombs in Israel. As for computers, hackers are among of the great threats to our security.

Off-the-shelf technology can be used to convert light aircraft into drones and, in conjunction with GPS, create a new threat.

When it comes to the big stuff, we are, again, in competition with ourselves. We pioneer a weapons system and, in due course, it is copied by other countries. A case in point is the cruise missile: for a long time, our smartest and most sophisticated precision weapon. Now, Defense Secretary Donald Rumsfeld warns that in the future cruise missiles may be as great a threat to our security as ballistic missiles. This is significant because potential aggressors will concentrate on cruise missiles, believing that eventually we will deploy an effective anti-ballistic-missile system.

After the Gulf War, former Defense Secretary James Schlesinger warned that in fighting that war we had revealed our hand, and that other nations would seek to replicate what had worked for us. As it happens, cruise missiles were among our most effective and accurate smart weapons.

Traditionally, the Pentagon has led the nation in developing technologies that had a major impact on civilian life. Oil exploration has improved beyond expectations because of the use of 3-D seismic technology; electric generation has been revolutionized by turbine technology developed for military aircraft; and every generation of new aircraft incorporates modifications developed by the military, such as fly-by wire and the so-called glass cockpit (the former is a system of computer-assisted flight controls, and the latter is the use of large display screens that displace dozens of gauges).

Now military experts believe there will be less civilian benefit from new programs, but that many civilian technologies can be used in military applications. The trend has been reversed.

In the days when the United States was squared off with the Soviet Union, American innovativeness and flexibility gave us an edge. Now in an age of terrorism, we have lost the flexibility advantage. Small groups of determined people can pervert seemingly innocent devices into lethal weapons. Who would have thought that the simple box cutter could be used to turn an airliner into a weapon?

The U.S. challenge has increased because its new enemies are not interested in winning a war but in inflicting hurt, making the challenge asymmetrical and pushing the United States into a reactionary mode.

Yet it is technology that offers the best defense against terrorism and random attack. Intercepts, biological identification and non-destructive materials analysis are the defensive weapons of the future, which may lead to beneficial medical discoveries.

The price is the loss of our civil liberties, as we move into the naked world of the future, where privacy is not what it has been and where Big Brother has been willingly empowered.

We are caught in a sad conundrum. We must develop new technologies to outwit our old technologies, and then technologies to outwit those technologies. This applies from the smallest terrorist weapon to very large systems, like cruise and ballistic missiles.

Technology is neither good nor bad in itself. But it can be perverted to terrible uses. The race is on.

September 17, 2002

WHATEVER HAPPENED TO THE WELL-STOCKED MIND?

The coming war with Iraq—and the talk in Washington is not of whether, but when—has overshadowed other issues in the mid-term elections. But that does not mean that voters are now unconcerned with prescription drug benefits, Social Security, and, of course, education.

Education has become a hardy perennial of our politics; yet it seems no closer to a fix than it was last year or the year before or, come to that, in 1948. Sloan Wilson, the novelist best known for "The Man in the Grey Flannel Suit," was hired in the late '40s by Henry Luce, the publisher of *Time* magazine, to go around the country proselytizing the need to fix the education system. After several years of this, Wilson gave up, saying in his autobiography that after hundreds of speeches and tens of thousands of miles, he realized he had had no impact on education and was wasting his time and Luce's money.

Wilson's account is interesting because he points to a breakdown in schools much earlier than most parents now believe it occurred, and the futility of talking about education. Yet talk about it people do. S. David Freeman, a big player in California's energy crisis, and a distinguished energy expert, told me years ago that he would never make another speech without referring to education, and he kept his word. Yet speeches about education do not seem to have any impact and the sense that we are failing to educate our children is pervasive.

Many universities are now little more than remedial high schools. Professors have told me that they have to teach simple English and math before they can tackle the coursework. That is the crisis. But it is not peculiarly an American crisis. Schools in Europe are also failing, and although we tend to think of the British as being superbly educated, as with the US, only the top percentile keep up the great tradition of learning.

What is particularly revealing about Wilson's foray into fixing education in the 1940s is that it was a time when television had very little penetration and electronic games and the Internet had yet to be invented. Today television is commonly blamed, as is the Internet. The problem has its genesis elsewhere.

Before fixing education, we need to know what it is we have in mind as an educated person. Is it, as is sought by industry, an automaton in science and math who can take a useful place in the workforce? Or is it, instead, someone with a well-stocked mind who can use education to help himself or herself through life? I lean toward the latter.

My father was not a lettered man. He could read and write, but only with difficulty, and he confined his reading to his Bible. At one stage in his life, he was living in Botswana, palpably lonely, and he would sit under a tree for many hours drinking tea and thinking. When I would visit him, this would so bother me that I urged him to read. His response was, "But I would only get other people's second-hand ideas." I had no recourse.

When I returned to Washington, a fellow journalist said, in an unrelated way one day, "Thank God I can read. When things are really awful, I have the luxury of going to bed with a good book, to find out that these things don't only happen to me." Alas, I was not quick enough to explain to my father that reading would have given him a connection to all of mankind and its pilgrimage.

Education, in my scheme of things, is about inner resources, defense against the world, and a connection to that world. It is also about the excitement of finding out and the fun of knowing. Were our educational system to focus more on these things—once thought of as a classic liberal education—it would seem to me we'd have the raw material to turn out as many scientists and engineers as we needed.

If we are to fix education, we have to kindle curiosity, nourish young minds, and instill a sense of excitement about just about everything. Nothing I have heard in the current education debate about examination standards, curricula, and the like, suggests that the marvelous adventure of learning is being inculcated into the young.

What, then, is the purpose of producing generations of students useful to the workforce and of little use to themselves? Democracy needs well-stocked minds. When did we lose sight of that? And how, without it, can we really discuss Iraq or anything else?

September 24, 2002

THERE'S SOMETHING OF THE NIGHT ABOUT THIS WHITE HOUSE

Secrecy is, in the end, its own worst enemy. When things go wrong, the public cries out for transparency. Indeed among those committed to fixing corporate America, those straightening out failing countries, even those fixing charities, transparency is held up as one of the great virtues. Ergo, secrecy is suspect.

The Bush administration is one of the most secretive in recent history. It has a cultural propensity to secrecy reminiscent of the Medieval Church, which believed that the less the parishioners knew the better. And the inclination to secrecy is at odds with the administration's goals of public rectitude and high moral endeavor.

So why should it choose to have something of the night about itself, especially now when President Bush is enormously popular, and the country is fairly united behind him on the great undertaking of war against Iraq?

Yet the secrecy is everywhere, from the tight control of administration officials speaking to the press to Attorney General John Ashcroft refusing to release the names of detainees, to Bush's own opaqueness about Iraq and much else on his agenda. A seemingly open man, he heads an administration that goes to lengths to be opaque, keeping information from Congress and the press and, of course by extension, the American people.

When the president came into office, there were allusions to a corporate-style of government—back when corporations were still admired, and their lack of transparency had not yet come to haunt them. Maybe here is a clue to the Bush administration and its zipped-up style. Even after nearly two years, the administration, and the White House staff in particular, act as though they are the new proprietors who have won a takeover battle and do not have to disclose their plans beyond the new management team.

It is a style that does not work for corporate America, and a style that has never worked for very long in politics. Most political scandals are worsened and become crises because of a lack of transparency early on. That was the story of Watergate, of Iran-Contra, and of President Clinton's impeachment: too little, grudgingly, too late.

The war against terrorism has fuelled the secretive tendencies of the administration— tendencies that make it appear arrogant and insensitive to law and precedent. But most of the administration's secrecy seems to be more in its culture than its service. One of Bush's great strengths is his down-home, regular-guy character: the sort of fellow that you would not think would keep secrets from you.

Here in Washington, as momentous events are underway, there is little information and what there is is pasteurized, packaged and handed out with an empty flourish. Take the proposed Department of Homeland Security. It was produced in the White House by a small team operating, yes, in secret. Or take the president's energy policy, which was produced by Vice President Cheney, after talking to a lot of his friends in the energy industry in secret. To this day, he will not say with whom he consulted.

Neither of these acts of secrecy has helped the resulting legislation. In the case of Cheney's deliberations, openness would have made the Democrats less suspicious of the product. Likewise, many of the problems with the Department of Homeland Security legislation could have been handled before it was encased in the legislative proposal.

In neither of these examples, and there are others, are state secrets an issue. But the administration grows more secretive, powered in that direction by forceful personalities such as Secretary of Defense Donald Rumsfeld, Ashcroft and Cheney.

When the books come to be written about the Bush years, they will doubtless dwell on this passion to do by stealth what can be done in broad daylight. Bush's problems with our allies began not when he said a regime change was necessary in Iraq but when he renounced the Kyoto treaty on climate change: a decision taken in such secrecy that not even the Environmental Protection Agency administrator, Christie Todd Whitman, knew it was coming. He could have broken with Kyoto in a less cavalier manner if the deliberations and rationale had been public.

Bush does not appear to be the kind of man who believes in changing doctrines, breaking treaties, and formulating policy by cabal in the White House. Yet we have to wonder. He and his administration will not open up to us. They are apparently sworn to secrecy.

October 1, 2002

THE LONG ROAD AHEAD TO DEMOCRACY IN IRAQ

Conquering Iraq, if the United States should go in, might be easy. The Iraqi army might lay down its arms and the population might welcome the liberation.

But establishing a democracy in Iraq will be the hardest of all tasks. There is along history of hothouse democracies and it is a dismal one. Ask the British. People who have never known democracy, in a country without strong institutions, do not take to it well.

When the British withdrew from their colonial possessions, they left behind in Asia and across Africa, many picture-perfect democracies, none of which survived for long. Across the world, democracy was an interim step to dictatorship: an easy way to seize power without a coup. This was the story in most of Africa, where democracy was immediately perverted to entrench the ruling elite and to subvert the will of the people.

"One man, one vote, once" was how old British colonial officers described what happened in Africa. Name the country: Ghana, Kenya, Malawi, Nigeria, Sierra Leone, Tanzania, Uganda, Zambia and Zimbabwe. All used democracy as a steppingstone to dictatorship.

In Asia, the story has not been much better. Malaysia has a modified democracy, as does Singapore. And democracy never took hold in Burma. In Hong Kong, the British did not bother with democracy, but did foster a strong judiciary and inviolable property rights. Just before China took over Hong Kong, the British tried quickie elections to stave off the inevitable consolidation of Communist Chinese rule. It is well underway now.

For a democracy to take hold, it requires strong independent institutions, especially a judiciary with the power to implement its decisions, a free press, and guaranteed property rights. Zimbabwe has a laudable judiciary but the vote-rigger, Robert Mugabe, simply ignores the courts and rules through gangs of thugs.

The sad lesson of the post-colonial era has been that democracy is a fragile plant that does not flourish in cultures that have no history of self-determination. It also suffers when there are ethnic or religious divisions—and people vote these loyalties axiomatically.

If one were to seek a country in the Arab world ripe for democracy-and there are no real democracies there-Iraq would be an unlikely candidate. It has ethnic and religious divisions, and no history of self-determination whatsoever. From the time Iraq was cobbled together by Lawrence of Arabia and the British government, rule has been authoritarian and oppressive.

Initially, the British established a king and shrugged when he was overthrown. They never attempted, as they did in Africa and Asia, to introduce democracy in Iraq or elsewhere in the Middle East.

The passion for quick democratization came after World War II, when the British wanted a plausible and dignified withdrawal from their empire. Only India has enjoyed a viable democracy since the departure of the British. But the same cannot be said for Pakistan. And Sri Lanka has veered between democracy and democratically assisted authoritarianism. Likewise Bangladesh.

There is a school of thought in Washington which holds that the establishment of democracy in Iraq will begin a democratic onslaught in the Middle East. But what sort of democracy will it be, given the divisions in Iraq, the poverty, the ignorance, and the pervasive presence of Islam? The specter of Algeria can be easily conjured up.

When the Algerians voted for an Islamic republic, the government set aside the elections and the West nodded approval. The dream of multiparty democracies was postponed. What would we do if there is a similar outcome in Iraq? Set aside the new democratically elected government until we find a dictator of our liking?

Those now working on a new constitution for Iraq are challenged by the improbability of democracy taking hold there, and by U.S. certainty that it can and must be done. The British and the French tried to leave viable democracies in the wake of their withdrawal from colonial rule, and it is hard to see a viable elected government coming to power in Baghdad. One has to hope that there will be a contingency plan.

The Middle East, with its monarchies and nepotistic dictatorships, needs upheaval that will lead to something better. It cries out for revolution to break the cycles of tyranny and to move the region towards open, viable government. In short, it cries out for democracy. But Iraq would seem to be an unlikely starting point, even if the incursion goes well.

Compared with democracy-building, nation-building is the easy part.

October 8, 2002

FEELING BETTER ABOUT AMERICA THE INVENTIVE

Prosecutors are building a formidable case against Martha Stewart, domestic diva and businesswoman extraordinaire. She may have been greedy or foolish, or both, but Stewart is emblematic of possibility in America. It is sad to see her fall.

Sad, that is, not because of who she is but what she is about: a woman who went for the brass ring and clutched it firmly. It is the Stewarts who exemplify the American culture of possibility.

Sure there are people in other countries who have promoted a little idea to a large success. But it is in America that this kind of extraordinary enterprise really blooms. Vidal Sassoon was a British hairdresser who made it big in Britain, but he had to come to America to make it huge.

It is the state of near constant upheaval that gives us the genius of possibility. The size of the market, of course, helps. But it is the changing, shifting nature of American society that means that the race is never over, and that the smallest of ideas can become the biggest winners.

Ray Kroc turned the humble hamburger into an international brand. Wally Amos did the same thing with the cookie. William Wrigley, Jr. scaled the heights by adding sugar to chewing gum. And Levi Strauss made a fortune from miners' pants.

These and a million more are American success stories that owed their origins to the openness of our society to new ideas. Possibility is not unique to America, but it is more abundant, more part of the culture, and more of an expectation than it is in other lands with greater rigidities, oppressive social systems and entrenched elites.

So, at a time when we are feeling badly about terrorism, repudiation by our allies, and a homicidal sniper in Washington, D.C., it is good to remember that there are no upper limits to American creativity, and that a market of magical proportions awaits the inventive.

One can salute Henry Ford or George Westinghouse, the great industrialists. But it is those who propelled a simpler idea into a grand scheme who keep the sense of expectation alive; the feeling that today or tomorrow, the individual can expand a humdrum activity into something glittering and special.

The enemies of the American state of inventive grace are rigidity, regulation and monopoly. It is a sad thing that Kroc's huge achievement with a hamburger should have prevented tens of thousands of small restaurateurs from finding a small place in the sun. But that is the other side of the mountain: the dark side. It can be conquered by the changing of fashion, better ideas, finer products, and finding the vacuums which monopoly itself produces.

Every upheaval breeds a new generation who will take advantage of it and go on to their place in the pantheon of successes. Inflation may be a national disaster, but there are those who have used it to their benefit. The crumbling stock market cuts off one avenue of investment but helps the small private company. Endless change feeds endless opportunities for the wise, and sometimes the lucky, to move in.

Blessings, then, on a society in perpetual change, and damnation on rigidity.

Somewhere someone is making something that will propel its inventor or promoter to great successes, and to that special fulfillment that is the North Star of this enterprising culture. Of course, you could invent something in South India, or in Nigeria, or even in France. But the road to market might be defeating.

The first thought I had when I arrived in the United States in 1963 was, "Wow, here you can be a success by making glass beads. The niches are big enough and there is always someone who will listen to your idea, even if they dismiss it."

I thought: "To succeed here, you do not need a formal education, family connections, or pots of money. You simply need to be enterprising about whatever you do—no menial task being without a possible pot of gold."

Back then, a guy called Bill Marriott was running a lunch counter in Washington, D.C. Today, such promoters of their own skills as chefs have become rich celebrities. Also back then, it took a whole day to get a car serviced because no one had yet imagined that it could be done in 20 minutes on a drive-in-drive-out basis. Now there is Jiffy Lube.

So let us celebrate opportunity, and celebrate Martha Stewart, who added a dash of glamour to the menial.

October 15, 2002

TRAVEL WITHOUT LEAVING HOME

TBILISI, Georgia—Back in the 19th century and the early part of the 20th century, the British traveling classes, who believed they had proprietorial rights to the world, favored what were known as the "grand hotels." These were lavish establishments where one could check in, complete with one's servants, for a long stay. They were, among others, the Peninsula in Hong Kong, Raffles in Singapore, Shepherd's in Cairo and The Grande Bretagne in Athens.

After World War II, the luxury hotels were in decline and frequently in the wrong place for the new community of business travelers who wanted less luxury, more anonymity and American services. Conrad Hilton obliged with Hilton hotels, closely followed by Juan Trippe, the then-boss of Pan American World Airways with his Intercontinental chain.

These were the precursors to today's international hotels, which are variously oases, garrisons and office extensions. They are in the front line of globalization. They were pioneered by Americans, and they are now patronized by a world business class: a class which liked to be characterized as men and women who wear suits, drink Scotch, insist on working out, and speak English.

Hilton and Trippe realized early that English was the key to attracting the new business class, particularly the Americans, to their new hotels. Americans were afflicted in the 1960s, and they still are today, with language fright—a fear of landing somewhere where they do not speak the language, or communicating is difficult. Handily for the hotels, English is also the lingua franca of the new Europe, and the language of business around the globe.

The hotels now scattered in every major city do not strive for luxury. They are instead utilitarian, comfortable and civil in the "have a nice day" genre of civility.

Their staffs look on the guests dispassionately, incuriously, grateful that they are there but without any sense of bonding.

That, too, is also the downside of the hotels. They nod to local cultures, maybe with a little artwork, possibly with one or two modified indigenous dishes on their menus, but they are there to serve the monoculture, almost to isolate a traveler from the people and culture of the visited land. You can travel the world, visit six continents, and have very little sense of having left home. Many do. Many with thousands of frequent-flier miles manage to circle the globe without ever getting acquainted with the people they hope to do business with, sell products to, and expand their own businesses among.

A price is paid for deals cut in hotels by similar people far from reality. Many electric utilities paid the price in their global expansion in the 1990s. They saw their new commercial domains in some way as an extension of the comfortable, orderly international hotels that hosted them. These companies were almost without local knowledge and without any grasp of the need to have real local knowledge, especially when investing in infrastructure projects. One smart Wall Streeter said of the electric deals: "We should take the CEOs' passports away."

His opinion was that the deals were being made in an artificial environment in the cosy conference rooms of the hotels' business centers, and that the executives were projecting the order and the efficiency of their surroundings onto the disorder and chaos of some of the countries, such as Indonesia, Brazil, Argentina and Pakistan.

To think that you can do the same kind of business in Pakistan that you can do in the United States or western Europe, you really do need the blinders provided by international hotels, with their homogenized service and pervasive sense that all the world is the same place.

In the United States, we have forgotten what the privately owned hotel is like—its uneven service, eccentric proprietors, but real feel of community. The small private hotels hang on in Italy, Germany and France, but they are not for the jet set. They enrich one's travels but are, in their own way, work—not for the international business class.

The business hotels are so important for emerging economies that they are the first investment allowed in. Eastern Europe had a rush to invite in the hotels after the collapse of the Soviet Union, in the sure knowledge they were the essential precursors to investment.

It is the business class which misunderstands the artificiality of the hotels; that they are, in their way, colonial outposts for the new ruling class of commerce. Sure, the fax works, the Internet is available and the exercise room is standard. What they miss is any sense that they are in another country, that the people passing by in the street are the customers for the new enterprise, and that there is something slightly imperial and somewhat offensive about the digs favored by the well-heeled few.

October 22, 2002

WHEN LOBBYISTS SUCCEED TOO WELL

Lobbying has been around since the early days of the republic. The premise is simple: You hire well-connected people to persuade legislators to see it your way.

At some level, all organized groups lobby Congress. Universities crawl over Capitol Hill looking for preference, labor unions are up there with their agenda, environmentalists push the green way, and churches are not beyond asking our elected representatives to be the agents of their God.

But it is corporations, directly and through their trade associations, which are most heard in the halls of Congress.

Lobbyists, like the organizations they represent, come in many shapes and sizes, from the bearded and sandaled to their corporate brethren in English suits and monogrammed shirts. This is not all an infestation on the body politic. Indeed, Congress would find it difficult to do its work without lobbyists to guide legislators through intricate subjects.

Also, unfortunately, today's elected officials would find it difficult to get elected without the money that lobbies funnel to their election campaigns.

A really good lobbyist is one who can give a congressman or a senator real information and not just a point of view. Before money became as critical as it has, legislators used lobbyists as a resource, often calling them in for advice and to counter the views of other lobbyists. It was a system that worked quite well, although woe betide the group which did not have the resources to hire a lobbyist.

Sometimes such groups can be quite large and either cannot afford a lobbyist or are in an inappropriate position to lobby. For example, consider the armed forces. Here the trouble begins: a certain pernicious asymmetry sets in. Retired Gen. Wesley Clark told me several years ago that he was hesitant about anti-missile defense. His reasoning was that he worried that the big defense lobbies would throw their weight behind these new programs and the services would be starved of the more routine upgrades and equipment they needed.

Equally as an individual or on behalf of a group of such individuals, it is difficult to petition the government. You will be elbowed out of the way by the super-petitioners: the lobbyists.

Paradoxically, business rails against the government and yet, year after year, petitions the government for more contracts, lighter regulation, less tax and other favors.

Often business gets what it wants in Washington, but is it good for it? Some of the most troubled industries—accounting, airlines, energy and telecoms—are those that have had the most success in getting their way in Congress and the regulatory agencies. Mostly they swept away the protections they once enjoyed, only to find that the free market was more efficient than they were. As someone once said, the free market is a great provider of goods and services, and also a ruthless exterminator.

As lobbying has become part of the strategic planning of companies, they may have lost sight of the importance of innovation, satisfying customers, and operating in a transparent environment, reassuring to investors.

In Washington, the trade associations have vied to locate their headquarters closer and closer to Capitol Hill, as the pace and pitch of lobbying has increased. But what do they have to show for it? Accounting standards? Airline, energy and telecom deregulation? What they would appear to have to show for their efforts is chaos, scandal and bankruptcy.

The two-edged sword of lobbying for what you think will do you good has hurt not only corporate interests. Environmentalists have tied themselves in knots by supporting courses of action that turn out to be more environmentally destructive than alternative routes.

What is the Chinese curse about being careful about what you wish for lest you get it? Better be careful about what you lobby for lest you get that—and Arthur Andersen, Enron, United Airlines and WorldCom.

Next year there will be some new faces on Capitol Hill: some of them naïve, fresh faces who believe that they can exist without lobbyists. They will learn that that is not so—that lobbyists are now as much part of the system of governance as the reporters who cover Congress. The wise ones will listen to their new best friends and ask a lot of hard questions. Then they will decide in their own minds.

In Washington, everyone is a friend at some time. But access to an enemy can impress a client as much as access to a friend.

October 29, 2002

TARNISHED GEORGIA: A JEWEL OF ANOTHER TIME

TBILISI, Georgia—There is something about small countries in extremis, like this one, which makes you feel that you should take them in your arms and tell them that everything will be all right. Unfortunately, that is not always the case.

Some small countries, like Ireland and Chile, have overcome their history and moved into prosperity and stability. Others, Nicaragua and Lebanon come to mind, are indefinitely lost.

Some just slide into that new category of "failed states." Malawi and Haiti are failed states; by definition, places where governance is almost nonexistent and people live as best they can beyond the pale of social order.

Georgia, an ancient land with its own alphabet, language and culture, trembles on the brink of failure. It gained independence when the Soviet Union broke up; had a nasty civil war along its Black Sea coast; and readied itself to enjoy a place in the sun, with inward investment, burgeoning exports, and an improving standard of living.

Instead, the closest it has come to enjoying the fruits of globalization are two incongruous McDonald's outlets here in the capital.

Georgia expected a flood of tourists to enjoy its mountainous beauty, its seaside resorts, and its distinguished wines and brandies. Instead, Russia has turned hostile, accusing the Georgians of harboring Chechen terrorists in the Pankisi Gorge, and of other national misdemeanors. Ten thousand Russian troops have failed to withdraw from Georgia's sovereign territory, despite assurances over many years that they would do so.

Today's Georgia feels unloved, hapless and sliding towards complete disintegration. Its economy has never taken off. The tourists have not come; the seaside resorts have been destroyed by war; and there has been no inward investment, partly, but not completely because there is nothing to invest in. The Soviet-era industries have collapsed, and the Georgians have failed to capitalize on the resources that they have: agricultural produce and a fairy tale landscape replete with castles, walled enclaves, and innumerable places of worship-mostly domed, Orthodox churches, and a smattering of synagogues and mosques.

This small city alone has more than 400 churches, all in need of refurbishment. While neighboring Azerbaijan looks forward to an oil bonanza, Georgia can only look forward to hosting an oil pipeline on its way to the Mediterranean. Another smaller pipeline already runs to the Black Sea.

The first thing you are told by almost anyone who speaks English—and they are few, as Georgian is the first language and Russian is the second—is that Georgia is choking on corruption. Indeed, the corruption is so pervasive that it is the only part of the economy that seems to work. Government paychecks arrive months and years later, and are miniscule.

Yet, Georgians are somehow surviving through a system of extended-family support. The corrupt, extorted currency goes a long way in Georgia. Diplomats are astounded that people turn up for work neatly dressed, and go about their business even though they may not have received a paycheck in many months.

Of course, the United Nations is here together with a phalanx of non-governmental organizations, who patronize the two luxury hotels—a Sheraton and a Marriott—and hold endless meetings on how the Georgians can help themselves. The Georgians oblige by attending the meetings, but have no faith that the remedies can be applied.

Georgia is waiting for its longtime president, Eduard Shevardnadze, to finish his term in 2005; for the Russians to calm down or do their worst; and to see whether the small American presence, now training a corps of what will become the Georgian military, has any intention of staying for the long haul. The conventional wisdom is that the Americans will lose interest in Georgia after Shevardnadze's term is up.

At present, the Bush administration is convinced that there are al-Qaeda forces mingled with the Chechen refugees in the Pankisi Gorge. Georgians are doubtful that al-Qaeda fighters are there in any number, although a few have reportedly been arrested. The Georgians point out that it is almost impossible to get to the gorge, and that they would face tremendous linguistic and physical difficulties in hooking up with Chechens who have fled across the Russian border.

The 4.4 million Georgians have become fatalistic about their future, fearing, probably correctly, that it may be decided in Washington or Moscow. They are a unique, ancient people without advocates on the outside, and without promising leaders on the inside.

A diplomat here said this puts them in such state of mind that Georgians are living for today, enjoying their wine and exceptional bread, without much hope for the future.

On the plus side, a former Georgian parliamentarian said that of the countries in the Caspian-Caucasus region, Georgia is the freest. "If we were next door in Azerbaijan, I would expect to have policemen watching me. But there is nothing like that here," he said, gesturing towards the street.

Ironic, really. Stalin was a Georgian.

November 5, 2002

HOW THE DEMOCRATS CAN
LOOK BEYOND THEIR OWN MISERY

The Democrats are in an ugly mood. They are a lost tribe, as interested in fratricide as they are in rebirth. There are unhappy parallels with the Conservative Party in the United Kingdom—although the Conservatives are in even worse shape than the Democrats.

The immediate cause of their disenchantment is, of course, the loss of the Senate to the Republicans. But this has laid bare underlying uncertainty in the Democratic Party and its leadership.

Democrats I talk to ask variously how the party can rid itself of Terry McAuliffe, chairman of the Democratic National Committee; find a viable candidate to run against George W. Bush in two years; and what is to be done about the ragged left wing of the party, which now feels itself in some ascendancy. If you want to further dispirit mainline Democrats, try these two words: Al Sharpton.

Lifelong Democrats fear that if Sharpton mounts a bid for the presidency—which he cannot win—it will remind the voters that Sharpton, too, is a Democrat. Since Ralph Nader ran as a spoiler, mainline Democrats are particularly sensitive to ego-driven incursions from the left.

There is also a deep chasm between Democrats on Capitol Hill, and the rank and file worrying about the future of the party and the Republican steamroller. They see problems in the economy, in international relations, in the potential war with Iraq, and with a host of treasured programs, like Medicare and Social Security. But they do not hear a rallying cry.

No one in the party's leadership has raised a standard around which they can gather. Tom Daschle is liked and respected, but he does not light the fires of political indignation—an all-important ingredient in elective politics.

The likely Democratic candidates for the presidency are as appealing as a meal on television's "Fear Factor." Al Gore, the undeclared frontrunner, has not yet been forgiven for running a dismal campaign against Bush, or for his near silence since then. John Kerry, whose principal virtue is that he served in Vietnam, reminds people of Michael Dukakis—too liberal, too Massachusetts, and without fire in his belly. Richard Gephardt, who failed as the Democratic leader in the House, still dreams of running for president, but his record suits him better for teaching politics than for practicing the craft.

And so it goes: a roll call of the unacceptable in pursuit of the unobtainable.

Democrats do draw some solace from the realization that Bush is now the sole proprietor of the national fortune. He can no longer blame former President Clinton or a recalcitrant Senate for failure. He is the man, and on his head rests the crown.

The president's victory in the midterm elections may prove to be one victory too many. No president has had both houses of Congress on his side since Dwight Eisenhower; and Ike was a remarkably ecumenical Republican, unlike Bush, who is an ideological conservative.

How will the Democrats, then, exploit their role as the loyal opposition? They would be advised to take on the Republicans selectively, rather than across the board. The filibuster is a clumsy weapon that has to be used sparingly. Belittling argument will keep their purpose alive even though it will not affect the Republican agenda. They would do well to save their most extreme parliamentary maneuvers for Supreme Court appointments, and the most grotesque aspects of the Republican agenda coming from the extreme right of the party.

Bush, himself, may want a little help with the far-right, now so emboldened.

The difficulty for Democrats is to wish to see Bush fail without relishing national discomfort. Like Bush, the Democrats should find and define a few key issues that can grow through repetition. For the future, they have to hope that a Lochinvar—maybe a governor—will ride into presidential politics, uplifting a dispirited party and invigorating those precious, elusive swing voters.

In short, the Democrats need to go on a blind date with a new, untrammeled candidate for the presidency. Blind dates have worked for them in the past. Both Jimmy Carter and Bill Clinton invigorated the party because they were largely unknown to it.

Of course, blind dates seldom work out, young people tell me.

November 12, 2002

ABBA WOULD HAVE HAD SOMETHING TO SAY

Abba Eban, who died Sunday in Tel Aviv, was variously a great orator, a great diplomat, a failed politician, and a man uncomfortable with Israel, the country he helped to bring into being.

In the early days of Israel, Eban was the voice of the new state, a fountainhead of its idealism, and its incredibly articulate spokesman at the United Nations and around the world. Although he was born in Cape Town, Eban grew up in Britain and absorbed two of the dominant features of his character there: a passionately idealistic view of what Israel should become, and an addiction to the intellectual life of Cambridge University.

He shone as a student at Cambridge, dominated its revered debating society, the Cambridge Union, and later taught at Cambridge. At the university, he studied the classics and Middle Eastern languages. There, he developed a deep respect for Arab culture and science, and a sympathy for the decline in Arab civilization.

These influences later lead to his ostracism from Israeli politics after years of distinction: He was too much the perfect Englishman, with too much sympathy for the Arabs.

While Israelis developed their own style, guttural and raw-boned, Eban remained the silver-tongued Cambridge don in a three-piece suit. He was also just too clever for many Israeli politicians. His command of many languages was flawless, and his speech incorporated classical references and arcane words. Indeed, when he was not pressing Israel's case at the United Nations or to the U.S. administration, he came across as pedantic-a multilingual showoff.

He could also be very rude. I can attest to that. At a cocktail party in Tel Aviv, I told Eban that he was the most brilliant speaker that I had ever heard in the flesh. In particular, I tried to pay homage to a quick retort he had made about remarks De Gaulle had made about Israel. When asked what he thought about De Gaulle's statement, Eban flashed back: "Among the general's many enormous qualities, impeccable veracity is not found." Eban looked at me with a mixture of dislike and distain, and said: "Stick around and I will say something even better."

I was dismayed, but it did not shift my opinion that Abba Eban—who was born Aubrey Solomon but adopted his stepfather's surname, Eban, and used his given Hebrew name, Abba—was one of the great orators of the 20th century, right up there with Winston Churchill and Martin Luther King Jr. Yes, he was grandiloquent and even pedantic. But he was disciplined enough to know exactly what he was doing at the podium, and the product was a divine concoction of English, history and wisdom. He was, in short, an enthralling speaker, a master of the craft.

Like Churchill, audiences came to hear him but not necessarily to be convinced. It is forgotten now but before 1940, the House of Commons would be packed when Churchill was to speak. However, his influence on policy was negligible. In Israel, the same fate befell Eban. Although he occupied several Cabinet positions in the Labor Party, including foreign minister and deputy prime minister, he was never destined to hold the highest office.

Democracies are suspicious of intellectuals who speak too well. And Eban failed by a wide margin on both counts. Eventually, he was not even offered a constituency by the Labor Party, having become something of a liability. He had opposed settlements on the West Bank and in Gaza, and had tried to maintain a dialogue with the Arabs. His last endeavor on behalf of Israel was to play an intermediary role in bringing about the Oslo peace agreement.

Had Eban not been imbued with a passion for a Jewish state from his earliest days, he might have become a classic Cambridge professor: brilliant, eccentric, and a delight to tens of thousands of students. As it was, he started his career, after serving in the British forces in World War II, with a view of the new state of Israel that owed more to the conceptions of British Jewry than it did to the realities of the new state. British Jews had a utopian vision of the new country: inhabited by a people of generous spirit, tempered by their own horrendous history; a place that was egalitarian, socialist, kind and accommodating. You might say, a Little England in the Levant.

Eban was unable to shake this vision of the country and faded from public life. True to that part of the world, he was a prophet without honor in his own land. Yet, he will always have honor where there is reverence for the classic uses of the English language.

November 19, 2002

BUSH AND FRIENDS: THE ENERGY ENIGMA

It is widely held in Washington that President Bush has promised France, Russia and China that their interests in Iraqi oil—especially the $9.5 billion owed by Iraq to Russia—will be safeguarded after an American-led invasion. It seems unlikely.

First, to make that kind of assurance the United States would have to be planning to administer Iraq as a subject nation, apportioning its wealth to foreigners. This would be at odds with the president's declared intention of setting up a free, democratic government in Baghdad. As a sovereign state, that government would presumably deal with Iraq's debts and the future exploitation of its oil wealth.

Certainly Iraq, which has the second largest proven reserves of oil next to Saudi Arabia, is of keen interest to France and Russia, and of some interest to China. In persuading these countries to support the new U.N. resolution on inspectors, Bush must have had to at least discuss their old debts in Iraq and new possibilities of supply from Iraq. But did he really tell Russian President Vladimir Putin that his money was assured? If he did, it is uncharacteristic of Bush, who is cautious about commitments.

Besides which, none of the three countries is naïve enough to believe the United States could guarantee the conduct of a post-Saddam Hussein Iraq.

More likely, France, Russia and China decided to go along with Bush in recognition of the inevitable. If they were acting in isolation, all the evidence is that they would let Hussein be, while providing him with whatever he wished to buy.

Also, their interests are not mutual. France wants Iraq, an old friend, as a market and a source of oil. Russia wants its money back and a role for Russian oil companies in Iraq, while protecting its domestic producers. Chinese interest in Iraq is more opaque. It is interested in markets and in long-term oil supply, if it is to continue its economic expansion. But, clearly, Iraq is not important enough for China to pick a fight with the United States at this time.

Meanwhile, American oil companies are wondering what, if any, role they will have in post-Hussein Iraq. That, too, is an unanswerable question. But what is certain is that early on, very early, the Bush administration hopes to use American oil-field service companies to secure the safe operation of Iraq's infrastructure—especially in the event that it is damaged by war or sabotage. The American military is good at many things, but running an oil terminal is not in its portfolio of skills.

The Bush administration has a clear interest in restoring Iraqi production as soon after hostilities cease as possible because the new administration will need money to stabilize the country and for reconstruction. The shortage of adequate funds has led to balkanization in Afghanistan, where there is no indigenous wealth to support its new and fleeting liberty.

At home, Bush is bound to try and push through some form of the energy legislation, which failed in the last Congress. The centerpiece would be as before: drilling in the Arctic National Wildlife Refuge. Republicans are pretty united on this. So this time, it will be Bush 1, caribou 0.

But the rest of the package is more problematic, particularly its electricity components.

Republicans are as divided as Democrats on the future shape of the electricity markets, with Southern and Western states already antagonized by Pat Wood, chairman of the Federal Energy Regulatory Commission. The Southern states want nothing do with further electric deregulation. And Western states want special recognition of the unique role of federal energy facilities in the West. In short, both groups say: One size does not fit all.

Also, there is to be considered the interests of Sen. Pete Domenici of New Mexico, who has special expertise in energy and particularly nuclear power, as a result of hosting two of the Department of Energy's national laboratories in his home state. Domenici is the new chairman of the Senate Energy and Natural Resources Committee.

So the energy outlook is as clouded as ever. The Bush administration cannot know for certain whether there will be a general disruption of oil supply from the Middle East, if there is an invasion. And it cannot tell the outcome of an energy bill in Congress beyond the probably drilling of ANWR. The Bush administration probably knows more about energy than any administration before it, but it has taken two years to learn—as others have—that making energy policy is an existentialist undertaking.

November 26, 2002

THE INSIDIOUS AFTERMATH OF MOMBASA

Tourism, that cash cow of countries large and small, that employer of so many semi-skilled and unskilled workers, is likely to be on a respirator by next summer. Al-Qaeda and its terrorism affiliates have seen to that.

Bali and Mombasa would have put a serious crimp in global tourism, if they had simply been the bombing of holiday resorts. But the failed missile attack on an Israeli charter jet in Mombasa raises public alarm to new highs.

The unintended consequence of the terrorists' escalation is to severely damage countries against which they have no argument. The United States will suffer, but only marginally compared to those countries that have nothing to sell except sunshine or snow.

Bali, Indonesia's principal tourist attraction, is suddenly a dead zone. And Kenya, already an economic disaster, is sustained only by its tourism, either to the coastal resorts or the game parks. Two terrorist attacks on its soil will terminate the flow of tourists' dollars.

All of Africa, the Caribbean, and parts of Latin America will see a dramatic drop in tourism from Europe and America, and with it, their flow of hard currency and vital jobs. Even the oil states of the Middle East can expect a hit. Tourism is a great consumer of oil, and so the terrorists have effectively damaged the world as an unintended consequence of their hatred for Israel and the West.

Prima facie, it is impossible to guard all the airports of the world or to equip all airliners with anti-missile shields. So travelers will protect themselves by staying at home.

The attack on the soft target of tourism is an attack also on some of the most desperate countries on earth. Think of the Bahamas, Botswana, South Africa and Thailand. Think also of the offshore islands of Europe, from the Isle of Wight to the Canaries, and you get some idea of the dislocation facing the cash-starved extremities of the world.

Ever since World War II, the World Bank and other international organizations have seen tourism as the quick fix for ailing economies; a solution that became even more viable with the jet airplane, and the development of large communities that depend exclusively on airborne tourists, such as Cancun, Mexico, and Spain's Costa Brava.

These will be among the worst hit because they have no alternative life, no industry, and no purpose but to coddle tourists and separate them from their pounds, euros and dollars. Now some of them may implode, as people grow ever more leery of air travel.

The collapse in tourism is also a collapse in the quality of life of those who can afford to travel. One of the great pleasures of the time in which we live is that ability to board an airliner and, at a reasonable cost, explore another country, get a nodding acquaintance of another culture, and kick back.

Americans, in particular, have shown themselves disinclined to travel in the face of terrorism. Northern Ireland, despite excellent facilities, has failed for nearly 30 years to attract Americans. In the days of the Red Brigade, Italy was crossed off American itineraries. And Israel, Jordan and Egypt suffer an American tourist drought every time violence escalates.

Even though there are dangers at home, we as a people would rather take our chances in the familiar than face an unquantifiable threat abroad. The expectation is that more Americans will travel by car next summer to U.S. destinations, and that the Europeans will climb aboard the trains that crisscross Europe before they venture on an overseas flight.

Before 9/11, tourism was at a peak, with distant destinations competing for vacation dollars. Now the whole prospect of air travel is fraught with apprehension, as well as inconvenience. And tens of thousands of resort workers will face a desperate future. It has already happened in Bali and it is beginning to happen in Kenya.

It will take several years without terrorist attacks on aircraft and resorts for confidence to return, by which time many hotels will have failed, and with them, more airlines.

The best attempts of governments to secure airports and aircraft will not reassure recreational travelers. Besides, the known fixes cannot protect all targets and are expensive.

The first time a shoulder-fired missile was used against a civilian airliner with lethal result was in Zimbabwe during the war against white rule. An airliner leaving a resort at Kariba was shot down with a substantial loss of life. Mercifully, this action did not produce any copycat attacks. But, clearly, al-Qaeda has brought a new degree of sophistication to the unspeakable work of killing innocent people — and throwing many equally innocent people out of work.

December 3, 2002

THE IMPERIAL ECHO OF CECIL JOHN RHODES

Thirty-two American students and 145 other students from around the world have just received, in time for Christmas, the gift that will keep on giving for the rest of their lives. They have been accepted as Rhodes Scholars and will study at Oxford University for two or three years.

These young people may not have been born with silver spoons in their mouths, but they have them now. A Rhodes scholarship is about the niftiest accolade one can get; a triumph on a resume, entrée to the movers and shakers of the world and, with a little work, a degree from Oxford. By and large, Rhodes Scholars never look back: Bill Clinton was one, as were Sen. Richard Lugar, former Sen. Bill Bradley, and former Librarian of Congress Daniel Boorstin.

Yet when Cecil John Rhodes, the British imperialist, created the scholarships in 1902, he had something less than academic utopia on his mind. The plan, which he handed to his ever-helpful sidekick, Dr. Leander Starr Jameson, was to produce a long line of imperialists. They would all be men. And except for the Germans and the Americans whom he thought were of the right stock, Rhodes Scholars would be British and white. They would excel academically and athletically.

In fact they would be just the kind of young men that Rhodes, who had no interest in women and who said derogatory things about them, like to surround himself with. His biographers have questioned whether Rhodes was actively gay and have concluded that he liked men more than women, and sex not at all.

His young scholars, he hoped, would go forth into the world and perpetuate the British imperial values of the late 19th century. They would be the leaders of tomorrow, imbued with the values of yesterday and committed to the imperial dream.

Today, all the countries that once were under British control now nominate candidates for the scholarships, so that a minority are white; moreover, women are included. Not quite what Rhodes had in mind.

Rhodes, who inspired Rudyard Kipling to some of his most grandiloquent writing on empire, was an uncontested imperialist. But his view of race appears to have been as ambivalent as his view of sex. When he was prime minister of Cape Colony, he opened the franchise to all adult males, without regard to race, provided they owned property worth 100 pounds sterling or could speak 100 words of English.

It is possible that Rhodes believed that the subject people of the empire would metamorphose into perfect little Englishmen with time, and hence his desire to democratize the Cape. However, there is no evidence that he had any such feelings of democracy for the indigenous inhabitants of Rhodesia, the country he named after himself, now Zimbabwe. Perhaps, like the Romans, he thought that the subject people would become citizens of the imperial project.

It was an accident of history that took Rhodes from Oxford to Southern Africa. His health was poor and doctors suggested a better climate, and he had a brother already living in South Africa.

He made one of the greatest fortunes of the world at the time from diamond mining, and plowed it and all the dividends from his De Beers Company, and later from his British South Africa Company, into colonizing Rhodesia.

Another historical chance saved what is now Botswana from falling under the Boers and being incorporated into South Africa. Botswana, inadvertently, owes much to Rhodes. The British had granted Botswana, then known as Bechuanaland, protectorate status. But Rhodes wanted to incorporate it into Rhodesia, and the Boers, during the Boer War, wanted to incorporate it into their country of the Transvaal. But thanks to the ill-advised raid under Jameson against the Boers, Rhodes and Jameson lost their credibility with the British government and the sanctity of Botswana was assured. Actually, that busy medic, Jameson, was imprisoned in Britain for his troubles, and Rhodes lost the ear of the British government.

Of Rhodes's ambitious handiwork, only two major edifices remain: The De Beers diamond cartel and the Rhodes scholarships. The thing he loved, expanding British control in Africa, is long gone; and it was 100 years before the franchise was again opened to all the people living in South Africa.

Given that Rhodes is reviled for the conquest of Rhodesia, and for his imperialistic plans to extend the British Empire from Cape Town to Cairo, the old expansionist still has a powerful influence in the world. You can argue about the diamond cartel, but his other legacy, the shiniest, thrives. To be named a Rhodes Scholar is the greatest gift a young person can receive and, happily, they are handed out just in time for Christmas.

December 10, 2002

WHY THIS FOOLISH TALK OF IMPERIALISM?

There is talk, lots of it, in Washington these days about American empire and how we will meet the challenge of governing Iraq after the ouster of Saddam Hussein and, possibly, how we will install governments in other Middle Eastern countries.

Unfortunately, there is no good paradigm for the Bush administration to follow. The plans all hint at getting in and getting out quickly, a replay of Grenada, Panama and Haiti. Nothing will be that simple in the Middle East, and it has not been that simple in Afghanistan. Nor has it been that simple for the Israelis in Gaza and the West Bank.

Forget about the old colonial models; they are not applicable. The global proliferation of small arms alone, particularly the ubiquitous AK-47, has made conquest and, yes, subjugation a much more dangerous affair. The great European empires were built not so much on the number of troops but on the monopoly of firearms. The initial imperial conquests in Africa and Asia relied on the weapons asymmetry between the conquerors and the indigenous peoples.

It also relied on something harder to quantify: the preparedness of certain peoples at certain times to come under the control of a European country. Sometimes it was for stability, sometimes it was to end internecine warfare, and sometimes it was conquest and defeat. But the colonial era began to end with the free flow of modern arms to previously unarmed people. Terrorism worked. In the end, it was terrorism that evicted the French from Algeria, the Portuguese from Mozambique, and the British from Zimbabwe.

The smart colonial powers began an orderly retreat early, as the British did in most of Africa. Those who had not thought out retreat abandoned their positions to chaos, such as the Belgians in the Congo and the Portuguese in Mozambique and Angola. The British tried to leave behind viable institutions, but they were often European institutions imposed on people who had no understanding of the delicate balances of democracy.

So the British also failed, but unevenly. Of British India, comprising Bangladesh, Pakistan and India itself, only the latter has enjoyed continuous democracy. Sri Lanka might have succeeded if it had not been torn with ethnic strife. Burma was a total failure and Singapore and Malaysia are half-successes. Africa has been more or less a disaster, producing such monsters as Idi Amin in Uganda and Hastings Banda in Malawi. Zambia has just mismanaged itself into utter poverty and Kenya is not far behind.

The picture of the British Empire is that it worked extraordinarily well until the British were forced to withdraw. France lost Indochina and Algeria in bloody conflicts. And its Central African holdings fell apart. Likewise, Portugal. There are no good exit strategies for post-colonialism.

These are lessons that the United States may learn again. But from the outset, the difficulties are larger than ever faced by a European power. Populations are larger, more sophisticated, armed and imbued with hatred. You cannot take blankets and beads to Baghdad. And you cannot expect a puppet government, formed in London, to install democracy where it is an alien concept.

There is no doubt that in short order we will defeat the forces in Iraq. But after that, what? A long war of attrition? Multiple acts of terrorism? The use of primitive weapons of mass destruction?

These are not things that were faced by any colonial European power. The modern world is a very different place. Just think back to the German occupation of Europe during World War II. Without weapons, the resistance made hell for the German invaders, and no German citizen felt secure outside of Germany.

I have my roots in colonialism. I grew up in the self-governing colony of Southern Rhodesia. My parents and my peers thought the British would be there for all time. But when the terrorist war of liberation began, it was greatly apparent that our days in the sun were numbered. Nationalism is not a logical emotion. You cannot argue with people that they will be better off under your regime than theirs. They will not buy it, any more than the 13 Colonies bought it from King George III.

This imperial talk is folly, and we should know it from our own history.

December 17, 2002

IS BUSH A BRAVE MAN OR DESTINY'S VICTIM?

By any measure, this has been a bumper year for President Bush. He ends his second year in office and 2002 with reason to be glad, even exultant. Although Bush may not be loved around the world, he is feared and respected. And at home, he has a Congress of his own party, high approval ratings and, suddenly, an ally in Bill Frist, the new Senate majority leader.

Yet Bush's head may not rest easy this holiday season. Next year promises to be the most difficult any American president has faced in a long time.

Having made regime change in Iraq the centerpiece of his foreign policy, the president has little choice but to prosecute an invasion, and to hope that it turns out as well as his advisers, the hawks, have said it will. His alternative to war is to accept a clean bill of health for Saddam Hussein in the matter of weapons of mass destruction, after a long period of inspections. It is not an attractive proposition.

The right wing of the Republican Party will see it as weakness and the world will wonder whether Bush is prepared to use his saber, after rattling it for so long. Only the demise or overthrow of Saddam can save Bush from the most difficult and fraught call he will have to make as president. Time is not on Bush's side.

The deteriorating situation in North Korea makes Bush's commitment to overthrow Saddam look more like a vendetta and less like a genuine decision to eradicate weapons of mass destruction.

Then there is the ever-delicate matter of the world's oil supply. The Bush plans did not allow for more than a million barrels a day of oil being taken out of the market due to the political unrest in Venezuela. That situation forces the administration to recalibrate the risks to the world oil supply of an invasion of Iraq. It is not that the trickle of oil out of Iraq will be halted—it will—but whether the Arab oil workers will sabotage distribution networks throughout the Gulf, including Saudi Arabia.

If this happens, the price of oil will rise to unimagined heights, with real supply interruptions for Europe, global inflation, and economic stagnation at home and abroad.

Oil may not be why the administration wishes to invade Iraq, but it is an ever-present reality. If the world oil supply is gravely interrupted, Bush will be blamed domestically and internationally. His presidency will be mortally wounded, and he will go into history as the president who went too far.

Oil will have more effect than casualties, the breakup of Iraq, or the seething of the Arab Street.

Other than an interruption in the flow of oil, Bush can survive any unintended consequences of an invasion of Iraq. If casualties are high, he will be forgiven on the grounds of patriotism. If Iraq breaks up, so what: it was an artificial country to begin with. Likewise, if it sinks into chaos and civil war: a probability. Americans are not going to worry about the strange passions and ethnicities of a faraway country that has been nothing but trouble since Iraq invaded Kuwait.

We are a generous and forgiving people, but we do not understand what seems like mindless bloodshed half a world away. We have never understood the passions of Northern Ireland, the hatreds of the Middle East, the struggle in East Timor, or the destruction of Yugoslavia. If we cannot tell the good from the bad, we withdraw wishing damnation on all the combatants. Our foreign policy, reflecting us as a people, has always been: if they cannot be more like us, to hell with them. That is not an unreasonable position for a nation that never aspired to empire, colonization and involvement across the globe.

As the president proceeds relentlessly with his plans to attack Iraq, he gambles all that he has won. If he is aware of the downsides, he is one of our bravest presidents. If he is motivated by a powerful sense of right, without regard to unintended consequences, he is a different kind of man: a presidential fatalist.

December 24, 2002

2003

THE REALLY BIG IDEA THAT IS CHANGING EUROPE

BRUSSELS—From Brussels, you can take a train to much of continental Europe without changing any money or producing a passport. This is extraordinary. It causes one to ask what the Europeans are up to and, with 10 more countries poised to join the European Union, whether the EU will work.

The answer to the first question is that they are engaged in the greatest act of detribalization in world history. The answer to the second is more problematic.

The big idea behind European integration is the end to thousands of years of internecine warfare, and the creation of a new kind of super-state beyond nationalism. At a time when the world is dissembling and petty rivalries are everywhere, the Europeans are pursuing an enormous concept. European integration is, by any measure, a giant idea: a reversal of history and an affirmation of faith in the future.

In reality, it is a little messier. Many issues are unresolved, including how to govern the new monster in a democratic way. Europe has a parliament, but it is ineffective. And the bureaucrats control things-a state of affairs the Europeans refer to as the "democratic deficit."

Likewise, the new European currency, the euro, is still untested after a year. The question that hung over it at its introduction remains: How can a central bank for many countries deal with economic excess or distress in one of those countries?

Still, it is extraordinary that 11 proud nations of Europe should have given up their francs and marks and guilders—all ancient currencies—for a new transnational currency. Of course, not everyone has joined the euro, most notably the United Kingdom. But there is pressure for all of Europe to join.

Small countries, such as Belgium, Holland and Finland, face not only losing their forms of currency but gradually losing distinct cultures and languages. The lingua franca of the New Europe is English, and one day it may be the first language of Europe. Giving up language is one of the great examples of detribalizing, closing a door on thousands of years and opening a door on a new, uncertain one. Yet Europe is doing it.

New members waiting in the wings pose peculiar problems for old members, mostly because the newcomers are poor and will bring no wealth into the union. Instead, they will take money out of it, and European taxpayers may grow unhappy under the burden of unification.

Another unresolved issue is defense. European countries spend far less on defense as a proportion of their gross domestic product than do the United States and many other nations. Having decided that they are beyond nationalism, the Europeans also have implicitly decided that they are beyond war—a dangerous assumption, as Europe found in the Balkans.

Yet detribalization does resolve some issues and will have its effect on long-running conflicts such as those of Northern Ireland and Basque separatists. The very goal of those nationalists tends to disappear in a bigger Europe.

Unfortunately, even as the traditional inhabitants of Europe bit by bit dispose of their tribal trappings, new tribes are appearing through immigration that have no sense of the greater whole, which is the idea behind the New Europe. In particular, these are immigrants from North Africa, the Middle East and parts of Asia, who have migrated into Europe since the end of World War II, but who remain separate and ghettoized in the cultures that have accommodated them.

In all European countries, there are now tribes from distant lands who reject assimilation. The Arabs stand out as the most conspicuous, but they are not alone among these tribal orchids, living on the boughs of the trees that host them. As immigrants flood into Europe, Europeans who are engaged in a great experiment to shed the rivalries of the past find they have to deal with imported cultures that have no interest in the great European project.

Hence the rise of right-wing parties throughout Europe that seek to limit immigration by reviving old nationalism.

With 10 new members scheduled to join Europe, the unresolved issues become more pressing: how to manage from a central bank the economic disparity of Europe, how to make this monster creation more democratic, and how to assimilate the new tribes even in the midst of detribalization.

Europe is much criticized in the United States these days for its social policies, its passivity and its preoccupation with itself. And yet Europe is also engaged in pursuing a multinational, multicultural commonwealth on a scale that has never been contemplated. It is the big idea and it is being tried.

January 7, 2003

THE NEW OLD AGE, FLORIDA-STYLE

FT. LAUDERDALE, Fla.—George W. Bush made a bad joke in Paris last year about not being able to remember a reporter's question because he had reached the age of 55. Standing on the podium with him was French President Jacques Chirac, who responded by glaring at Bush, mindful of the fact that he was 69.

When do you know you are old? Is it when a young person offers you a seat on public transport? Or when a young person you want to flirt with says, "You must have had an interesting life."

When I was a boy, old people were old—the men were crotchety and the women were full of sighs. Now, there is a new culture of age: a determination to live intensely in the last years. And it is on display in Florida. Florida's retirees are determined, if not to cheat the Grim Reaper of his harvest, at least to hold him off.

In Ft. Lauderdale, for example, septuagenarians and octogenarians weave through the traffic on bicycles. The more daring go down the sidewalks on roller blades. There is a pervasive sense of late-life adventure. To keep the Grim Reaper at a distance, the retirees of the Sunshine State in the tens of thousands, if not the hundreds of thousands, practice yoga and Tai Chi, and fill the health clubs, where they bicycle, lift weights, and deny the passage of time.

There is something very special about these men and women, who have laid down the burden of appearances. They parade the streets in shorts and sandals without regard to the physical imperfections they might have hidden when younger. Bowed legs, varicose-veined legs, cellulite-dimpled legs are all on display. It is as if their owners are saying, "This is me, and I am without apology."

To those who still have their health, retirement is a state of grace; a club, a special place to be. At a dinner in Delray Beach with a group of retirees, I was asked when I retired. When I told them that I had not and was not planning to do so, they looked at me differently. Clearly, I was an outsider, a philistine and not a member of the club.

There is no publication in America to celebrate the old. But the English have a splendid one. It is called The Oldie, founded by Richard Ingrams, who also founded the satirical magazine Private Eye. He has made The Oldie a thing of joy—heavy on reminiscences; tut-tutting at modern life; and full of travel, adventure and literature. By contrast, our publications for the old have a terminal quality about them. They dwell on health, living wills, funeral plots and other dismal necessities. They fail to put any gold into the golden years. And they are at odds with the determined resourcefulness of the tens of thousands of people who are going hard at their lives in Florida.

I mention Florida, and not Arizona or California, because the Floridian retirees epitomize the best of the culture of the old.

Of course, there is a caveat to all of this autumnal joy: money. The ancients doing yoga on the beach, mastering windsurfing and taking courses are the lucky ones who secured good pensions, made money or, by some means, came to have the resources to finance their last flings. These are the people you see enjoying life, sometimes as they never enjoyed it before. But God help those without pensions, eking it out on Social Security, eating badly, unable to afford their medicines and waiting for the inevitable in poverty, discomfort and sorrow. Theirs is not a culture of second youth, but often the sad end to a long, hard story. If they are lucky and they find the sun, it will be a trailer park or some inland community, far from the boutiques, health clubs and first-class doctors who have made old age more bearable for the fortunate.

But the inequality is not a reason not to celebrate those who are making something of age in a way that has never been seen before. So, I celebrate them: the gutsy oldsters who are learning instead of whining and going about the business of living while their lease on life runs. In Florida, they have created a proud and bold society: Men and women determined not to go gentle into that good night.

January 14, 2003

DIRTY BOMBS: OLD TECHNOLOGY IN A NEW WORLD

When it comes to making nuclear weapons, it is the ingredients not the recipe that counts. The recipe is well known and can be found on the Internet. The ingredients, though, are tricky.

There are two routes to acquire a "dirty" bomb. The term "dirty bomb," when used the nuclear fraternity, refers to the kind of weapon the United States dropped on Hiroshima and Nagasaki during World War II. Some politicians now refer to a stick of dynamite encased in a radioactive material as a dirty bomb. But that is not a nuclear weapon.

There are two ingredients, either of which can be used to make a dirty bomb. One is plutonium, with a concentration of the isotope 239. The other is so-called highly enriched uranium, with a concentration of over 97 percent of the uranium isotope 235.

The way to obtain plutonium is to "breed" it in a nuclear reactor, which uses low concentrations of uranium. However, one of the by-products of nuclear fission is plutonium, and that is the course that North Korea appears to be embarked on.

Iraq started down the plutonium route with two reactors, but when the Israelis took them out, the Iraqis switched to the highly enriched uranium route.

Uranium is enriched in a variety of ways, two of which dominate. The first is the technology adopted by the United States during World War II. It is called diffusion in which uranium hexafluoride gas is forced through a series of membranes, each on removing a small quantity of 235. This process takes huge quantities of electricity and very large factories, covering many acres. It is now regarded as obsolete.

The currently favored legal means of enriching uranium is with centrifuges, which spin a gas at tremendous speed and separate the fissionable isotope. The Europeans have several commercial centrifuge facilities, and some are to be built in the United States.

Then, there are the more exotic separation technologies. The South Africans, before they abandoned their nuclear program, were said to be using nozzle technology in which the gas is squirted through narrow apertures.

When Saddam was frustrated in his attempts to get plutonium, he decided to take the highly enriched uranium path. To do this, he built Calutrons, originally developed by the great American physicist, David Lawrence, in 1941.

The United States did not use the Calutron, believing there were technical difficulties: it is an electro-magnetic process, where relatively small machines grouped together would enrich the uranium.

All of the enrichment processes use a lot of energy. Iraq, being rich in energy, can contemplate an enriched uranium bomb. But energy-short North Korea has no choice but to take the plutonium path.

The weapon dropped on Nagasaki was a pure plutonium bomb, and the one dropped on Hiroshima was an enriched uranium bomb. Both were considered by their makers as extremely dangerous to handle and transport. So much so that final assembly took place on the delivering aircraft for fear of a premature detonation.

A senior American weapons designer told me that any weapon developed in a Third World country, from either plutonium or highly enriched uranium, would be very dangerous to handle. To initiate the nuclear reaction, high explosive is used, and the United States has spent decades developing insensitive high explosives that will not detonate accidentally. A primitive weapon, such as a Third World country might make, could be detonated by falling off a truck or even in severe air turbulence, if the makers did not have access to insensitive explosives and sophisticated electronic switches.

By contrast, advanced nuclear weapons have a complex cocktail of isotopes, including tritium, layers of fail-safe switching, and very subdued high explosives.

In short, according to American bomb designers, Third World nations can make their bombs—they are dirty because of the high amount of radiation they would release—and even do the calculations on a laptop computer, if they have the materials.

Any rogue-nation bomb is likely to be big, as were the early American ones, and would not easily be fitted onto a rocket. However, they could be propelled small distances, or dropped from commercial or military aircraft.

The first threat in this new age of proliferation is to the bomb makers, and the second threat is to their immediate neighbors. As for suitcase bombs, these are almost certain beyond the reach of countries like Iraq and North Korea, at least for now.

January 21, 2003

TOM DASCHLE: A LEGISLATOR, NOT A LEADER

Mark Twain said: "Give a man the reputation that he is an early riser, and that man can sleep till noon."

The Bush administration has mastered this ploy. By using a number of key, evocative words, it has been able to create an aura of commitment, where the facts are at odds with the performance.

President Bush has used the ploy lavishly on his domestic agenda. His frequent use of words such as education, security and diversity, give the impression that he is really doing something about these issues.

By contrast, Senate Minority Leader Tom Daschle, and titular leader of the Democrats, is conspicuously lacking in Bush's ability to cloak himself in virtue. Daschle's approach is that of a mechanic, rebutting the president line by line. He does not have Bush's skill in using a single word to create a transcendental image.

While Bush is criticized for bad syntax, he knows the impact of individual words and the cumulative effect of repeating them often. When he is in trouble at the podium, he falls back on a vague and repetitive discussion of values, integrity and commitment. It serves him well.

By contrast, Daschle does not talk about overriding Democratic values. Instead, he falls back on data and statistics. It does not serve him well.

There is a strange juxtaposition here. If there is a time for sweeping vision and grand oratory, it should be when one is in opposition. But Bush has sold himself better in office than he ever did during the campaign. He has made so much of his values and his integrity, his family and his faith that he has projected himself as a rare and caring leader.

Daschle attacks the policies and programs of the administration, but seems too modest to suggest that a Democrat would do a better job. There is something tentative about Daschle; something that suggests he has no jugular instinct.

Dasche's weakness as the leader of the Democrats is that he is a consummate legislator. He would rather work things out with his opponents than belabor them in public. His manners seem to preclude a frontal attack.

At a luncheon in Washington, D.C. this week, Daschle could find only nice things to say about Sen. Bill Frist, the majority leader, and about Sen Trent Lott, the fallen majority leader. Like the gentleman he is, Daschle quickly accepted Lott's apology for his remarks at an event celebrating Sen. Strom Thurmond's 100th birthday. A more combative politician would have sensed the political opportunity: think of Rep. Sam Rayburn or Sen. Lyndon Johnson. The president did not let his friend Lott off the hook. You can be too decent in politics.

It is just as well that Daschle is not seeking the Democratic nomination for president in 2004. Wisely, he has decided that his work is in the Senate.

Unfortunately for the Democrats, none of the present field seems to have the ability to take the high ground away from Bush. To beat Bush, a Democrat has to be able to speak the new language of integrity and to wrest back the white working class: to convince them that their interests lie with the Democrats and not with the Republicans.

To do this, the candidate has to be sufficiently convincing to win these swing voters away from the right-wing broadcasters who have entranced them. The voters the Democrats need are unduly influenced by Rush Limbaugh, Bill O'Reilly and Sean Hannity. It will take oratory, conviction and passion. These are not qualities that the Democratic field appears to have any more than that good man in the Senate, Daschle, has them.

Too much Democratic strategy, if you can call it that, is relying on Bush to stumble. There is not enough thought given to tripping him. The Democrats can triumph if they borrow Bush's techniques, while eschewing his policies.

That is why if Sen. Bob Graham of Florida were to enter the 2004 race, the White House would have reason to worry. Graham has not conceded moral superiority to Bush, and has been hard on his weaknesses in homeland security. Somehow Graham, though a Democrat through and through, has managed to appear to the right of Bush.

But it is not certain that Graham, who is due to have heart surgery, will run. He, alone, may be able to provide what the Democrats need: a vision from a candidate with fire in his belly.

January 28, 2003

THOSE MAGNIFICENT MEN AND
WOMEN AND THEIR FLYING MACHINES

An old argument is rekindled. There are those who say that space flight should be automated and that the heavens should be probed only with unmanned vehicles.

But those who would end manned-space flight would seal off another frontier and deny generations the last great adventure left.

To understand the lure of flight, one must understand the motivation of pilots. Whether they are flying around the moon or taking a hot-air balloon ride, the flying is the thing.

To pilots, flying has a spiritual dimension. It is not for nothing that they quote the poet John Gillespie Magee Jr. He was the author of the lines, "Oh! I have slipped the surly bonds of Earth ... Put out my hand and touched the face of God." Magee may not have been the greatest poet, but he wrote the pilot's creed and is quoted to every flight student.

Pilots fly because they can; because since time immemorial, humans have wanted to fly, and for a nearly a century, it has been possible. Pilots—they come is all shapes and sizes in both genders—will climb into just about anything that leaves the ground: a hot-air balloon, an ultra-light, a helicopter, a small plane, a Boeing-747, or a space shuttle. The irreducible is that it leaves the ground, seemingly reverses human fortunes, and takes pilots into that metaphysical paradise called flight.

There are common bonds between pilots, whether they fly military jets or single-engine, private planes. In learning to fly, they have joined a select company of men and women who have known extreme fear and wild exhilaration.

In the lexicon of flying, there are fixed-wing pilots (the standard), helicopter pilots (admired), fighter pilots (greatly admired), and astronauts (worshipped). To ordinary pilots, astronauts are the epitome of the craft for their courage, their skill, and conquest of the last frontier.

All the astronauts I have known are bonded to and consumed by aviation, whether it is in space flight or Sunday afternoon puddle-jumping. When I was learning to fly, astronaut Bill Anders called me almost daily to monitor my progress and to urge extreme safety. "Don't fly into weather you can't handle," he said often.

Last year, I spent time with three astronauts at the Barron Hilton Soaring Championships, which are held every two years at the hotelier's Nevada ranch. After the soaring, the guests—all of them were pilots, from the actor Cliff Robertson to the astronauts Gene Cernan and Anders—played with every kind of flying machine. There were aerobatic aircraft, hot-air balloons, gliders, old airplanes, and helicopters. The astronauts would get behind the controls of anything that left the ground. They were first and foremost pilots and, needless to say, enthusiasts for manned space flight.

Even as we mourn the crew of the Columbia, are we to deny the brave and the bold the great adventure? From the beginning of the Space Age, pilots have fought for their place in it, insisting on windows in the first space capsules, a flyable launch vehicle, and resumption in space exploration-back to the Moon and on to Mars.

Occasionally, the very love of flight has limited progress. The U.S. Air Force was slow to develop unmanned combat vehicles because of it. The pilot-dominated Air Force was reluctant to admit that there were some jobs that were better done without men and women at the controls. Now, unmanned vehicles are a part of our arsenal. There is the technology today for freight aircraft to be flown remotely, but it is a hard sell to those who take the controls of airplanes.

After the Comet, the first jet airliner, blew up, Winston Churchill, who learned to fly during World War I, said: "The cost of solving the Comet mystery must be reckoned neither in money nor in manpower."

So it must be with the Columbia. But to astronauts and aspiring astronauts, it must also be a new beginning in space exploration-with men and women.

We can hope that the numbing tragedy of the shuttle breakup will be remembered with a revival of interest in space exploration. I have no doubt that is what the seven who perished would have wanted. And, ultimately, even those who stay on the ground will be richer for it.

February 4, 2003

SAFETY HAS BECOME OUR NATIONAL DISEASE

The argument against a manned space program is being heard everywhere these days. The argument is all over the lot, but its central points are that we would get more bang for our buck with unmanned vehicles and there would be no risk to human life.

As to the first point, the history of government funding teaches us that if a scientific endeavor does not excite the public, politicians happily put it on a kind of life-support system that keeps it breathing but supine. I have watched many such science programs die the slow death that is reserved for pure science. If people are not involved, politicians will limit the funds until there is no purpose in continuing the program. Our great national laboratories are littered with the skeletons of once-exciting programs that fell out of favor and were starved into abandonment.

The second point has to do with the nation's preoccupation with safety. Nuclear power plants are not built, innovative aircraft are not introduced, and genetic engineering is not fully pursued due to the quest for absolute safety.

Pressure groups have made safety a central plank of their endeavors. Alarming the public about safety is a sure fundraiser and bait for the media. Safety has become a kind of American disease, wherein danger is viewed hypothetically. Ergo, we have an asymmetry between life as it is lived and the introduction of any new dimension to that life. Automobiles and motorcycles are inherently dangerous, but they are grandfathered by experience and toleration. Light aircraft are constantly under attack from those worried about the safety of passenger jets, but they are beloved by those who actually fly them. We cringe before hypothetical danger and face the real thing bravely.

The Mercury and Apollo space missions were more dangerous than the routine launch of the space shuttle. Yet, because of two unfortunate accidents, there are those who would close the door on this great human adventure.

It is probably time to re-examine the space program, but with a view to establishing lofty new goals in space, not ever-safer ones. None of those who have climbed into a space capsule or the shuttle have done so because they craved a safe, sedentary, Earth-bound life. Instead, they were responding to an ancient, fundamental, human challenge: exploration.

While institutions yearn for safety and have made an industry of its pursuit, individuals are always seeking to break out of the confines of an oh-so-safe existence. Why do high-wire walkers seek the tallest towers, bungee jumpers the highest bridges? Why do singular people try to fly around the world in balloons? Extreme sports suggest a yearning to escape the bonds of safety. By any measure, Charles Lindbergh was foolhardy, but he fed the imagination of the world, authenticated the concept of a hero, and ushered in the era of intercontinental flight.

Yes, manned space exploration should be made as safe as possible, but not so safe that it does not take place. John Glenn, the former astronaut and U.S. senator, who is now 81 years old, said after the Columbia disaster that he would go into space again if it would serve any useful purpose. The writer Tom Wolfe called that attitude "the right stuff."

Future manned space exploration should return to the Moon and aim for Mars. A dissembling and unhappy world needs a sense of its common invincibility; of the dauntless human spirit, literally and figuratively, soaring away. Happily, there are plenty of men and women who have "the right stuff," and who know the risks. Or, as the poet Robert Browning wrote: "Ah, but a man's reach should exceed his grasp, or what's a heaven for?"

February 11, 2003

THE HISTORICAL LEDGER IS BALANCED WITH FRANCE

The foul winds of Francophobia are blowing everywhere. France, suddenly, is the country we love to hate. Ironically, the present mood of hostility to France is a mirror-image of the anti-Americanism that has pervaded the political left in France for 50 years. It is angry, sometimes vicious, and baseless.

The French have a well-honed capacity to be perverse. This capacity was epitomized by Charles de Gaulle, who sometimes seemed nearly as large a problem to his allies as he was to his enemies. During World War II, Winston Churchill sent de Gaulle, the leader of the Free French, to visit Franklin D. Roosevelt. "Why," Roosevelt asked Churchill, "would you do this to me?" Churchill replied that he had borne the Cross of Lorraine long enough and needed a respite. It was the same de Gaulle who refused to have NATO troops in France and who pursued a French nuclear weapons capacity, known as the "Force de Frappe."

The British and the French, harkening back to medieval times, have enjoyed a convivial but rude relationship. The British call the French "Frogs" and the French call the British "Roast Beef."

Napoleon said: "England is a nation of shopkeepers." But he was more accurately describing France, which is made up of highly individualistic, small entrepreneurs. If French commercial life has a failing, it is because it has lacked an entrepreneurial class at the top. There are not many great French multinational corporations, but France abounds in small businesses—boutiques, hotels and restaurants. In short, shopkeepers.

Next only to Britain, France has produced some of the greatest intellectuals, and has a permanent claim to greatness among artists, philosophers, scientists and writers of literature. The artists include Jean August Ingres, Claude Monet and Paul Gaugin; the philosophers include Jean-Jacques Rousseau, Baron de Montesquieu and Jean-Paul Sartre; the scientists include Louis Pasteur and Marie Curie; and the literary figures include Racine, Moliere, Voltaire, Balzac, Hugo and Proust.

A great and ancient player in the world of ideas, France is joyously self-confident in its culture.

While the French made a botch of colonialism, they were our staunch ally in the Revolutionary War. And while members of Congress and the Bush administration sit around and try to punish the French by eschewing their food and wine (inadvertently punishing themselves), they might consider that the White House looks out on Lafayette Square and is located in a city designed by L'Enfant. They might also consider that the symbol of the freedom we cherish is the Statue of Liberty: a gift from France.

Most of the institutions and practices adopted by the Founding Fathers were derived from British traditions, dating to the Magna Carta. But they were modified and humanized by French philosophical ideas.

If the approximate cause of the rash of Francophobia is the perversity of Jacques Chirac, the French president, there was a latent hostility to France in

American conservative circles. For nearly a decade, conservative writers and the denizens of think tanks have been sniping at the French.

The independence of France and its welfare society have annoyed American conservatives. It is a tenet of their conservatism that state health systems do not work. Yet France, which spends only 8 percent of its gross domestic product on health, compared to 14 percent in the United States, has one of the most effective systems of nationalized medicine in the world. Another conservative anathema, public transportation, has worked extremely well for France, which boasts the best intercity rail system in the world.

Of course, American conservatives may be right: France's social net may be too expensive for it to afford, and its public transportation is highly subsidized. But for now, these things contribute to the quality of life in France.

Then, there is the widely-held view that the French are rude to Americans. Here the evidence can be only anecdotal. In more than 40 years of visiting France at least once a year, one man was rude to me once—a night porter in a hotel in Normandy.

The Francophobes are doing a little judicious rewriting of history, implying that the United States entered both world wars for the purpose of saving France. Hardly. The defeat of the Germans in World War I to the benefit of France was a byproduct of that awful conflict, much of it fought on Belgian and French soil. And the liberation of France in World War II was a byproduct of our throwing in with the British against the Nazi axis.

Sure the posturing of French politicians is annoying, but posturing by politicians is the price of democracy. It is appropriate that the French remember our sacrifices for them during World War I and II. It is as appropriate for us to remember the French who sacrificed for us during our War of Independence, and who added Gallic charm to the American enterprise.

February 18, 2003

WHEREFORE ART THOU, TEDDY ROOSEVELT?

"Like all Americans, I like big things. Big prairies. Big forests and mountains. Big wheat fields, railroads, big factories, steamboats, and everything else." So said the 27-year-old Theodore Roosevelt, reported *The Badlands Cowboy*.

When he became president, the first big domestic political battle Teddy Roosevelt fought was to build a big dam on the Great Salt River. It was not easy: Congress was skittish and the financing was unorthodox.

The river either ran dry or flooded. The landowners along the river saw that it had to be tamed if they were to prosper and if that part of Arizona was to grow. They had petitioned Congress for help in damming the river and had been rejected. So they went to the new president with their plan, and he embraced it.

Under the plan, the landowners would pledge their property as security for the dam bonds, and it would be up to Roosevelt to bludgeon Congress into agreement. He bludgeoned, Congress acceded. And 100 years ago, the Roosevelt Dam was opened by the Rough Rider himself.

With the dam came the Salt River Project, which still manages water in the region and supplies 800,000 customers with electricity. Without it and Roosevelt's foresight, Phoenix might not have evolved into the great city it is today. He also had a vision of how the West might develop, although it was his distant nephew, Franklin D. Roosevelt, who took to fruition the concept of taming the West through water management.

Teddy Roosevelt's biographer, Edmund Morris, at the Salt River Project's centennial ceremony, added a caveat to T.R.'s love of big things. He said: "And one of the things he most liked was big government, with plenty of power ... plenty of anti-trust power. Insofar as the GOP of his day was protectionist and stood for emancipation, he was a party faithful. But he was very happy to blaspheme against the conservative tenets of *laissez-faire*."

In the presidential message calling for a National Reclamation Act, the vehicle that established the Salt River Project, Roosevelt wrote: "The doctrine of private ownership of water, apart from land, cannot prevail without causing enduring harm."

But the point of Roosevelt's first big domestic achievement was not his doubting of conservative orthodoxy, but his belief in big projects producing great public dividends.

Nowadays, great public infrastructural projects, if proposed at all, tend to be dead-on-arrival. Big shopping centers and big subdivisions sprout everywhere. But big public works are distained politically and frustrated by local coalitions when they are tried. So we have no new airports, no new dams, no new major electric transmission, and no additional highways and bridges. This is known by the acronym NIMBY (not in my backyard). The British, similarly frustrated, have added another acronym, DADA (decide, announce, defend, abandon).

The spirit of T.R. is not marching through the land. Not since the creation of the national highway system, sold as a defense project, has a truly visionary public-infrastructure project been undertaken. The French have built their high-speed rail service, which now reaches much of Europe. The Germans have built their autobahn. And the Japanese have their bullet trains. In the last three decades, a new airport in Denver is about as much as we have achieved in terms of big projects for a big people.

Sure, Congress appropriates billions of dollars for highways, but most of those funds are absorbed in maintenance and repair. Amtrak is maintained with such frugality that it cannot improve its service, let alone add new high-speed-rail services, which would make it competitive with air transport between cities 400 miles apart.

There is not a major city in the country that is not suffering from crippling, expensive congestion. But is not just transportation where the spirit of T.R. is missing. The older cities have antiquated sewers, which give out in flood conditions, as they have just done along the East Coast. And the nation's electric transmission grid is only just holding its own and is in need of upgrading.

President Bush plans to stimulate investment through tax cuts. But if those investments do come, they will not come in the form of public infrastructure. The spirit of T.R. is not abroad in the land, although it is much needed.

February 25, 2003

CLOUD OVER IRISH PRIME MINISTER'S VISIT

It has become a tradition for the Irish prime minister to visit Washington and exchange pleasantries with the president on or around St. Patrick's Day. This year will be no exception. Irish Prime Minister Bertie Ahern is scheduled meet with his friend, President George W. Bush, at the White House on March 13.

But this may be the most difficult visit an Irish prime minister has ever made to Washington. And although Ahern will be smiling in public, the message he has for Bush is one of gloom. Ireland is rent with anti-war activism: the first major wave of anti-Americanism since the 1980s has spread across the country. In the 1980s, there was anti-American feeling, largely fed by Irish missionary priests, over President Ronald Reagan's Central American policy.

Now the feeling is more widespread and the anger more visceral. In particular, Shannon Airport is under siege by anti-war activists, who are accusing the Ahern administration of violating Ireland's neutrality constitution by allowing American warplanes to refuel at Shannon. A peace camp has been established at Shannon. And the airport's perimeter has been breached several times, leading to attacks on U.S. military aircraft with paint and hammers.

The anti-Americanism violates what has been a very special relationship between Ireland and America: a relationship that has found its strongest expression around St. Patrick's Day. On the evening of an attack on Iraq, at 6 p.m., Irish activists plan protests in every village, town and city across the country, according to the Irish Anti-War Movement's Web site. The day following the attack, at noon, they plan a 10-minute, countrywide work stoppage. And on the Saturday following the start of the war, they plan mass demonstrations in every major city and town in Ireland.

During his White House meeting, Ahern will tell Bush that he, like other democratically elected leaders, cannot totally ignore the wishes of his people. Irish sentiment against a war is as complete as it is in France, and Ahern is aware that he may have to answer to the electorate at the next election.

On the other hand, Ahern, who has no international standing, depends on his connection with Bush to give him, and by extension Ireland, stature. The Irish prime minister would like to be seen as a friend and confidante of Bush. But too much friendship may doom Ahern politically, particularly if the anti-war demonstrations turn violent.

Ahern's predicament highlights an irony in today's fragile international community. Bush wishes to invade Iraq to establish democracy. But the citizens of most of the world's democracies are ambivalent or hostile to his plan. Do you vitiate democratic will in order to create a new democracy?

Alone among democratic leaders, British Prime Minister Tony Blair has shown himself to be prepared to take the consequences of standing strong with Bush. Even so, British public opinion is sharply divided, and hostility in Blair's own Labor Party to the Bush position is growing daily. Those close to Blair say that he is nervous and unsure of how to reassert his leadership of the Labor Party. In London, it is believed that if a war against Iraq goes badly, particularly for British troops, Blair will be removed.

Across Europe, elected leaders are upset with the Bush administration's insensitivity, bordering on indifference, to their plight.

Although Ireland is a small country, it exemplifies the democratic crisis in Europe, where it is damaging for leaders to oppose Bush, and possibly suicidal for them not to. In Ireland there is an additional emotional imbroglio. The Irish are often accused of never forgetting their history, and they remember that it was America that provided a haven for their starving people in the 19th century. They revel in the fact that more than 40 million Americans trace their ancestry to Ireland.

The Irish even thank America for teaching them how to celebrate St. Patrick's Day. Before the big parades and the festivity that came to characterize the holiday in America, it was a dour saint's day in the Old Sod. The Irish sent delegations to New York to find out how to spruce up their celebrations.

It is the Irish, rather than the British, who have always felt that they had a special relationship with America. Respecting America, Irish passions run strong; the question is whether those passions have turned negative in an irredeemable way.

March 4, 2003

ADM. LOY, YOU KNOW BETTER: RESCIND THIS RULE

The Transportation Security Administration (TSA), a Homeland Security agency headed by former Coast Guard Admiral James Loy, has infuriated pilots across the nation by what appears to be the draconian imposition of a new rule in the war against terrorism.

The rule gives the TSA the authority to ask the Federal Aviation Administration to revoke an American citizen's pilot's license if the agency considers the flyer to be a "security threat." The TSA need not produce evidence to prove its allegation. What is more, the only appeals procedure is to the TSA itself, without any third-party judicial review.

Ron Laurenzo, a colleague of mine and a reporter for *Defense Week*, and a pilot like myself, reported that the ruling took effect upon its publication in the *Federal Register* on Jan. 24. This is very unusual, Laurenzo wrote. "The public's period for commenting on the rule, which normally occurs before a rule takes effect, started after this rule became binding."

The TSA now holds sway over who will fly and who will not fly, and it does not have to explain why a license is revoked. It need not state what evidence it has, nor why, if it has suspicions of a pilot, it does not convey them to the normal law-enforcement authorities for action. If the TSA thinks you are a security threat, your career as a professional pilot or your recreational flying can be ended in an airless procedure by nameless bureaucrats.

Confronting your accuser does not enter into the matter. Up in arms, not surprisingly, are the two organizations that represent the most pilots: the Air Line Pilots Association, which represents 66,000 professionals, and the Aircraft Owners and Pilots Association, which represents almost 400,000 members.

As well as violating constitutional norms, the TSA's action suggests very little understanding of how aircraft are operated. It is one of those actions that will only penalize the law-abiding, and will do nothing to deter those with malicious intentions.

Any more than with automobiles, no one checks a pilot's credential every time he or she climbs into an airplane. As with automobile drivers, most pilots only have to present their credentials when there is an accident or a safety violation. As with automobiles, there are a few pilots who fly without licenses, but probably far fewer in percentage terms than those who drive cars without them or while their licenses are revoked. The purpose of these licenses is simple: they prove only that the operator has the training to be safe.

The TSA rule would suggest that the agency has a very poor understanding of the air traffic system. Would a pilot who was taking up an aircraft to commit an act of terrorism worry that his or her paperwork was not in order?

Over many decades, the air traffic system in the United States has depended on trust, camaraderie, and the discipline that comes from knowing the price of getting it wrong. In light of this, the TSA, with what probably is an unconstitutional rule, has wantonly sought to abridge the civil rights of pilots without any regard to the underlying absurdity of their rule.

Having met Loy, I am astounded to find that so gentle and thoughtful a man would lend his authority to such a vicious and pointless regulation. The good admiral must know that there is no licensing of recreational boating, and that, in a crowded port, a powerboat can be used as lethally as an airplane.

Happily, the chairman of the House Transportation Committee, Don Young, has called the ruling "unfair and probably unconstitutional." The Alaska Republican has said that the TSA has gone beyond its congressional mandate. Young has reason to be sensitive to the pilots' lobbies: commercial and private aviation are essential to Alaska's economy.

TSA spokesman Brian Turmail told Laurenzo, "The bottom line is: 'If you're not a terrorist, you don't have to worry about this.' "

Oh yes, you do. I remember in the bad old days, when I covered the Atomic Energy Commission, how perfectly patriotic people would have their security clearances pulled on "national security" grounds. Even if they fought and got their clearances back, these luckless people were at the end of their nuclear careers.

Now suppose you are an airline pilot and a union activist, and someone who does not like unions finds that you once vacationed in a troubled part of the world. Bang! You are a security risk: end of your career.

How quickly we forget the wicked ways of J. Edgar Hoover and Richard Nixon. Here is a government agency amassing a power it should not have against a threat it cannot eliminate. Every stupid action, such as this one, is in its way a victory for the very terrorists we are all committed to fighting.

March 11, 2003

THE ODD COUPLE: HOW BLAIR, BUSH DIFFER

Even as the nation applauds British Prime Minister Tony Blair for standing shoulder-to-shoulder with President Bush, it behooves us to understand that Blair is not a neo-conservative with a British accent.

Neither is he Winston Churchill, nor Margaret Thatcher, nor any of the other prime ministers with whom he has been compared. If he has a political antecedent, it might be Clement Atlee, the prime minister who succeeded Churchill after World War II. Not a figure to inspire Americans.

But Atlee was a transformational prime minister with a clear vision of the kind of Britain he wanted. In that, he was Blair-like. For Blair has been working hard at transforming Britain in radical ways—more radical than even Thatcher. Thatcher broke the unions, favored free enterprise, privatized state industries, and left the structure of Britain largely alone. When she attempted to change the structure, through changing local government and its tax system, she failed.

Blair has built on the Thatcher inheritance, but has been far more successful at structural change. Consider:

- He has revolutionized the House of Lords, although he has not finished the task.
- He has devolved political power to Scotland and Wales.
- He has freed the Bank of England from political control.
- He has chosen to bypass the House of Commons by governing around it rather than through it and, symbolically, reduced "Question Time" from twice to once a week.
- In a blow to a great British tradition, he has given the green light to the banning of foxhunting.
- And he has stood his Labor Party on its head, offering it the carrot of winning as an incentive for moderating its deeply held trade unionist and socialist views.

All of this Blair refers to as "the project." The project, it turns out, is the modernizing of Britain. He is first and foremost a modernizer. Although he went to a distinguished private school in Scotland and graduated from Oxford, he has no bondage to the past: neither the bondage of British tradition nor the bondage of Labor Party tradition.

He has been helped in his quest by the collapse of the Conservative Party and his own large and inexperienced majority in the House of Commons. Most who sit in that hallowed place today have no experience of politics or the traditions of the House of Commons. In short, his majority is malleable. And except for the grumbling over Iraq, his parliamentary colleagues are submissive.

Blair's political philosophy rests on three legs: one, winning; two, modified Christian Democratic pragmatism; and three, a quiet religious faith blended with the social philosophy of John Rawls, the late American political philosopher.

Blair also has a thoroughly modern family, including a wife with a high-powered career as a barrister. If he had chosen another path for himself, one could imagine Blair staying home and playing Mr. Mum.

Rather than being George W. Bush East, he is closer to being Bill Clinton East. He likes to be a man of the world, and take his vacations throughout it.

And despite the current contretemps with France, Blair is a Francophile. He worked in France as a student and speaks excellent French.

He is also an environmentalist and has promised to reduce carbon dioxide emissions from the United Kingdom below the levels targeted by the Kyoto Protocol.

Blair is fascinated by business, but, like Rawls, is committed to social justice; a catchment net woven so fine that none will fall through it.

What neither his fans nor detractors knew of Blair was his extraordinary political courage. There have been hints of it when he has stood by unpopular and compromised colleagues, and when he, the Labor Party leader, sent his children to private schools.

But it is his support for Bush that has revealed the full range of his political courage. With 60 percent of the British people opposed to a war in Iraq, Blair has done the unthinkable: he has thrown in with the Americans.

It is possible for the Labor Party in Parliament to show Blair the door. But that is unlikely to happen. While they may be deeply unhappy with his stance on Iraq and his closeness with Bush, his Labor colleagues fear that without him they would return to the bad old days of a party dominated by trade unionists and socialist ideologues.

Members of the party know that Middle England likes Blair, and that he is their ticket to future electoral success. If Blair were to be moved aside, his successor almost certainly would be the chancellor of the exchequer, Gordon Brown: a dour and canny Scot with a deep investment in old-fashioned socialism.

March 18, 2003

THE GREENING OF GEORGE W. BUSH IS OVERDUE

It is almost unimaginable: a hugely popular president loses a vote for oil drilling in Alaska on the eve of going to war in the Middle East. Yet that is what happened when the Senate rejected the Bush administration's proposal to drill for oil in the Arctic National Wildlife Refuge (ANWR).

It should have been a slam-dunk, given the timing and the Republican control of the Senate. But it was not: the proposal lost by 52 to 48. And what had been the centerpiece of President Bush's energy policy when he assumed office has again failed in the Senate.

The ANWR vote points up one of the administration's largest vulnerabilities: the environment.

If Bush's father had difficulty with the "vision thing," his son seems to have difficulty with the "environment thing." Bush does not understand the depth of feeling that many people have about the environment. The administration simply does not get it.

The culture of this administration owes much to the president's early years in West Texas, where environmental laws often seemed to the oil industry to be cumbersome and counterproductive. Deep down, Bush and his vice president, Dick Cheney, appear to believe generally that much environmental legislation has been counterproductive, and that regulations promulgated in the Clinton years were particularly so. It is a cultural schism as much as a scientific one.

In a recent book, New America Foundation fellow Michael Lind argues that the culture of the new Republicans and their leader, Bush, was formed by the extractive industries: oil, gas and mining. These industries feel cribbed by the government, and chafe against what they feel are excessive and frustrating regulations.

The administration wants to fix that and still do its bit for the environment. Unfortunately, the administration came out swinging—abandoning regulations and, symbolically, turning its back on the Kyoto Protocol. The administration may be no less Green than many Democrats, but it had a terrible beginning. It appeared to be overly sympathetic to industry and indifferent to the direction in which the country had been going, and Bush appeared to cut the legs out from under his own Environmental Protection Agency administrator, Christie Todd Whitman.

It is hard to believe that Bush and Cheney, both of them outdoorsmen, are really indifferent to the environment. It is just that they see it very differently, and see the environmental movement as political, effete and self-serving.

The president's defeat in the Senate also pointed up another problem: the administration has not cultivated good relations with the Senate. This is not uniquely a Bush problem, but one that most governors who become president go through. They think of Congress as a whole, and the Senate in particular, in the way they thought about their state legislatures: as malleable bodies that, in a pinch, could be arm-wrestled into submission.

Not the Senate. It is jealous of its prerogatives and its unique constitutional role. The care and feeding of senators is important for presidents to do. The administration has not done a good job of it. Senators of both parties complain that executive agencies do not respond to their letters, nor answer their questions fully when their people testify.

Bush tried to claim the environmental high ground when he came out in support of hydrogen-powered vehicles in his State of the Union speech. But he still needs to present a comprehensive environmental position that shows that he cares and that he has thought about the environmental challenge.

After the economy, the environment is the big domestic issue. People do wonder what sort of world their children will grow up in. While they may not wish to give up their SUVs, they would like to think that progress is being made in cleaning the air and the water. From the first, the administration has failed to assure people on these issues. It seemed unduly anxious to bury Kyoto, to reverse regulations on arsenic in drinking water, and to open up national forests to logging.

Bush, who can be a great persuader, as we have seen with the war in Iraq, has not made the effort to persuade anyone on the environment, probably because he does not see the problem. He drives around his ranch in Texas in a propane-powered pickup truck, but has kept this piece of environmentalism, this persuasive piece of symbolism, quiet. Personal virtue, you might say. But he has to go beyond personal virtue, as the Senate vote showed.

March 25, 2003

THAT WAS THE CHURCHILL THAT WAS

What do President Bush, his chief political counselor, Karl Rove, and the neoconservative *Weekly Standard* have in common? Answer: an averred passion for Winston Spencer Churchill.

Bush is said to believe in a Churchillian model. Rove is said to keep a picture of Churchill in his office and a copy of his quotations handy. *The Weekly Standard* uses a picture of the great man on its subscription order form.

All of this suggests that today's conservative movement in America is Churchillian in nature and that if Churchill were alive today, he would be counted in their number. Their scholarship may be wanting, and suggests that their only knowledge of Churchill consists of the great speeches of World War II.

What, I wonder, do they make of the fact that Churchill always described himself as a liberal, even when he was leader of the Conservative and Unionist Party (the Conservative Party's full name—and a name he debunked).

Churchill joined the Conservatives because the Liberals were collapsing from severe internal dissention over free trade and other issues. He needed a home and a constituency, and Stanley Baldwin's Conservatives offered him refuge. But his liberalism always showed through. For example, Churchill was opposed to putting Britain back on the gold standard (although he acquiesced) because he feared its impact on working people. And he was right.

He fought the coal owners of Britain during the coal strike, which followed the general strike of 1926. His political rivals painted him as the hard man of the government, but his sympathies were with the workers.

Likewise, Churchill championed national health insurance, although it was the post-war Labor government that brought it into being. More: In the 1920s,

Churchill opposed the size of Britain's military budget because it drained the resources needed for social programs.

It was not until the rise of Hitler that he began to champion rearmament.

Yet when it came to the British Empire, Churchill was a peculiarly 19th-century man, taking particular pride in the British role in India. But, even here, there was a contradiction, for he played a critical role in the creation of the Irish republic.

In life, as in politics, there were contradictions suggesting that not everything about Churchill the man would sit well with today's conservatives. He seldom invoked the name of God, and there was no evidence that he had deep, or any, religious convictions.

He also drank like a fish; starting with champagne at breakfast and continuing unabated during the day, varying the intake between Champagne, Scotch, claret (Bordeaux wine) and Cognac. Churchill was ecumenical about drink, so long as it was abundant. At Yalta, he drank the wines and brandies of the Caucasus region, augmented with the product of Scotland.

While he was always drinking, he was always working. Shorthand secretaries had to follow him around to take a stream of memoranda, newspaper articles, and chapters for his books. After long and liquid dinner parties, he would dictate for as much as four hours-and repeat the whole cycle the next day.

While he was chancellor of the exchequer (finance minister), he was also building walls at his country home, painting and taking painting lessons, and writing books. His official biographer, Martin Gilbert, said you could not understand Churchill in any normal way. Gilbert said he was simply "a phenomenon."

When you think of Churchill, you have to think of people like Leonardo da Vinci, Shakespeare and Mozart—people of such energy and talent that we cannot understand how they did it.

Although Churchill was often loud and ebullient, full of fun and exuding energy, he had his dark moments. He would suffer from depression, which he referred to as his "black dog," as in "the black dog has been here."

Something else, Churchill was a disaster with money; always in debt, and frequently saved from bankruptcy by rich friends, such as the publisher, Lord Beaverbrook.

One thing that the neoconservatives would like: Churchill was utterly faithful to his wife, Clementine. Although some of his children had terrible problems in later life, he provided a great family life to them when they were young.

Servants, secretaries and bureaucrats were not enamored of Churchill's indifference to them and to the hours he demanded of them. One of his weaknesses, besides ego, was insensitivity to those who served him.

But would he fit the neocon mold? I doubt it. If you saw the way his name and image is invoked nowadays, he might have resorted to one of his famous retorts: "Up with this I will not put."

April 1, 2003

WHY SHOULD WE DO ALL THIS HEAVY LIFTING?

The Bush administration, if it is not careful, may seize defeat from the jaws of victory in Iraq. It has already decided to play the lead role in the reconstruction of Iraq, and it may yet rue the day.

In rejecting a lead role for the United Nations, the administration is undertaking possibly the most difficult job of nation-building ever attempted.

All historical analogies are flawed. The reconstruction of Europe after World War II was an assist to the status quo ante. The reconstruction of Japan required the de facto pardoning of the Emperor to maintain Japanese cohesion and pride.

And the experience of colonial powers in the 17th, 18th and 19th centuries bore no relationship to Iraq today. The colonial powers had the advantage of state-of-the-art weapons and projected effectively an aura of cultural and technical superiority.

This worked even with the British in India, until insensitivity to local mores and religious beliefs led to the Indian Mutiny of 1857-58. But the British still held the upper hand, controlling the advanced weaponry and having a monopoly on information.

Unfortunately, and symbolically, it is Northern Ireland, where President Bush and British Prime Minister Tony Blair just met, that shows the difficulty of bringing about political change without absolute control of weaponry, and without any control of information. Good intentions, Northern Ireland proved, are no asset.

The British Army entered Northern Ireland in 1970 to support the Catholic minority. But after some blunders, it became a symbol of oppression, and the Troubles were underway—a partial insurrection in which 3,600 people, out of a population of only 1.5 million, have lost their lives. It is a foreboding example of what can go wrong in the name of right.

Iraq poses all the problems of Northern Ireland on a grander scale, without common heritage, without the security forces having intimate local knowledge, and without a common language among the combatants. It can be argued that had it not been for the ubiquitous availability of small arms and explosives, peace would have come earlier and have been more durable in Northern Ireland.

Even though the Iraqis may have been oppressed by Saddam Hussein's regime, they are now to be asked to accommodate a totally alien conqueror after much loss of life among their people. We do not plan to stay in Iraq any more than the British Army had planned to stay in Northern Ireland—as it has for more than 30 years.

We come to Iraq with noble intentions, a political ideal, and very little experience in administering any country other than our own. The National Rifle Association likes to make the point that American freedoms are stronger because of the abundance of small arms among the population. In this state, the gun lobby says, we cannot be oppressed. Unfortunately, the Iraqi population is awash in small and medium arms and a sizable portion of it may feel oppressed. Ergo, Iraq will remain a very dangerous place throughout our involvement there.

Democracy has an appeal in oppressed nations where political redress is expected to be the route of liberation. It is the secular solution. But in a nation where religion comforts the oppressed, religious rule beckons. An example of the former is Eastern Europe and of the latter, Iran.

Winston Churchill said that mankind is not to be spared the rigors of the human pilgrimage. Despite our best efforts in Iraq at establishing civil order, reviving the economy, rebuilding the infrastructure, and hothousing a democracy, it is hard to believe that that nation will be spared the rigors of its pilgrimage, which is about to become ours as well.

The president has yet to explain to us why, simply because we played the lead in overthrowing the regime, we have to take on the lead role in repairing the nation. What is the American interest in this? Why is it not prima facie harder for those who bore the battle to do the cleanup than for a multinational force of noncombatants to come in and start rebuilding? They would not have to endure the bitterness of a proud but conquered people. And several of the nations that are keen to help—France, Germany and Russia—have long in-country experience with Iraq.

Of course, these are the countries with which we have been at odds, but there would be elegance in letting them take up the burden in peace that they rejected in war. One of history's lessons is that a bad peace undoes a good war.

April 8, 2003

LET US NOW PRAISE THE REPORTERS IN IRAQ

Cornered, most journalists would confess that they are part of a craft that attracts an eclectic bunch of misfits; an irregular army of wayward partisans, redeemed only by getting the story.

You might describe journalists as egotistical, cynical, anti-authoritarian, undisciplined, sometimes drunken, and the proprietors of untidy lives. Their marriages are often rocky and frequent, their finances chaotic, and their employment security nebulous. Not for nothing is the patron saint of journalists, Jude, also the patron saint of hopeless causes.

But not in peace would you describe journalists collectively as brave and sentimental. Yet when there is war, there is bravery and sentimentality.

The sheer courage of the reporters who have stayed in Baghdad throughout the current war is a thing of beauty, a thing to be marveled at and to be lavished with praise. To go to bed every night in the Palestine Hotel, not knowing whether an errant bomb would make it your last night, or to walk the streets when someone in the crowds could turn on you and kill you on the spot, is courage in the extreme. It is also beyond the call of duty. No man or woman has to be there. But dozens of extraordinary individuals—reporters, news technicians and columnists—have put their lives on the line for weeks now to give us the news.

It has something to do with that part of the job that verges on a higher calling; of serving the imperatives of the story, above safety, above comfort, and above sense. It is that bit of journalism that is antithetical to the cynicism that is held to be the trademark of journalists.

Over the decades, many journalists have been killed in many conflicts; many of their names are now forgotten. At its offices in Washington, Reuters news agency maintains an honor roll of its staff who have given their lives for the news. Others news organizations do likewise. They commemorate journalists in their prime who have died far from home in Congo, Korea, Vietnam, and across South America.

Now two American journalists, at the peak of their powers, the engaging David Bloom of NBC and the pugnacious columnist Michael Kelly, have died. Neither was killed by fire, but they both died because they were in Iraq, doing what they had to do, covering the news.

Their deaths have produced sorrow and mourning among their colleagues, opening a vein of sentimentality that you might not have known existed. Both Bloom and Kelly were well known and liked in Washington; Bloom, in the White House press corps, and Kelly, just about everywhere. The tears are real and the sentiment honest. Their deaths also remind us of our friends and colleagues who are still in Iraq, filing and surviving.

Kimberly Dozier, who is with CBS Radio in Baghdad, touches me every time I hear her on the radio. She used to work with me when she was fresh from college. Now she is a seasoned war correspondent and, like her colleagues, gallant. When I knew her, she covered technology and the energy industry—a far cry from the lethality of war.

Journalists are accused of being too liberal, too conservative, too aggressive, too prying, too addicted to society's failures: on the whole, a reprehensible lot. But nobody can say that they do not rise to the occasion and exhibit the same incredible courage as our troops.

Rudyard Kipling, who knew a thing or two about war, defended the British soldier in his poem "Tommy." He castigated the shameful way the troops were treated until they were needed. As in this stanza: *While its Tommy this, an' Tommy that, an' "Tommy, fall be'ind," But it's "Please to walk in front, sir," when there's trouble in the wind.*

Those lines make me feel sentimental about all heroes. But particularly, at this time, about those who carry notebooks, cameras and tape-recorders. Soldiers armed only with words.

April 15, 2003

MEMORIES OF THE CONCORDE: A TALE OF THE TIMES

After nearly three decades, the world's fastest passenger jet airplane, the Anglo-French Concorde, is on final. The French Concorde will fly for the last time in May, and the British Concorde will terminate service in October.

The story of the Concorde is a chronicle of our times: It is all about technology, politics and money. As these last Concorde flights take place, the aircraft flying them are out-of-date and still wondrous.

The Concorde was conceived in 1965, and the first prototype was completed two years later. But early in its life, it hit political turbulence, with disagreements between the French and British. But more important, there were dramatic attempts to deny the aircraft U.S. landing rights.

At the end of the '60s, the Senate killed an administration request to build a U.S. supersonic transport. That made the European Concorde a commercial and prestige threat to America, and an alliance of U.S. aviation and environmental interests waged a mighty campaign to deny the Concorde landing rights in the United States. These rights were granted in 1976, but Congress did ban supersonic flights by commercial aircraft over the United States, thus impairing Concorde's commercial viability.

As the Concorde settled into primarily serving New York and Washington, D.C., seats became progressively more expensive, until the cabin of the aircraft was transformed into a club for the super-rich. At over $10,000 per roundtrip, the Concorde was not to be for ordinary people in a hurry. It became, like the Rolls Royce, a status symbol, an indicator of financial well-being, more treasured for that reason than for the three hours it clipped off of transatlantic flight.

The Concorde, the only civilian airplane with a delta wing, was a technological masterpiece in its day. But it arrived too early for computer controls, quiet engines and some of the other technical refinements reflected in new aircraft today.

But it was always fast and it was always beautiful. In its early flights—I was on one of them—passengers stood and applauded when a meter in the cabin showed that the aircraft had reached Mach 2.3. That is going something.

Both British Airways and Air France matched the speed of the aircraft with superlative service. Nothing was too much for a Concorde passenger on the ground or in the air. The wine lists were incomparable, the food magnificent and the staff supremely obliging. In all, I flew the Concorde three times, but I never bought a roundtrip ticket. I always took the cheapest coach fare one way in order to be able to afford the experience of Concorde the other.

In the cockpit, I once found the captain of a French Concorde with his feet up, reading a newspaper, while the copilot was nowhere to be seen. What, he asked reasonably, could he do at Mach 2.3 and 62,000 feet?

For all of its grandeur, the 100-seat Concorde is a small airplane with the cabin divided in three sections, not for the reason of class but for the reason of structure.

Other pilots and air-traffic controllers have had a love-hate relationship with the Concorde. Pilots always have thought that air traffic controllers give the Concorde special treatment and preference in landing. Air traffic controllers always have been wary of the Concorde, because it is low-and-slow on takeoff and has to be guided through air traffic patterns to its exclusive altitude. They also know that it is low on fuel when it has completed its transatlantic crossing, and they want to get it landed expeditiously.

Had the politics been different, the costs more contained, and had the Concorde been the symbol of American rather than European prestige, we might today take for granted crossing the Atlantic in under four hours. Nonetheless, for those of us who were privileged to do it, it was a very special experience. Flying the fastest civilian airplane in the world with the best service on earth.

Now, my most personal Concorde story. During the Iranian Revolution, I was landing a small airplane at Dulles International Airport, outside of Washington, D.C. The Concorde was waiting impatiently to take the runway. The captain of the Concorde, in a clipped British accent, asked the tower: "Dulles, in view of the energy crisis, don't you think you should land your airplanes somewhere else?"

"Speedbird One [Concorde's call sign], in view of the energy crisis, why don't you take that thing over to the British Museum and park it?" rejoined the air traffic controller.

Yes, there was ambivalence about the Concorde. But now that civilian supersonic flight is unlikely to return in our lifetime, there is sadness. Like the Apollo program, it was something that collectively humankind aspired to and achieved. Now it has been relegated to history. There is something wrong when the cutting edge is in the past.

April 22, 2003

GEPHARDT REKINDLES HEALTH CARE DEBATE

My friend Norman Macrae identified the central problem of health care in *The Economist* many years ago. The problem, he argued, was simple and the fix impossible.

Macrae identified the obvious, which is seldom mentioned: at the time of delivery, neither the health provider nor the patient is interested in the cost. Ergo, health care costs are the most difficult to contain.

People who do not have insurance, or who do not live in a country where the government pays, do without the health care they need. In that respect, the market works. But if you are lying on the gurney and you have insurance, when the nice radiologist asks you if you want more X-rays before the operation, you do not ask what they cost nor do you suggest that the surgeon proceed without additional X-rays.

The previous statement is not hypothetical. I fell off of my horse and broke my leg badly and before I was wheeled into the operating room, I was asked if I wanted the additional X-rays. Damn right, I did.

Way back, when most of the advanced countries introduced government-financed, single-payer health care systems, medicine was simpler and ran more to comfort than to cure. Today we can cure almost anything and prolong life to an astounding extent—at a price. The only country to go to nationalized health insurance in this new regime of high-science medicine is Canada.

Most of the others, including nearly all of western Europe and Japan, introduced national health care after World War II. The common political reality is that people who have nationalized health care love it and would not vote for an alternative private system. In Britain, for example, where the National Health Service is plagued with problems, no politician dares breathe the thought that it be abandoned.

Think about Americans and Social Security and you will get the picture about how the British feel about their health care system. It is the third rail of British politics.

Surprisingly, none of the countries with nationalized systems spend as much money on health care as a percentage of gross domestic product as does the United States, with its private insurance that is alleged to leave out 41 million people.

We spend a whopping 14 percent of our GDP on health care compared with between 6 and 11 percent for those with single-payer systems.

As my friend and colleague, Martin Walker of United Press International, points out, it comes down to rationing and where and how you do the rationing. In Europe and elsewhere, elective surgery and the very old bear the brunt of the rationing. You can wait two years in Britain for elective surgery. And if granny needs artificial knees at age 85, she will have to wait until the point is moot.

By contrast, we ration health care to young uninsured people. It is the ghetto child, the minimum-wage earner and the seasonally employed who do without in our system.

Yet American medicine is the best in the world and the time when we might have tried a European or Canadian system is long past. Therefore, Democratic presidential contender Richard Gephardt deserves credit for putting health care back on the national agenda and coming up with a thoughtful plan for compulsory insurance underwritten with tax credits. Not since the debacle of the Clinton health care scheme has any politician at the national level had the courage to raise the health care issue.

Gephardt asserts that his plan would be good for the economy. You might say, "He would, wouldn't he?" But most small businesses—revered in the abstract by politicians—would welcome some variant of the Gephardt plan. Yes, good, entrepreneurial, right-of-center small business owners.

As one myself, I would much rather be relieved of some of the burden of providing health insurance for my small staff than receive additional tax cuts. In this economy, many of us are not making enough money to pay taxes, but we have to pay health insurance for employees in good years and bad years. It gets inexorably more expensive, even if part of the increased cost is shared with the beneficiaries.

Probably not very many small business owners could bring themselves to vote for Gephardt for president because of many of his protectionist positions. But we should give him full recognition for raising the issue of national health insurance. It is the crisis that does not quit.

April 29, 2003

THE OTHER INTERNATIONAL CRISIS: CRIME

I can tell you, I think, why democracy fails in the Third World. I can tell you, I think, why conservatism has become the central political idea of American politics. I can tell you, I think, why the British Conservative Party has imploded, and why the Democrats in the United States are in such sorry shape.

But I cannot tell you why, for more than 30 years, crime has risen inexorably around the world. I do not know why London, and much of southeast England, is in the grip of a crime wave; why Rio de Janeiro is one of the most dangerous cities in the world; or why Johannesburg is practically a no-go zone for the law-abiding.

But I can tell you when it was different. I can tell you when, in the 1950s and 1960s, you could walk in New York's Central Park at night, you could roam Rio and Mexico City at 3 a.m. and crime was de minimis in London.

Liberals believe that the rise of crime has to do with poverty and injustice, and to fight crime you must root out its causes. The problem is the causes are elusive.

Conservatives will tell you that crime is the product of coddling criminals. Well, when there was less crime, there was more mercy in the justice system.

Let me take you back. When I was a young man, I hitchhiked all over central and southern Africa and never had a thought for safety. Houses were unlocked, keys were left in cars and crime was not a concern. Yet, my liberal friends, there was grinding poverty and huge inequality.

As a young man, I worked in the East End of London, then a thriving dock area with ships and their crews from around the world. At night, often after midnight, I would walk through Swedenborg Square, which has now become the respectable Tower Hamlets section of the city. The police considered Swedenborg Square to be the roughest section of London. Although it was overrun with prostitutes, violent crime was rare.

As a reporter, I covered the police court, where the miscreants of the area appeared for summary justice, mostly for prostitution, occasionally for fencing. Nearly all of the defendants cheerfully pleaded guilty and were fined or jailed for less than a week. In fact, they were coddled. Nonetheless, London's ugliest area was a safe place.

Today, you dare not walk far from your hotel in Rio or many other Latin American cities. But in the 1960s, I used to walk around Rio in the early hours of the morning, without knowing a word of Portuguese or having any thought for my security.

What I am trying to get at here is that crime has risen globally and no major city, from Moscow to San Francisco, is as safe as it was 30 years and more ago.

The literature on crime does not answer the universal rise in violent street crime, burglary, bodily assault and murder. It is not as though just one country lost its head, but that much of the world has lost its head. Gentle forbearance, the hallmark of civilized places and some that were not so civilized, has given way to civic barbarity. No one anywhere is absolutely safe in any urban environment.

Paris, which used to be as safe as London, is less so. Purse-snatchings, muggings and assaults are now as much a part of daily life in Paris as they are in London or New York. Only Tokyo comes to mind as a major city as safe as the rest of the world was in the 1950s and 1960s.

Criminologists, sociologists and anthropologists have not satisfactorily answered why so much of the world has turned criminal and violent, and why law-abiding people have accepted this departure from what was the norm in such a passive way. Worse, we have curtailed our freedoms in pursuit of security. We live in gated communities, select our housing based on security and find comfort in automobiles.

We talk about freedom but we have accepted an enormous erosion of our freedom, as we have come to believe that crime is a natural state.

Crime probably has something to do with the change in morality and with the death of shame. But how can this be in such disparate places as the African savannah and the London Underground?

May 6, 2003

THE PERDITION TRAIL—ONE BET AT A TIME

Gambling is in the news these days, because virtue czar William Bennett was a gambler, because many states are trying to balance their budgets with gambling revenues, and because gambling is beginning to edge out pornography as the big money winner on the Internet.

Ladbroke, the big British bookmakers, has seen a huge rise in its income from its Internet operations. But that is the tip of a vast iceberg of offshore casinos, homegrown bookmakers and those who simply bet among themselves.

I do not know whether Bennett is an addicted gambler. But I hope he is not, because it is one of the most frightening addictions. The wreckage it causes is as complete as the destruction of drug addiction or severe alcoholism.

It is more frightening, perhaps, because there is no changed state, no visible high, no palpable loss of control. Yet it is as absolute as any substance abuse.

This is not a confession. I am not a gambling addict. But back in the 1960s, I was very close to a young newspaper reporter who was in the thrall of gambling. His name was William Hoffman and he later, by way of expiation, wrote a book called "The Loser," which stands alongside Charles R. Jackson's tale of alcoholism, "The Lost Weekend." But "The Lost Weekend" was fiction and "The Loser" was fact.

Hoffman was energetic, talented and, more is the pity, plausible. I do not recall when his gambling spree began. By the time I met him, when he was a reporter for *The Baltimore News-American* and a part-time reporter for *The Washington Daily News*, he was well down the road to ruin. He had abandoned his wife and four children and was living a criminal life in which he deceived people out of money, bounced checks, and left a trail of deception through many racetracks around the country and at the Las Vegas casinos.

Hoffman would starve himself to have money for gambling and, for a while, slept on the fire escape of *The Daily News* to avoid paying rent. Yet he was a productive reporter. And until the police began investigating his attempt to sell a vehicle belonging to *The News-American*, he managed to survive.

After some time, Hoffman confided in me about the precarious, addicted life he was living. For him, gambling was everything and it did not matter what the game of chance was-cards, horses, slot machines. If he had any money whatsoever, he bet it. If you stopped in a bar to have a beer with him, he would want to bet. My saddest recollection is when he wanted to wager on who could drink a beer the fastest.

Finally, he took me to see his wife and four young children. It was a scene of crying, despair and recrimination. She showed me a great pile of those notices that banks send you when a check is returned.

Without knowing what we were doing, some of us on the newspapers tried what might be called an intervention. Trouble was, he needed money to stay out of jail and if we gave him money, we knew what would happen to it.

There were little moments of comedy, like when he took a third job in a debt-collection agency, chasing American Express credit card deadbeats.

"None of the people in the boiler room would ever get an American Express credit card the first time," he reported.

Finally, it was all too much and Hoffman disappeared. He was not heard from again until his book, "The Loser," became a best-seller—even being favorably reviewed by Mario Puzo in *The New York Times*. On the success of the book, Hoffman said he was cured. But he refused to pay back any of his friends. He cast himself as a victim of his addiction, which somehow he believed absolved him from any moral responsibility.

I have known a lot of alcoholics and a few drug addicts. But I have never seen anyone so possessed by a relentless dybuuk as my gambling friend.

He comes to mind when I see governments shirking their responsibility of progressive taxation and substituting gambling revenue. And I thought of him when I read about Bennett. Hoffman did gamble the milk money. Bennett appears to have had enough money never to have had to make the choice.

May 13, 2003

RAMSEY CLARK: LIBERAL LION IN WINTER

It is a lonely voice; urbane, cultured, moralistic and isolated. It is the voice of Ramsey Clark, who served as the attorney general of the United States under President Lyndon Johnson. Even in those days, he was known as the anti-attorney general. He was the lawyer's lawyer and the liberal's liberal.

So much so that he did not participate in Cabinet meetings, where the Vietnam War was an issue. His father was a Supreme Court justice. As a young lawyer in Texas, Clark chose to defend minor criminals and cases that would not migrate to the Supreme Court, compromising his father. It was his father, Tom, who swore him in as attorney general.

To Clark, the law is next to godliness and the Constitution is close to holy writ.

So it happens that Clark, who is regarded as a traitor by supporters of President Bush, is waging a quixotic campaign to impeach Bush. He talked about it in a speech at the National Press Club in Washington, D.C.; a speech with echoes of the 1960s, a reprise of the struggles of that time.

His audience, too, was a throwback: aging activists with a hankering for the barricades, despite their grayed hair and fattened middles. To be fair, there were young activists in the audience too—mostly minorities. But it was the veterans of earlier struggles who came to get the word from their leader.

Although the venue was the National Press Club, the media were thin on the ground and Clark's indictment of the Bush administration did not make the evening news or the front pages. He is suffering from that most painful of punishments in our media-conscious society: Ramsey Clark has been marginalized.

Yet he plows ahead, demanding nothing less than impeachment and trial of the president, citing law and the Constitution and backing it up with examples from the Nuremberg trials. He is deadly serious.

Said Clark: "As a young Marine, I sat briefly on two occasions in the Nuremberg hearings. And we really need to refer back to the constitution of the Nuremberg tribunal, because there we will find that the first crime to be prosecuted, the most important crime to prevent, was set forth in Section 6(a), described generally as crimes of peace. And the first crime against peace is war of aggression, and a war of aggression is an attack on another country that presents no threat of imminent danger to you. And I don't believe any objective person, on the evidence available, could believe that Iraq was an imminent threat or danger to the United States."

It is Clark's deeply held belief that the U.S. invasion of Iraq was an illegal act of aggression and that the holding of prisoners in Guantanamo Bay, Cuba, without counsel and trial, is a violation of the Geneva Conventions, U.S. law and the Constitution.

There is nothing oblique about Clark's attack on the administration. It is frontal and direct.

He said: "It's time that we recognize that the Constitution of the United States, at length and more than with any other single issue it addressed, dealt with the problem of the imperial presidency, the possibility of that, or of crimes by officers of the United States. They dealt with it at length because they were concerned about it. The Articles of Confederation hadn't worked. There was no executive. The government was dysfunctional. They didn't like the idea of a king. They had had some problems with George III. And, in fact, if you look at it, the Declaration of Independence is basically a bill of impeachment by the United States against George III. That's all it is. That's what it says."

Like that other great critic of this administration, Sen. Robert Byrd (D-W. Va.), Ramsey Clark is an old man and, in a sense, a free one because he does not seek to avoid the consequences of his association with left-wing causes, nor to compromise his views to fit the times.

Whether you agree with Clark—and he is very much in the minority—there is something courageous and, to my mind, very American in his iconoclastic stand against the political emotions of the time. Ignored, he battles on, buttressed by the 250,000 signatures he says he has collected for impeachment.

Clark's views are so far from the mainstream of the time that it is quite startling to hear them—an untrammeled liberal when most liberals are trying to pass for something else.

May 20, 2003

THE MISERY OF THE DEMOCRATIC INTELLIGENTSIA

They mutter, they grumble and sometimes they give way to almost incandescent rage. Yet they feel voiceless and leaderless. No, they are not a minority in Iraq, nor French wine producers. They are the Democratic Party intelligentsia in Washington, D.C.

I have been exposed to a lot of them lately, and they give breadth and depth to the phrase "unhappy campers."

These Democrats feel that the famously liberal media have gone missing; that the party cannot find a strong, declarative voice among its congressional leaders; and that the Democratic National Committee, under Terry MacAuliffe, is ineffectual—that it whines but does not fight.

Their list of grievances with the Bush administration is as long as their sense of impotence is real. Mention the nine Democratic candidates for president and they groan. In fact, having studied them, the Democratic intelligentsia can tell you why each one of them would be defeated by George W. Bush.

They brighten at the mention of an undeclared outsider like retired Gen. Wesley Clark. But they cannot conceive of a mechanism to bring in an outsider.

At one cocktail party, the group was enlivened only by the thought that eventually Bush would be overtaken by events; demolished by a self-inflicted wound. But the Democratic thoughtful are tempered in predicting catastrophe because it might involve wishing ill to the United States. As they are patriots, that is not their way.

These Democrats are angry with Bush over profoundly philosophical issues— issues they see as being above and beyond the normal cut-and-thrust of politics. These include: the preemptive war against Iraq; the failure of the military to locate weapons of mass destruction; the administration's hostility to Europe; the failure to restore order and to reconstruct Afghanistan; the treatment of unindicted, suspected terrorists; and the perceived violation of civil liberties by the Department of Justice.

As much as the Democratic intelligentsia is angered by the administration, it is perplexed by the enduring public approval of Bush. Deep down, they believe that the president will win a second term, and that what they believe is a wrecking crew will continue with historic changes at home and abroad.

They see the Bush policies ending not in a glorious realignment of the world, but in a world united in its hatred of an isolated United States that has betrayed its own values.

However, among this group of Democrats, there is no idea of how to stop the Bush juggernaut. They have no faith in their party structure or its leaders. They worry that the party will become known not for its Clinton-era centrism but for its extreme and noisy left wing-to them epitomized by the Rev. Al Sharpton and Rep. Dennis Kucinich of Ohio. These, they feel, are the people who will draw the whole party into disrepute.

Worse, they feel the Democratic Party will not raise enough money to fight the next presidential election because of its tarnished image and the reluctance of big donors to support hopeless candidates.

If you see the president as a man riding a tiger that he uncaged, as these Democrats do, it is more than galling to note that the public has a different vision; that the public sees Bush as a heroic figure, spreading American virtue and values throughout the world.

Some of the Democratic bitterness is not directed at the administration but at the apparent implosion of the Democratic Party and the lack of strong, clear voices on Capitol Hill. The Senate minority leader, Tom Daschle, is liked but is thought to have the political weight of helium. Likewise Nancy Pelosi, the House minority leader, is not seen as having the gravitas for the job.

Who are these disgruntled Democrats? They are lawyers, economists, former ambassadors, retired military officers and Clinton and Carter appointees. They believe that the neoconservatives, who have orchestrated the Bush agenda, are leading the nation into an abyss, but they are well aware that they have no one to articulate the trouble they see.

They may take heart if they reflect on the sorry fortunes of the British Labor Party in the days of Conservative supremacy, before an unlikely white knight, in the person of Tony Blair, rode into London. The rest, as they say, is history.

May 27, 2003

BIG BUSINESS IS OK, BUT SMALL IS INNOVATIVE

An Englishman, E.F. Schumacher, captured the attention of a generation with his book "Small is Beautiful: Economics as if People Mattered." The Federal Communications Commission, in deciding to lift the restrictions on broadcast ownership, has taken the opposite view: Big is beautiful.

These should not be absolute positions. There are times when size, corporate size, is imperative to undertake great things, such as the laying of transatlantic cable or putting a satellite into orbit.

But bigness has proven to be the enemy of innovation. It also stultifies personal growth.

No one of sound mind nowadays would try to open a grocery store, a hardware shop, or even a cut-price hamburger stand. The economies of scale of the supermarkets, the chain hardware stores and chain restaurants would doom these enterprises.

I have been trying to calculate how many small hardware stores are put out of business on average by the arrival of a Home Depot. Using where I live as a gauge, it is upwards of a dozen. That is upwards of a dozen dreams of self-employment ended.

However, the greater damage of consolidation may be to innovation. After all, if people want to shop in supermarkets, at Wal-Marts and at Home Depots, they should have the freedom to do so. But how do you develop a culture of innovation in a big corporation?

Yes, a good idea might see the light of day at the 3M company, which makes its money on bringing new ideas to market. But how about Boeing, General Motors or McDonald's? An engineer at Boeing may have the greatest difficulty in moving through the bureaucracy a better idea for an airplane. When Detroit is faced with an innovative idea, I know for a fact, the inertia is overwhelming. And to launch a new menu item at McDonald's is a Herculean task.

Sorry, big companies do not innovate.

Great periods of innovation in our history have been when a new technology, or idea, arrives unfettered by tradition and is executed by dozens of eager inventors with an entrepreneurial spirit. In the early part of the 20th century, automobiles developed by leaps and bounds from dozens of manufacturers.

By the time the airplane became viable, sclerosis already had set into the car industry. In theory, it was the carmakers who should have capitalized on aviation: they had the money, the engineering and the technology in engines and sheet metal. But no. It was entirely new people, with names such as Cessna, Piper, McDonnell and Sikorsky, who would challenge the skies.

Now that the first wave of computing is maturing, would there be room for Steve Jobs or Bill Gates if they were subsumed into existing corporations? IBM went from the avant-garde to the rear guard as new, untrammeled inventors ran away with the personal computer.

So to the concentration in broadcasting. As the few dominant broadcasters grow bigger, the chances of innovative programming dim. Had Ted Turner been an employee of a big broadcaster, would his memo about starting a cable news network have reached the boardroom? Probably not.

The pain will be felt especially in radio. Television requires a certain concentration of wealth to execute new programming. But radio always has been delightfully eccentric, and the mom-and-pop radio station is as important a part of Americana as the diner.

I am less sympathetic to the loss of editorial freedom in broadcasting concentration. There never has been much of that, except at the mom-and-pop radio station. Thanks to the Internet, there are more diverse opinions available than there have been since newspaper competition began to decline, market by market. Instead, what we face with the broadcasting competition are more spin-offs and—here is an oxymoron—creativity by committee.

There are something like 25 new reality television programs in preparation. Welcome to corporate creativity.

The argument favored by FCC Chairman Michael Powell is that the broadcasters need consolidation for financial viability. Oh, yeah? When did you last hear of a TV station going broke? And even the smallest radio station has managed to survive on local advertising.

Technology has given us many more news and entertainment outlets and much more repetitive programming. Rupert Murdoch, a vulgarian but an auteur, whether you like it or not, has changed the programming landscape by encouraging different dimensions in broadcasting. When he leaves the scene, his company will revert from creative vulgarity to repetitive vulgarity.

If Powell had wanted to improve broadcasting, he would have investigated the possibility of breaking up the broadcasting behemoths, which might have unleashed a new Golden Age of Creativity. Remember, if you would, how telephony exploded after the breakup of AT&T. Let us not forget the reason we have the FCC is because the airwaves are public not private property.

June 3, 2003

TIDE IS UP FOR HILLARY; IS SHE UP FOR IT?

Shakespeare said there is a tide in the affairs of men that, if taken at the flood, leads on to victory. Unfortunately, for Hillary Rodham Clinton, her waters are cresting early, and there may not be another moment in her political career at which she can seize with ease the Democratic nomination for president.

The thinking in Washington always has been that Clinton would run for president, but not until 2008. According to the Washington reasoning, she would have a full term as senator from New York under her belt; the indiscretions of her husband, Bill Clinton, would be old history; and the public, assuming that President Bush is re-elected, would be tired of Republican governance. Also, if Bush runs with Dick Cheney, as is expected, there will be no Republican heir apparent.

This is a nice and reasonable thinking. But it is washed away by the torrent of publicity surrounding the publication of Clinton's memoir "Living History": Her tide is at flood. Can she afford to waste it? Will she ever again be the woman of the hour?

If Clinton declares her presidential candidacy for 2004, she will reinvigorate the Democrats and eclipse the nine political minnows now seeking the party's nomination. If she runs and is nominated, not only will Clinton be the first woman seriously to seek the presidency, but she will also become the titular leader of the Democratic Party, filling the vacuum gracelessly left by former Vice President Gore.

On the downside, Clinton must know that the Republicans will go after her with fury and malice. And if she loses, even with a good showing, and returns to the

Senate, things could be touchy with the senior Democratic senator from New York, Chuck Schumer.

Then, there is the problem of what to do with her husband during the campaign and if, against the odds, she were to win. A former president, especially one with Bill Clinton's baggage, presents a historical challenge. The ideal solution would have been if the former president had been made chancellor of Oxford University. Now, Hillary would have to think of where to send Bill. Another overseas university? A non-governmental organization headquartered abroad? Or an ambassadorship?

The Clintons present a political conundrum without precedent. But for the Democrats, Hillary could ride at the head of their column, invigorating them and redefining the political landscape. What is more, she could raise the money needed to compete with the Bush war chest.

"Damned if I do and damned if I don't," Hillary must be thinking to herself, as her book soars in popularity and her public persona is enhanced.

The question her political advisers have to answer is whether she will be a bigger force if she runs for president in 2004 and loses, than if she waits to run until 2008. The rank and file of the party probably have no doubts: they need a standard-bearer and they do not have one.

The unknowns of the Clinton candidacy revolve around whether the country is ready for a woman president; whether she can put enough distance between herself and her husband; and whether women voters, who have moved towards George W. Bush, will turn out for one of their own.

The media and the political spectator class would be enthralled by a Clinton vs. Bush presidential race. Neither candidate would have to complain that the media were ignoring them, or that their position papers weren't getting any attention.

Clinton vs. Bush would be the greatest political spectacle since Nixon vs. John F. Kennedy.

GOP mastermind Karl Rove would have to rethink the president's re-election strategy. He beat Democrat Ann Richards for governor of Texas. But that was hardly a prologue for battling with a former first lady under an incandescent media spotlight.

As Clinton and her advisers debate whether they should take her tide at the flood, she herself must wonder whether she should walk into history now or hope that the opportunity exists in five years. Shakespeare was clear on this.

June 10, 2003

GAS SHORTAGE PUTS WHITE HOUSE UNDER PRESSURE

A new fear is stalking the White House. It is unconnected with the war on terrorism, the war in Iraq or the Israeli-Palestinian road map.

Instead, it is about today's high prices for natural gas and the prospect of severe shortages this winter.

Already, the White House has mobilized the Department of Energy to talk up the need for conservation and for fuel switching. Statements from Energy Secretary Spence Abraham have been categorical about the need for conservation, and are at odds with the White House's previous indifference to energy conservation of any kind.

The White House has come under pressure from natural gas users in the pharmaceutical, chemical and fertilizer industries. Other large users of natural gas, in what might be called the "finishing industries"—printing, packaging, wood-treatment—are hurting and are letting it be known. Right behind them will come the electric utilities, which have been encouraged, for environmental reasons, to install gas turbines as the preferred source of new electric generation.

When cold weather arrives at the end of the year, residential consumers may have to pay three times more for gas than they did two years ago—and political pressure for relief will follow. Even the normally obtuse chairman of the Federal Reserve Board, Alan Greenspan, has warned about the economic impact of sustained high natural gas prices.

There are many complex ingredients in the run-up of natural gas pricing. But the simple underlying one is that we are using more natural gas and producing less. Unless great new resources come to market or we can import gas in its liquefied form quickly, prices may remain high for a long time.

Natural gas is a commodity and is acting like all commodities: small shortages produce remarkably high prices and tempt traders and producers to manage the shortages for their gain.

Last week, the chief executive officer of a large gas distribution company in the Northeast told me that he expects gas prices to be 80 percent higher this winter than last, as he passes through the increased price of the commodity. It will, he said, be a catastrophe for his company, which, he fears, will take the brunt of political accusations, investigations and, especially, criticism from fuel oil suppliers, who have in the past lost heating customers to natural gas when gas prices were low.

Natural gas has not been in such short supply since the 1970s, when Congress passed the Fuel Use Act, which sought to save natural gas for manufacturing purposes and home heating. Electricity producers were forbidden from using natural gas. The shortage affected even trivial uses such as pilot lights in appliances, which manufacturers had to replace with electronic igniters.

By the 1980s, the price of natural gas had fallen and the supply appeared to be much larger than Congress had believed. Congress repealed the Fuel Use Act.

Shortly afterward, a new technology began to sweep the electricity generating business: the aeroderivative turbine. This technology—essentially a military jet engine operating on the ground—offered greater efficiencies than traditional turbines and the lowest environment impact of any fossil fuel. The craze for turbines swept the electricity generating business. And an eager gas industry reassured them there was plenty of gas.

Even so, the price of gas remained low, discouraging investment in new drilling, pipelines and storage facilities. The result is that demand has overtaken supply, abetted by a harsh winter last year in much of the country.

Just how severe the shortage will be next winter and how high the prices will go depends on the severity of the weather. The Bush administration is hoping for a mild winter and an increase in drilling activity. But the gas producers have been slow to respond with new investment, as in previous years of price volatility. Likewise, investment has lagged in pipelines and storage facilities.

The best chances for new domestic sources of gas lie in the Gulf of Mexico and in the Rockies. But it will take years for any of this gas to reach market.

The United States imports a small amount of gas in liquefied form and certainly will have to import much more. But liquefied natural gas imports require a sophisticated and expensive infrastructure. Gas coming from, say, Venezuela, has to be developed and liquefied in that country; loaded onto purpose-specific tankers; and discharged at big, ideally remote terminals and re-gasified. One of these "trains," from field to consumer, can cost around $10 billion.

President Bush, faced with this crisis, may have reason to feel angry with his friends in the gas industry, who have been issuing assurances for years that there is plenty of gas. Now there is a shortage, and it is on George W. Bush's watch.

June 17, 2003

THREE FACES OF EVE AND TIES THAT BIND

Three women have commanded our attention for weeks and months. They are J.K. Rowling, author of the Harry Potter books; Hillary Rodham Clinton, a New York senator and former first lady; and Martha Stewart, the domestic diva.

At a glance, they are a disparate trio. But they are bound together in some cosmic way: They are women of giant achievement.

Rowling is the embodiment of the human dream, having moved herself off welfare to become a celebrated children's author, whose books will enter the pantheon of the genre for all time. Untrammeled, Rowling is everyone's heroine—her own story outdoing fiction. So far, no graceless contrarians have assaulted her achievement nor laid bare anything unseemly in her private life.

Not so for Clinton and Stewart. They have been under merciless attack for years.

From her arrival in Washington on the arm of her president-elect husband, Clinton inspired jealousy and hatred. Her ambition was her downfall. Did she marry her husband because she had political ambitions, or was she a full partner in the realization of his political rise? Missteps over the healthcare advisory committee and a pack of merciless political and journalistic dogs were upon her.

Yet Clinton persevered, endured the humiliation of her husband's philandering and won a seat in her own right in the U.S. Senate. Real achievement. Now, Clinton is the first woman in history openly talked about as a viable Democratic presidential candidate. Whether she runs or not, she has reached a place that no other woman in U.S. political life has approached. Clinton might say to her critics, in the words of the Gershwin song, "They can't take that away from me."

If Rowling climbed to great heights in the unlikely métier of children's fiction and Clinton on the greasy rungs of politics and marriage, Stewart's achievement is even more wondrous. She created an enormous public media company out of the most mundane of endeavors: household chores.

Stewart, so much the cookie-baking-lady-next-door on television, stepped on many toes on her way but she got to a unique place of her own making. Her genius has been to infuse little home rituals with glamour.

Now, Stewart has fallen. She is to be tried in New York for obstruction of justice, arising out of her sale of ImClone stock on an insider tip. The money on the table was pathetic, considering that Stewart, at the time of the stock sale, was worth more than $1 billion. The prosecutors are going after her for the cover-up and not the offense, which suggests a political dimension to the prosecution. When many of those involved in corporate scandals, like Enron, are walking free after wiping out tens of thousands of investors, Stewart's alleged offenses are as light as her own meringues. Even if she wins in court, Stewart is damaged—a sad end to a woman who really created her own wealth.

It is fashionable to write about women of achievement in terms of their struggle in and against a male-dominated world. The first question asked of a female chief executive officer or an airline captain is a clichéd one about gender. Yet history is filled with women of achievement who never sought nor found the famous glass ceiling. Ceilings were not part of the architecture of their lives.

In just recent history, Coco Chanel, Margaret Thatcher and Oprah Winfrey come to mind as women who moved the earth to make a passage for themselves. No complaints, just heavy lifting.

Oddly, the women's movement is slow to recognize its own, as it is keen to see the human condition as combat between the sexes. Surely, there is discrimination against women or, to be more exact, prejudice. But that is not a reason for organized womanhood to deny the successes of their own. "Come, you spirits, that tend on mortal thoughts, unsex me here," Lady Macbeth said, reflecting the attitude of the women's movement towards successful women: they are no longer sisters.

I worked for the best part of 10 years on women's issues in the 1960s and 1970s, and found it discomforting how the movement denied who should be its heroines.

You may never read a Harry Potter book, vote for Hillary Clinton, or buy a Martha Stewart magazine, but that is not a reason not to realize that they are in the headlines for good and sufficient reason: achievement.

June 24, 2003

INTO AFRICA: WHAT BUSH SHOULD SAY

President Bush is off to Africa. If he had time, the continent would steal his heart and break it also. It does that. So many wonderful people, such appealing children and such misery is the story of Africa. There are islands of wonder in oceans of despair.

On the upside, the president will find that his quick humor goes down well. Probably nowhere in the world do people love a joke more. Indeed, they do not just love it at first telling, but go on savoring it, bursting into spontaneous laughter long after the joke has been told. If the president comes up with nicknames for his African hosts, people will love it and will laugh again and again.

If Bush tells African audiences that the answer to the AIDS epidemic is abstinence, they will laugh at that too—again and again.

What they want to hear is that the United States, which they believe to be limitlessly wealthy, is going to shower money on Africa, from the Sahara to Cape Point. One of the ugly legacies of the last half-century in Africa is that the whole continent south of the Sahara has descended into a collective victimhood, entitling the countries of the continent to a stipend from the industrialized world.

Bush may lecture the Africans on the need for democracy, but he would be well advised to lecture them also on property rights, self-sufficiency, and a sense of national purpose beyond going to war with their immediate neighbors. They will offer, in explanation of their situation, old saws about colonialism, artificial borders and international indifference.

Now that hope has almost gone out of Africa, Bush could inspire Africans with a vision of a productive, well-fed future if they fix their leadership and abandon the corrosive effects of the socialism most African countries adopted in the wake of colonialism. Socialism/communism appealed to African nations because it offered their leaders total control of their hapless populations.

Bush might also take it upon himself to speak up for the women of Africa, who hold their societies together but have little role outside of their homes.

Then he might lay out a plan that would work: aid and investment only in islands of excellence. Bush could tell his African hosts that investment respects stability, honesty, property rights, the expatriation of profits, incorruptible government, and an independent judiciary with real appellate authority.

Bush should tell Africans unequivocally that these are the conditions under which great societies can be built, and the absence of one or more of them will deter investment and lead to ruin, which is everywhere to be seen. He should also tell them that he knows that Africans can live in peace and that they should renounce the petty revolutions that plague so much of the continent.

For himself, Bush should realize that Africa consists of some four dozen countries, 2,000 languages and as many tribes as a supercomputer can count. Only its suffering is monolithic, fed by folly, greed, corruption and an insane proliferation of small arms.

As it is, the president has found precious few African countries to visit that pass the democracy and stability test. Leaving aside South Africa, the most conspicuous of these is Botswana, which is enjoying a mineral-fed boom. But by the standards of the United States or the rest of the industrialized world, even this showcase is wanting. There is corruption, inefficiency and an elite that is indifferent to the well-being of the whole.

Bush should speak firmly when he gets to Nigeria. It is the most populous country in Africa, with possibly the most talented people. But it has turned itself into a vast criminal enterprise. Somehow, to Nigerians, capitalism and crime are the same thing. He should caution them that oil alone will not bring wealth, and across the globe, Nigeria is regarded as a fraught place to do business. Nigeria needs to know that it must mend its ways beyond establishing a fragile democracy: Some form of honesty has to underpin democracy.

In an odd choice, the Bush entourage will visit only Pretoria in South Africa. A country in which there is a lot of American investment, a functioning democracy and a more promising future might have deserved a few more stops. Pretoria is peculiar in many ways. It was laid out by Edward Luytens, who also designed New Delhi, after the Boer War and it became the administrative capital. While the politicians and the media were off in Cape Town, the bureaucrats in Pretoria got on with the heinous business of implementing apartheid. If there was any city that was peculiarly the home of apartheid, it was Pretoria.

Africa may be brutal and chaotic, but those of us who were born there have not given up on it. And it is a net good when an American president visits the continent of enchantment and agony.

July 1, 2003

ACTUALLY, IT'S THE ATLANTIC, NOT MARS OR VENUS

DUBLIN—Europe and America are at odds, and the academic writer Robert Kagan has tied it all neatly together in a catch phrase: "Americans are from Mars and Europeans are from Venus." Defense Secretary Donald Rumsfeld has chosen to dismiss much of Europe as geriatic, irrelevant and timid with his own catch phrase: Old Europe.

But like most truisms, these clever metaphors do not tell the story. Heritage binds, but so does social experience. And the social experience in Europe today parallels that of America.

After Iraq is forgotten or forgiven, when the contention over genetically modified foods is resolved, America and Europe will find their commonalities indistinguishable and binding.

There is hardly a social issue in Europe today that is not duplicated in America. Consider: falling academic standards, suffocating traffic, rickety health-care systems and low birth rates from the traditional people. The latter issue threatens both continents, and compels the young to pay for the old and to shoulder the burden of the baby boom, which was a phenomenon in both Europe and America.

After World War II, women returned from their wartime jobs to do what women always had done: have babies and raise families. But as domestic appliances and new concepts of the role of women in society arrived, along with advanced contraception, birth rates fell.

Indeed, in Europe as in America today, there are powerful economic disincentives against raising more than one or two children. In America, children mean hefty college tuitions. And in Europe, if you want the affluence of the middle class, you cannot enjoy it with a large brood.

This has produced many social gains. The most notable is that with women fully integrated into the workforce, the pool of the most talented has doubled in size. But this shift has been hell on procreation.

In good times, European societies rewarded themselves with generous social benefits, free medicine and state pensions. American were more circumspect, but only in degree: Social Security and Medicare are the same programs under different titles, although somewhat more parsimonious than those the Europeans enjoy.

The common fact is that in the years ahead, there may not be enough native-born new taxpayers to support ageing and infirm populations.

The answer, of course, is replacement populations: Let in the immigrants to top up the working pool. But here is the rub on both sides of the Atlantic. Immigrant populations enter at the low end of the economic scale, and they bring with them languages and religions that change the host country and endanger its traditional culture.

In America, we have replacement population aplenty trying to cross the Rio Grande — fine people all, but they bring with them a different language and a different set of values. Here we depart from Europe, for our situation and our traditions are different than those in Europe.

Europe easily can top up its declining population with enthusiastic immigrants: in Spain and France, from North Africa; in Germany, from Turkey; and in Britain, from South Asia. Tens of millions of North Africans would like to move to Europe and as many as a billion English-speaking Asians and Africans would like to move to the British Isles. But the population of Britain, including its minorities, is only 58 million.

The unspoken fear of mainstream European politicians is that their homelands will be swamped. Once the flow of replacement population begins, as most of Europe has learned, there is no ending it neatly when enough have been absorbed to become the taxpayers of the future.

In Belgium, North African immigrants already are campaigning to have Arabic made an official language; terrorists were recruited in the Finsbury Park mosque in London; and illegal immigrants continue to penetrate all of Europe, seeking a better life, but not committing to assimilation.

It will take another generation before America finds what has been the degree of assimilation of the new wave of immigrants. Or are we ourselves headed for balkanization?

It is not evil or malicious for people to seek a better standard of living in just and orderly countries. But those countries are irrevocably changed if assimilation does not take place.

These are the challenges that face successful countries in the 21st century — and they will be compounded by the need to balance the tax rolls. For America and Europe, these are common problems, not competitive issues. They are problems that transcend brief crises, and they suggest that Western culture and commonality is neither from Mars nor Venus but from the Atlantic rim.

July 8, 2003

BUSH'S TROUBLES: SO FAR,
THEY ARE JUST HAIRLINE CRACKS

Engineers call them hairline fractures: minute cracks that do not affect the load-bearing ability of a structure but that bear watching, in case they should propagate.

Last week, Washington began to notice hairline cracks in the Bush White House—nothing so severe that the president is threatened by the Democrats. But, by any measure, it has been a terrible time for the White House. And the pollsters are beginning to pick up the public's doubts.

The immediate impact has been a toning down in the truculence of the president's keenest supporters. Talk of a new imperialism has evaporated and the doctrine of pre-emption has been put back on the shelf.

The immediate cause of the White House discomfort is the faulty intelligence on Saddam Hussein's alleged attempts to buy uranium in Niger, and Bush's referencing this fiction in his State of the Union address. The White House blames the CIA and a nasty spat has broken out between CIA Director George Tenet and National Security Adviser Condoleezza Rice. It seems unlikely that both of them can remain in the administration.

Then there is the situation on the ground in Iraq, which does not look to be improving soon, and the continued U.S. fatalities, running at about one a day. No administration can believe that this will not have a sobering impact on the public and call into question the administration's pre-invasion plans. The neo-conservatives, who were the most vociferous and articulate in advocating war, are on the defensive. Their Bible, *The Weekly Standard*, has gone from lavish enthusiasm about the war to claiming that things are going better on the ground than we are being told.

In light of these difficulties, the administration has been forced to tread lightly around such thorny issues as Syria, Iran and North Korea. Even the most bellicose of conservatives are not suggesting that the doctrine of pre-emption be given another outing while Iraq remains an open sore. Mercifully for the administration, the public and the politicians are overlooking Afghanistan, where our allies-now seen as warlords-have upped the production of heroin.

On the domestic front, things are not going any better. Such economic recovery as there is has not produced new jobs. And no less an oracle than Federal Reserve Chairman Alan Greenspan twice has warned about the dampening effects of an anticipated natural gas shortage this fall and winter. Heavy users of natural gas, such as the chemical industry and the wood products industry, already are severely impacted by gas prices, which are high by traditional summer standards. The chemical industry is losing production and moving offshore.

If Greenspan is right, we will face a winter of discontent. And the benefits of Bush's tax cut will be negated by the cost of people heating their homes. What is worse, there is no quick fix, and the White House has to hope for the mildest of winters.

There are other issues that impact individuals and families besides the cost of home heating, and the White House appears to have been slow to grasp them. They include Medicare, welfare and transportation. Unlike foreign policy, which is an abstraction to most people, these are voter issues.

Joyous Democrats tell me that we may be at the beginning of real trouble for the president. Maybe. But the Democrats look weak and disorganized without resounding alternatives. Democrats have no more idea of what to do in Iraq than anyone else. And they consistently have underestimated Bush both as a politician and as someone who can communicate with the population.

To think that the president's current troubles signal an end to Republican dominance in Washington is naïve. What the White House's troubles may signal is a closer election than appeared possible before the invasion of Iraq.

Of the nine declared Democratic presidential candidates, none inspires confidence. The party is still hoping for a savior from outside. They bandy about retired General Wes Clark's name. And Delaware Sen. Joe Biden is hovering. Clark is a political amateur and Biden has tried his luck before and failed. The Democrats' biggest difficulty is that Bush has monopolized patriotism. It is patriotism that Bush has been most skillful at exploiting. He has ridden high from 9/11 to the present day not on tax cuts and the rest of his domestic agenda, but on the war on terrorism, which to-date has included the invasion of Iraq.

Bush is not in trouble, but he is not as strong as he was. It will take a further deterioration for any of the tiny cracks in Bush's governance to open wide enough for his opponents to insert a crowbar.

July 15, 2003

FIRST THING'S FIRST IN IRAQ:
FIX THE ELECTRIC SUPPLY SYSTEM

The guerrillas, or whatever they are to be called, in Iraq understand one thing very clearly: the supply of electricity may hold the key to the outcome of their struggle. Already insurgents have blown up pylons and murdered the woman who ran the electric utility in Baghdad. They clearly believe that disrupting Iraq's feeble electric supply will help turn the populace against the Americans.

Electricity often is the key both to winning wars and to hastening the peace. The Marshall Plan put heavy emphasis on rebuilding Europe's electric infrastructure after World War II. Urgent emphasis, drawing on all the talent available in the United States and Europe, ought now to be directed at getting and keeping the electricity on in Iraq. If we fail at this, we may fail altogether.

In a modern war, the most effective way to utilize precision bombing is to take out the electric system before attacking bridges and factories. Once a population is dependent on electricity, that dependence becomes its greatest vulnerability. Under Saddam Hussein, electric supply may have been feeble in Iraq, but most of the time, for most of the day, it worked. Ergo, Iraqis know the comfort of air-conditioning, the utility of operational elevators, and the value of getting their news by radio and television rather than by rumor or from disingenuous clerics.

The Bush administration claims that it is working assiduously—and certainly under traumatic conditions—to restore the electric supply in Iraq. But is it doing all that can be done?

We are a nation rich in electric technology, with tens of thousands of skilled professionals. Those men and women swing into action selflessly after natural disasters at home, but they have not been tapped to help in Iraq.

The administration's two principal contractors in Iraq—Brown & Root, a subsidiary of Halliburton, and Bechtel—both are experienced with electricity. But they are not operators of electric plant; neither do they respond to emergencies, nor do they have enormous teams of dedicated professionals whose life's work is to keep the current flowing. Instead, Brown & Root and Bechtel have their expertise in plant design and systems architecture. They are not peopled with hands-on linemen, shift bosses, maintenance engineers and spur-of-the-moment innovators.

During the 2000 presidential election, many U.S. electric utility executives met with George W. Bush and supported his campaign. Now President Bush should call them back in to form an industry task force on electricity for Iraq. He also should not overlook the 2,000 or so public power companies that have special expertise in small, and sometimes cantankerous, electric supply systems.

As each day goes by, with more abysmal news from Iraq, our project looks more imperiled. Many Iraqis are in the dark, literally and figuratively. Without electricity they have no reliable sources of news, have no way to escape the heat of the night except to sleep on the roof, and nothing to do by day but join the demonstrations in the streets.

L. Paul Bremer, the top U.S. official in Iraq, has the least enviable job on earth and, by accounts, not all the tools he needs. Securing the electric supply is a job for the army. Making it work is a job for those who have not yet been asked. An American utility task force, clearly civilian, with skill, supplies and security, could begin to turn the tide in Iraq by bringing the lights, air-conditioners, elevators, televisions and traffic-control systems back on line, hopefully 24/7.

Hot, angry, discomforted, ill-informed Iraqis are a fertile population for guerrilla recruitment. People who see the quality of their lives improving are less likely to be so.

Electricity is the gauge of well-being in societies who are used to it. The United States has the greatest reservoir of electricity expertise on earth. At the operational level, American utilities are remarkable for their can-do ability. They demonstrate it every time there is an earthquake, a hurricane or an ice storm. Those gallant men and women need to be let loose in Iraq to repair, to upgrade, to get the generators rolling and to restore the integrity of the power lines.

The battle for electricity could be the battle that turns events in our favor in Iraq. Time is critical.

Bremer has said he expects the electricity to be back at pre-war levels in the entire country in the next six weeks or so. But the electric supply system, which Saddam starved of investment, needs more than a return to its pre-war condition. It needs to be a modern, reliable system; a palpable demonstration of U.S. ability and concern for the people of Iraq.

It is more important that electricity becomes a showpiece of U.S. ability and intent in the short term than it is to increase the production of oil. The latter confirms Arab suspicions that we invaded Iraq not to bring liberty but to secure oil. Electricity would be a gift to the people.

July 22, 2003

THE SPECIAL AGONY AND ISOLATION OF TONY BLAIR

No British prime minister besides Winston Churchill and, to a lesser extent, Margaret Thatcher has been so revered in the United States as Tony Blair. He was there when we needed him and we have been conspicuous in our gratitude.

Unfortunately, in Britain, Blair is reviled in many quarters and is isolated within his own Labor Party. He would probably lose his job if the rank and file of the party felt there were another leader who could win a general election. For the most part, they have concluded that they must stick with Blair because he is their best chance for remaining in power.

The opposition Conservative Party would like to see Blair go—although they supported him more fervently than the Labor Party did in the Iraq war—for the same reason. The Conservatives calculate that if Blair were to fall, they would have a chance in the next general election.

Blair is the loneliest of men, even as he continues to lead the Labor Party. Gradually the allies, who helped him mastermind two general election victories, have left the scene for political and personal reasons. He is left with a party that is in revolt and a Cabinet that he does not feel close to.

British prime ministers pick their Cabinets, but they are confined to choosing from among the members of Parliament. Often these are men and women who would like to bring down their leader and take his or her job. Unlike the president of the United States, who is secure for his elected term, British prime ministers are not. They can fall at any time and they have a limited number of capable people to staff the administration.

In addition, British prime ministers have to face down a permanent and intransigent bureaucracy with agendas and policies of its own. Therefore, they need to pick Cabinet members who are strong and ambitious, and who will dictate to their departments.

Then there is the British media. Prime ministers have to spend as much time soothing and cultivating newspaper proprietors as they do cajoling and supporting members of their Cabinets. Blair owed much of his initial success to the fact that he had been able to win over Rupert Murdoch and persuade him that "New Labor" was a better bet than the Conservatives. Murdoch's defection was, in its way, as big a political upheaval as Blair's quieting of the trade unionists in the Labor Party.

Traditionally, newspaper proprietors in Britain have expected and gotten direct access to the prime minister, and they have traded their support for assurances in things that they care about. There is nothing subtle in the process.

If a British press baron throws the support of his newspapers to a politician, he delivers not just an editorial page that is favorable but an entire newspaper, which is slanted to favor a candidate. The editorial opinion of the proprietor permeates the whole newspaper with ferocity.

Since the 19th century, British newspaper proprietors—among them three Canadians and one Australian—have believed that it was their right and duty to make and break British prime ministers. This power of the press barons in Britain, reminiscent of the days of William Randolph Hearst in the United States, remains uncontained.

But, whereas the newspaper proprietors have their political preferences, they are also somewhat sensitive to their readers. Hence, Murdoch's British newspapers—*The Sun, The News of the World, The Times* and *The Sunday Times*—along with his satellite television station, BSkyB, are beginning to attack Blair. It is not an all-out, proprietor-ordered assault—after all, they supported the war in Iraq— but they are not as lavish in their praise of Blair as they once were.

Murdoch, Blair must have noticed, is keeping his options open. By contrast, Murdoch-controlled Fox News in the United States is unfaltering in its support of the Bush administration.

Newspaper proprietors want things from government, but they also want to finish elections in the winners' circle, and thus are sensitive to prime ministers who are showing isolation or weakness. The British press barons turned on John Major, Thatcher's successor, when they sensed his vulnerability. Blair must wonder how much he can trust them.

Blair would be stronger and less isolated if his domestic programs were working. But big new public expenditures have not fixed the British public health and transportation systems, the high crime rate or illegal immigration.

Blair's support of Bush may not be fatal to his political career, but it has been damaging. And it has left him oh-so-isolated in London.

July 29, 2003

WHEN ONE VISION FADES, GET ANOTHER

In life, it is never the thing you fear that comes and bites you. It is something else.

So too in war. The Bush administration feared in invading Iraq that U.S. forces would face heavy resistance from the Republican Guard and dedicated units of the regular Iraqi army. It also feared that our forces would be subject to chemical and biological attack. None of this was to be.

It did not fear the peace, and the peace has come to bite it.

The administration, with its sense of high moral purpose, really did not believe that enough Iraqis would place the humiliation of defeat over the toppling of a dictator, and therefore launch into guerrilla warfare against their liberators.

It is a development the administration was not prepared for—despite the protestations of Arabists around the country and the world—and for which it is psychologically and imaginatively unprepared. This is an administration that believes in good and evil, and that triumph comes to the decisive. It is an administration that believes in getting tough, doing the right thing and kicking a little behind to get the job done.

It is not just President Bush who feels this way, but his whole administration— maybe with the exception of Secretary of State Colin Powell. This administration draws its metaphors and its modus operandi from the sports field and the executive suite. In those places, there is no gain without pain, and getting tough means getting it right.

But how do you get tough with a recalcitrant civilian population that is awash in small arms, ranging from AK-47s to mortars? The administration clearly has been broadsided by the reality of the peace when it was focused on the geography of the war.

As with many nations before them, the administration is taking the hard line, believing that it can mop up the resistance, mollify the guerrillas, and march Iraq towards the unity and freedom that it conceived when it launched the war.

Some of this optimism must have come from the Iraqi exiles who urged on the administration and assured those in office and those close to those in office that Iraq without Saddam Hussein could be converted quickly and easily into a democracy, a beacon for other Arab nations. Maybe one day. But will any American president have the time and the political support to persevere with a long war of attrition?

Already, some of the graybeards in Washington are beginning to think that if the loss of American life continues in Iraq, at some time there will be pressure— mounting pressure-simply to walk away; to declare a victory and bring our troops home.

To abandon Iraq, as we have largely abandoned the countryside in Afghanistan, will debilitate our foreign policy, possibly catastrophically. It was not until Margaret Thatcher sent troops to the Falklands, a decade after the Vietnam War, that the world was reassured that democracies could and would fight. A poor result in Iraq will move us back to the decade after the Vietnam War, when foreign policy was dominated by fear of involvement.

Unfairly, the administration is criticized for not having a post-war plan for Iraq. It had a plan, but that plan was predicated on an erroneous assumption: the assumption that the people of Iraq would be universally elated by the fall of Saddam and the prospect of a free and open society. Enough Iraqis are not of this persuasion for it to be a huge problem for the United States.

The administration is faced with the prospect of an Iraq very different from the vision that dominated the White House and the Pentagon. Unfortunately, reappraisal, implying as it does an admission of error, is an anathema to the administration. Men and women formed on the sports field and in executive suites do not easily tear up the game plan or throw out the business plan.

Before the 2000 election, a stream of thinkers and executives made their way to Austin, Tex. to advise presidential candidate Bush on what to do if he won. Now it is time for Bush to consult, quietly, some of the old and ignored diplomatic establishment about a new course in Iraq. The United Nations does not want to govern Iraq because it is still smarting from the insults it endured in the run-up to the war.

The big new idea is not immediately visible, but it should be sought. For example, there is some virtue in casting the Arab League in a greater role, thereby enhancing all Arabs' sense of themselves and bringing Iraq towards self-government.

August 5, 2003

IMPERIALISM? NOT THIS TIME AROUND

A debate is raging in Washington over what should be the underlying principles of U.S. foreign policy. There is a school of thought that says the United States is a de facto imperial power and should accept that role. This appeals to the neoconservatives, in a theoretical way.

The debate is nourished by the British historian Niall Ferguson, who has written extensively on British imperialism. But the first post-Iraq war test, Liberia, has the new imperialists saying, "Stay out." Like so much else in Washington, the new imperialism is invoked when it suits a favored course of action—for example, the invasion of Iraq—and abrogated when it does not serve the agenda of its proponents.

As somebody who was born into the British Empire, and witnessed its closing days, I say this is all so much nonsense. The large moral choice in foreign policy is not going to be whether we are going to control great swathes of the globe, settle foreign lands or pursue globalization through military force. No. It is whether we will intervene not as an imperial power but as a Good Samaritan.

The empires that were established from the 16th to 19th centuries were imperial, in the sense that Rome was imperial: the purpose was to hold and control territory, and spread the culture and religion of the conqueror.

To achieve this, the conquerors had to believe absolutely—as the Romans did, and the British very much did—in the superiority of their culture. They saw conquest as a gift to the indigenous inhabitants; a treasure they were spreading around. It required not only a huge sense of ethnic superiority by the conqueror, but also a sense of the inferiority of the conquered.

The French, the Belgians, the Dutch, and belatedly the Germans and Italians, were more mercantile in their imperialism: the purpose was exploitation. The Spanish were committed to exploitation and to settlement, somewhat like the British.

The colonial ethos that imperial colonization was a net good for the people who were conquered was a trick that was easily pulled off where people were fairly primitive. In India, the British were astounding: They persuaded a sophisticated people with a complex society that they, the British, were in some way a master race which had conquered the human condition.

That enabled the subject peoples to be governed by few troops and even fewer administrators. A friend of mine, who was once the editor of *The Times of India* and who had lived through the last part of the British occupation, always wondered to me how a single, young British administrator in India could control 3 million people in his care. The question, I would tell him, was, "Why did the Indians swallow the British line of moral superiority?"

Unrest would come to India when Indians visited Britain and saw that the master race was less than admirable at home: There was poverty and deprivation in Britain just as there was in India.

Growing up in Southern Rhodesia, now Zimbabwe, I knew all about the sense of British moral superiority. As time went on, the British, like the Romans, believed they could share power and prosperity with the indigenous inhabitants so long as they thought of themselves as happily British, loyal servants of the Crown. Many a revolutionary started life trying to be a perfect little Englishman.

What passes for American imperialism is simply our power in arms and money. Our task, and it is onerous, is to keep failing states from sliding into anarchy. Those states will destabilize the neighborhood, provide a haven for terrorists, and lead to untold human suffering.

As we are not an imperial power and have no desire to be, the challenge is how do we withdraw, having stopped the killing and fed the starving? Fareed Zakaria of *Newsweek* suggests we hand them over to the United Nations, which has some skill in nation-building. But the very people who talk of the new American imperialism are the same people who declared the UN irrelevant. That, too, is not a solution for all time, but the hope is that stability will allow local institutions to mature.

When we had the Soviet Union as an adversary, failing states were swept into one or the other orbit. We may not want to be the world's policeman, but can we avoid being its Good Samaritan?

August 12, 2003

THE AMERICAN WAY: FOR BLACKOUT, READ BONANZA

The new law of American governance is: Failure should be handsomely rewarded. Those in intelligence who failed to sound the alarm before 9/11 were not punished for their failure but, rather, were rewarded with draconian authority that they had long coveted. Those who told President Bush that Iraq was bristling with weapons of mass destruction are happily at their desks working towards retirement.

Now the electric utility industry, after a catastrophic failure, will get rewards beyond its wildest dreams. As few members of Congress opposed the Patriot Act, or were disapproving of the carte blanche for war handed to the president, few will oppose a long shopping list that is coming from the electric utilities. After all, who wants to be said to be in favor of blackouts?

Everything that is said about the rickety condition of the electric grid is true. But it is not what caused the debilitating blackout in Northeastern United States and Canada last week. That was not overload, but a lack of oversight. It was poor load management.

But as heads have not rolled in the intelligence community or at the Pentagon, heads will not roll in the electric utility industry. Rewards will be handed out. The utilities will demand and get tough rights of eminent domain; relief from environmental standards, such as the contentious New Source Review procedures; and utilities will demand and get a guaranteed right of return on new transmission lines and on the upgrading of the old ones.

Over the years, I have watched the relentless erosion of the sense of civic responsibility, which was once the hallmark of the electric utility industry. From the passage of the Public Utilities Holding Company Act of 1935, until the scattershot deregulation of the 1990s, utilities set the standard for corporate responsibility. They attracted management with a highly developed sense of the public good and of the moral obligation of monopoly.

After the blackouts of 1965 and 1977, they were humiliated. By contrast, their immediate reaction after this latest disaster has been to blame everyone who can be blamed—from the Canadians to the environmentalists—and not a breath of mea culpa.

The compact that underwrote years of efficient electric service frayed quickly with deregulation, even in utilities that were not deregulated. The performance of the companies' stock became more important than the performance of their systems. Deregulation, not inherently a bad idea, turned into a gold rush for a new breed of upwardly mobile executives, investment bankers, consultants and traders.

A once noble industry traded away its decency and good reputation in the hope of large stock gains. Those who were not sufficiently inspired by Enron, looked over their shoulders at the telecommunications industry and rolled the dice.

As the industry sailed into uncharted waters, it looked overseas for guidance. This came from the United Kingdom (where Margaret Thatcher privatized the state utilities) and—get this—New Zealand. I remember sitting in a meeting of the Aspen Institute when a persuasive advocate of deregulation from that small country was urging American utilities—many of whom have more customers than New Zealand has people—to sign on and follow the New Zealand example.

The administration needs to address the transmission issue but with caution. Consumers' best hope for not being stuck with a bill for concessions to the electric utility industry lies with the states and their determination not to trade away states' rights. Unfortunately, to date state regulators have been more interested in protecting their fiefdoms than they have been in solving a regional problem.

Pat Wood, the embattled chairman of the Federal Energy Regulatory Commission, a sometime Texas regulator, recognizes the need for regional solutions and has been working diligently to bring them about, while being sniped at by the states and many utilities, and stymied by Congress. Wood should be allowed to finish his work and to present a comprehensive plan that can be incorporated into national legislation.

However, as the utilities smell the possibility of reduced regulation, federal guarantees, and abrogated environmental laws, Wood's task will be harder. Failure demands its payout.

August 19, 2003

AN ADMINISTRATION TOO RIGID FOR THE TIMES

George W. Bush has turned out to be a better president than his detractors anticipated. But now he is a president in trouble; not in the polls, but in the world.

The virtues of resolution, decisiveness and moral-grounding that have served Bush so well are beginning to hamper his ability to respond to new realities. People with a high sense of principle also suffer from a certain rigidity. The rigidities of this administration are becoming apparent and they are counterproductive.

It is rigidity that has kept the administration from extending the post-war coalition in Iraq. And rigid beliefs about business, tax-cutting and regulation stymie the administration at home.

It is time Bush persuaded his loyalists that you have to give a little in politics and diplomacy. Politics is about compromise and diplomacy is about flexibility. Bush's two most powerful lieutenants are Vice President Dick Cheney and Secretary of Defense Don Rumsfeld. Both are rigid men. They believe, maybe more so than the president, that if the underlying principle is correct, the outcome must be victorious. It is a philosophy that works in war and fails in peace.

As Bush prepares for the battles of this fall, he might want to urge a little more flexibility from his followers. It is not just Cheney and Rumsfeld who are inflexible, it is the whole ethos of the administration.

The principles of "character" and "resolution," along with "good" and "evil"—all so beloved by Bush's speechwriters with their biblical sense of right and wrong—have nothing to offer the mounting problems at home and abroad.

Let us visit some examples:

- In the vexing question of North Korea, we are going to have to talk directly to the North Koreans at some point. That or war. It is rigid and unrewarding to accuse the North Koreans of blackmail, and to try and pressure them through a clumsy alliance of Asian countries. All through the 20th century, unpleasant regimes had to be dealt with either directly or through war. It has not been easy, for example, for the British to talk to the IRA, nor was it easy for the United States to open a dialogue with the North Vietnamese. But it had to be done.
- The administration has bought—often from marginal advocates-an inflexible attitude toward taxation. Historically, taxes have risen and fallen in accordance with the national agenda and the national need. They have not been cut arbitrarily to serve a rigid philosophical point. Presidents should not paint themselves into this kind of corner.

- The environment is another issue where rigidity is undermining the president. The attitude of this administration—that all environmentalists are loony tree-huggers seeking to cripple U.S. industry—is one of the rigidities that is counterproductive. Standards produce better engineering, less pollution and more innovation. Lowering them to accommodate industries that are seeking the easy way out only enhances the appearance that the administration has sold out to its cronies.
- Then there is the matter of appointments. The administration has not done badly with appointments—judicial or otherwise. But it would have done better if it had recognized that every Democratic concern was not an act of war.

It goes on an on. Take the USA Patriot Act. At a time when both conservatives and Democrats have concerns about the intrusiveness about this piece of rushed legislation, rather than sitting down with its critics, the administration has sent its most inflexible advocate, Attorney General John Ashcroft, on the road to defend the act in its entirety.

The most immediate problem Bush has is the continuing chaos in Iraq, where the assumptions underlying the war have proven to be wrong: weapons of mass destruction ready to be used and joyous Iraqis welcoming their liberators. No weapons of mass destruction have been found and many Iraqis are keen to kill their liberators.

Time, you would think, for Bush to call in the best minds on the Middle East and to come up with a new concept for the future of Iraq, such as an interim government administered by the Arab League or the Organization of the Islamic Conference. The rigidities of the original concept need to be abandoned in light of new realities. Likewise, the president needs to level with us about the anticipated costs of Iraq and Afghanistan.

The president is liked because he is likeable. He has shown flashes of greatness because he believes. Now he needs to show that he can be flexible without being unprincipled.

September 2, 2003

BUSH'S GOLDEN TWO YEARS DRAW TO AN END

In a sense, 9/11 thrust greatness upon President George W. Bush. He rose to the occasion, giving Americans faith and confidence that there was muscle and wisdom in the White House.

Now his golden two years are over. Bush is under hostile fire from emboldened Democrats and friendly fire from his loyalists. The sense that the administration was in command and knew where it was going has given way to a sense of drift and uncertainty.

The bold invasion of Afghanistan and the more contentious invasion of Iraq enhanced Bush's image as a resolute and brave leader. His adamancy in pushing for tax cuts suggested that at home and abroad he had vision as well as courage. Now with Afghanistan in chaos and Iraq on the threshold of anarchy, Bush is not as assuring as he was. Events that conspired to elevate the president are, in their aftermath, debilitating him.

Add to Bush's foreign woes the collapse of his Middle East policy and the economic uncertainty in the United States.

For the president, the unkindest cuts of all must be those now coming from conservatives who have supported him monolithically in every endeavor of the last two years. They are criticizing the administration of Iraq, demanding more money and more troops, even as they are beginning to worry about the surging national debt.

Conservatives exulted in the quick military victories in Afghanistan and Iraq. They supported Israeli Prime Minister Ariel Sharon while he antagonized the Palestinians, ignoring Bush's pleas for moderation.

But now the conservative movement is in a kind of low-grade crisis. It still loves Bush, but its columnists and commentators no longer find him invincible. The surge of advice—from radio talk show hosts to the influential *Weekly Standard* editors—implies that they are no longer certain that the administration as now constituted is up to the job. The old comfort they once achieved in beating up the liberals is exhausted. They are beginning, albeit gently, to beat up the administration.

The brutal truth is that Bush, beset by problems, has lost credibility among the faithful.

Nothing has turned out as it should. Weapons of mass destruction do not litter Iraq. The mighty U.S. military machine is more or less pinned down there. And in Afghanistan, the Taliban and al Qaeda are showing renewed life. This is not how it was supposed to be: The Lilliputians were not supposed to prostrate Gulliver. It is disquieting to conservatives.

Then there is the growing friction between traditional conservatives and the so-called neoconservatives. The neoconservatives seized the initiative in informing the early Bush administration on foreign policy and the economy. Traditional conservatives contented themselves with being the voice of business in the administration, while both factions kept a wary eye on the Christian right: a great voting machine but a difficult ally.

Now traditional conservatives feel that the late-arriving neoconservatives— with their command of the debate and their ideological preferences—hijacked the administration. Traditional conservatives were wary of foreign involvement and given to hyperventilation over budgetary deficits. They are the people who support the balanced budget amendment and they are unhappy to be applauding budget deficits that are reaching toward 5 percent of Gross Domestic Product.

The three conservative alignments—traditional-business, Christian right and neoconservative—are becoming suspicious of each other. Who, they wonder, led

Bush into the present difficulties? The Department of State—the happy target of the Christian right and the neoconservatives for nearly two years—is now embraced by Bush as he seeks help in Iraq.

Enter Howard Dean, the Democratic front-runner for the presidential nomination. Dean is a kind of godsend for disgruntled conservatives. They are convinced that he is George McGovern with a medical degree and a deliciously soft target. Whether he is a peace candidate who can be easily trounced or something more dangerous is yet to be known. But he is a gorgeous antidote to conservative misgivings about their own predicament. *The Economist* magazine warns that Dean may be more the reincarnation of Jimmy Carter, who won a term, than McGovern. But, for now, he will do to cheer up the conservatives.

September 9, 2003

EDWARD TELLER: REGRETS, A FEW

I first met Edward Teller in 1973 at a conference on nuclear energy in Geneva. I was to introduce him, so we agreed to have breakfast. He seemed to be old, defensive and tired. I wondered whether he was up to making a speech at all. Yet when he stepped onto the platform, he had the vigor of a man half his age.

Teller will be remembered as the "father of the H-bomb." But to me, he will always be a consummate performer; a public figure both avuncular and passionate. And, it must be said, a great American patriot.

Over the years, Teller came to many meetings that I attended or organized to talk about his passions: nuclear power, the Strategic Defense Initiative, and research and technology transfer from government laboratories to the marketplace. He never seemed to change. He was a big man, with even bigger eyebrows, who liked to slouch in his chair as though he was sleeping. I believe he developed his demeanor as a protection against being ceaselessly pounded with questions about the development of the hydrogen bomb.

At each of those meetings, when his time came to speak, Teller was transformed. He would mount the platform with a long stick—think a shepherd's crook without a hook—which he used in lieu of a conventional cane. While a student in Germany, he had lost a foot in a streetcar accident and needed assistance in walking on his prosthetic. His stick became his trademark, and with it he would perch on a table—not quite sitting on it, but certainly supported by it—and speak from that position.

Teller, I came to believe, was a passionate convert to the concept of American exceptionalism. He believed that the best in civilized values and moral virtue existed in the United States and had been betrayed in Europe. And so it had for him. Born to wealthy Jewish parents in Budapest, he was scarred by the early Communist uprisings in Hungary. He left Budapest to study at a number of German universities, where his mathematical genius became apparent and, in turn, led him to be fascinated with the new science of quantum mechanics.

With the rise of Nazism, Teller fled to the United States and taught at The George Washington University in Washington, D.C., until he became involved in the Manhattan Project in 1942. Whereas many scientists involved in the development of the atomic bomb suffered moral queasiness, Teller had no doubts. At the Los Alamos (N.M.) Scientific Laboratory, he was noted for his zeal: Hitler had to be defeated and, before the threat was recognized in the United States, the Soviet Union had to be contained.

The Soviet occupation of his native Hungary was the final reinforcement of his political view. It was probably his hatred of the Soviets that led him to betray his co-worker and former boss, J. Robert Oppenheimer, for foot-dragging on the hydrogen bomb.

Ironically, a lecture Teller gave on the theory of the hydrogen bomb may have alerted the Soviets to the fact that the United States was working on a much more sophisticated weapon. In the audience was Klaus Fuchs, a Soviet spy. Although Teller's outline for a weapon turned out to be technically flawed, it probably spurred on the Soviets.

Late in his life, Teller expressed some regrets but none about the atomic bomb. He regretted the fate that befell Oppenheimer and he, like many other scientists, believed that the bomb should have been detonated off the coast of Japan, rather than being dropped on Nagasaki and Hiroshima.

Teller took full credit for selling President Reagan on the Strategic Defense Initiative, dubbed "Star Wars." He told a colleague of mine that Reagan had said that he wished he could put a glass bowl over the United States to keep villainous people and their weapons out. "You can do so," Teller told the president. And Star Wars was born. But when my colleague asked Teller whether it would work, he shrugged and replied, "Probably not. The technology is not there."

What he probably meant was that the technology could be forced, and he loved to see big enterprises in science. He had a role in forcing the development of computers. I read a memorandum he wrote in 1955 in which he complained about the inadequacy of "computing machines" to develop weapons and other science applications. In his memo, he urged greater efforts to improve these computing machines.

The Fuchs episode may have been an indication that Teller himself was not too respectful of secrecy. Another colleague of mine was driving him to a conference I had arranged on the Strategic Defense Initiative and asked Teller whether he would be inhibited in his talk about the classified aspects of the project. Teller replied, "No. I have been trying to teach students the Second Law of Thermodynamics for 50 years and they can't get that. So why would anybody understand this?"

By any measure, Teller was a phenomenon: a giant mind with a passionate heart. His faith in America was formed by the rise of communism in his youth, the horror of Hitler and the expansionism of the Soviet Union. To him, the hydrogen bomb was as necessary for his beloved, adopted homeland as a coat in winter.

September 16, 2003

A NEW WAR FOR AN OLD SOLDIER

For a man who has only just put his head above the parapet, retired General Wesley K. Clark is taking a wicked amount of fire. He is the 10th Democrat to enter his party's race for the presidential nomination and he has upset a lot of the political establishment, especially the punditry.

No aspect of his distinguished and fairly blameless military career has not been projected as a character flaw. The mostly liberal columnist, Richard Cohen, threw himself into the fight to find out that Clark has a short fuse and does not suffer fools gladly. His subordinates, Cohen revealed, often chafed under his command, finding Clark ambitious and abrasive—the same criticism that dogged Winston Churchill.

Robert Novak, the mostly conservative columnist, has retreaded the old story about Clark getting a little chummy with the Serbian war criminal, Gen. Ratko Mladic. They swapped caps and Clark accepted a bottle of wine and a pistol as gifts. His well-known sense of fun did not serve him well in that encounter. And none of his political enemies intend to let him forget it.

It is probably Clark's late entry into the race that has upset the Democratic establishment, many of whom already have committed to one of Clark's nine opponents, politically or in the media. The Republicans fear that he will take away the national security issue from President Bush and leave him exposed.

The first thing you notice about Clark when you meet him is that he does not have *the presence* that is the mark of many former generals, most especially Secretary of State Colin Powell and former Secretary of State Alexander Haig. Powell dominates a room when he walks into it. And many other generals stand out as being military men first and all the time.

Clark, I found, when I spent some time with him several years ago, to be wiry and erect: He could be taken for a lawyer or a banker as easily as a four-star general. In civvies, Clark comes across as a civilian, while the others are always generals. Clark reminded me more of the astronauts I have known than the generals: smart, witty and urbane. Sure he is a good-looking man, but he did not shine any more than others at this year's White House Correspondents' Association dinner. He fit right in, rather than standing out.

When I talked to him over a lunch several years ago, the conversation turned to anti-ballistic missile defense. Then he said he was not in favor of the president's plan because he feared that the defense lobbies would throw all of their resources behind the big technology systems and ignore the fighting soldier. Like many army men, he focused his concern on the survivability of the grunt on the battlefield, whose equipment has not improved much since Vietnam. That conversation was before 9/11, before Afghanistan and Iraq and, therefore, before warfighting would point up the vulnerability of troops on the ground. It is the kind of thing you want generals to worry about.

By and large, politics is a learned art and amateurs crash and burn early. Clark must know this, and his challenge is to learn the art before he is shot down. George Romney and Al Haig both thought they could convert their success in other fields into a run for the presidency. They perished politically from a combination of self-inflicted wounds and hostile fire.

Clark is going to have to learn the game, and learn it quickly; the whole game, from kissing babies to suffering foolish local politicians. Oxford and West Point do not teach this brand of street smarts. Clark has lived his whole life in a world of clever contemporaries and subservient inferiors. Now he must remember that absolutely every player in politics must be taken seriously, and even the most annoying or foolish journalist must be answered with caution and skill.

Any slip or error at this precarious point in Clark's political life could doom him. He may yearn to tangle with Bush, but first he must dance around his opponents—any one of whom could bring him down in debate. Initially, his big problem will not be the frontrunners but the laggards: Dick Gephardt, Dennis Kucinich, Carol Moseley Braun and Al Sharpton. They may not have much chance at the nomination but they know how to use a trip wire and they are steeped in domestic policy, where Clark is weakest.

If Clark gets the nomination, he will have won one of the great battles of his life. In a field of battle that has defeated many gifted amateurs, including Ross Perot and Steve Forbes, Clark will need skills that neither we know nor he knows he has. Presidential elections are simple: the enemy is in front. In primaries, the enemy is all around.

September 23, 2003

JUST TRY TALKING POLITICS
AT THE LIVESTOCK EXCHANGE

It is that time in the election cycle when the television networks are in search of the real America: the down-home crowd they find in diners and at lunch counters. No matter that most Americans eat in fast-food restaurants, and old-fashioned diners and lunch counters are few and far between.

Almost daily now on TV, you can see a farmer in Iowa chewing on a toothpick or a construction worker in New Hampshire finishing his eggs and bacon. Fair enough. It may not be the whole of real America, or even a substantial fraction of it, but it is real.

For my political soundings, I go to the lunch counter at the livestock exchange in Fauquier County, Va., 60 miles west of Washington, D.C. and 50 years behind it. Here, Kevin Whitener serves up what is, to my mind, the best breakfast in America. You can get ham, bacon, sausage, pork chops, steak, catfish and scrapple with your eggs. The grits are classic and the homefries are four-star. As a concession to sophistication, Kevin also offers up excellent Eggs Benedict on the weekend.

But this year, politics is not on the menu. At the horseshoe-shaped counter with its dilapidated stools, the conversation ranges over horses, pickup trucks, the hay supply, sports, the encroachment of the suburbs into the country and the worsening traffic. Politics has not had a run at the counter since Bill Clinton and Monica Lewinsky were in the headlines.

The patrons of the lunch counter are not all farmers and horse people: some are wealthy landowners and others, like myself, commute to Washington every day. "Are things still a mess in Washington?" someone will ask one of the commuters. The answer is likely to be, "Always."

If you expect to hear a great debate about Wesley Clark or Howard Dean, you have come to the wrong place. If you try to initiate one, the conversation soon will turn back to veterinarians and farriers, the impact of Home Depot on local hardware stores, and the virtue of having a diesel-fueled truck rather than a gas-fueled one.

If you want politics, you will have to be content at the livestock exchange with a desultory conversation about whether the incumbent sheriff should be re-elected or voted out.

In the parking lot, you will find that patriotism is alive and well if you count the number of American flag and God Bless America bumper stickers. People seem to be queasy about the government, but they are quite comfortable with George W. Bush and the war in Iraq. This lunch counter may be a backwater of Americana, but it is a serious reflection of the Democrats' largest problem: political apathy. The time was when these people, and others like them across the country, held passionate political views; when they believed that the government would seriously affect their lives, for better or worse. They are hard-working people whose last vocal view was the belief that welfare recipients were indulged shirkers. Now they seem content to let things play out, convinced that government is beyond their reach, that their views are not important, and that their votes will change nothing.

My suspicion is that my companions at the lunch counter find today's political arguments impenetrable. They do not know whether free trade is in their interest or not. They do not know whether the nation's deficit will hurt them or not. And they have no clue about the real state of Social Security: They just hope it will be there when their time comes.

However, there is one political story that has them animated: the gubernatorial recall in California. Of course, they are not interested in the complexities of the California constitution, but they are interested in Arnold Schwarzenegger. They know his name and they have enjoyed his movies. If they lived in California, they would vote for him—that is, the local people, not the Washington commuters.

There is a lesson in this for Democrats and Republicans alike. It is no good decrying the effect of celebrity in politics. Just learn the lesson: The public is fed up with politicians who speak the language of professional politics—the kind of thing you can hear every Sunday morning on the talk shows.

The future belongs not to party politicians, but to self-financing candidates with big name recognition. So expect to see more actors, sports figures and celebrity CEOs seeking the final trophy: political office.

September 30, 2003

THE COMING ENERGY BILL: WHAT IT WILL AND WON'T DO

Shortly, Congress will deliver itself of an energy bill. It is now in a House-Senate conference, where contentious issues, like drilling in the Arctic National Wildlife Refuge, are holding it up.

When it is finally passed and signed into law, the new energy bill will be highly praised. The bill is a buffet of goodies for the energy industries, with tax incentives and loan guarantees worth about $20 billion. It will smooth out some rough spots for utilities and gas producers, and it may provide incentives for nuclear power. All the Washington energy trade associations—from coal to oil—have endorsed it.

Early in his administration, President Bush identified an "energy crisis," and Vice President Cheney established a controversial task force to produce recommendations for a new national energy policy. Many of these recommendations are reflected in the bill, plus sweeteners for environmentalists and others who might have impeded its passage.

It is so complete and so generous to so many that criticism has been muted. But will it really help the fundamental energy problem facing all industrialized nations? Well, here and there, it will help by stimulating natural gas production, improving the electric grid and other small fixes. The big issue of nuclear power is still in the balance and whether the proposed loan guarantees in the bill will lead to new nuclear power plants is an open question.

Yet the energy picture is not as bleak as it was in the 1970s—thanks not to politics but to technology. Although the versions of the bill now floating around Washington do not seem to grasp this, consider:

- Wind-generated electricity is now a reality and is now gaining apace, despite the visual impact of wind turbines and their tendency to chop up birds.
- Nuclear power remains the unawakened giant of electric generation, which, absent some better technology, will have to be called upon sooner or later.
- Hybrid cars and trucks, using extant technology, can make a dent in our appetite for oil for the first time ever.
- Small technologies, such as cryogenic electric transmission, coal-bed methane extraction and possibly natural gas production from hydrates, combine to offer supply solutions that were not available in the 1970s.

Yet our consumption of energy is awesome—particularly of oil, closely followed by natural gas. There is a hope that hydrogen, operating through fuel cells, will alleviate the demand for oil. But there is no easy source of hydrogen. The only known way to get it in very large quantities is by "cracking" water and that takes huge amounts of electricity, suggesting a resurgence of nuclear power and a change in public confidence in nuclear waste disposal.

The Cheney task force report was a supply-side document: more gas, more oil, more electricity. The energy bill will almost certainly recognize that conservation is an important part of this equation. The environmentalists have been pushing conservation, hydrogen and wind power for years. They will now have the establishment on their side.

The bill that is likely to emerge will give the environmentalists a yellow light, but not a green one. Deep down, the administration and Republicans on Capitol Hill have yet to accept that there is an alternative to ever-increasing supplies of traditional fuels.

Conservation has never been an easy sell because it implies doing without: driving underpowered vehicles, enduring cold or hot homes and tolerating inconvenience. It seems un-American. Yet, in fuels, the era of the hunter-gatherers is inexorably coming to an end. There are more hunters than gatherers, and they have been forced far from the homestead to insecure parts of the world, such as the Persian Gulf and the Caspian Sea. China and India are in full pursuit of more traditional energy as their economies and middle classes expand.

Even in a secure world, there is bound to be volatility in energy prices. In an insecure one, volatility is a given. High prices ration energy, cut productivity and are devastating to weak economies. They also have political consequences. In 1974, 23 heads of state lost their jobs as a direct result of energy induced inflation.

Even at today's firm natural gas prices, the chemical and fertilizer industries are suffering. While end users, like farmers, will feel the pain next year, consumers will feel it this winter.

While computers, pharmaceuticals and telecommunications have benefited from technological revolution, energy of all kinds has benefited only on the periphery. The energy equivalent of fiber optic has yet to be invented.

The new energy bill may nudge some things in the right direction, but scientific energy alchemy is not in sight.

October 7, 2003

THE CURIOUS MATTER OF BUSH'S INCURIOSITY

An American journalist is addressing an audience in Ireland about the Bush administration. The audience is hostile to President Bush, the war in Iraq and the detentions in Guantanamo Bay, Cuba.

The journalist does not want to be severely critical of his president and his government to an overseas audience. He defends and deflects. But finally he blurts out, "What I do not understand about George W. Bush is how he can be so incredibly incurious."

Indeed, Bush is not the rube, the dunce or the victim of his advisers that his most liberal critics have tried to paint him. But he is a man who is clinically incurious. Although Bush spent the first decades of his life with the resources to travel the world, while knowing people who could have told him anything, he chose to abstain. Texas and the company of his oil and sports friends was world enough for Bush.

On his first European trip, in a joint press conference with French President Jacques Chirac, Bush regretted in public that he had had no time to see Paris and that as president he "traveled in a bubble," which precluded him from really see-ing the city. Wait a minute. Bush had a lifetime in which he could have visited Paris. Tens of thousands of American students have done it year after year, often with little money.

In a recent interview with Fox Television's Brit Hume, Bush revealed that his incuriosity remains intact. Bush told Hume that he does not read newspapers or watch television news, and that he relies on briefings from his chief of staff, An-drew Card, and National Security Adviser Condoleezza Rice. The pair, he said, give him news objectively. They would do it, he said, without opinions. He said: "I appreciate people's opinions, but I'm more interested in news. And the best way to get the news is from objective sources. And the most objective sources I have are people on my staff, who tell me what's happening in the world."

Whoa! Card and Rice may try to be objective, but often they *are* the news. And when they are not the news, they make the news. Objective?

Former Presidents Kennedy, Johnson, Nixon and Clinton, among many others, were seriously curious and voracious consumers of periodicals and newspapers. For one thing, they wanted to know what their own staffs were up to.

Bush's loyalist supporters flinch when you ask them about the president's lack of curiosity. It worries them in proportion to their own curiosity about domestic and foreign affairs.

I have always been curious about the incurious. When I was 20 years old, I lived in a rooming house in South London. One of my fellow lodgers was a 72-year-old man—a nice man of impeccable conduct; neat, polite and considerate. I traveled the short distance across the Thames River to my newspaper on Fleet Street, on the North Bank of the Thames. He thought this was amazing and told me that although he had never lived anywhere but South London, he had never ventured across the Thames.

Therefore, my lodger friend had never visited the Houses of Parliament, West-minster Abbey, St. Paul's Cathedral, Buckingham Palace, the great hotels, the British Museum or even Madame Tussaud's. He stunned me not because he was self-satisfied: just incurious.

One wonders what is stocked in the incurious mind, how it accumulates intel-lectual capital, and what strange fate of development obliterates the common hu-man desire to know? After all, education is the collective expression of centuries of curiosity.

I was the reporter struggling to defend Bush's judgment in Ireland—while won-dering how judgments can be made if the groundwork of knowledge has not been laid down by assuaging curiosity.

In foreign policy, Bush is remaking a world that did not exist for him before his election. In U.S. education policy, he is trying to light a passion for knowledge without having seen the flame himself.

October 14, 2003

TIME MANAGEMENT: THE BOTSWANA EXTREME

There was plenty of time in Botswana. At one point, all Botswana seemed to *have* was time. With a little imagination, you could see it stacked up in the desert as far as the horizon and much more beyond that.

I had the time phenomenon explained to me by a student in Gabarone, Botswana, who thought I was shortening my life by always trying to get to the next project. The source of the problem, he claimed, was that I had lived too long in Europe and America, and had lost the gift of time.

"In Europe there is no time. In South Africa there is no time. And in America there is no time at all," he said declaratively.

Then he sat down in the shade of a building to enjoy a couple of hours of Botswana time before opening his books.

Washington used to be a city that had a lot of time. But that was decades ago, when legislative disputes were settled over bourbon and a reporter could walk around the corridors of the West Wing without an official minder. These days, the only person in Washington who seems to have any time is George W. Bush. He has time to run on his treadmill for more than an hour a day, or to jog and often to play golf. He also watches ballgames on television. What luxury.

I am not suggesting that the president is lazy, but he is a throwback to a time where you could delegate your work. Technology has increased our productivity by destroying our ability to delegate.

Thirty years ago, middle managers were surrounded by a support network consisting of a dynamite secretary and various typists and gofers. Today, the same person is self-contained, walled in by e-mail, voice mail and some combination of both on a handheld instrument. These technologies say that we must be self-contained; they frustrate the concept of delegation, even if there were somebody left to delegate to.

The first blow against leisurely executive work was struck by the women's movement, when secretaries themselves became executives and joined the ranks of the upwardly mobile. That put an end to the three-martini lunch and many other perquisites of being a major or minor "boss."

Today, you do all your own work, and no one is going to bail you out. When messages came on pink slips, it was easy enough for someone to return a call on your behalf and letters could be answered without the addressee ever seeing them today. Today, if you really want someone to listen to your voice mail or read your e-mail, chances are there is no one left in the structure to do it: all secretarial work has been internalized.

Prima facie this means that we are all hugely efficient. Maybe. Or is it that the race now goes to those who are good with gadgets, not those who, in the large sense, are productive? Can it be that schmoozing with colleagues or customers was of no value? How do you float a new idea in this straightened workplace, where we are judged by the number of electrons we put in motion? Winston Churchill worked in the night and talked in the day. Can we imagine that great man banging away on e-mail, returning innumerable phone calls and checking his Blackberry every 20 minutes?

By one measure, today we have the most efficient White House in history, where the greatest internal compliment for a worker is that he or she is "focused." Clearly if you are focused, discursive discussion and meandering thought have no place. The scheme of things is this: You got the message, now focus on disseminating it.

Ironically, the man who should be the busiest man in the world—the president—is the one who has a little downtime. The question is, how does he use it? Is he like my student friend in Botswana, reveling in time for time's sake? Or is he just being busy with that treadmill—another technological creation dominating human life?

The secret of the man sitting in the shade in Botswana is tied up in the realities of a harsh life in a hard land. In a country like that, even if a man or a woman in adversity makes it to adult life, chances of wealth are slight. Therefore, one likes to take the abundant time available to celebrate survival.

They know a thing or two in Botswana.

October 21, 2003

BUSH HAS TO FIND A WAY TO TALK TO IRAQIS

The ship of state has not capsized, but it has been taking on some heavy seas in the last several days. President Bush has tentatively acknowledged this by being more open with reporters and by sending out signals through that route that the United States wants to be a good world citizen, collaborating with other nations on its problems.

To use his father's phrase, this is a kinder, gentler George W. Bush, maybe even one who feels that the harshness of his posture before the invasion of Iraq was overdone.

Then, there is the extraordinary matter of Defense Secretary Donald Rumsfeld's introspective memorandum. In this he wonders aloud whether the U.S. policy of hunting down terrorists one by one was doomed to fail, as the terrorist-breeding lands can mint them faster than the United States can neutralize them—somewhat the way metropolitan police departments feel about taking out drug dealers.

Rumsfeld may have been writing his memo for those to whom it was addressed; he may have been writing it with the thought that it would leak; or he may have been writing it to the files for history. One way or the other, it is an extraordinary document, in which a bold warrior wonders about the frailty of his own campaign. Rumsfeld may have been compelled into retrospection by the president's decision to give National Security Adviser Condoleezza Rice ultimate responsibility over the Iraq conflict.

For the first time since it has been in power, the Bush administration appears to have real doubts about the efficacy of its policies. It is alone in the world and neither Afghanistan nor Iraq is turning out well. The bloodshed in Baghdad, the close call for Deputy Defense Secretary Paul Wolfowitz, and an increasingly hostile media are taking a toll on the administration's self-confidence. Resolve and military superiority, the basis of the administration's confidence, are challenged.

Those who were opposed to the Iraq war from the start might take malicious pleasure in the administration's discomfort. But Afghanistan and Iraq are not peculiarly Bush problems; they are problems now for the nation as a whole, and still would be problems even if the president were to be voted out of office next fall. The test of the administration will be whether it can come up with big new ideas to deal with big new problems.

Most Americans care little about Afghanistan and enormously about Iraq. The whole concept of American international authority will be undermined if Iraq, rather than progressing to democracy, falls to factional warlordism.

So far, the administration has looked to the post-World War II experiences of Germany and Japan. Unfortunately, these are inapplicable in Iraq. More applicable is the situation the British have faced for more than a quarter of a century in Northern Ireland, or the chaotic conditions that prevail in Algeria. Germany and Japan were cohesive countries that accepted defeat and desperately wanted to rebuild. They also were not littered with small and medium arms that any malcontent could use against the occupying forces. Moreover, the Germans and the Japanese were not infused with religious zeal—let alone a religious belief that sanctifies martyrdom.

Until the recent massive bloodshed in Iraq, the administration could comfort itself with the belief that the media were telling only the bad news and concealing the good news. Now, the bad news is so bad that it is its own messenger. And the message is clearly getting through to thoughtful people in the administration, as evidenced by the Rumsfeld memo.

When the Vietnam War began to go sour, Sen. George Aiken of Vermont espoused the idea that the United States should declare a victory and withdraw. That was an option and, in hindsight, a good one in Vietnam. Unfortunately, it is not an option in Iraq; not until something like a legitimate government has been installed, even if it should not last.

The thousands of American demonstrators who call for withdrawal from Iraq now are wrong. Withdrawal now would be read across the world as a victory for terrorism and the most extreme religious belligerents.

What the administration needs now is a big elegant idea coupled with a steadfast timetable for the assumption of authority by Iraqis. It is no good going on about American ideals, what a bastard Saddam Hussein was, and what a great job we are doing rebuilding Iraq. Humiliated people do not think logically and they are not full of gratitude. Bush needs to tell the Iraqis that he feels their pain and that the Americans are going home in short order—as soon as something that looks like a legitimate government has been put in place. After that, it is not our affair. Maybe it never was, but it is too late for that argument.

October 28, 2003

MICHAEL HOWARD, CAT LOVER,
IS NEW HOPE FOR UK TORIES

Michael Howard almost certainly will be the next leader of Britain's Conservative Party. If times were normal (but they are not) this would cause jubilation in American conservative circles.

If times were normal, Michael Howard's e-mail would be jammed with invitations to speak at right-wing think tanks in the United States before conservative groups and at private universities. As it is, Howard, who is well known in American conservative circles, will get his congratulations in private. American conservatism is too indebted to Labor Prime Minister Tony Blair to risk feting the man who will challenge him for his job in the next general election.

Challenge is the operative word, for it is unlikely that the Conservatives, who have a poor image in Britain, will beat Labor in the next general election. Despite widespread opposition to Blair's participation in the Iraq war, the prime minister is a popular man who reflects contemporary Britain, whereas Howard is a throwback to the Thatcher years and a different time. Their ages tell the story: Blair turned 50 this year and Howard is 62.

Yet Howard is exactly what the Conservative Party needs in order to pull itself back together. He is a skilled politician and a deft performer in the House of Commons, where he will be able to engage Blair, who has had an easy ride under the two previous Tory leaders Iain Duncan Smith and William Hague—the former inept and the latter callow.

Whereas the Conservatives struggled to make a leader out of mild-mannered Duncan Smith, hiring image consultants and even asking President Bush for advice on how to project authority when you walk into a room, Howard is a finished product ready for work. And he will have a lot of work to do to sew together a party that is divided over Europe and almost every other issue. In fact, the only thing the Conservatives seem to agree on is the virtue of fox hunting, which Blair is trying to ban.

Howard is a gunship of words with extraordinary courage in debate. I have seen him at work in the Commons and standing down Benjamin Netanyahu, the bellicose former Israeli prime minister. A barrister, Howard has awesome skills in the Commons. It is not necessary for American political leaders to be exceptional debaters, but it is a prerequisite for their British counterparts. No prisoners are taken in the Commons.

Nonetheless, Michael Howard's role as chief Tory will be to mend his broken and ailing party, to reconnect it with its constituency, and to convince voters that the Tories still have something to offer Britain. If he is lucky, Howard will reduce the government's majority in the next general election, which could come any time in the next 18 months, but probably towards the end of that time. (It is the prime minister's prerogative to set the next election date.)

If the Tories can make inroads on the government's majority, they will set the stage for victory in the election after that, by which time Howard probably will be considered too old to lead the government. In private, Howard, who is married to a glamorous former model, is soft and avuncular, elegant and curious.

In public, he is seen as harsh: he brought much opprobrium on himself when he was Home secretary in the John Major government. He was attacked for being insensitive to prisoners' rights and on other civil liberties issues.

One of his junior ministers, Ann Widdicombe, hung a tag on Howard that he has not been able to remove. "There is something of the night about Michael," she said. It is equivalent to the label "Prince of Darkness," which was applied to the neoconservative Richard Perle when he was in the Reagan administration, and which has stuck. Indeed, comparisons to Howard and Perle are not out of place. Both can sound unsympathetic in public, although they are soft in private.

Both Howard and Perle see public service as a high calling, not a vehicle of personal ambition. Howard, the son of a Jewish immigrant to Britain, makes a point that he joined the Conservative Party out of choice, not out of heritage. Likewise, Perle serves the Republican Party cause but remains a registered Democrat.

If Michael Howard does become prime minister, he will be the first Jew to do so since Benjamin Disraeli occupied the position in the 19th century. And Howard is a cat fancier in a party traditionally inclined to dogs. The British Conservatives may be barking up the right tree at last.

November 4, 2003

IT IS FAR BETTER TO BE LIKED THAN RIGHT

Howard Dean was a physician before he became a governor. George W. Bush, before he became a governor, was a bit of a playboy, a bit of a businessman and, first and foremost, his father's son.

Dean, like Bush, grew up well insulated from the needy. But somewhere along the line, Bush abandoned his wealthy upbringing to become a regular guy: a Texas manure-kicker. The two sides of Bush, as president, serve him well. Easy humor and locker-room bravura combine in Bush to make him magically likeable.

You can find Bush's grasp of world affairs risible, his command of English tenuous and his lack of curiosity appalling, but he is still hard to dislike. He is hugely, damnably, annoyingly likeable.

By contrast, Dean is cold, fairly humorless and given to fits of pique. Somehow when they were training the good doctor, they left out the instructions on bedside manner. Even those who work for Dean are not sure that they like him; that they would like to pass their off-hours with him. If there is a warm and cuddly Dean, it is time he showed it.

Dean The Man is obscured by Dean The Fundraiser, Dean The Bush Critic and Dean The Compulsive Commentator.

Dean has chosen the big issues, such as the war in Iraq, which shows some temerity, given that on NBC's "Meet The Press" he did not know how many men and women there are in uniform. We know what he was trying to say about pickup trucks and the Confederate flag, but he botched it. He would have been no worse off if he had said what he meant: "I want the redneck vote." He might have been more easily forgiven if he had been more truthful and less pandering.

The net result of Dean's faux pas was to reveal that he had no feeling for the South and may not know more about Democratic Party demographics than he did about U.S. military manpower.

Bush has had his share of faux pas, but they do not stick to him. The president grins, jokes and gets away with them. In this he has the skill of Ronald Reagan: an innate ability to deflect with personal charm.

Bush may be the least informed man to be elected president of the United States. He may also have a naïve vision of the future of the world and a simplistic grasp of economic reality, but he remains intensely likeable.

They do not teach it in political science, but if a politician is liked, he or she is halfway home. The best hope for a politician who is not liked is that his or her opponent should be equally deficient in likeability. By contrast, Al Gore knew everything, had a sophisticated vision, and scored close to zero on likeability. Bill Clinton, who carried a lot of unsavory baggage, scored well on likeability. Jimmy Carter, who was admired but not liked, had to run for re-election on his record, not his smile.

Now that Dean is beginning to pull ahead of his rivals for the Democratic nomination, it is time for him to make two telephone calls. The first: to Gore, to find out why he projected an image that invoked no public passion. And the second: to Clinton, to find out how he got away with so much and was still loved by a majority of the electorate.

In the age of television and celebrity worship, likeability is essential to the pursuit of the presidency even as it dumfounds policy. A rogue, a fool or a charlatan can go a long way in politics on likeability. People really liked Edwin Edwards, the former governor of Louisiana, and voted for him although they knew he was not of good character. Edwards is now serving a prison term for racketeering.

It is the bedevilment of democracy that the best candidate does not win: the most liked one does. This is the more so in the television age. When we knew our politicians only through the newspapers, we had one view of them. Now we see them in our living rooms day after day and if they seem likeable, we are swayed.

Bush may have been wrong on tax cuts, wrong on Iraq, wrong on Russian President Vladimir Putin's soul, wrong on supporting the USA Patriot Act, wrong in not commuting any death sentences while he was governor of Texas, but he is liked. Howard Dean, take note.

November 12, 2003

ANGLICANISM IS NOT IMPLODING

By reading the great journals of opinion, it is hard not to believe that the Anglican Communion, known in the United States as the Episcopal Church and in Britain as the Church of England, is in tatters. The Nigerian Church, we are advised, is set to break away, as may Episcopal congregations in Pennsylvania and Texas.

The cause of the controversy is the consecration of an openly gay Episcopal bishop, Gene Robinson, in New Hampshire. Conservative commentators, such as George Will, have argued that if the church does not hold to Biblical writ and doctrinal law, it will implode.

Well, they must be talking about some other church. The church has been in violation of doctrinal law since Henry VIII created it in 1534, for his own dishonorable purposes.

Over the centuries, the Anglican faith has, more than any other organized Christian religion, become a house of many mansions. In its quiet way, it has also been quite revolutionary. In the 19th century, it consecrated its first black bishop in America, and it broke with apostolic doctrine by ordaining women in the 1970s.

Nowhere is the church more convoluted, tolerant and endearing as it is in England. The queen, in theory, still appoints the bishops, even though the job falls to the prime minister. The gulf between the High Church and the Low Church is vast and unbridged. The High Church is very close to Catholicism in liturgy, and the Low Church is more akin to Protestant churches.

There is something else: The High Church does not regard itself as a Protestant church but, dating back to Henry VIII's rule, as a reformed Catholic church, which is reflected in the catechism.

Outside of Britain, most Anglicans are described, and accept the definition, as Protestants. Traditionally, doctrine has varied within bounds in accordance with the preferred liturgy.

The surprise about the bishopric in New Hampshire is that it has taken so long, for the Anglican Communion has survived by embracing secular values. It was in the forefront of the fight against slavery and the great social issues that have transformed the world in the past 200 years. While its leaders may have been establishment figures, at the pastoral level the flock is progressive and outreaching.

The Anglican Church traveled on the wings of imperialism and was divided about the enterprise. Its establishment wing lauded British expansion around the globe, while its missionaries and priests often led the opposition in their far-flung parishes. Dichotomy has never been a problem for the church that has valued its social role as much as its spiritual one.

It was by this mechanism that the Anglican faith spread to Nigeria, and it is ironic that the Nigerian Church should now be held up as offering a purer doctrine than the church in America. In opposing Bishop Robinson, the Nigerian Communion is affirming not scripture but the homophobic social values of Africa, which is famous for a primitive and savage intolerance of gays. There was something ludicrous about seeing Anglicans gathered in London worrying more about the values of the church in that troubled country than about its worldwide tradition of accommodating the needs and realities of secular life.

There are not many Episcopalians in America, and they have been mostly on the high end of the social order—as they say, the good and the great. Eleven presidents and an impressive number of high officeholders have been Episcopalians. In the

United States, more than anywhere else, including Britain, the church has been elitist.

In ordaining women and now in consecrating a gay bishop, the church is reaching ou, not turning inward. The church has survived because of its sensible and reasonable approach to the social storms of the time.

There is something very comforting about the Anglican Church; unthreatening, forgiving and questing. The idea of "the twice found" sums up the best of the church. Almost alone, it allows and accepts the concept that its members will have crises of faith, as have its bishops and priests, but they will come back to the church. Come back to this ramshackle, caring bridge between the elites of the faith and the common, secular Christian.

Over time, those with deep religious faith, such as Cardinal Newman through Malcolm Muggeridge, have left Anglicanism for the more absolute doctrines of Catholicism or the greater evangelical zeal of the newer Christian churches.

Yet Anglicanism, illegitimately conceived, has kept the lights on in its many mansions.

November 18, 2003

THE ENERGY PIG OUT HAS BEEN DELAYED

The energy bill, which has been put on a respirator and deferred until next year, deserves a special place in the history of legislation. It should be held up in political science classes as an example of how not to legislate, and of what happens when vote-buying among politicians becomes manic.

Congress acted as though it were looting a department store, frenetically dividing up the stock among eager hands—flatware for some, appliances for others, clothes and shoes for all. The bill contains subsidies for every interest group, from bicyclists to big oil.

Nuclear power, coal, gas, oil, Alaska, wind and sun all would get their share as Congress abandoned any pretense of fiscal responsibility. It was pork for all—and lots of it. All justified by the myth that these excesses were helping the nation's energy predicament. Some of the great excesses, such as doubling subsidies for ethanol produced from corn, were championed by Democrats as well as Republicans, and they spurred some very disingenuous reasoning.

House Speaker Dennis Hastert got emotional on television about the ethanol subsidies, claiming that this would help save the United States from dependence on imported oil. Surely the speaker knows that it takes as much or more energy to make ethanol from corn as it produces. It takes natural gas to make fertilizer, diesel for farm operations, and more natural gas to dry and ferment the harvested corn. In short, it is an energy sink with an environmental consequence.

The least corrupted title in the bill was the electric one—putting some discipline into the management of the electric grid and modestly extending the power of the hard-pressed Federal Energy Regulatory Commission.

But on the supply side, the only thing that would be supplied would be hand-outs to special interests. Some of the Bush administration's most loyal supporters at the end came down hard on the bill. Irwin M. Stelzer, director of regulation at the Hudson Institute and a columnist for the London *Sunday Times,* who has championed President Bush, excoriated the bill in *The Weekly Standard.* Robert Novak, another dedicated conservative, whipped the measure in his syndicated column. And newspapers generally supportive of the Republican cause weighed in against the bill. These include: *The Economist, The Houston Chronicle, The Wall Street Journal,* and even *USA Today.*

Sen. John McCain (R-Ariz.) called the measure "the no-lobbyist-left-behind bill." But his characterization may be unfair. Sure, the lobbyists were all over the bill—writing parts of it, cajoling members of Congress. But they cannot be blamed for the porcine instincts of those members. Lobbyists are paid to seek preferment for their clients. Members of Congress are not obliged to cave into every lobbyist. They are supposed to weigh the national interest. However, local interest trumps the national interest. And when intoxicated with the prospect of taking the pork home, the pols go and produce something like this energy bill.

Some blame must rest with the White House and Vice President Cheney, whose taskforce, meeting in secret with energy industry leaders, wrote the libretto for the bill. With this bad beginning, things rapidly got worse, with every project seman-tically linked to energy finding favor. More secrecy among Republican members of the House-Senate conference on the bill added to the suspicion surrounding it. When the report on the bill finally was published, the suspicion was well-founded.

Stelzer, writing in *The Weekly Standard,* described the bill as "grotesquely irre-sponsible."

"The major liability of this bill is not what it contains, but what it doesn't. It leaves our energy policy stuck where it has been ever since Presidents Nixon, Ford, Carter and their successors talk the talk but fail to walk the walk towards a sensible response towards our dependence on imports," he wrote.

It is my experience that when a bill before Congress seeks to do too much, it does nothing but serve a panoply of special interests. The bill should have been broken down into separate manageable bills aimed at remediating specific situa-tions, such as the weakness in the national electric grid, beginning the process of bringing natural gas south from Alaska, and restraining bad science at the service of dubious interests.

After the great blackout in the Northeast, Rep. John Dingell (D-Mich.) sug-gested sensibly that the electric provisions of the bill be considered separately, but those who smelled the pork would have none of it. Now, we may not fix what needs fixing.

November 25, 2003

LOVING AND HATING PUBLIC BROADCASTING

No one would seriously seek to advance the welfare of taxpayers by suggesting the withdrawal of public financing from education. But when it comes to public broadcasting—both National Public Radio and the Public Broadcasting Service—there is no such inhibition.

As public broadcasting maintains a fragile link with Western culture and operates as something of an open university, it is extraordinary that American conservative organizations regard it as needing to be starved, and possibly expunged. It is the desire of those opposed to public broadcasting, presumably, to end classical music in many cities of the nation, to eviscerate the little broadcast drama that is available anywhere in the United States, and to cut news coverage from the global reach of NPR to the thoughtful coverage provided by "The NewsHour with Jim Lehrer"—all because of an alleged political bias.

If you scratch the opponents of public broadcasting, the final argument beneath their skin is always that it is too liberal. Yet it was PBS that incubated "The McLaughlin Group" and carried William F. Buckley's "Crossfire" until he retired.

Certainly, PBS carries the only avowedly liberal program on television: "Now with Bill Moyers." Is the airing of a different opinion a sin in a democracy? Should the BBC News be punished along with "Masterpiece Theater" because of the pathological obsession of some conservatives with liberalism, the nation's competing political philosophy?

Since the inception of broadcasting, governments around the world have wrestled with the problem of providing a service that gives continuity to the cultural threads of history without government intruding on either the artistic or journalistic function. The British opted for a license fee that finances the BBC, and variations of this approach are found throughout the world. In the United States, we came to realize this cultural and educational need late, and public broadcasting, as we know it—under-funded, overanalyzed and precarious—came into being.

Here, I must declare that I am the executive producer and host of a weekly public affairs program, "White House Chronicle," which airs on a PBS station in Washington, D.C. and cable around the country. I get no public funding for the program. And I have to find sponsors just to cover the production costs.

NPR, with lower costs than its television counterpart, is growing in audience and is now the most important radio broadcaster, largely because its commercial rivals simply have declined to do the job.

While I believe more federal funding for public broadcasting is a worthwhile national investment, indeed an essential one, I take a back seat to no one as a critic of the genre, and particularly of PBS. It is an archipelago of fiefdoms, self-perpetuating management, favorites, and confused program objectives. How many tired old British comedies must we endure? Why is PBS slavishly devoted to the BBC, when there is English-language broadcasting around the world? Particularly, why are NPR and PBS so afraid of producing original American drama, which would cultivate new writers?

If conservatives succeed in de-funding public broadcasting, it will become a self-perpetuating non-governmental organization with all the moral superiority and elitism of other NGOs.

A small beginning to improve public broadcasting might consist of two things: providing reliable, predictable funding, and giving its "members"—the people who send money to NPR and PBS—real membership rights. Every station ought to sign up members with the understanding, as with all other membership organizations, that they get a vote that can be exercised in a duly constituted annual election and meeting.

De-funding public broadcasting only will add to its quirkiness and inaccessibility to the public it serves. It also will damage the critical cultural and educational dimension of broadcasting.

December 2, 2003

THE COMMONWEALTH FINDS THE LIGHT IS FAILING

It has been said of the Commonwealth, formerly the British Commonwealth, that it is as soft as gossamer, but held together by ties as strong as piano wire. With Zimbabwe's President Robert Mugabe quitting, the 53-nation organization is being tested as never before.

The Commonwealth, which was cobbled together by Britain as its empire shrank, is made up almost exclusively of former British possessions and bound together as much by sentiment as by reality. It is all of these things: a mini United Nations; a pint-sized Davos World Economic Forum; a sports promoter via the Commonwealth Games; and an operator of various modest welfare programs, including its own Peace Corps.

In its latest and most contentious meeting last week in Abuja, Nigeria, presided over by Queen Elizabeth II and attended by Prime Minister Tony Blair, the organization ran into the limits of its comity. It divided along racial lines in an ugly exhibition that the interests and values of the Westernized members, including some in Asia, were not those of Southern Africa.

North and South were, as so often, continents apart. Even the Commonwealth's most cherished institution, the Commonwealth Retreat, during which heads of states spend days causally conferring with each other, failed to produce healing. If anything, it emphasized the differences.

The proximate cause of the Commonwealth schism was a reluctantly adopted move to continue the suspension of Zimbabwe for vote-rigging and other unconstitutional practices. But for years, except by force of will and forced camaraderie, the Commonwealth has been on the verge of disintegration, as the founding standards of Britain have been mocked by members.

In 1991, ironically in Harare, Zimbabwe, the Commonwealth decided it had to get serious about constitutional government and the rule of law. It had taken no serious disciplinary action since the eviction of South Africa over apartheid. But, as the recent meeting in Abuja showed, one country's sinner is another country's saint.

In Southern Africa, Mugabe is not a man who has brought the country to failure but one who has wrested it from its white settlers. To his neighbors in Botswana, Malawi, South Africa and Zambia, Mugabe is an inconvenience, an embarrassment, but above all else, he is still a freedom-fighter and a hero of the anti-colonial struggle. Also, his anti-white racism plays well in the region.

Years ago, I asked then Prime Minister Margaret Thatcher whether the Commonwealth could survive. She retorted that it was strong, prospering and a force for good. As he struggled to find consensus in Abuja, Blair might have wondered whether that is still so, and whether a club that was founded in the twilight of colonialism can survive when anti-colonialism, and by extension anti-white racism, is a virulent creed.

In Zimbabwe, animals and people are dying by the tens of thousands from starvation and disease. But the Commonwealth members that surround the tortured country, prefer to see Mugabe as a freedom-fighter and a revolutionary hero rather than an incompetent, corrupt mass-murderer. Now he has quit the Commonwealth, accusing it of racism and bias, while his country continues to implode.

In the Southern African tragedy and the discomfort of the Commonwealth is a bitter lesson for those who believe that the great liberal principles of democracy and the rule of law will triumph over hate and a state-sponsored interpretation of history.

Successful members of the Commonwealth, say, Sri Lanka and Singapore, are not consumed with pathological hatred of members like Australia, Canada and New Zealand. But even the northern and eastern African countries barely saw eye to eye with the non-African Commonwealth on Zimbabwe.

The Commonwealth will probably limp along as a communications tool between heads of state, but it will not fulfill its idealistic promise. It is a house divided by race.

December 9, 2003

SUCCUMBING TO CHRISTMAS, ONE MORE TIME

Memo to Christmas:

You are at hand again, and I am dancing to the old choreography. It has been this way for five decades: You enchanting and me resisting, until I abandon my resistance and submit to the joys and delights of your visitation. I start the holiday with "bah, humbug" and rattle on about commercialization, cheap trinkets and bad music until I capitulate—as I know I will—and get swept up in your embrace of hope, joy and good feeling.

Indubitably, you are the greatest of all festivals, springing from a baby in a manger in a faraway torrid land more than 2,000 years ago to encompass nearly all people, Christian and other faiths alike. What magic of continuity you give to an individual's life as well as to the national and international family of mankind.

The continuity extends from the first Christmas remembered to the impending one. The memory of Christmas is the strong sinew that binds the years together, dims the sorrows and elevates the joys. For each and every one of us, the first Christmases we remember are the abiding ones—the key in which all other Christmases are written. That is why northern expatriates in southern climes make mock snow with cotton wool and change your hue to white, as snow, that is. Southerners laugh at these northern expatriates and declaim: "There was no snow in the Holy Land."

My mother, who was born and lived all of her life in Africa, was one who insisted on her vision of authenticity at Christmas. She believed that the ambiance of the stable was appropriate for Christmas; no tinsel, no bells, no fir trees—just what might have been in Bethlehem. Her one concession was to pin ferns from the African bush around the doors of our house. She allowed mistletoe, but was ambiguous about it, fearing its pagan message.

A devoutly abstemious woman, my mother was disposed for that one day of the year to tolerate alcohol. Nobody dared suggest that a tipple was one of the gifts borne by the Wise Men. We let that one go. She actually took a drink: a thimble of sweet sherry. On swallowing the sherry, long before it could have entered the bloodstream, she would declare that she was dizzy and that she might have to lie down. My father, my brother and I believed this was a placebo effect: tipsy by expectation.

At Christmastime, most of us plan to drink a little more than we normally would. For a few, it is a misadventure. Christmas is the time of year when the lonely feel particularly so and the unhappy are more so. That Christmas drink does not help the bereaved and the alienated. For the rest of us, it is the best time to open a bottle.

Some love the embrace of their families, and odd characters like myself love to travel at Christmas-to laugh and celebrate with strangers made close friends by the specialness of the occasion. Cities have their own ethos for the celebration: Paris even gayer than usual; New York energetically pursuing its celebration; London, well, out to lunch; and Harare putting on a healing face, despite its anguish.

The sweetest place for Christmas I know? Gabarone, Botswana. There, a barefoot child can invoke the great spirit of the occasion with a piece of wrapping paper tied on a stick. Toys are us, not them.

But you, Christmas, are everyone, from that kid with the stick to my late mother with her sip of sherry. Thanks from all of the world.

December 16, 2003

2004

THE UNCERTAIN FUTURE OF TONY BLAIR

LAVENHAM, England—As they say, a year makes a difference. A year ago, British Prime Minister Tony Blair was so unassailable, with such a large majority in the House of Commons, that it appeared that he could be prime minister for years, if not decades. Now there is speculation that he might be gone by next Christmas, a victim of his own work habits as much as of political opposition.

For President Bush, the loss of Blair would be immense. Not that Britain would automatically repudiate its close affinity with the United States, but it is hard to imagine any other prime minister, let alone Blair's potential successor, the mercurial Chancellor of the Exchequer Gordon Brown, hewing so closely to the Bush line. Blair has been a godsend to Bush: an exuberant partner in the war against terrorism, the Iraqi war and the overthrow of the Taliban in Afghanistan.

If there has been periodic tension between these two, as there was between Winston Churchill and Franklin Roosevelt during World War II, not a hint of it has emerged. Blair always seems to be there for Bush. But the past year has taken a terrible toll on the prime minister, with problems in Europe, domestic problems in reforming the education and national health systems, plus constant criticism of his war policies from members of his own party. Whereas Bush is a master at delegating, Blair seems not to trust his own Cabinet and feels that he has to do everything himself. He does take vacations—the latest in Egypt—but he often works through weekends, travels incessantly and is Britain's man at the table, whether it is a Commonwealth meeting in Nigeria or a wrangle over the European constitution in Brussels.

Blair's style of governance is to work outside of the traditional channels of government. He is criticized for not attending the House of Commons frequently enough and for not enjoying it as prime ministers are supposed to; for holding brief, perfunctory Cabinet meetings; and for relentlessly taking the responsibilities of the country on to himself.

Although the Brits are deeply confused about Blair's Bush connection, they still seem to like him. But Blair has entered that dangerous neverland of politics, where he is liked but not trusted. It means he stands on a slippery slope and will be tested severely in the weeks ahead when an independent inquiry conducted by Lord Hutton looks into whether British intelligence was hyped to support the war in Iraq. A scientist critically involved in the assessment, David Kelly, committed suicide after suggesting to a BBC correspondent that the intelligence had been "sexed up" to support the war. It is unlikely that the prime minister will come out of the inquiry untarnished—and possibly he could emerge quite damaged.

Far more than Bush, Blair emphasized weapons of mass destruction as a justification for the invasion of Iraq. It was Blair who offered up the false information that Saddam Hussein was trying to buy uranium in Niger and that he had weapons of mass destruction that could be launched in 45 minutes.

Yet British analysts believe Blair's physical problems, not his political ones, may cause him to step down in the coming year. He has a mild heart condition, as been losing weight, and looks haggard. The burdens of his office have increased as his early team of confidantes have drifted away through scandal or normal attrition. The latest to go was his press secretary, Alastair Campbell. But the most missed may be Peter Mandelson, one of the authors of the Labor Party's revival and an alter ego. He was caught up in a scandal involving a house loan from another Labor member of Parliament and had to leave the inner circle.

It appears sometimes that Blair may be closer to Bush than he is to his own Cabinet and Labor Party operatives. It is an odd precariousness into which Blair, a devout Christian and clearly well-meaning man, has maneuvered himself.

The situation is summed up by Peter Oborne, the political editor of the venerable Spectator magazine: "The summer marks the prime minister's 10th anniversary as Labor leader, an elegant opportunity for him to make an exit with as much grace as he can muster. There's no more than a 50:50 chance that he will be in Downing Street by this time next Christmas."

In cricket, the equivalent of a homerun is a ball in the air to the boundary, counting for six runs. Tony Blair needs to hit a six if he is to stay on and fulfill his potential as one of Britain's more extraordinary prime ministers. If he does not, it may be Britain's loss—and it certainly will be America's loss.

January 6, 2004

BUSH LIGHTS FUSES, BUT IS IT POLICY?

There is a presumption around the White House and in Republican circles of President Bush's invincibility; that every action taken will lead on to triumph.

In this mythology, if the president says that a temporary worker plan is immigration reform, reform it is. If the president says that come June the governance of Iraq will be handed over to its people, that is so and it will work. If the president says that tax cuts will bolster the economy in the long term, then the economy is set to thrive.

The president lights fuses connected to devices that are expected to burst into beautiful light, but instead they could explode with devastating results. This is the year when at least two of these devices will be tested and the portents for success are dubious.

His biggest test will come in Iraq, where he hopes to hand over much of the governance to Iraqis by the end of June under a structure yet to be determined, with authority yet to be outlined, and with consequences yet to be speculated upon. Bush is anxious to move Iraq from its unhappy state of occupation to the first glimmers of the democracy he plans to establish. This is a tricky undertaking at best. A false move in Iraq would go from the violence of the current insurgency to a full-blown civil war, with the three constituencies in Iraq fighting each other as well as the occupation.

The crucial handover will take place just as the U.S. military is recycling its personnel—in itself a huge undertaking, which will replace what are now hardened Iraqi hands with fresh troops inexperienced in peacekeeping. The Bush administration is giving no answers, but the questions pile up: To whom will American and British troops be answerable? What are the expectations that lead the administration to believe that troop strength can be reduced without security catastrophe?

All we have, so far, is a naïve, theatrical proposition that "it will be all right on the night." Chances of it being all right are slim in the extreme.

Then there is the weakening dollar, which is losing ground daily to the euro and on most days to the yen. In public, the president says he favors a strong dollar, but his business friends, to whom he is extremely attuned, think they will reap a bonanza from a weak dollar favoring U.S. exports. Not quite so. There is a price to be paid and that price is already being extracted by the Organization of Petroleum Exporting Countries.

OPEC has abandoned its commitment to increase production to hold the price of oil to $28 a barrel. Because oil is denominated in dollars, OPEC is feeling the draft from the weak dollar and is pushing up the price. The immediate effect will be on the U.S. economy, where the price of oil affects everything—notably inflation. If the oil price triggers the onset of inflation, the Federal Reserve will have to raise interest rates, which will crimp the anticipated economic recovery.

Up to this point in time, the president has been able to shield himself from criticism by invoking the war on terrorism as a defense. This will not wash if an economic crisis can be laid to his policies of tax cuts and deficits. One cannot invoke heroism for self-inflicted wounds.

Bush has enjoyed three extraordinary years in power without suffering the unintended consequences of his actions. This year could be a year of accounting-the year in which political philosophy encounters hard reality. Iraq and the economy will decide whether the president has done well by us. And Bush should be advised to beware the ides of June.

January 13, 2004

TOO MANY HOUSES; BEWARE OF CEO INSANITY

The great protectors of the public health, including the World Health Organization and the Centers for Disease Control, preoccupied as they are with transnational diseases, such as avian flu, SARS and Mad Cow Disease, have overlooked a new and virulent epidemic: Mad Financier Disease.

An important minority of the world's chief executive officers have come down with the contagion in recent years, felling along with themselves small investors, employees, accounting firms, law firms and government regulators.

After the fall Michael Milliken, who was convicted of securities fraud in the 1980s, those who look after the health of corporations thought the disease had been arrested; that those who were showing symptoms of larceny would take themselves in hand for fear that the jailhouse doors would close behind them as well.

Then there was Enron, where the love of money knew no bounds. After so spectacular a collapse, it seemed that in future those entrusted to run public companies would do so with rectitude. Alas, no. Along came Tyco, WorldCom, and maybe the biggest corporate heist of all, Parmalat.

What, one wonders, possesses those who, with more money than they (perhaps even their descendants) can spend in their lifetimes, to grab for more?

The tip-off that the disease of greed has ousted reason would appear to be in the frenetic collection of homes: great big houses, scattered around the world, maintained by teams of servants, for occasional visits by the owner. Two houses seems reasonable, but three suggests some imbalance is afoot. And more than three homes is a strong indication that the captain of industry now believes that he or she is a monarch, or at least a dictator.

Oddly, history judges the megalomania of tycoons not on the skill with which they built their empires but on the passion with which they acquire homes—lavish pavilions with indoor basketball courts, movie theaters and marble bathrooms by the dozen, intimating that the owners suffer either from an obsession with hygiene or recurring diarrhea. Mostly these mini palaces sit idle, tended and burnished by an army of servants, who stand ready should the great man or woman decide that it is time for a night in Palm Beach, Fla., or New York City, or a foxhunt in Virginia.

In the scheme of lavish success, a large house in London, costing tens of millions of dollars, is *de rigeur*, as is a ski chalet in the Rockies—even if the owner doesn't ski. It's the heights, not the slopes.

Of course, a corporate jet is necessary to ferry the oligarchs among their sacred bathrooms.

What possesses otherwise gifted entrepreneurs to seek lifestyles beyond reason and, in the ultimate phase of their diseased excess, to loot the companies that enable them to furnish their homes and lives?

Andrew Fastow of Enron has pleaded guilty. Bernard Ebbers of WorldCom and Dennis Kozlowski of Tyco have taken the perp walk. Calisto Tanzi of Parmalat has been arrested.

Now, sadly, a man of real talent, Conrad Black, the newspaper proprietor, is being sued by Hollinger, the company he headed, for $200 million. He also is being investigated by the Securities and Exchange Commission, and by authorities in his native Canada and Britain.

Black, who has denied any wrongdoing, and who is a man of substantial intellect, has fallen when he should be enjoying the successes he earned. He owns important newspapers: Britain's *Daily Telegraph,* Canada's *National Post, The Jerusalem Post,* and *The Chicago Sun-Times* and its affiliated suburban newspapers. He has just published a well-received biography of Franklin D. Roosevelt, and recently was raised to the peerage in Britain.

Yet Black, the intellectual, the canny publisher, the crusader for political causes, a man whose dinner table was graced by the great, the good and the witty, is accused of taking money from his public company to which he was not entitled.

There is something tragic about a man who can write with sympathy and grace about FDR and yet persist in living a life of conspicuous, in-your-face excess — and boast about it.

In London, Black has two houses that are joined together to make a mighty mansion. In Palm Beach, he has an estate he bought from Donald Trump — which even Black has described as vulgar. And in New York, Black owns a sumptuous apartment. The value of his homes exceeds $70 million.

The moral: Before you invest, check on the living arrangements of the CEO: they appear to be a statement of intent.

January 20, 2004

BROWN: BRITAIN FACES ENTREPRENEURIAL DEFICIT

Gordon Brown, Britain's canny chancellor of the exchequer, would like the British to be more like the Americans. In particular, he would like the British to be more entrepreneurial and more prepared to deal with globalization and labor competition from Asia.

In a speech at a conference in London, Brown advised his countrymen to get with the free-enterprise program.

Brown is right. There is less entrepreneurship in the British Isles than there is in the United States, where, in turn, there may be less entrepreneurship than there is in Asia.

One of the problems is that government red tape is not friendly to business start-ups in the United Kingdom. But there are other barriers — the most important of which are cultural. Indeed, worldwide, culture may be the determining factor in the zeal to start a business.

Another problem is a lack of competing banks. The United Kingdom has only a handful of retail banks. In the United States, there are thousands. So it is harder for a British entrepreneur to get a loan.

Returning to the cultural barrier, the British simply do not wish to be associated with endeavors that they believe to be socially inferior. They are happy working for large companies or in local or national government. But they do not want to be known for running the dry-cleaner on the street corner, the furniture shop on the main street, or the neighborhood trucking company.

A legacy of Britain's class system says: You shall be defined by what you do, not by the money you take home or the wealth you create. As a result, the most talented people in Britain do not apply themselves to entrepreneurial endeavor. Instead, they seek institutional employment. Ergo, small business is often in the hands of the remnants of the working class: good people, but not people who are going to grow their companies and expand their enterprises.

That is why Asian immigrants to Britain have done so extraordinarily well—and many have become multimillionaires, often by developing businesses the British shunned. Case in point: convenience stores and late-closing restaurants. Britain was famous for rolling up its sidewalks at 5 p.m.—and God forbid you needed bread on Sunday. The Asian influx of the 1960s and 1970s revolutionized retailing.

If Brown wants to energize the British and restore commercial vigor, he needs to look not only to the United States, but also to those nations that have an innate passion to be in business, without regard to the social status of the entrepreneur. He may want to know why the Chinese, the Georgians, the Indians and the Lebanese are such extraordinary entrepreneurs. Even when oppressed by war and stultifying central planning, these cultures throw off entrepreneurs.

Brown would like to start a government program to encourage entrepreneurs. He would like to join the problem, not the solution.

It is not just Brown who has a lesson to be learned here. We do, too. As we have grown wealthier, we have grown more selective about our areas of endeavor. We look not to ourselves to invigorate commerce, but to first-generation immigrants—people who cannot spell entrepreneur, do not know what an MBA is, and amass fortunes.

We are not immune to the British problem of being defined by what we do. But luckily, we have people on the way up who want to be defined not by what they do, but by where they will educate their children. Gordon Brown, copy.

January 27, 2004

THE END OF THE BBC AS WE HAVE KNOWN IT

Collateral damage is the term the military chooses to use when areas adjacent to a target are destroyed or damaged. Well, the debate over weapons of mass destruction has produced its own collateral damage: the British Broadcasting Corporation has been hard hit—its structure damaged, its veracity questioned and its staff demoralized.

As journalistic sins go, the one that has caused all the trouble at the BBC is pretty minor. A BBC reporter, Andrew Gilligan, said on the BBC's morning radio program, "Today," that the Blair government had "sexed up" intelligence data about weapons of mass destruction in Iraq. The prime minister's then-press secretary, Alastair Campbell, heard the broadcast and was infuriated.

Later, it came out the Gilligan did indeed have a source for part of his allegations. When Gilligan's source was revealed to be David Kelly, a dignified and quiet government scientist, the distraught Kelly committed suicide. The government looked to be in trouble and the BBC defended its reporter. Some independent investigation was called for, and Blair appointed a well-known British jurist, Lord Hutton, to investigate. Hutton reported last week.

Everyone in political and journalistic circles expected Hutton to exonerate the BBC and castigate the government. Instead, he did the reverse. The report has been a blow for the BBC like none other it has received in its 77-year history. The chairman of the BBC's board of governors, Gavyn Davies, Director-General Greg Dyke, and Gilligan resigned. The dispirited governors issued a groveling apology to the prime minister and the government.

The apology may have satisfied the government but it has infuriated journalists throughout Britain. Members of Parliament and leading commentators, many of whom have been critical in the past, have savaged Hutton and defended the BBC.

The BBC's problems begin with the strange nature of its structure. In the early days of radio, the government decided to have an independent public monopoly control the new medium. It would be freestanding and financed in a new way — with a tax of its own called a "license fee." If you owned a radio, you would have to pay for the privilege of listening to it.

When television came along, the BBC simply extended its monopoly to that new medium and the fee went up accordingly. After World War II, the BBC was riding high with a global reputation for veracity and objectivity, the like of which no news organization ever had enjoyed. It was an icon; it was the gold standard; it was without peer; and it was an example of the best of Britain.

In the 1950s, commercial television was introduced and in the 1980s, commercial radio came to Britain. But people who watched or listened to only the new programming still had to pay the license fee (now $180 a year), and commercial broadcasters campaigned increasingly against the BBC and its privileged position. The BBC responded not by seeking the high ground of quality programming, but by trying to be all things to all viewers and listeners. It also has tried to expand abroad, ostensibly without using the license fee, but it would not have made inroads, as it has in the United States, without linkage to the home networks.

In recent times, the BBC has been criticized for not knowing what it is trying to do; for trying to resist its commercial rivals at every turn, usually without success. It went into a 24-hour, CNN-type global news broadcast that has won hardly a smidgen of audience. Meantime, it has become a retailer of its own products, and of products it thinks are quintessentially British: Did you know that you can buy jam from the BBC as well as books, tapes and gift cards?

In 2007, when its charter comes up for review, the BBC almost certainly will be cut down to size, discouraged from filling its channels with American sitcoms and old movies and encouraged to get on with what it is good at—news, drama and current affairs. It almost definitely will be restricted to one television channel and three radio channels.

The BBC has been at odds with both Conservative and Labor governments over many years because of its efforts at "moral equivalency" in its news coverage. It infuriated Margaret Thatcher, when she was prime minister, for interviewing Irish terrorists. In the same way, it has infuriated the Blair government by implying manipulated intelligence.

But if it had not been for the fuss over Gilligan and weapons of mass destruction, the world's largest broadcasting operation might have avoided the paring, which is undoubtedly coming to it in 2007. It will be the end of a remarkable era in broadcasting; of great programs, great mistakes and a great role in the history of the 20th century.

February 3, 2004

HOW "GOOD MAN" BUSH GETS ALL TIED UP IN GOODNESS

Samuel Johnson, the great British writer and lexicographer, supposedly said: "I hate mankind, for I think myself one of the best of them, and I know how bad I am." One has the feeling that George W. Bush, the 43rd president of the United States, would rephrase that remark to say: "I am one of the best of men, and I know how good I am."

We do not know if that is so, because Bush does not deal in realm of the contemplative. That he has told us. After more than three years of watching him, we know that he is a man of certainty, a man who believes in goodness just as much as he believes in evil.

If Bush approves of you, he describes you as a good person. How many heads of state has he proclaimed to be "a good man"? Bush appears to feel that these "good people" are like himself: good through and through. Likewise, evil people are evil through and through—their motivation being a satanic hatred for the freedoms that Bush cherishes.

It is from this division between good and evil that Bush was not able to find enough good in any death-row inmate in Texas to commute a death sentence. Bush admires Winston Churchill, but he is not attended by the self-doubt that visited Churchill. Nor is he visited by the despondency and despair, which Churchill called his "black dog."

Some of Bush's confidence may be related to his religious convictions. But it is more likely that he would be much the same if he had not undergone a religious conversion. He is just one of those lucky people untrammeled by doubt.

As a human being, all this is great for Bush. However, as an international leader, it has its limits—devastating limits.

Bush has no pangs that he invaded Iraq, despite the false rationale of Saddam Hussein's weapons of mass destruction. Saddam was palpably evil, and the war was justified to Bush.

However, when he is confronted with evil in countries he cannot invade, because of their size or importance, Bush has to look away. So he cannot find it in himself to criticize Russian President Vladmir Putin for agglomerating power, brutalizing the Chechens or suppressing the press. Either he still believes that Putin is a good man, or Bush has no tools with which to tackle the growing authoritarianism in Russia.

Likewise, Pakistani President Pervez Musharraf. When Abdul Qadeer Khan was exposed as the chief proliferator in the world (surely a crime against humanity), Bush bit his tongue and swallowed Musharraf's cynical pardoning of Khan. Intelligence sources knew that Khan was up to no good for decades, and it would have been impossible for Musharraf to wonder from where the nuclear scientist's huge and conspicuous wealth was coming. But Bush would not move Musharraf from the "good column" any more than he was prepared to move Putin.

North Korean dictator Kim Jong-il is firmly in the "evil column." But Bush has no remedy and possibly exacerbates the situation by refusing to negotiate directly with the North Koreans. This might not work, but it won't hurt. Trapped, Bush looks the other way.

It was the same belief that good guys cannot do bad things that led Bush, as the former diplomat Richard Holbrooke has said, to fracture our relations with our allies. The Old Europeans were as offended by getting back of Bush's hand on Kyoto as they were by the Iraq invasion. Bronwen Maddox, foreign editor of *The Times* of London, has pointed out that it was as much Bush's style as his policies that caused the initial offense in Old Europe.

In some parts of the world, good men are supposed to have good manners as part of the package. The Bush administration has never been so much arrogant as mannerless.

A leader other than Bush, as he goes into the next election, might have a long night of the soul and see what has gone wrong.

More and more economists are expressing doubt about the runaway expenses of the government in the face of declining revenue. But Bush will have none of it. His self-confidence extends from reshaping the Middle East to rethinking the laws of economics.

Around Washington, it is believed that Bush's gutsy appearance on NBC's "Meet the Press" satisfied the faithful, but did not convert the skeptical. He said nothing about how he would govern if he is given another four years. More of the same? A good man—in this case, George W. Bush—will do good things, won't he?

February 10, 2004

GAS PRICES HIGH? YOU AIN'T SEEN NOTHING YET

It may be a tsunami. It may just be high water. And it could (though it's unlikely) dissipate without serious effect. But the White House and the energy producers are bracing for what they fear could be disastrously high oil prices this summer— prices between $2.50 and $3.00 a gallon for gasoline.

The White House is rumored to have commissioned a special study from a consulting firm, which put the gasoline price at $3.00. Already it is flirting with $2.00.

Oil anxiety in the administration was heightened by last week's meeting of the Organization of Petroleum Exporting Countries in Algiers. At that meeting, OPEC, in a surprise move, said it would cut oil production by 1.5 million barrels a day, thus breaking with its previous commitment to a target price of between $22 and $28 a barrel. As it is, oil has been trading just below $35 a barrel, and there is no price relief in sight.

OPEC's rationale for raising the price is this: Oil is traded in dollars, and its members are hurting because of the weakened dollar. Another explanation might be opportunism.

A cold winter in the Northern Hemisphere, political instability in Venezuela, increased demand in both Japan and China, and declining production in places such as Alaska's North Slope and Europe's North Sea, together mean that inventories are low, traders are jittery, and predators are circling.

Of course, high prices will dampen demand—particularly for gasoline, as motorists decide not to take that cross-country trip. But the economic and political consequences could be severe.

Irwin Stelzer of The Hudson Institute believes that the economy can absorb $35-a-barrel oil, and that oil at that price will only cut into economic growth by a half of a percent. But the political impact could be more severe, because there is very little that the Bush administration can do to tamp down energy prices.

High oil prices lead to high prices for natural gas—and very specific economic damage. Manufacturing, which has been trying to get out of its sickbed, would be clobbered along with chemical, fertilizer and electric production. More obviously, high prices hurt air, rail and road transportation.

Unlike the case with other commodity prices, consumers are immediately affected by energy prices, which can dampen their all-important confidence.

The Democrats may see the impending oil shock as an opportunity and a gift to front-runner John Kerry. Unfortunately for Kerry and his party, they haven't espoused an energy strategy and always have been keen to say what they will not do rather than what they will do: witness the Democratic position on drilling the Arctic National Wildlife Refuge and Kerry's already-stated opposition to nuclear power.

A crisis will require the Democrats to produce an energy strategy that is convincing and unburdened with talk of solar and wind power, hydrogen cars, and regulation. An energy shock will be an embarrassment to President Bush and his administration, revealing its impotence in controlling prices that are set overseas. But it won't necessarily be a gift to the Democrats.

One of the hard-to-measure consequences of high prices is that they stimulate the transference of industry overseas, where manufacturers will substitute cheap labor for what was once cheap energy in the United States. Chemicals are going and fertilizers may not be far behind. Traditionally, cheap energy has been one of the strong pillars of American prosperity. Likewise, trucks and SUVs, the most profitable segment of the automobile market, may take a bath.

All of this is really bad news for Vice President Cheney, who has spearheaded, controversially, U.S. energy policy in the administration. At a time when Washington is swirling in rumors that Cheney may be dropped from the ticket, an energy crisis won't help his standing within the administration. He has been very contemptuous of conservation—the only short-term remedy in an overheated market.

During the energy crisis of 30 years ago, the oil-exporting nations believed that the United States, the largest energy consumer, could make dramatic technological and conservation efforts to wean itself from imported fuels. Instead, we've increased our oil imports from 30 to 60 percent, and we're about to begin importing liquefied natural gas from the same foreign oil suppliers. It isn't a pretty picture.

Many American families may join the conservation effort this summer when they choose not to load up the family in the SUV and drive to Disney World in Orlando, Fla. from, say, New York. That's conservation and a market solution to the market rigidity of OPEC.

February 17, 2004

LED BY DRUDGE, FEARLESS PRESS IS ON BEDROOM PATROL

Matt Drudge, the Internet gossip, worded his rumor cleverly. He did not claim that presidential hopeful John Kerry had had an affair with an intern. Instead, he said that several news organizations were looking into it.

Well, they certainly were after Drudge's sly innuendo. As it is, the woman came forward and denied any part of Drudge's implication, as did Kerry. And the whole thing has gone away. But it is an important illustration of how things work nowadays, and why any public figure who does have skeletons in his or her closet has to live in daily fear of exposure.

This is not exactly new, but it has viciousness and a hypocrisy about it that has reached an all-time high.

Public figures always have been subject to dethronement by scandal. At one time, they were somewhat protected by fears of libel. But progressively, the courts have held that public figures are fair game—and game they are.

At the end of the 19th century, Charles Stewart Parnell, the great Irish leader, who might have changed the history of Ireland and saved much bloodshed, was brought down by his love affair with a married woman.

Most allegations of sexual impropriety have no bearing on the fitness for high office of the perpetrator. Public officials are held to a standard that does not exist for entertainers, or for the journalists who are the accusers in these cases.

Only one case comes to mind where the public was served by the revelations-and it was a case I came to know well. In the summer of 1963, at the London *Sunday Mirror*, where I worked, two exquisite young women haunted our offices. They had a story to tell that involved high jinks at the highest level in government and society. And for money and recognition, they were keen to tell their tale.

The women were Christine Keeler and Mandy Rice-Davies. Christine was lissome and beautiful and Mandy was chubby and sexy. Their story was this: They had both been sleeping with important people, engaging in orgies, and generally living it up in a way that would make Hugh Heffner blush. Mandy was having a good time, largely at the Cliveden estate of Lord and Lady Astor, while Christine was sleeping with the war minister, John Profumo, and the Soviet military attaché, Yevgeny Ivanov.

It was juicy and well documented stuff. Yet *The Sunday Mirror* declined to publish their story—not because it cared a fig for intrusion into private lives, but because it feared both libel writs and reprisals from high government officials.

Then as now, British tabloid newspapers believe that intrusion into the private lives of anyone of importance was part of their mission, and a great help to circulation.

Eventually, what came to be known as the Profumo Affair got into the British press by the back door. The story leaked out by dribs and drabs, and the whole press went mad.

The public good was not so much saving Britain from the pillow-talk of the war minister being conveyed to the Soviet Embassy, but rather that the trusting British public got a hard look at its ruling class and its excesses.

In the United States, the press once observed a code of silence about our leaders here. Congressmen frequently dallied, with the knowledge of the press, and nothing was said. Jack Kennedy trysted with abandon, to the knowledge of many newspaper people, and silence prevailed. Was that so bad?

Were the members of Congress better or worse for their excesses? Was Kennedy an inferior president because of it?

The real damage comes because the most gifted often have been struck untimely—sometimes frequently—by Cupid's arrow. As a result, they do not offer themselves as candidates for public office because of fear of hurtful revelations. This denies the nation a huge reservoir of talent and hands government over to the gray sons and daughters of rectitude. And, oh, the hypocrisy!

The members of the Fourth Estate never have found it necessary to practice abstention any more than public officials. Public office should not be for the saintly but for the gifted and able.

February 24, 2004

DEMOCRACY IS A HARD SELL—ASK THE BRITISH

I went to Vietnam a few years ago with a colleague. He had spent the Vietnam War on the campus of the University of California, Berkeley. And he had one purpose:

to apologize to the Vietnamese for the war. He apologized to government officials, the staff of the guesthouse in Hanoi where we stayed, and to every Vietnamese we interviewed. They all stared back blankly at him.

The war was over and the Vietnamese had other things on their mind—like penetrating the American market, attracting American investment, and wondering concernedly about what America was going to do about China. After all, they had been fighting with the Chinese for 4,000 years and they saw China, not the United States, as their problem.

In the end, I took my colleague to one side and said: "Forget it, they don't care."

The time has come for someone to take the right people in Bush administration to one side and explain to them that the world is not yearning for democracy. There are nations that have shown a predisposition to democracy, and they mostly have achieved it through struggle. But there are great areas where democracy is just a word, not an aspiration; where there are other longstanding items on the agenda that do not include the form of government that works so well in the West, but that has not been embraced in the Middle East, much of Africa, or large parts of Asia.

Before Hong Kong reverted to Chinese control, the wily Hong Kongans embraced British Common Law, capitalism and civil liberties, but not democracy. They were content to be ruled with a loose rein from London. The business of Hong Kong was business. And so long as the political arrangements favored the pursuit of wealth, the residents of Hong Kong didn't care.

Britain tried to introduce democracy before Hong Kong was handed over to China, but that was an afterthought. It was never part of the bargain between the people and their administration.

The British knew something about this indifference to democracy, but dutifully installed democratic systems of government among the departing members of the British Empire. With the notable exception of India, most of these democracies were short-lived. A lack of a sense of the virtue of a democratic system, combined with the absence of strong independent institutions in these former colonies, doomed them. Some of these democracies sputter intermittently, like Malaysia and Pakistan. But there are more Burmas and Zimbabwes than there are shining lights of government-for-the-people-by-the-people.

The enemies of democracy are corruption, theocracy, tribalism, and the normal inclination of the powerful to solidify power. In Africa, democracy was the easy route to a single-party state under an autocratic ruler. Malawi, Tanzania, Zambia and Zimbabwe all fell victim to that infection.

Now the United States is zealously promoting democracy in the Middle East and Afghanistan, where it has never taken root, and probably once more in Haiti. The chances of success are not good.

Then there is the problem of democracies that do not behave has their sponsors in the West had hoped: Allende's Chile, Chavez's Venezuela, and, yes, Aristide's Haiti.

In some of the failed democracies, the ballot box simply has been the route to dictatorship.

Where Islam is the dominant religion, it can be the route to theocracy. That is why free elections were set aside in Algeria, why elections are fraught in Turkey and Pakistan, and why George W. Bush may have a footnote in history as the man who won and lost Iraq and Afghanistan.

Churchill famously said that democracy was the worst form of government, except for all those other forms that have been tried from time to time. Unfortunately, in much of the world, despite the ardent salesmanship in this administration, Churchill's meaning is not understood. In a country where a coup d'etat seems a more efficient way to change the government than an election campaign, democracy is a hard sell.

One day, China may embrace democracy, under pressure from its private sector. But it needs to get there without revolution. Even as we are selling democracy in much of the world, a really important country, Russia, appears to be going the other way, under the autocratic and self-satisfied Vladimir Putin.

Telling the world that it will be a better place if it is democratic can be remarkably like apologizing for the Vietnam War, when our erstwhile enemy already has moved on to a new agenda.

March 2, 2004

TO HAVE AND HAVE NOT—PAPERWORK AS DESTINY

I cannot remember now whether I was nine or 10 when I first, in my uncertain hand, wrote a note that would have sway over another man's liberty. Certainly, it was before I was 11.

The place was Rhodesia, now Zimbabwe, and domestic servants had to have a "pass" to travel freely in residential areas. The notes were routine, but they fit into a system of racial separation and management.

If you were white, you had the authority to grant dispensation to black domestic servants. More onerous were the passes, or "stupas," which every indigenous inhabitant of that British colony had to carry. It was a single sheet, lined on both sides, on which each date of the bearer's employment or dismissal was noted, along with the annual poll tax payment of 1 pound sterling.

The insult was not so much that this document—really an identity card—had to be carried by every adult who sought employment or held a job. It was that it was only black males who were singled out for the indignity. Whites, people of mixed race and Asians were exempt.

Rhodesia was not as oppressive in its racial laws as neighboring South Africa, but they were there. They also instilled in me a horror of people's lives' being dependent on a piece of paper. I have seen refugees clutching their documents, whether they had escaped from Iron Curtain countries or war or famine, or other upheaval. In 1956, I saw refugees from Hungary coming off airplanes in Rhodesia. Frightened, alarmed and hopeful, they clutched the paperwork they had been given as the only enduring statement of their being.

In the 1980s, I traveled out of Cuba on a plane which every night ferried Cuban refugee parents to Miami in a little-publicized humanitarian undertaking. But, oh, the paperwork. The crew on the charter flight would spend hours checking it, assuring its holders that it was in order, and helping them fill out the forms they would need in Miami. They were frightened people, defined by a sheaf of paperwork, which they were scared to let the cabin crew lift off their tray tables.

The first time I crossed the Allenby Bridge from Jordan into Israel, my bus, loaded with American journalists, swept by a checkpoint where hundreds of Arabs sat on the ground clutching their papers, waiting to be admitted.

It is the paper that legitimizes, the more so for the illiterate and the have-nothings. The last line on those Rhodesian identity papers read: "His signature or mark." I never saw one that was not signed with an "X."

For many years, my father lived in Botswana, where a stream of vagrant young men would come to him to write them a reference. They were not references. They were pieces of paper that defined and comforted the holder. They usually read something like this: "The bearer is (his name), to the best of my knowledge, an upstanding person. He is in great need and would appreciate any work, however lowly, that you could give him. He is hungry and needs food."

These simple notes, plus a meal, would seemingly restart a failed life and conveyed immediate dignity. In Africa, in Latin America, in Eastern Europe, I have felt guilty for no more indulgence than being entitled first to a British passport, and later to an American passport. British passports used to carry the imperial inscription: "Let the bearer pass without let or hindrance on command of Her Majesty the Queen." American passports, of course, are less grandiose. Now the British carry utilitarian European Union passports.

Yet, you can feel guilt for that little book that establishes that you can come and go in the world as you please. And should you lose it, you can have it replaced in a timely fashion.

Those who are not born to accept the normality of their legitimacy, those who clutch such documents as they can, know all about "let and hindrance."

One wonders how many illegal immigrants in the United States crave the documents that will make them whole and safe. Of course, they have broken the law in coming here without documentation. But it is hard to avoid the thought that the motive for their wrongdoing was the common human aspiration for betterment.

These thoughts came to me while I was waiting for a blood test at a commercial laboratory with a cross-section of rural Americans clutching their primary-care-physicians' referral papers, if they had insurance cards. They appeared to be worried about whether their insurance would cover the costs and what the blood tests would reveal—from HIV to cancer to diabetes.

As refugees surge across the frontiers of the world, I am glad that I have my paperwork in order. I would not want to be part of the fraternity of the dispossessed by documentation.

March 17, 2004

CONSERVATIVES ARE FROM MARS, LIBERALS FROM VENUS

Conservatives are from Mars and liberals are from Venus. Honestly. Because they are culturally and dogmatically opposed, they both feel aggrieved by the media.

What makes conservatives so mad is they believe that mainstream newspapers and television are biased against them. What makes liberals so mad is the domination of talk radio by right-wing commentators and the ascendancy of Fox News.

More interesting than the charges traded are the cultural preferences of Martians and Venusians. Martians clearly have affinity for radio. They are assuaged or stimulated by Rush Limbaugh, Sean Hannity, and their many imitators. They have nearly given up the fight over newspapers. Avowedly politically conservative newspapers, like *The Washington Times* and *The New York Sun,* have failed to penetrate very far in their markets. *The Washington Post* is not threatened by *The Washington Times,* and *The New York Times* is scarcely aware of *The New York Sun.*

Radio is another matter. Commercial radio belongs to the conservatives in content and audience, and it is probably unassailable. But assailed it is being, albeit in a rather quixotic way.

On March 31, Air America Radio goes on the air in four markets: New York, Chicago, Los Angeles and San Francisco. It is planned to be liberal talk radio, liberal satire, with the occasional old-fashioned discussion group. The name on the marquee is Al Franken, the former "Saturday Night Live" comedian, who has found a niche in bashing conservatives. He is Ann Coulter's counterpoint.

Traditional talk radio is syndicated, but Air America is trying for network—all-liberal-all-the-time. It is both ambitious and improbable. Rather than penetrating the market with specific programs, Air America is trying to do something quite different. And the only way it can do it is to buy broadcast time from weak stations broadcasting to minority communities.

This, says Adam Clayton Powell III, is an illiberal act to begin with. He castigated the plan on the Washington PBS program "Evening Exchange." So, the project has begun with controversy among liberals before a word has been broadcast.

Liberals have been saying for a long time that they needed to find an alternative on the dial to Limbaugh. But they seem to be planning something much more expensive and less likely to succeed than if they had developed individual programs in syndication.

There is no doubt that Franken can find an audience: he has with his books. So, it is surprising that investors in Air America did not put their money behind a daily, syndicated Franken rather than going for something much grander being aired on bought time to select audiences. It is a mystery, and we shall see.

My guess is that Franken and some other individuals, like Liz Winstead, may find an audience and even a loyal following. But who wants 16 hours a day of unremittant political diatribe. Even Limbaugh failed in television and has had to withdraw to radio.

Where the liberals do seem to be gaining-and substantially-is on the Internet. Howard Dean proved the power of the liberal Internet community. And it is on the

Internet that one of the truly liberal U.S. publications, *Salon.com,* has established itself with millions of hits, making it a major daily contender.

Stuart Stevens, consulting producer of TV's "K-Street," has cleverly illustrated the difference between conservatives and liberals, and their respective attitudes to the media. He says that the difference between liberals and conservatives over the vexing media issue is that most liberals would like to be journalists, and most conservatives would never dream of it.

There, I think, is the cultural divide that informs political attitudes to journalism. And somewhere in the cultural divide is the Republican support for rightwing journals of opinion (*The Weekly Standard, The National Review, The American Spectator, Human Events, Insight, National Spotlight,* etc.) and hundreds of talk shows.

So, good luck, Air America Radio, but you may not be producing the product liberals feel deprived of—they favor different media.

Finally, the Martians, true-blue critics of the allegedly liberal mainstream media, conveniently forget that the powerful spokesmen for their cause, people like Cal Thomas, George Will, Charles Krauthammer, are known to us all because they are carried on the op-ed pages of these, er, liberal newspapers.

March 24, 2004

WHY IRAQ? THE DEBATE IS RE-OPENED

There is something awesome about the administration, any administration, when it mobilizes. The Bush administration has mobilized against one man and one book. It has thrown its enormous capacity to command the attention of the media into high gear.

One can imagine the excitement in the White House. One can imagine the thrill of finding a remark that contradicts Richard Clarke's book, by the author when he worked at the White House. One can imagine the high-fives when Condoleezza Rice acquits herself well on a television program. One can imagine the sense of "we've got him now" that must permeate the West Wing after a smooth and statesmanlike performance by Colin Powell. One can imagine the rush when Dick Cheney appears on the Limbaugh show. Red meat for the base.

If Clarke, himself, were less urbane, skillful and assured, there would be a moment of sympathy for him. As it is, he is a very capable David against the White House's Goliath.

But when it is all finished, when it is simmered down, when the news cycle has a different topic, what did it all mean? Did the White House serve its own purpose in throwing its best into the fray and did it exacerbate its own vulnerability rather than dispose of Clarke and his charges?

This modus operandi is now a Washington standard: denigrate your accuser; intimidate his or her supporters; question his or her veracity; impugn his or her motives; hint at venality; and leave your accuser unemployed and unemployable, tainted for all time. Nixon tried it, Clinton indulged in it, and with the barrage against Clarke, the Bush White House has perfected it. Yet, Clarke has left his mark.

Clarke's mark is to indelibly associate George W. Bush with a pathological passion for invading Iraq. Foreign policy circles in Washington suspected this from the company Bush kept during his presidential election campaign. But event he doubters were thrown off by weapons of mass destruction. And importantly, by British Prime Minister Tony Blair's unflinching commitment to the Bush agenda.

There is a resident confidence among the Washington intelligentsia that the British enjoy a unique enlightenment in foreign affairs. It worked like this: Bush is suspect but Blair is the gold standard.

The Clarke book has reopened the debate on why we invaded Iraq. Was it because Bush and Blair really believed Saddam Hussein had weapons of mass destruction? Or was it because they believed that Saddam and his heirs were so heinously evil that there was a moral duty to end their rule?

The debate is raging again, as it did before the invasion. What was the real agenda? Was it really about oil, about Israel, or was it about the assassination attempt on the first President Bush? Or was it an overwhelming sense of unfinished business from the people who were in charge during the Persian Gulf War, and who have resurfaced in this administration—Cheney, Powell and Donald Rumsfeld, and their intellectual spear-carriers, Douglas Feith, Richard Perle and Paul Wolfowitz?

The Israel argument is winning in Washington salons. It goes like this: If the status quo were to continue in the Middle East, eventually a weapon of mass destruction would find its way to Palestinian hands, and it would be used against Tel Aviv—killing untold numbers of Israelis and Palestinians, but effectively ending the viability of the state of Israel.

This argument holds that the Bush team believed that a show of American strength in the region was imperative; that a democracy in Iraq would lead to reform throughout the region; and that with this changed dynamic, an Israeli-Palestinian accord could be reached. Anyway, that is what the political scientists, professional and amateur, are arguing about at present.

Richard Clarke, whatever his fate under the Bush administration barrage, has triggered that debate, which fathers the question about why the administration was so anxious to invade Iraq.

March 31, 2004

IRAQ: THE HORROR TODAY, THE CATASTROPHE TOMORROW

The situation in Iraq is deteriorating faster than even the most pessimistic had anticipated. The word "quagmire," as it was used during the Vietnam War, is again current. It is inappropriate. In Vietnam, we were fighting communist nationalists with leaders, a mission and a goal.

Iraq is something else. It is as though we have knocked over dozens of lethal wasps' nests and more angry wasps are taking to the air every day.

Even the most severe pessimists about the outcome of the U.S. invasion of Iraq had not calculated on the diversity of the uprising against coalition forces and embryonic Iraqi police force. Martyrdom is in the air in Iraq and it fuels a pernicious lust to kill and be killed. This is outside of the Western experience and beyond military resolution.

No matter how tolerant a religion Islam has been historically, and despite the prohibition against killing in the Koran, the Islam now manifested in Iraq is fired by a religious vision of very palpable rewards in the afterlife—rewards more defined than they are in Judaism and Christianity.

Cristina Odone, deputy editor of the British magazine *New Statesman*, writes in that magazine: "The martyr regards torture, interrogation or a spell in prison as merely a temporary, insignificant setback before the overwhelming and eternal happiness that awaits the defender of the faith."

Odone points out that all three of the major monotheistic religions have recognized martyrdom, and even used it for political purposes. But she says that it is at a high point in current Middle Eastern Moslem theology. Also, she says that the distinction between temporal existence and eternity is well articulated in Islam, and particularly Shi'a Islam, and is reiterated in contemporary sermons.

Whereas Judaism and Christianity seem to have put martyrdom aside, it has become a primary weapon for those who seek to damage or overthrow the Western ideal. Odone says: "The message, deriding the status quo and despising earthly power, is inevitably subversive. . . . The dramatic contrast between the here-and-now and the hereafter offers plenty of scope for unscrupulous interpretation by leaders with a political agenda."

So it is that power has passed to the imams who have no hesitation in telling their followers that the present life is worthless and that they must hurry to the next in order to receive their real being. The imams codify heaven with a certainty that no rabbi or Christian preacher would think of doing.

Young Moslems are given very certain guarantees of the benefits of life after martyrdom. Imams preach the hereafter as though they were selling luxury automobiles on television. The good times begin to roll on death, and the rewards of martyrdom can be calibrated.

In the West, many of us have laughed when have learned that imams have told their followers that they can expect to be given 72 virgins in heaven. That is a much harder sell than clouds and angels with harps. Virulent Islamic fundamentalism, therefore, degrades the value of life and works against the development of a livable civil society.

Critics of the Bush administration feared that post-Saddam Hussein Iraq would descend into civil war between the contesting Shi'a and Sunni branches of Islam and the ethnic Kurds. What is transpiring is a hell not even conceived by the Bush critics. It is a hell of factional fighting between independent religious militias against each other and against coalition forces. There is no place to sue for peace or to terminate the violence by eradicating its leadership.

President Bush said that no matter what, the United States would hand over civil authority to the Iraqi authorities on June 30 and that U.S. troops would remain to keep order. But now, all the troops can do is to swat at individual wasps and knock over more nests, producing more wasps. Laying the blame on al-Qaeda, which now has a role, and taking out its leadership will not subdue the forces that have been unleashed.

Things could not have gone worse in Iraq. Its future is gloomy in the extreme: bloodshed today and more bloodshed tomorrow.

When the British withdrew from India, dividing the country into Pakistan and East Pakistan (now Bangladesh), they expected violence. But they did not contemplate its extent nor the loss of 3 million lives.

When U.S. forces are finally withdrawn from Iraq, we will have to contemplate similar consequences except, unlike the British experience in India, with the power of martyrdom unleashed, we know it will be very terrible.

April 7, 2004

RADIO: THE REALLY SHOCKING JOCK IS MICHAEL POWELL

The fact that Clear Channel Communications has dropped shock jock Howard Stern from its stations that carry him should be of no concern. The suits at Clear Channel should have rung up Stern years ago and said, "You're boorish and heavy-handed, and your endless sexual suggestiveness grates."

If they had done that and then cancelled Stern for good broadcasting reasons, one would applaud Clear Channel—which owns more than 1,000 radio stations—for trying to do something about the quality of programming. Instead, they canned Stern to appease members of Congress and to rekindle their love affair with Michael Powell, the chairman of the Federal Communications Commission.

Clear Channel, with revenues of over $8 billion, hopes that Powell will prevail not in improving the quality of broadcasting, nor in saving sensitive listeners from Stern's crudities, but in allowing Clear Channel to own even more radio stations. Neither Powell nor Clear Channel has shown any interest whatsoever in the quality, diversity, creativity or community service of American broadcasting.

Since broadcasting has been deregulated, the broadcasting industry has treated Powell as its agent in Washington, D.C. And he has not let them down.

At its best, radio is one of the truly great media. It is flexible and inexpensive. Radio reporters do not have to lug great quantities of equipment; they can be on the scene of the news faster than television reporters, and they can file way ahead of newspaper reporters.

Yet the broadcasting industry has reduced radio to inconsequence. Its formula is Top 40; in country, jazz, rock. And for the few stations that play classical music, the formula is—you guessed it—Top 40.

But Powell's intention is to reward the giants in broadcasting, letting them acquire even more stations for even more formula broadcasting. Right behind Clear Channel in the station stakes is Infinity, which is owned by Viacom International Inc., and which competes with Clear Channel for the rush to the bottom.

If Powell has ever used his office to advocate better broadcasting, the development and promotion of local talent, or innovation in music and community service, that speech has not been reported. Does he really believe that we have the best radio that we possibly could have? He has just leveled a $495,000 fine on Clear Channel for Stern's transgressions. Shock, horror! The FCC has decided that while it is quite all right to insult people who listen to radio by appealing to the lowest common denominator, it, under Powell, is going to save listeners from dirty words and sexual innuendo. That should improve the moral fiber of the nation.

The hypocrisy of the FCC's action against Clear Channel, and Clear Channel's pusillanimity in censoring its shock jocks in the name of decency is on par with Claude Rains's discovery that people are gambling in Rick's Café in "Casablanca."

Ostensibly, these money moralists are out to save the children. Give us a break, Chairman Powell. One cannot turn on a computer without being besieged with pornography, and obscene language spews from cable television and is beyond the reach of Powell and his merry men.

There is obscenity in radio. It is the obscenity that this local medium of entertainment and service has been confiscated by companies like Clear Channel, Infinity Broadcasting Corporation, Westwood One, Inc., and Bonneville International Corporation for the greater enrichment of their principals.

Quality broadcasting does not pay, they say. That is not true. It is just more expensive and more of a risk to experiment with alternative programs; and there is no mechanism in companies that own hundreds of stations to cultivate interesting alternatives. Are we never to have another radio play produced in America? Are we never to have original music played on any station? Is there no future for talented people in any part of radio except advertising sales?

If the broadcasting conglomerates could raise their eyes briefly from the bottom line, they would learn that National Public Radio, with all of its faults, has 10 million listeners-and it manages that with one station in each market. Perchance, it is on to something. Now the avowedly dull C-SPAN radio is finding an audience that commercial broadcasting does not want to believe exists.

The FCC, our public defender, should worry less about sex and more about the needs of listeners. Whose airwaves are they, anyway?

April 14, 2004

THE DEMOCRATIC ANGUISH
THAT DARE NOT SPEAK ITS NAME

There is a pain in the breast of the Democratic Party; a lump that reminds the professionals that all is not well. There is a fear among Democrats, which they dare not speak of in public, that they may have chosen the wrong candidate for the presidency in Sen. John Kerry. In brief, they worry that he is a clunker.

These fears, private and profound, have risen in the last three weeks as George W. Bush has had the most tumultuous time of his presidency.

First, things became unglued in Iraq; second, Richard Clarke lifted the veil in the war on terror; and third, Bob Woodward tore the veil off, revealing an obsessed president more concerned with taking out Saddam Hussein than with prosecuting the war on terrorism.

Bush's defenses have been down, the Democrats argue, yet Kerry has failed to land a blow. He is lost in a fog of words, explaining himself, seeking the middle ground when the time for that has passed, and generally is failing to invigorate his own base, let alone convert those precious swing voters who will decide all in November.

Additionally, even Kerry's own supporters find it hard to argue that he is likeable. Indeed, they recycle smart remarks about his woodenness, elitist background and confused record in voting, it would seem, both for and against the war in Iraq, or at least the money to pay for it.

The waspish columnist, Tina Brown, likens Kerry to a medieval cardinal. And another journalist says he looks like none of the Novocain he has ever had from a dentist has worn off.

Words are vital in politics and have been since the time of the Greeks. Oratory is nearly all in elections. The problem with Kerry, his detractors in the Democratic Party say, is that his Niagara Falls of words is incoherent, suggesting that the underlying ideas are also shapeless. Can Kerry get on message if he is unclear about what his message is?

Kerry's slow and confused start in the campaign has left many of his Democratic supporters believing that a Democrat will return to the White House only if Bush implodes, not because Kerry is able to signpost a better path.

Kerry, without the benefit of having been a governor, and having to subdue his adversaries, talks and campaigns as though he were deliberating in the Senate. The campaign trail does not lend itself to deliberation. It lends itself to simple, repetitive messages delivered with as much rhetorical flourish as the candidate can muster.

Kerry may have studied Bush's technique of infinite repetition, but he has not learned from it. He comes across as a remote, rich man who empathizes with those in adversity but who does not understand their conditions. Liberals are gladdened by his Senate record in the same measure that they are distraught by his inability to go for the jugular or to explain a superior course of action.

While many Democrats want Kerry to go after Bush on his war in Iraq, his homeland security mess, and his endorsement of Israeli Prime Minister Ariel Sharon's plan for Palestine, they have been fed only fuzzy positions and unexpected endorsements of some of Bush's most controversial policies.

So it is that Democrats are muttering among themselves, heaping derision on Bush and struggling to find a passion for Kerry. Privately, they admit that Kerry—almost a man of another world—is a hard leader to follow. He is a difficult man for people who are angry and hurt, and who believe that there has been a tragic abandonment of the finest in American ideals, from the encroachment on civil liberties to preemptive war. They believe that Kerry needs to borrow from the Bush technique of simple messages delivered in clear, unambiguous language. They have fallen in behind Kerry's standard; now they desperately want him to raise it.

As Mike Allen of *The Washington Post* said recently, Democratic leaders admit that Kerry is less likeable than Bush. They even talk about a "likeability deficit."

So the Democrats march to November, believing that we are facing one of the most important elections ever, with a sense that somehow they may have chosen the wrong leader.

They know if Kerry wins in November, it will be because he is The Other Candidate, not because he is John Kerry.

April 21, 2004

AFRICA: THE CONTINENT THAT KEEPS LOSING ITS HEAD

Western cameras capture only a thimbleful of Africa's oceans of suffering. Yet they are busy bringing out more images of misery and death than their audience can comprehend. There is genocide in Sudan, killing and mutilation in Congo, starvation in Malawi, Zambia and Zimbabwe, and murder in Uganda.

Where, old Africa hands like myself ask, are the hopeful and kind people of yesteryear? Where are the people who took back their land from colonialism, expecting to build great civilizations, to end subsistence farming, to see industry flourish and education transform expectations from the humble to the magnificent?

Gone, it appears, to the Kalashnikov and the land mine, the dictator and the fool, who have more often than not marched their countries and their people to destitution and violence, while ignoring the ravages of disease and hunger. Their tools are tribal hatred, racial hatred, superhuman indifference and monumental self-aggrandizement. Amin, Banda, Mobutu, Taylor and a string of other strongmen have come, destroyed and gone. They have left little behind that anyone can build on.

We call them failed states, but they are beyond that. They are uncountries. They are places where abused people squat on eroded land, hoping for the generosity of others to feed them and the mercy of God to protect them.

How does it all start? When did Robert Mugabe, the leader of Zimbabwe, who came to power looking wise and profound, begin his journey south, taking with him a once-prosperous and harmonious country that seemed immune to the ills that spread from his northern border to East and West Africa, and as far as the Sahara Desert? Maybe it was the moment when he decided that legal process was an affront to his presidential authority and his stature as the man who ended colonialism in Rhodesia (now Zimbabwe), my homeland.

From wise leader and protector of a small jewel of a country, Mugabe became incensed—and maybe insane—about the slow rate at which farms owned by whites were being turned over to landless Africans. He encouraged gangs of thugs to destroy the farms, uproot the farmers and drive off their workers.

As the pace picked up, so did the brutality and insanity. The infrastructure of the farms was destroyed, animals—both livestock and pets—were mutilated and left to die, and many farmers and their workers were murdered. Most of those taking over the farms had neither the inclination nor the resources to farm. Now the farms lie derelict, subject to severe soil erosion.

The very best farms were given to Mugabe's cronies. Now after all the horror, all the bloodshed, Zimbabwe, once a net exporter of corn and other cereal crops, faces annual starvation and needs world food aid to keep its people alive. AIDS is ravaging the country, foreign currency reserves are all but dried up, and Mugabe is building himself a retirement palace.

But Mugabe has one export left. He has sent a delegation of "land resettlement experts" to his neighbor Namibia to get the whole business of catastrophe started there. Already the president of Namibia—a vast desert country in the southwest of Africa, with a sparse population and huge mineral wealth—has a campaign to drive out his commercial (white) farmers in the name of agrarian justice. Some land redistribution has been going on with proper compensation. But the Namibian president, Sam Nujoma, has felt outclassed by Mugabe, less of an African patriot. Now he has upped his rhetoric against the farmers and has imported Zimbabwean thugs to affect land seizure—so he can take his place as an African despot.

Not only is Namibia hugely rich in diamonds, tungsten, iron, uranium and other metals, but it also has a population of less than 2 million people in a land area half the size of California. In good years, when it rains, Namibia can feed itself. In bad years, it must import food. The Bushmen and some European sailors called Namibia (formerly Southwest Africa) "the land that God hated." But God packed it with mineral wealth as no other part of the world; and there is plenty of land for everyone to farm, if they can deal with the adversity of the climate.

One would think that Nujoma would concentrate on exploitation of the mineral wealth and the welfare of the 22 percent of the population who are HIV-positive rather than try to emulate Mugabe's disasters. But he plans to go ahead and, in due course, we will send photographers there to capture all the horrors of human starvation: distended bellies, stick limbs, sunken cheeks and eyes, waiting in the dirt for death.

What in God's name motivates African "leaders"?

April 28, 2004

THE EXTRAORDINARY TURMOIL
IN IRAQ AND THE CALM AT HOME

April was the cruelest month.

For the Bush administration, everything that could go wrong in Iraq did. The American death toll went up, a young cleric in Fallujah defied the United States, kidnapping became a tool of the insurgency, and allegations of abuse in U.S. military-controlled prisons damaged U.S. credibility.

Add to that defections from the alliance and emboldened supporters of the president second-guessing the Pentagon. Sens. Richard Lugar and Chuck Hagel, among others, joined the chorus of those calling for more troops to be sent to Iraq. Feisty William Kristol, editor of the pro-war *Weekly Standard*, accused the administration of "panicking" and also demanded, as he has for a long time, more troops.

Meanwhile, the deadline for handing over sovereignty to the Iraqis is approaching inexorably. While the president's supporters believe there should be flexibility on the date of the handover, Bush himself insists it will take place on June 30, no matter what or to whom.

Bush, at his East Room press conference, laid the responsibility for the next Iraqi government, which will hold power until elections are held in January 2005, on United Nations' envoy Lakhdar Brahimi.

Incredibly, Bush is looking to the U.N. to solve the governing crisis, to disband the U.S.-appointed governing council and to replace it with a whole government, including a president, a prime minister and 25 Cabinet secretaries. The administration has devolved this critical responsibility on one man, who will have to exercise superhuman judgment in a country where the U.N. is still very unpopular because of its corrupt administration of the oil-for-food program during Saddam Hussein's last decade in power. John Cushman of *The New York Times* said on the PBS television program "White House Chronicle" that the U.N. is so hated in Iraq today that when it announced a press conference in Baghdad recently, it described itself only as a "friendly international organization."

Brahimi may lose sleep at night, wondering how he will bring off the greatest diplomatic coup in modern history. He may pace the floor, identifying with the predicament of another U.N. servant, Hans Blix, who was charged with locating Iraqi weapons of mass destruction and who was reviled by the Bush administration when he came up empty-handed.

Will Brahimi face the same fate: the fall guy if his new Iraqi government does not take root? Brahimi may want to have a word with Blix about the lot of international diplomats. He may also want to get the name of Blix's literary agent: Blix at least came out with a best-selling book.

After a year of occupation, and quite stupendous zig-zagging on appointments, caucuses and elections, the United States has handed the whole responsibility for the future political arrangements of Iraq to a lone Egyptian: Brahimi.

The events of April have not checked the president's insouciance, but they have diminished the self-confidence of the administration. As the summer rolls in, and U.S. troops face greater adversity, administration figures are, for the first time, asking themselves, "Where will it end?" The president has said time and again that it will end in freedom and democracy for Iraq. It is getting harder and harder to find anyone who, off the record, will agree with him.

Officially, "quagmire" is a dirty word around the White House, but it is used quite freely in private conversations. Speculation is no longer about democracy in Iraq, but about the two unacceptable options: civil war and theocracy. One White House staffer told me, "After all this, we could end up with a mirror image of Iran."

Yet at home, the political skills which seem so lacking abroad are everywhere in evidence. Bush has recovered in the polls and his operatives have effectively kept the presumptive Democratic nominee, Sen. John Kerry, wallowing in Vietnam. Kerry has yet to reach Iraq.

Kerry could learn something from his opponent. The Bush strategy, which is deadly effective, is to "stay on message." Kerry seems in need of refining his message and then sticking with it. For all of the pain and turmoil of Iraq, the Bush campaign has distanced the president from the day-to-day travails in the Middle East and has promoted him as a leader.

If Republicans have their problems abroad, Democrats have them at home. And the Bushites know that elections are seldom decided on foreign policy.

May 5, 2004

EMPIRE, ANYONE? I DON'T THINK SO

I grew up in Southern Rhodesia (now Zimbabwe) in the remains of the day of the British Empire. Now as talk of American empire ricochets around Washington, even as we are aghast at the excesses in the Abu Ghraib prison, I wonder if anyone has any idea of what made the British Empire work.

Britain controlled first and foremost the technology. Firearms belonged to the British and they were kept in British hands. Later came the telegraph and the railroads: technologies that opened up the land but were the exclusive province of the European conquerors.

But there was more to it than that. The British believed in building on what they found, not in dismantling indigenous institutions. They hung chains of office around the necks of tribal chiefs and enhanced their status rather than diminishing it.

More important was the philosophy of empire. At its core, it believed in the superiority of its own race and institutions. But it was moderated by a belief, deeply held, that with empire went responsibility to indigenous people.

To control its excesses, it evolved a language of empire, of colonization, which promoted nobility in action and words.

Officers who failed, or committed abuses, were expected to "fall on their swords." By the 19th century, it no longer meant suicide, but it did mean resignation and disgrace. The phrase *noblesse oblige* permeated government thought and action, and established protections and dignities for the subjugated peoples. Their "kith and kin" were to be respected and handed out justice equal to that meted out to the colonizers. At all times, one was to be a lady or a gentleman.

Some of the British implementation in Africa was positively socialist. Domestic servants, in addition to their meager wages, by law had to be fed—and generously fed. A domestic servant had to be given stewing beef twice a week and 15 pounds of maize meal (cornmeal) once a week. Of course, this was much more than any individual could eat, and it provided for many hungry mouths among the unemployed.

Likewise, medicine, though limited in its availability to large urban hospitals, was free to Africans. Schooling, also limited, was free, too. In addition to government schools, there were dozens of Christian mission schools that augmented the public effort. It was not universal health care and it was not universal education. But it was a reflection of the settlers' sense of moral responsibility.

In Southern Rhodesia, police were few and far between, until the outbreak of the war of independence in the 1970s. Until then, the police were proud that no prisoner had lost his or her life in custody—a record just slightly better than that in Great Britain itself.

On the upside, these settlers operated their outpost of empire with wisdom and generosity. On the downside, they seized for themselves the riches of the country, taking some of the best land, and imposed a system of dominance by a small white minority over a much larger indigenous population. There was racial segregation and denial of political rights. It was benign but futile.

Britain's colonial experience was uneven. Some countries were conquered. Others, such as Northern Rhodesia (now Zambia) and Nyasaland (now Malawi), sought the protection of the British Crown and became protectorates. Still, other parts of Africa, of less interest to Britain, were said to be held under the Queen's suzerainty—a loose arrangement to keep out other colonial powers and to protect trade.

By the 1960s, whatever the nomenclature of empire, the Empire was collapsing. British Prime Minister Harold Macmillan acknowledged this when he spoke of "winds of change." One by one, the colonies, protectorates and other entities began life as independent countries. Ghana, Kenya, Malawi, Nigeria, Tanganyika, Zambia, Zanzibar, in Africa alone, said farewell to the Empire. India had departed in 1948, followed in due course by Burma, Malaysia, Singapore and Sri Lanka.

Oddly, the imperial experience was probably happiest in Sri Lanka, then known as Ceylon. The only execution ever carried out, I was told by a Sri Lankan historian, was of an Englishman by the English for crimes against the regime.

There was good and there was evil in the Empire. But it could not have been brought about without the fundamental respect for human rights that it embodied-before human rights was so titled.

The British learned to administer empire, and they often learned it at a high cost, from the Muslim rebellion in India in 1857 all the way to the Mau Mau uprising in Kenya around 100 years later. It is worth remembering that two of the most ignominious failures of the British Empire were in the Middle East, when it simply abandoned its responsibilities. The first was the withdrawal from Palestine in 1948. The second was 16 years earlier, when the mighty Empire threw up its hands and pulled out of a place called Iraq.

To talk of empire today is to talk nonsense; and if one is to try it, the conqueror must be conditioned for the burden of the undertaking.

May 12, 2004

MEMORIAL DAY ECHOES ON THE NATIONAL MALL

Monuments are tricky. One hopes that art and architecture combine to capture the genius of an individual or the sentiment of the essence of the horror and sacrifice of war. Most fail in some measure.

Washington, D.C., is full of monuments that are mostly ignored: the Civil War Nurses Memorial, the Titanic Memorial and the Boy Scouts Memorial, to name a few. The Lincoln Memorial broods over all and symbolizes the clash in monuments between the neoclassical and the romantic.

But it is the Vietnam Veterans Memorial that has raised the monumental bar. Emotional and evocative, it speaks to the division that war created. For the veterans, it is the recognition of blood and heroism denied to them in their homecoming. To opponents of that war, it is an indictment of it.

Now, belatedly, comes the World War II Memorial, nestled in the middle of one of the greatest city vistas anywhere: the National Mall. To reduce the cataclysm of that war, which affected every corner of the globe, to stone and water may be an undertaking too far.

The architect, Friedrich St. Florian, has been brave and bold. But in the judgment of many, particularly architecture critics, he has fallen short. It is almost as though he approached his work with so much sensitivity to concerns about the memorial that he has drained it of any emotion. It has been called stiff and sterile. The columns, marking the states and territories that contributed 16 million men and women, are stark. They edify without capturing the human dimension of that great struggle.

In time we will come to love this permanent addition to the Washington landscape, just as we have come to love the Washington Monument, which scarcely captures George Washington and does not make it as great architecture.

What was important this Memorial Day weekend was that it focused the nation once more on sacrifice and selflessness. Between the advertisements for car sales and store discounts, we remembered those who died-many too young to vote and too young to have known love.

I went to the World War II Memorial hoping that I would find an echo of my father and his friends, who survived the war but never quite got over it. I found my echo in the old men of the "greatest generation" acknowledging each other—some still sprightly, some confined to wheelchairs. They were satisfied and solemn; having been forgotten, they are now remembered. And the spirit of their generation and their time is enshrined in the heart of their nation's capital.

We should be rebuked by them; rebuked for mislaying the everyday spirit of duty and sacrifice of the 1940s. Young men lied about their ages, their health and their family commitments to do their bit for the war effort. For those who are still with us, this was a weekend of sentiment and majesty—a celebration of the human spirit ascendant.

I found the memorial, for all of its dancing fountains, dry and empty. But in the end, I am much more glad of it than I am critical. Glad because we can raise people of such humble, noble selflessness, and they are remembered.

June 2, 2004

REAGAN: A LOCHINVAR FOR HIS TIME

PARIS—Now, let Reagan be Reagan: the man and the myth at one in death.

The measure of Ronald Reagan should be not so much by his devoted associates as by those who found virtue in him when they could have found fault and enmity. Two stand out, each remarkable in their own way: Margaret Thatcher and Mikhail Gorbachev. Their endorsement—Thatcher's devotion and Gorbachev's respect—marks Reagan as standing very tall in the world. Even here in Paris, where Republican presidents traditionally are seen as dangerous, there is recognition that this cowboy, this film star turned statesman, did great things in the world.

History will take a long time in its assessment of Reagan. He is clearly not easy for historians, because of the simplicity of his programs and the untrammeled idealism of his philosophy. Already, Edmund Morris has failed with Reagan. Morris found so much of Reagan's life repetitive and simplistic that he was unable to produce the biography that he set out to write. To deal with what were the silent years during Reagan's ascent, Morris, respected and competent, had to revert to non-traditional artifice to fill out his book. Morris found no there there. But Thatcher and Gorbachev found a lot there.

There is no mystery. Reagan served big, sweeping, simple ideas, repeated them often and, for the rest, filled in with jokes and anecdotes. There was no long political struggle. He selected political ideas as he might have selected movie roles. Then he played them completely.

Reagan's gift to America was his simplest tenet: hopefulness. Appropriately, the bitterness of his years in the White House, the anger and fear among those who did not agree with him, is now laid aside, as the myth and the reality garland him as one of the great presidents.

More than most, Reagan had the genius to play to his strengths and to ignore all else; hence his detachment, his refuge in comedy and the flow of anecdotes. A nuclear scientist I know came out from briefing Reagan in near hysterics. He had wanted to enlighten the president about the safety of civilian nuclear technology. When he explained the internals of a light-water reactor to Reagan, the president interrupted with a long anecdote about a can opener and how he saw this as being analogous to what the speaker was trying to tell him. Reagan believed that he did not need to know about nuclear reactors because he employed people who did know and would make the right decisions.

So it was with much of Reagan's presidency. And two of its great blots reflect his incuriosity about the details of events: Lebanon and Iran-Contra. He was quick to take responsibility for the appalling loss of life at the Marine encampment in Beirut. But he was never able to tell Americans why the Marines were there or what the American role and purpose were. Likewise, Iran-Contra remained a mystery to him. He is quoted by Matthew Parris, the English writer, as saying in March 1987: "A few months ago I told the American people I did not trade arms for hostages. My heart and my best intentions still tell me that this is true, but the facts and the evidence tell me it is not."

Yet, we mourn Reagan almost as much for his naivete as for his steadfast opposition to communism, for his role in the downfall of the Soviet Union and, above all, for giving us a myth to believe in when we needed one.

People the world over long for mythological figures who stand above the fray. The world wept when Princess Diana was killed, but it wept for someone who did not actually exist. The myth was that Diana was a caring princess: unlike the rest of the aristocratic jet set, totally human and caring. The world deleted the fact that she was a manipulative, selfish and spoiled royal.

With Reagan, there is less to delete. He proved that sometimes there are simple solutions to complex problems. In that way, he was above politics.

But Reagan has left a legacy that is not worthy of his myth. Today's conservatism is Reagan stripped of the kindness and the good humor of the enterprise of government. Reagan, who loved to ride horses, said: "There is nothing so good for the inside of a man as the outside of a horse." He might be paraphrased to say: "There is nothing so good for a nation as a leader who can create myth."

John F. Kennedy gave us the first Camelot. The second was Reagan's.

June 9, 2004

CHITTY CHITTY BANG BANG ISN'T AN ENERGY POLICY

National Public Radio's delightful Tappet Brothers, Click & Clack, dissolved into laughter when a caller said he'd heard that a car could run on woodchips. The brothers just laughed and laughed—the hallmark of their very funny program, "Car Talk."

Alas, for once, the brothers were wrong. A vehicle can run on woodchips, but you wouldn't want to do it. It simply isn't a good way to go.

The technology was developed during World War II in both Germany and Japan. And it was used on some military vehicles. The technology is based on a low-grade gas, made from wood, charcoal or other organic material, which is gasified on the vehicle. The gas—methane not dissimilar from that which is found in landfills-will operate a normal engine with a power loss of about 50 percent and more environmental issues than can be thought up at an EPA Christmas party.

I know about this. My father, an inventive mechanic, got hold of one of these gasifiers and mounted it in the bed of a Ford pickup truck. It sort of worked. He would set off using gasoline and then switch to methane. The gasifier, stoked with charcoal, would start up with frightening noises and other disturbing side effects, including a 4-foot flame that shot out of it when he applied the truck's brakes. The family called it the "horrid, livid monster." It started brushfires, terrified other road users and caused the fire brigade to take an interest. Finally, it was retired so that it could be "perfected."

I mention the charcoal-fired truck only because I'm reminded of it every time a politician promotes some new-and-wacky alternative energy source.

Conservatives, like Vice President Cheney, and probably President Bush, believe there is more and more oil and gas to be discovered, and that subsidies and other encouragements for the extractive industries will bring these to market. The conservative cheering section hints at all sorts of technological wonders that will bring this about, plus, of course, relaxed regulation. A science writer in the conservative London *Daily Mail* recently proclaimed that there were no oil and gas shortages and that oil and gas would be released in huge quantities momentarily. A contributor to the ultra-right-wing magazine *Human Events* unearthed the old theory that oil and gas shortages are idiotic because microbial organisms in the earth are replenishing the reserves as we go. Meaning, in short, that oil and gas are self-renewing fossil fuels. The only known self-renewing fossil fuel is peat, and that takes thousands of years to replenish itself.

The administration now talks about conservation. But in a May 2001 speech, in Toronto, Cheney set the tone when he said: "Conservation may be a sign of personal virtue, but it is not sufficient basis for sound energy policy." With Saudi Arabia, the world's largest energy producer, wobbling, the vice president may be considering recanting, but he hasn't done so yet.

The Democrats, for their part, have swallowed the "alternative" energy concept whole. Sen. John Kerry and other Democrats talk about renewable energy in bland and general terms. They embrace the concept of using hydrogen for transportation. Bush also embraced it, in an act of political cunning. Neither side will admit that there is no source of hydrogen beyond reforming fossil fuels or cracking water with prodigious quantities of electricity. Prodigious quantities of electricity can only be obtained through nuclear power. And there's the rub.

The Democrats abhor nuclear power and the Republicans can't find anyone who will build one nuclear power plant, let alone dozens of them. If this continues, the hydrogen economy will be stillborn.

The other two renewables that have promise are photovoltaic solar cells and wind power. Both work extremely well but only when the sun is shining or the wind is blowing. Wind is the superior of the two technologies because it's cheaper and more available. The inconvenient thing about weather is that on the hottest and coldest days of the year, the wind doesn't blow. The East Coast of the United States gets very little wind in July and August, when it has its highest electricity demand. Go figure.

A sensible energy policy suggests more efficient cars, led by hybrids; more electrified railroads; a limit on the amount of natural gas used to produce electricity; and a fleet of new nuclear power plants that have passive safety features—i.e. plants that don't need mechanical devices to shut them down. Wind would have a secondary place; it can't be a primary electricity provider. Its place may indeed be in making hydrogen, where a windless day or month wouldn't be catastrophic.

The charcoal-burning car is an energy alternative. But like many energy alternatives, it isn't one worthy of consideration or political enthusiasm. That, I do know.

June 16, 2004

THE DAYS OF GLORY FOR THE NEOCONS ARE PAST

The neoconservatives, who have dominated foreign policy in the Bush administration, are under attack, not only from Democrats but also from old-line Republicans.

This loose confederation of like minds was more or less invented by the philosopher and author Irving Kristol. He became disillusioned with liberalism and moved to the right, espousing a new philosophy of American unilateralism in the context of free markets and overwhelming U.S. military strength.

Kristol's views attracted other disillusioned thinkers, who conceived a new vision of America in the world that placed Israel as a cornerstone in American foreign policy.

As this federation formed, it attracted Democrats who had supported the late Sen. Henry "Scoop" Jackson and his policies of liberalism-at-home and strength abroad. However, they turned against the liberalism at home philosophy and what they saw as the Nanny State. They attracted Richard Perle, former chairman of the Defense Policy Board, and Paul Wolfowitz, deputy secretary of defense.

Others pushed neoconservative philosophy from think tanks, notably the American Enterprise Institute. Soon they had their own media. Financed by Rupert Murdoch, *The Weekly Standard* was launched under the editorship of William Kristol, Irving's son. Murdoch's Fox News provided a television platform for the journalists and philosophers of the neocon movement.

Older conservative publications were eclipsed. And less intellectual conservative commentators, led by radio talk show hosts, fell in behind the neocon vanguard.

Although some of the neocons—particularly William Kristol—had doubts about Bush, they were in place and ready for action when Bush was elected. The battle for a new foreign policy was joined.

The first test of neocon strategy was the downing of an American spy plane off China. The neocons were ready for a fight. And if that fight was to be with China, so be it. However, in that incident, the neocons' house enemy, Secretary of State Colin Powell, prevailed.

Then came 9/11. The neocons, validated, led the charge for the invasion of Afghanistan and pressed for tough action against Iraq. When Bush bought in, the neocons had reached the apex of their influence; they would reshape the world as a whole and the Middle East in particular to forms of conduct and government to their liking, always mindful of the interests of Israel.

But things have been going badly for the neocons, and the administration has become weary of them. At the outset of the war in Iraq, the necons were talking happily about invading not only Saddam Hussein's roost, but also those of the leaders of Syria and Saudi Arabia. European nations that objected were denigrated. The op-ed pieces flew, the books were written, and the talk show hosts gave our European allies the backs of their hands. "Who needs them?" was the cry.

Bush's willingness to wield force, abrogate treaties and ignore the ties that had bound Europe and America for so long elated the neocons. This was a president of their own imaginings.

The reluctance of the Department of State to sign on to the new world confirmed their view that Powell was an equivocator, a fifth columnist within the administration.

Now the heady days of neoconservatism appear over. An intellectual counterattack has been launched by people like Jonathan Clarke of the Cato Institute and his collaborator Stephan Halper of Cambridge University. They lament the new American isolationism, the anti-Americanism around the world and the hijacking of foreign policy by what is a very small movement.

Old-fashioned conservatives, intoxicated at the time of Bush's election, are sobering up and wondering what is going on. Particularly, the business community is voicing frustration with U.S. insensitivity to their customers and suppliers abroad.

But as Iraq has dragged on and it has become apparent that neither the neocons nor the administration had thought through the aftermath of shock-and-awe, the necons have lost credibility. Their favorite Iraqi, Ahmad Chalabi, is the target of administration allegations that he had been communicating with Iranian intelligence.

Also, the country and the world have been deeply unnerved by the prison scandals in Iraq and the support for torture from within the administration. To the business community and to old-line conservatives, these practices, and the suggestion that they had support high in the Pentagon and the Department of Justice, are shocking, immoral and downright un-American.

Belatedly, the administration has recognized the scope of the bad feeling about prison abuse and torture and is working to distance the president from these practices and to condemn them.

Alas for the neocons, their media had encouraged extreme interrogation and suggested that if Americans were too squeamish to do it, Israelis and others should be brought in.

These schisms in the conservative movement have not translated into better poll numbers for John Kerry, but they have caused soul-searching in the White House and led to something of a redemption for professionals in the State Department and their embattled secretary.

June 23, 2004

"OLD EUROPE" IS FEELING A LOT BETTER ABOUT ITSELF

MUNICH, Germany—In hindsight, Europeans are divided as to the greatest offense caused them by the Bush administration. To ordinary people, it is unquestionably the war in Iraq and prisoner abuse. To the intelligentsia and the business class, it was the offhanded repudiation of the Kyoto treaty early in Bush's presidency.

Despite all that has happened since then, Kyoto still rankles as the first indication of the fraying of Atlantic comity—the first indication that U.S. foreign policy would not respect the delicate balances established over 50 years.

For this ruling class of Europeans, the other great offense was Defense Secretary Donald Rumsfeld's dismissal of France and Germany, along with other original members of the European Union, as "Old Europe." Those two words have caused offense and anger beyond anything that Rumsfeld might have intended.

Europe's business elite has digested the war in Iraq with greater equanimity than it has the attitude conveyed by Bush's unilateral withdrawal from Kyoto and Rumsfeld's offhand comment. Those, taken together with Bush's withdrawal from the Anti-Ballistic Missile Treaty, convinced the Europeans that the Atlantic alliance was not as durable and as trustworthy as it had been.

Treaties are important in Europe—particularly in the European Union—where compromise, collaboration and extravagant civility are essential to the progress of the enterprise.

Europeans have been less offended by the incessant conservative U.S. media attack on Europe's institutions, its currency and its defense posture. That they take as political; an entitlement of a free press. Besides, they are used to it.

Continental Europe is under relentless media attack in the United Kingdom, where the newspapers are dominated by Rupert Murdoch, the media magnate, who has mined a vein of British chauvinism and ancient hostility to the people across the English Channel.

In reality, Europe is doing relatively well and is beginning, hesitantly, to address its structural problems, most of which boil down to its social services, which it no longer can afford in an age of competition, aging populations and declining birthrates. In Germany and France—Europe's heavyweights—the problem is clearly identified. The resolution will take a little longer.

The debate is whether the reforms, which are opposed by the unions and the public services, can be effected gradually, as the Germans and French are trying, or whether they have to be done cataclysmically, after the fashion of Margaret Thatcher in the United Kingdom.

In a period of political apathy across Europe, recently demonstrated in local and transnational elections, it is unlikely that a continental Thatcher will appear. Instead, Europe is resigned to the idea that the reforms will have to wait until they can no longer be avoided. Deficits are plaguing the EU members, as they have missed deficit targets-mandated under European treaties—routinely. Italy has just been hauled over the coals by its fellow European Unionists for particularly dubious accounting.

But there is a quiet optimism that the reforms will come eventually and that Europe will emerge strong and competitive, not as a purveyor of cheese and wine, but as a serious, high-technology competitor. Europeans point to the European Aeronautic Defense and Space Company EADS as a bellwether of the future of Europe. Certainly, the company is enjoying extraordinary success. It is the principal manufacturer of light helicopters in the world. It is also the manufacturer of Airbus, the civilian jets, which have given Boeing unexpected and devastating competition. Next year, when EADS rolls out the 550-seat A-380, it will become the dominant manufacturer of civilian aircraft.

If the A-380 is a commercial success, as it appears it will be, European confidence will take to the sky with it. Europe, regarded for so long as the technological laggard, will be the aviation leader in the eyes of much of the world.

The extraordinary thing about EADS is that its genesis was in a clumsy marriage of the aerospace interests of four countries—Britain, France, Germany and Spain. How these diverse interests have been molded into a single company is a fine example of inter-European cooperation, political accommodation and sheer will to succeed. EADS is also producing a highly-competitive twin-engine, air-to-surface fighter, known as the Eurofighter.

This new generation of European aircraft employ cutting-edge sophistication in manufacture, composite material, and pilot-friendly cockpits.

The EADS achievement is inspiring other European countries to look across their borders for collaboration and out beyond them for markets. Given the very high wage structure in Europe, the company has had to go to advanced manufacturing techniques, and these have paid off for it.

The next leap forward in European competitiveness may well be in biotechnology. Already the use of stem cells, limited in the United States, offers another leadership role for Europe.

The kind of inter-country collaboration that has made EADS a success has also reinforced the European proclivity for alliances and collaboration-alliances and cooperative ventures that they once looked to the United States for.

So Europe has extraordinary structural problems and yet a new will to compete. To do this effectively, it has to enact what are called "the reforms" in social security, the pervasive government provision of free services, and its ludicrous and debilitating agricultural policies. Europe is not cleared for takeoff, but it knows where the runway is and how to get there.

July 7, 2004

MY FRIEND IN HANDCUFFS: KEN LAY'S FALL

There is some place in us where we register hurt of a special kind. Mercifully, it is seldom touched. But it was for me recently, when I saw my friend Ken Lay, former chief executive officer of Enron, being ushered into a federal courthouse in handcuffs. Your friend in handcuffs-that hurts.

I do not know any of the legal issues surrounding the collapse of Enron, nor to what extent Lay was a party to the greed and insanity that overtook that once-proud company. But I have known Lay for more than 30 years. And it grieves me to see him fallen.

I first met him when he was a government employee, and kept in touch with him throughout the Enron years. This I know: Lay was kind, considerate, friendly, outgoing, and entirely without the self-importance and self-regard that characterizes most of the captains of industry that I have known as a journalist.

Recently, a financial writer inferred that Lay rode around in limousines with a retinue. He got that wrong. Over the years, Lay spoke at many conferences that I organized, and his *modus operandi* was anything but regal. He liked to rent his own car—often a sports car or a Jeep—and drive himself to his destination.

Whereas most CEOs I have known arrive at conferences with a phalanx of aides and assistants, Lay, who could be both jaunty and serious at the same time, just popped up. He did not seek or seem to want special deference. His manners were flawless. They were the manners of the Old South, not of brash Texas.

He was genuinely interested in you, and always seemed to be really glad to see friends and acquaintances from another time. Indeed, Lay was sensitive to those around him. On one occasion, he was speaking at one of my conferences and he called up to inquire whether it would be inconvenient to bring one of his daughters, then a Washington energy lawyer. Compare that with one CEO who arrived with 14 people and a television crew to record his every action and utterance. Another came by private jet, helicopter and limousine. He was a big shot.

I never benefited financially from my association with Lay. Enron was not a big purchaser of *The Energy Daily*, an energy newsletter that I founded and publish. You might think that Enron would have been, but it did not turn out like that. And I never wanted to raise it with the only person I knew well at Enron, Lay.

Although I was not the beneficiary of the lavish expenditures that Enron was famous for, I was the beneficiary of a great deal of Lay's time. He would rearrange schedules and inconvenience himself to attend my events, in what amounted to extraordinary generosity.

I was always giving Lay offhand advice, such as "do not go into India" and "avoid the water business," he politely ignored me. In turn, I ignored the only advice Lay ever gave me. When I was thinking of starting *The Energy Daily*, I went to see Lay, who was then a deputy undersecretary of energy at the Department of Interior. "Don't do it," he advised. "There is too much competition." Later, when he left the government, I told him that I did not think one could make much progress in the highly regulated natural gas business.

Newspapers, magazines and radio stations have called me to ask whether I think Lay is guilty of the charges brought against him. I do not know. But I do know that most of us remember kindness long after we have forgotten everything else. That there was massive fraud and connivance at Enron, I do know. I hope that the guilty are punished and that Lay is as blameless as his defense says.

July 14, 2004

AFTER CENTURIES OF TRAVAIL,
A BITTERSWEET BOOM IN IRELAND

BALLINA, Ireland—Dreams fulfilled for people and countries alike are anticlimactic. Ireland, once one of the poorest countries in Europe, is tasting the bittersweet fruit of a commercial revolution that had eluded it for all of its long and troubled history.

Just over a decade ago, Ireland begged for the charity of its descendents living abroad (about 40 million in America alone), exported its workers (as it had done for hundreds of years) and beseeched its partners in Europe for development aid. The Irish government told the people that structural unemployment of 22 percent was immutable.

Then, quick as you can order a Guinness, Ireland began a phenomenal economic surge—as dramatic in its way as the current economic growth in China. Computer companies worldwide discovered that Ireland's legendary literacy was just what they needed, and the Celtic Tiger was let loose.

Today, at 5 percent, Ireland's unemployment is the lowest in the European Union, its expatriates are returning home, and all of history seems to be stood on its head. Gross domestic product is an extraordinary $30,000 per capita, 10 percent above the four largest European economies. Industrial and service exports are running at 75 percent of GDP. Irish butter, cheese and bacon are still exported around the world, but the importance of the agricultural sector has faded away.

Dublin and Galway, the nation's computer center, are boomtowns with high-rise office buildings and condominiums sprouting everywhere. The world of William Butler Yeats, James Joyce and Samuel Beckett has given way to computers, networks and all the paraphernalia of an IT society. With 3 million cell phones and 4 million people, the Irish are no longer just talking up a storm in the pubs.

However, Ireland is also beginning to pay the piper. Drugs, long a problem, are endemic, especially in Dublin. Crime, once about the theft of a cow or a minor burglary, is vicious, lethal and organized. The Gardai, the Irish police force, is overwhelmed and corrupted by the new class of criminal.

When immigrants once poured out of Ireland, they are now pouring in. The Irish, so proud of their ancestry and culture, are struggling to assimilate Africans, Chinese, Cubans, Middle Easterners and Middle Europeans. The Irish have yet to recognize that these refugees are after the same economic salvation that the Irish themselves sought around the world, and particularly in the United States.

Irish nationalism, the strength of its people under centuries of English exploitation, is defensive and racial incidents are common. The world that Ireland longed to join has joined Ireland, and it is unexpected and shocking for the Irish.

The Irish also are dealing with the inflationary impact of their new prosperity. Office space in Dublin and Galway is renting for prices that prevail in Washington, D.C. and Mumbai, India. Housing, once so affordable, is hard to come by and expensive. Small country roads are jammed with traffic. Sweet Molly Malone would have difficulty getting her wheelbarrow through Dublin's streets broad and narrow (and they are narrow).

Here in the northwest of Ireland, along the Atlantic, the computer boom has not arrived. But every day prices have risen, from food to housing to the price of a drink. So much so that they are affecting the mainstay of the region's economy: tourism. Irish tourists are finding it cheaper to travel to Spain's Costa Brava than to the west coast of their own country. Publicans and hoteliers lament the affects of "New Ireland" over the ways of "Old Ireland."

Increasingly, conversations throughout Ireland have a nostalgic ring, as people discuss fondly Old Ireland and its gentle ways. They like the full employment, the cars and the notoriety of being the greatest economic success story outside of Asia. But there is, in a sentimental country, a deep sense that something has been lost.

Yes, Irish eyes are smiling. But if you look deeply into them, you also can see tears.

July 28, 2004

BUSH IS FELINE, KERRY CANINE. YOU DECIDE

If you are one of those cherished unaligned voters, you may decide to align not on the basis of the wit and wisdom of the candidates, but on your predisposition as a dog or cat person.

If you are a dog person, the pull of John Kerry will be at play. He is canine by disposition and in performance. In appearance, there are hints of the Irish wolfhound; lean and imposing, yet deferential. His eyes cry, "Love me for what I am, and what I have done."

By contrast, George W. Bush is essentially feline—purring in the company of his choosing and aloof when he wishes to be. Ever seen Bush talking to the Christian right? He is light and nimble, quick to retreat into his own comfort zone when he is not approving of company.

My way or the highway is the Bush way. It is also the way of all cats. While dogs wish to convert all people, to seek approval from all and to offer obeisance to many, cats select. While cats do not tolerate those who are not of their persuasion, dogs haplessly crave approbation. Self-confidence comes and goes with dogs. A kind word and a loving touch-and, instantly, rapture.

Not so with cats. They select those from whom they will accept approbation—on their time and in a place of their choosing. Ask any White House reporter about Bush's relationship with the media and they will tell you about his feline ways: his reticence to get close and his sense of a higher, feline, calling. The world on his terms is the Bush way.

There is something plaintive about Kerry: a dog among strangers. Even when his script says something else, Kerry's eyes and his body plead: "If only you knew me, you would love me. Can I bring you my bone? Let me lick your hand."

Bush, buttressed by the innate sense of nine lives, swaggers on, sure of where he is going and indifferent to those who are not going with him. While Kerry wishes to share his world with the voters, Bush expects the voters to qualify for it.

Unlike a dog, Bush caught in the act is not repentant. There are no repentant cats. That loveable pet caught killing a small bird is indifferent to remonstration. Dogs, though, tremble at the raised voice, the pointed finger, and will suffer remorse for hours: victims of their masters' opprobrium.

When Bush was asked by reporters whether there was anything he regretted or any mistake he had made, he could think of none. That was Bush the Cat. But dog-like Kerry has been trying to explain his votes on the war in Iraq and his post-Vietnam peace activities.

Kerry sniffs out ideas and paws at them. Bush pounces on an idea—anyone's idea—and makes it his own, as he did with Kerry's call for a national intelligence director.

When it comes to the vice-presidential contenders, there is Sen. John Edwards, the puppy-man, doing his tricks. "Would you like a paw, or would you like me to roll on my back?" By contrast, Vice President Cheney is the ultimate cat who walks by himself: cantankerous, furtive and mean in an alley fight.

Where Edwards exudes a desire to be loved, and is ready to reciprocate, Cheney is stealthy and taciturn. Only his wife can tell us if he ever purrs.

The pollsters should go forth and establish whether the undecided voters are cat or dog people. When they separate out those who love cats and dogs equally, they will have identified the real swing voters. If your heart belongs equally to Puss and Fido, you are one of the few who will decide the next election.

August 4, 2004

A WRITER WITHOUT A PEDESTRIAN GENE

The English journalist Bernard Levin died this week. He was not well known in the United States, except indirectly through the phrases he brought to the English language and the way he changed writing about politics, the theater and the way we live.

It was Levin who gave us the phrase the "Nanny State." And it was Levin, arguably, who gave us Arianna Huffington.

Levin burst on the journalistic scene in the 1960s with indignation as high as Everest, a vocabulary as great as all outdoors, and a wit as sharp as a Gurkha's knife. When he was the acerbic, revolutionary theater critic of *The Daily Express,* he could be seen walking in London's Fleet Street, then the home of all British national newspapers, lost in thought—the large head almost too big for the body that bore it.

So was it, too, with his writing. It was almost too big, too incredibly clever for his editors—and sometimes too much of an irritant to his publishers. He loved Wagner and he wrote on an operatic scale. Sometimes he ventured a sentence of more than 1,000 words and no copy editor had the temerity to try to deconstruct the behemoth sentence.

As a theater critic, he approached the task as no one has before or has since. He waged war on the cozy theater of French doors, pregnant maids and dutiful butlers. No one had ever experienced theater criticism that employed the ballistic devices that came naturally to Levin. Once he wrote about the scenery in a play without ever mentioning the actors. On another occasion, he concluded that the author's thinking was upside-down and had his review published upside-down. At the time, the theater world hated him. Although, in hindsight, he did much to reinvigorate English theater, to give a hearing to the avant-garde of his day, and to increase theater audiences.

As no critic had done since George Bernard Shaw, Levin made the theater once again a vital, exciting place where people wanted to be and where the audience felt it had an affinity for, indeed a role in, the performance.

Earlier, in London's *Spectator* magazine, he had revolutionized political writing in "sketches," which treated Parliament and politicians as theater, verging on cabaret. This approach affected political writing on both sides of the Atlantic and is alive to this day.

Levin began with a political predisposition to socialism and moved to the right, but he remained indignant about all injustice, the pomp of establishments and the hypocrisy of politicians. It can be said that he was ecumenical in his indignation.

Levin never married but had a number of long and intense relationships, one of which was with Arianna Stassinopoulos, who was later to become Arianna Huffington. She is alleged to have contributed to a rather strange phase in Levin's life when he became associated with a California-based Indian "guru," Bhagwan Shree Rajneesh. In some of his least memorable columns at the time, he praised Eastern mysticism.

It was writing for the London *Times*, under the heading "How We Live Now," that Levin achieved his fullest expression. He wrote about a great diversity of subjects with erudition, passion and soaring metaphor. His was the column every reader read, whether Levin was denouncing the closing of a newspaper, the evils of communism or the unintended consequences of the Nanny State.

In 1983, he wrote in *The Times* about Labor leader Michael Foot: "The sight of Mr. Foot hanging himself higher and higher and higher with every shifting, gaseous, unfinished verbless unintelligible sentence which he emitted like ectoplasm . . . was so distressing that I switched off two-thirds of the way through: I felt like a member of Greenpeace watching a month- old seal pup beating its own brains out."

British and American journalists borrowed generously from Levin in both style and ideas. His final gift to journalism was to make it clear that journalism itself is a work in progress, always struggling to get out of the bonds of its own manufacture. For Levin, the newspaper page was a place for creation and invention—exactly what he had demanded earlier of the theater.

Sadly, he had to abandon his craft when he fell into the evil embrace of Alzheimer's disease. In his final years, he was nursed by his last love, journalist Liz Anderson.

August 11, 2004

THE MYTH AND MYSTERY OF WASHINGTON "ACCESS"

Washington has a pulse, but it is barely discernible. This self-regarding capital of the free world has, as always, shut down for August.

President Bush is running for re-election somewhere else, as is his Democratic challenger. Likewise, the entire House of Representatives is seeking job-approval, as is a third of the Senate.

So, the denizens of Washington lawyers, lobbyists, think-tankers and journalists are scattered between Maine and Key West, Fla. A few find their way inland. But mostly, no matter where they originate, once they have taken on the coloring of the nation's capital, they wind up vacationing on the East Coast.

The well-heeled favor Martha's Vineyard, Nantucket, The Hamptons and Block Island. The rest stay closer to home: the Maryland shore, the Delaware and New Jersey beaches, and North Carolina's Outer Banks.

The intensely busy Washington professionals have traded their suits (English or Brooks Brothers for the men and Chanel or Talbots for the women) for Levi's 501 jeans and cutoffs.

Everything that was so critical and urgent in July is of no consequence in August. Al Qaeda, Iraq, U.S. health care, the national deficit, and the price of oil demanded instant action last month. But this month, they are all postponeable.

In Washington, everything matters all the time, except when it doesn't, which is in August. The voices that were raised over stem-cell research, gay marriage, Canadian prescription drugs and the Arctic National Wildlife Refuge are quieted. Blissfully so.

Even the trade in Washington's permanent commodity, "access," is quiet. Washington's worker bees believe that they deal in the honey of power, but the route to the sweet stuff is through the pollen of access.

Washington lawyers, lobbyists, think-tankers and journalists cultivate the idea that they have access. And if they can find enough gullible corporations, some of them become wealthy, indeed, selling this access.

Access to members of congressional committees is gold. Access to chairpersons of committees is platinum. Access to White House officials is prized for its prestige, but it does not affect legislation, lower a tax burden, deliver pork, nor cement a subsidy. That battleground is in Congress.

Those with the best access are former members of Congress. They have floor privileges and can buttonhole their former colleagues any time they feel like it. They are in a class by themselves.

Next in the access lineup come the former congressional staffers. They just know a lot of people on Capitol Hill.

Then there are those who have made it their business to have access. They have opened their homes to members of Congress, golfed with them, sailed with them, played tennis with them, and used every ingratiation trick in the book.

Of course, all of this is skewed by money. Give enough money to political campaigns, and access comes with a thank-you note. Forgotten is the fact that members of Congress, like the rest of us, sometimes just like to talk to a friend, share a joke, or chew the fat with somebody who knows something. Not every member of Congress wants to be dragged around a golf course, be bored on a sailboat, or be exhausted on a tennis court. Many have told friends how much they like being left alone.

Still, the fact is that of all the great capitals of the world, access is easier in Washington than anywhere else. The first route to access is not an elaborate entertainment. A simple phone call will do.

More, members of Congress can be found all over Washington: at charitable events, conferences, parties and receptions. They are easily approached. While you may not get more than a few minutes with them, you can sow the seeds of an idea or state a position.

Speaking to a legislator does not mean you will get what you want, especially if you are not backed up by a powerful political action committee. But they are not inaccessible, just unreachable.

After the Republican National Convention, Washington will leap to life. And the access salesmen will be back in business, confiding to clients, "We are close to the committee chairman."

August 18, 2004

THE MOVE TO IMPEACH BLAIR: GOOD, CLEAN FUN

According to English law, a man can relieve himself on the offside rear wheel of a taxi. That same taxi is obliged to carry a bale of hay and a sack of oats. Both laws made a great deal of sense in the time of horse-drawn cabs. They are now part of the eccentricity of English law, which the English are slow to update because they rather enjoy the anomalies.

Likewise, the English constitution is a sort of virtual arrangement. It is so virtual that it is not written down in any one place. Instead, it is an agglomeration of precedents dating back to the Magna Carta of 1215. This does not mean that the English are not proud of their constitution, do not defend this shady arrangement, and do not have a plethora of constitutional academics and lawyers prepared to pop up on television at a few seconds notice to discuss it and to identify passing political issues as representing a "constitutional crisis."

In fact, most of these constitutional crises have involved the royal family. The abdication of Edward VIII in 1936 was held to be a full-blown constitutional crisis. And if Prince Charles marries his longtime love, Camilla Parker Bowles, it is held that this will provoke a constitutional crisis because as king, Charles would be head of the Church of England, which in theory frowns on divorce.

Now a rag-bag group of MPs, supported by their own constitutional experts, has dusted off Britain's ancient laws of impeachment and is going after Prime Minister Tony Blair, alleging "high crimes and misdemeanors." (Yes, the framers of our constitution borrowed heavily from British concepts.) Their plan is to ask the House of Commons to impeach Blair for lying about the war in Iraq and entering into secret agreements with President Bush.

Unlike the American version of impeachment, the British one is decidedly rusty. It was last given an unsuccessful airing in the 1840s, when Lord Palmerston, a foreign secretary and later prime minister, was accused of doing a secret deal with the Germans. It was only effectively used during the English Civil War in the 1640s.

The present attempt to have the prime minister impeached by the House of Commons and tried by the House of Lords has little more chance of success than an Englishman would have exercising his right to urinate on a taxi.

Nonetheless, the spectacle is enlivening the pages of English newspapers and has brought forth some of the obscure minds of academe to expound on the virtues of impeachment and the right of members of Parliament to pursue the option.

The group has produced an 80-page document detailing the high crimes and misdemeanors alleged against the prime minister. At this point, the battle for impeachment is being waged by a coalition of Welsh and Scottish nationalists and one notable Tory MP, Boris Johnson, who is also the editor of *The Spectator,* the redoubtable London magazine.

Johnson has not been joined by other members of his party because the English conservatives supported the invasion of Iraq. Many left-wing Labor members would like to join the group but risk expulsion from the party.

The real purpose of the move to impeach the prime minister is to establish a device in which he can be called a liar. While speech in the House of Commons is protected, so too are its members from personal attack. The speaker of the House, who serves only as the moderator, has not allowed members to attack the veracity of the prime minister, only his policies. Those who are angry with Blair, for many reasons, believe they can discredit his word through the move to impeach.

But do not get too worked up about all this. It is mostly good, clean fun in the tradition of English public life. Blair is unlikely to be led by sergeants in arms from the Commons to the Lords to be tried at the bar of the upper house, nor to be taken afterwards to the Tower of London for beheading. The Commons will not hear the impeachment because Blair enjoys an enormous majority, and the Conservative Party is inconveniently on his side in this one. Also, that messy old English constitution was amended in the 1980s to prohibit the death penalty.

Blair will not lose any sleep over impeachment, but he probably would rather do without the implicit ridicule of the proceedings.

September 8, 2004

CBS FRACAS: SAY GOOD NIGHT, DAN

In journalism we live by the sword and, in fairness, we deserve to die by it. No one in public life is safe, if they falter, from the scrutiny and by extension the censure of the media. Ergo, Dan Rather, his producer Mary Mapes and unknown numbers of others at CBS News should be sacked. They should be sacked not out of malice but out of justice.

Instead CBS is taking what is a new route in troubled journalism. It has commissioned an independent inquiry into the discredited *60 Minutes* segment and the

now discredited memos about President Bush's service in the Texas National
Guard. The new rule in journalism seems to be "sin in haste and repent at leisure."
The New York Times, USA Today and now *60 Minutes* have all favored the "inves-
tigation" route out of their troubles.

Television journalism is a collective enterprise—unlike print, where an individual works alone and submits his or her reporting to an editor or several editors at
the end of a lonely quest. In television a whole staff is involved and, by extension,
a whole staff is guilty when they have thrown themselves behind a story that is
wrong and that had to be suspect from the beginning. The excuse "the pressure of
time" is not an excuse. The "pressure of time" is simply a fact of life in journalism, and a veteran like Dan Rather has lived with it all his career.

Rather must, in his early days, have worked with manual typewriters and known
how different the result is from computer-generated type or even type generated
from an electric typewriter. Manual typewriters, as Rather knew, left distinct signatures. The *e*'s were often worn out because *e* is the most frequently used letter;
o's were filled in; some letters punctured the page. To get a good copy from a manual typewriter you required a well-serviced machine, quality paper and a typist with
a soft touch. These were things found neither in newsrooms nor in military offices.

The manual typewriter was a workhouse and lasted for years but it did not produce pretty, well-spaced type, and the chances that the National Guard had a state-
of-the-art typewriter are slim. At least flags should have gone up from the older
hands when they first saw the memos. Second, the veracity of the source should
have been checked, rechecked and scrutinized with deep suspicion.

This was a big story which could move an election, and every newshound at
CBS must have known it, all the way up to the suits. No news organization goes
out with a story that can affect a presidential election without the whole chain of
command being sensitive to what they are about. That is what happened with Watergate. Katherine Graham, the publisher of the *Post*, and Ben Bradlee, its editor,
were as involved as the two reporters, Bob Woodward and Carl Bernstein, and the
desk editor, Barry Sussman. They had two things going: a great story and a sense
of its significance.

There is in all news organizations an imperative to get the story out; the story is
the driver, but it cannot take over the entire institution. Excitement, zeal and a
sense of mission prevail when a news organization is closing in on a big story. One
senses that at CBS a lot of people wanted the story to be true, not because they
were politically motivated but because the narcotic of news had intoxicated them.

Although journalists hold political opinions, as does everyone else, these have
not traditionally been the driving force behind a great expose. The story is the
thing, the source of the adrenaline.

Imagine an old-fashioned newspaper and a young Dan Rather. He rushes in
with incriminating documents. The city editor, scarred and cynical, tears into the
young Rather. Where did he get these documents? How good is the source? How
many other sources does he have? Has he pulled the clippings on this source to see
if he has been involved in any dirty tricks, has an axe to grind or is a malcontent?
Then he would demand to know where the source got the documents, and if these

questions were not answered to his satisfaction before he departed for the nearest watering hole, the story would be spiked or it would be rewritten, couched in doubt. That is journalism 101 and it is a simple procedure that somehow didn't take place at Blackrock, as the CBS building on the Avenue of the Americas is known.

The pressure in journalism is always to publish, always to push the envelope but somehow to stay just within it.

Journalism is in crisis generally from politicization, because of competition from new media and because the public has tired of old formulas and the over-abundance of political news. The new breed of politicized reporter says "good riddance" to the old media with its struggle to be fair. Look how the bloggers brought down CBS, they say; but the bloggers are not a new medium, they are something else. They are at their best in attack, at their worst in conveying news. News needs to emanate from established organs of fixed address which are subject to the courts and where the provenance of a story is known.

Bloggers will not cover the war in Iraq, investigate renegade corporations or seek out malfeasance across the government. Even if they had the training, they do not have the resources to keep the public informed. And there's the rub. Now more than ever the public needs news that it can trust from institutions of verifiable impartiality. CBS News moved itself out of that column into another place and has damaged the standing of all news sources and, with it, public confidence in their veracity.

September 22, 2004

THE DARING MEN WHO PUT THE LIGHTS BACK ON

It is 4 a.m. In a great swath across Florida, thousands of men—and a few women—are struggling out of bed in the state's less salubrious hotels and motels. They dress with care, like combat troops. Their garb is not ideal for the weather, but it is essential: heavy protective suits, special hardhats, rough leather gloves and ponderous boots with hooks on them. They are not dressed to enjoy Florida's sunny clime but to stay alive.

These are the utility linemen who have been heading south, since before Labor Day, to repair Florida's ravaged electric network. They are angels to the more than 2 million Floridians who are without power or who have been without power.

Subtropical Florida presents peculiar problems aside from those normally associated with downed power lines. The combination of heat and humidity knocks out a lot of linemen and is a constant concern for supervisors. Then there are the snakes and alligators-the biggest threat is from snakes that may be waiting up a pole for the unsuspecting repairman, looking all the while like a piece of wire. Recently, a lineman was bitten twice in the neck by a snake that had to be captured in order to verify that it was not poisonous.

When an electric utility encounters a natural disaster, it sends out a call to its sister utilities for relief workers. According to Carl Zatkulak of Dominion Power, these requests can be for between 7,000 and 10,000 men, who head to the troubled area, in what are known as "contingents" of 50 men with their vehicles and equipment. These consist of bucket trucks, mobile machine shops, wire-pulling winches and first aid stations.

However, in many instances the trucks cannot get to the downed wires and the men have to proceed on foot, climb the poles with safety belts, and attach themselves to the pole tops with their belts and the hooks on their boots. While it is widely believed that bucket trucks have replaced climbing, in fact many poles have to be climbed in the old-fashioned way. Supplies are hoisted up with a rope and pulley and can include water, tools, replacement parts and wire-drawing equipment. It is hot, dangerous work, conducted in emergencies in shifts that begin at 5 a.m. and end at 10 p.m.

Working an emergency crew is not a vacation. It is an avocation. Linemen have the same sense of duty as firemen and policemen. They also are fiercely proud of their skills, especially their ability to shimmy up a pole. Many do this until the age of 60 or older, and they tend to spend their entire career with the same utility. Usually they are local men and women, earning around $20 an hour.

Apart from the hazards of heat and reptiles, a constant concern is whether the line they are repairing is de-energized. And there are accidents. A live wire can have fallen across a cold wire and many wires may be carrying some electricity that is feeding back from portable generators. According to those in the industry, feedback electricity is becoming more of a problem as more and more homeowners install generators without cutting their homes off from the mains.

"Repairing lines is hard, dangerous, physical work. And these heroes go unsung," said a spokesman for the Edison Electric Institute in Washington, D.C.

Zatkulak, who supervises Dominion's line crews, said the utility had linemen returning from Florida who were so exhausted that they thought they could never do it again. But a week later, the same men headed south for more hurricane repairs.

I feel close to linemen because my father, though not a lineman, did similar work all of his life—before safety had become the priority it is today. He climbed every imaginable structure, from bridges to windmills; hung by one hand while he worked with another; and had to deal with bees, snakes and many other natural problems. The risks increase with fatigue, repetition and past good luck.

President Bush is fond of celebrating ordinary Americans by giving them prized seats at events, like the State of the Union, and receiving them at the White House. Well, the fellows up the poles are heroes and are emblematic of all that is best in our national character.

Here is my suggestion: Let's celebrate them for the phenomenal job they have done restoring electricity after many months of hurricanes, and before they tackle their next great challenge: the ice storms of winter.

September 29, 2004

THE AGONY—AND THE ECSTASY—OF
FINDING A TOILET IN WASHINGTON

Washington is a city with great monuments in granite and marble, but it is decidedly short on porcelain. It is a city that sanctions the spending of hundreds of billions of dollars without a shrug. But it is a bad place to try to spend a penny.

The millions of visitors who come here every year to enjoy the majesty of the nation's capital are well advised to have a strategy for going to the bathroom. There is one public facility on the Mall, and that is all there is for the tourist areas of the city. The unsuspecting must throw themselves on the mercy of the hotels and restaurants. But these establishments are getting increasingly intolerant of the incontinent.

Whereas London and Paris and other capital cities have public toilets aplenty for their visitors, Washington is willingly blind to this human need—and so are many other American cities. Once Washington boasted a smattering of public facilities, but these have fallen prey to crime and vandalism, and they have been closed down.

The Europeans have dealt with the public toilet problem by developing kiosks where the entire internal structure is flushed after each use. A test model for one of these is reputed to be located somewhere inaccessible on Washington's subway system. However, very few people have encountered it, and the management of the subway system thought it would be a good idea to move the device to a more traveled location. But at $70,000 just to move it, we learn that the idea has been abandoned.

The real problem throughout the nation with self-cleaning toilets of the European type is that they do not meet the requirements of the Americans with Disabilities Act. Ergo, we must all cross our legs.

If you are well-dressed and appear to be well-heeled, you can march boldly into any hotel or restaurant and use the facilities with impunity. But if you are casually dressed, you will be interdicted before you reach the porcelain haven.

In our cities, the homeless are also toiletless. They do the best they can, and we all know the problem with that.

The toilet cuckoo is not a new phenomenon. A hundred years ago or so, the great British jurist F.E. Smith, later Lord Birkenhead, would prance into London's Atheneum Club every day at lunch and use the toilets. As he was not a member, this perturbed the doorman. The latter finally mastered the courage, after years of abuse, to approach the great man and tell him: "Sir, this is a private club." To which Smith replied: "Oh, it's a club as well!"

At that time, it took chutzpah to take a pee in London, much as it does in Washington nowadays. The skilled illicit invader bent on exercising his or her innocent desire is well advised not to ask for the toilets but to inquire as to the whereabouts of the bar. This deception has two virtues: it implies imminent patronage, and it takes advantage of the fact that toilets are usually located close to the watering spot. It is a brave soul who walks right off the street and inquires about the toilets. Some subterfuge helps.

The closest point the to White House to find relief is the venerable Hay Adams Hotel, which replaces the former public toilet across the street in Lafayette Park. The hotel is an easy mark because it is filled with so many important visitors that the staff cannot ask too many questions. Your destination is left at the lobby and down the stairs. Clean and agreeable, too. However, you may find yourself back on the street if you are not well-clad.

Avoid at all costs the fast-food restaurants, where you might expect to find easy access. They are unfriendly to the wayfarer seeking the most basic human service. You have to go to the counter to get a token, which means that you have to buy something you do not want in order to get relief. Upmarket venues are more penetrable than downmarket.

Barbara Castle, the British socialist, believed that spending a penny (the toilets used to require a penny in a slot) was antisocial, and she campaigned for years to have toilet service offered gratis. After decades in the House of Commons, that is what Castle will be remembered for, despite her many campaigns on the great issues of the day. Of course, she would have had no legacy if she had been a member of Congress in a nation that has, so to speak, flushed the concept of the public convenience down the drain.

October 6, 2004

WHAT IF BLAIR WERE PRESIDENT, AND BUSH PRIME MINISTER

Together they stand shoulder to shoulder, remarkable allies in a war that is unpopular in much of the world: British Prime Minister Tony Blair and President George Bush. Yet there are commonalities that bind them. Bush, in a gauche moment, blurted out that they used the same brand of toothpaste. They are both physically vigorous, and like to project physical energy. But the real commonality may be religious faith, a biblical concept of right and wrong, and the destiny of Christendom.

Even so, it is hard to see how quick, urbane Blair, with his socialist heritage, can find so much in common with Bush's ersatz Texas rancher persona. Blair has just presided over the first stage in the banning of fox hunting in England and Wales. It is hard to imagine Bush favoring the banning of any hunting, anywhere. Blair passed legislation banning the private ownership of guns in the United Kingdom, except in very limited instances involving gun clubs. Bush, in contrast, let the assault weapons ban die.

There is probably not a single thought in the Labor Party manifesto that you would find in the Bush platform. For example, Blair is tolerant of gay rights and Bush wants a constitutional amendment to limit these.

Winston Churchill speculated to a joint session of Congress that if his father had been American instead of his mother, he might have got to Congress earlier than he did to address it after World War II. Churchill, with his love of America and his enormous knowledge of American history, clearly believed that he would at least have made it into the Senate, and possibly into the White House. But of which party?

Churchill's lifetime record suggests that he would have been a Democrat. He started as a Whig, i.e. liberal, and never felt very comfortable in the Conservative Party, which he used to mock by using its formal name: the Conservative and Unionist Party. He favored the old aristocratic world to which he was born, but he was passionate about social issues: ambivalent about the death penalty, supportive of nationalized medicine and many of the pillars of the welfare state.

Churchill was a phenomenon and a contradiction. He felt for the working classes and moved among the elite aristocrats, publishers and classicists. His close friends included newspaper proprietor Lord Beaverbrook, publisher of the *Financial Times* Brendan Bracken, and T.E. Lawrence (Lawrence of Arabia).

And it was a Democrat, Franklin Delano Roosevelt, of the many American politicians then active, who was Churchill's soul mate in World War II. They were men of privilege who reached out to the masses.

So how would Bush do as prime minister of Great Britain and Blair do as president of the United States? Blair would be appalled at the role of money in politics in the United States, although his own hands are not entirely clean; he would be shocked by the gun lobby; and he would be distressed at the lack of national health insurance. If he could swallow these political realities, he would do just fine as an American president. Articulate, boyish, family-oriented, optimistic, religious and fascinated by business, Blair would find much agreeable in America.

Once Bush had swallowed the indifference to religion in Britain, and digested the complexities of a system that maintains a monarch, an aristocracy and a class structure, while in many ways being more egalitarian than the United States, he might find the work of the British prime minister enjoyable. His frustrations would be that he would have to pick a cabinet from elected members of Parliament, some of whom are not too talented, and he might be sobered to realize that members of his own party could remove him at will.

And, oh dear, there is one challenge that Bush might find too onerous: the unruly, contentious House of Commons, where the great legislators are not beyond yelling out to a prime minister, "Sit down you little git!" or, after a well-thought-out phrase, rendering loud and clamorous shouts of "Shame! Shame! Shame!" Then there is the horror of Question Time, when the prime minister stands alone before his peers, his only defense against a hostile mob his own deft repartee, command of facts and skill at ridiculing his accusers.

On second thoughts, Bush and Blair are not interchangeable. The Atlantic is a wide ocean.

October 13, 2004

OH, THE WATTAGE OF THE RELIGION SALESMANSHIP

While a whopping 70 percent of Americans claim some religious faith, less than 10 percent of western Europeans do likewise. The great cathedrals of western Europe draw few worshippers on Sundays, and most of these people are old. Churchgoing is simply not a regular western European activity.

This is the case, despite the fact that most western European countries have official or established religions. European politicians do not invoke the Almighty, nor ask blessings on their nations with the frequency—indeed the routine—that American politicians beseech God. What American politician who hopes to be elected would not end his or her speech with "God bless America?" God bless France, God bless Italy, God bless Germany are not invocations that are heard across the Atlantic.

While European churches are near empty, American churches are crowded, especially those in suburban and urban areas. Are Americans a more pious people, or is there some other explanation? There may be no data, but there is intimation: Religion gets a hard sell in the United States.

It is on sale 24-7 on television and radio, especially on the AM frequencies. And full-time religious broadcasting is an American phenomenon. On DirecTV, I find at least three full-time religious broadcasts and many who buy time for their programs. If you stray from the networks and the cable news channels, you are into the big religious sell.

Now I would not have the temerity to make an absolute judgment about the religiosity of my fellow Americans, but I do know that it is very hard to avoid the proselytizers of the airwaves. I know of no country in Europe that has 24-7 religion on television. And the few religious broadcasts that can be found on radio generally originate in the United States, or are offshoots of American religious broadcasting.

In the United States, religion is sold a lot harder than soap. It is the No. 1 product available over the airwaves. More so south of the Mason-Dixon Line, but pretty pervasive everywhere.

In the early days of radio, preachers of every persuasion realized that this was a medium for them: a superb extension of the pulpit. Religious broadcasting has grown and grown ever since. The trouble with it is that, like all broadcasting, it is unsuited to complexity. So the religion that comes over the airwaves and by cable is simplistic, ergo fundamentalist. Great discussions of liturgy, dogma, and concepts of God are not to be found in Christian broadcasting.

It is hard to imagine St. Augustine expounding his views in a studio. Cardinal Newman and C.S. Lewis, both great Christian philosophers, chose the quiet of academe to explore concepts of God and the great mystery of divinity. Episcopalians and Catholics are anchored in an examination of the *magnum mysterium*.

Broadcast religion, like all broadcasting, seeks simple answers to complex questions and it finds it in a literal interpretation of Scripture. Call it "God said" religion.

But the greatest mystery of our broadcast religion is the affinity it has found with political conservatism, a digression from the charity, humanity and humility of the New Testament. Non-broadcast or traditional churches, influenced by their pastoral ministry, have always tended to be liberal but not political. Political religious liberalism reached its zenith not in the United States, but in Latin America in Liberation Theology.

The issue is not so much what religion is broadcast but that there is so much of it: the relentless sale of the product, self-financing and self-justifying. Are we more pious or more persuaded by the relentless marketing?

October 20, 2004

THE NEWS AS AN AUTEUR ENTERPRISE

In December, Brian Williams will replace Tom Brokaw as the anchor of "NBC Nightly News." Wow. Reading about this, one would believe that a new truth would be revealed. *The Washington Post* among other newspapers, has analyzed Williams' style, doted on his history, and lauded his excellence as a journalist. It is probably all true.

What is not true is that the person who reads the news controls the news, reports the news, or brings insights into the news. Mostly anchors read the news, which is assembled by an army of producers and correspondents, massaged in committee, typed in final form on sheets of paper, and fed into a TelePrompTer. The news anchor—usually with a grand title like managing editor—can add to and change the package, but cannot assemble it. It takes a team to put a television news program on the air. The idea that the anchor is a superjournalist—who reports, writes and reads the evening news—is a fiction.

It is a fiction that probably originated in the major networks' publicity departments, and has grown since the days when Walter Cronkite left the impression that every night he was speaking his own words from his heart.

A realistic job description for a television news anchor goes something like this: The candidate must be of nice appearance, inoffensive, credible-sounding, and able to convey an impression of authority. But first and foremost, the candidate must be able to real aloud flawlessly and to vary his or her reading speed according to the time dictates of the broadcast. General knowledge of the events of the day is desirable, and the ability to conduct a live interview is a plus.

Network news anchors are encouraged to convey the impression that when they are not on air, they are working the phones, confronting corruption, assessing the views of the common person, and holding politicians to account. Nonsense.

Anchors are treated like aristocracy. They ride around in limousines, have their telephone calls placed for them, and contribute very little to the news before the cameras come on. True, they go to trouble spots and love to be seen dressed in fatigues, trench coats or foul-weather gear. But viewers never see the caravan of assistants, producers, video and sound operators, and satellite technicians. When the great of television are standing on a sand dune in Iraq, they are not alone.

Of the anchor qualifications, the most important is the ability to sight-read without effort, in a slightly conversational way. The second most important qualification is the ability to ad-lib for long periods after a tragedy—9/11 highlighted that ability—and at national political conventions. Here the pros come into their own; talking for hours, listening to the small speaker in their ears, known as an IFB (interruptible fallback), and marshaling, in real time, incoming and often contradictory information.

While anchors insist on doing this themselves, there are many correspondents in any network who can handle the job. Having been cast as the superjournalist by the networks, the superjournalist must be on hand to impart the gravitas of the time.

As every network says that its anchor is the journalist par excellence, the tendency is to believe that all network anchors are created equal. Brokaw, Dan Rather and Peter Jennings have become interchangeable to the viewers-the best of the best on each network. That cannot be. Brokaw is unassuming and scholarly. Jennings can be tetchy and critical of his staff. Rather loves to cover hurricanes, and has been in the eye of a few himself.

I used to write for news anchors, and I can tell you that they are as different as any other group of people. One was vain; one insisted on completely rewriting the news before the broadcast; one was often drunk; and one would ask me to delete long words because he worried about stumbling over them. For the viewers, the most loved, and therefore the most trusted, of these anchors was the one who was terrified by polysyllabic words.

George Bernard Shaw, at a time when orchestral conductors were being fussed over the way news anchors are today, said: "The purpose of the conductor is to give the beat to the band. That is all." The purpose of the news anchor is to read the news. That is all. One wishes Brian Williams the best of luck.

October 27, 2004

GEORGE W. BUSH: THE MAN AND HIS WORLD

George W. Bush, now set to be the most powerful man in the world for the next four years, gives the illusion of being shorter than his 6 feet. Sometimes it is because he is standing with very tall people, such as Mexican President Vicente Fox, his erstwhile opponent Sen. John Kerry, or his secretary of state, Colin Powell. Even when he is in the company of people who are actually shorter than he is, Bush appears small. It is an illusion.

It is one of many illusions that cloak the president. He is never quite the man that anyone thinks he is. When George W. Bush burst on the national scene, his opponents greatly undermeasured him. Privately, editors at *The Weekly Standard*, a conservative journal, speculated among themselves that Bush would either be the most reviled candidate in history or the most reviled president. He was neither.

Liberals delighted in what they saw as his stupidity. They got that wrong. Even some Republican supporters believed that they would have to surround their president with minders, who would make the tough decisions and do the heavy lifting for Bush. They thought he would govern as a constitutional monarch; the emblem of power, but not the player who exercised it. Again, they were wrong. Bush does not care to be told what to do, but he does like to be told that what he is doing is right.

The search for the real Bush was as active on the right as it was on the left. People on the right, who were acquainted with Bush during the early days of his presidency, were confused by him. If you asked them how he was and how he was doing, they answered in a kind of jargon minted to deal with the elusive Bush. They said things like "He's focused," and "He's concentrating on the agenda." In fact, they had come away unenlightened about the president's frame of mind or his concept of governance. What was in Bush's mind remained in Bush's mind.

And Bush's mind has a lot to do with Bush's comfort zone. To reach this zone, throughout his life Bush has sought a role in which to immerse himself. As a young man, he played the buffoon, the party animal, the tipsy ne'er-do-well, the frat brat. It was a role that borrowed nothing from his upbringing and revealed nothing of his elite pedigree and patrician home life. In fact, Bush seems to have had a lifelong aversion to the mores of his own provenance.

He began to find comfort as a baseball team owner, where he was the cheerleader in the moneyed world of those who owned sports teams. He had reached some kind of comfort zone, and it was more dignified than being just a party animal.

It was Texas that was to provide Bush with a role that he could live with—a zone of extreme comfort. As Texas adopted Bush, Bush adopted Texas. Being more Texan than the Texans was the role that Bush fit nicely and into which he disappeared. Bush did not pretend to be a Texan, he became the embodiment of one. And along with the persona, he adopted a set of values and myths, which are part of the Texas ethos.

Bush the Texan became Bush the Man Wrapped Up In Texas. Everything fit well, from the jeans to the belt with the silver buckle to the locker-room towel-flicking wit. The discomfort he had felt in New England evaporated. He took a personality off the shelf and it fit as finely as though it were bespoke. He did not have to work on George W. Bush. The Texas package took care of everything.

Unfortunately as Bush's comfort grew, so did his greatest weakness: an astounding lack of curiosity. The Texan role answered all his doubts, provided easy rationales, and in time delivered a simplistic but passionate Christianity. If Bush had had a contemplative side, it was put to rest. If Bush had been curious about life outside of Texas, it was stifled by the satisfying new role. Only ambition was not extinguished by the charms of Texas certainty.

Having distanced himself from this family and his upbringing, Bush could contemplate the family enterprise, politics, as an outsider not an insider. He failed to win a seat in Congress. But steeped in the myth that good things happen to good people, he knew that it would all fall into place. And it did: He was twice elected governor of Texas. Then others dreamed of the presidency for Bush, and he liked the dream and made it his own.

Bush has demonic energy for the things he enjoys, like campaigning and working out. He has an almost equal lack of energy for debating difficult issues, reading long documents, and dealing with the intricacies of governance. It is not Texan. It is not necessary.

It is these things taken together which alarm other nations and comfort the American heartland. For a man who has difficulty with words, Bush has an extraordinary ability to speak folk. He charms them in West Virginia, Kansas and the South. He knows how to make empty words, like resolve, sound sincere and enabling.

As we have watched Bush as candidate and president, we are gradually becoming aware that he has found another role that he likes: president. But it is not as easy and fulfilling as the Texan role. It is not an extreme comfort zone. But Bush seeks comfort in it by brooking no criticism in his inner circle, tuning out disagreements and overlooking fiascos. Bush does not think he has made any significant mistakes. He eliminates them by the deft practice, honed in Texas, of assertive incuriosity. For Bush, there is no bad news, just degrees of good news.

November 3, 2004

WANTED: BIG FEET FOR THE EMPTY SHOES AT DOE

Andrew Card, President Bush's indefatigable chief of staff, has been on the phone to prospective candidates to be the new secretary of energy. If Card is seeking the most qualified person for one of the most difficult jobs in Washington, he will be departing from a long history of treating the Department of Energy as a second-rate Cabinet agency.

The department was cobbled together during the Carter administration by James Schlesinger, its first secretary. Schlesinger brought a phenomenal knowledge of all the components of the new department, from nuclear weapons to the need to establish a strategic petroleum reserve. He had a great feel for geopolitics and for the contending constituencies in the energy mix.

Of course, Schlesinger had been chairman of the Atomic Energy Commission, director of the Central Intelligence Agency and secretary of defense. He was aware that the new department was held together by semantics as much as it was held together by energy output. He knew that it was a vast archipelago of disassociated islands. And he worked for as much cohesion as could be achieved in the political framework of the time.

President Carter could not solve the energy problem, but he could create a department that by its very existence implied that the problem was in hand. Unfortunately, the department required a leader of Schlesinger's depth and breath to function effectively.

As there have been no other candidates with Schlesinger's resume, successive administrations have filled the DOE headquarters, at the Forrestal Building in Washington, with a series of secretaries selected more for political reasons than because they had either a passion for the subject or a comprehensive grasp of the portfolio. Don Hodel, in some respects, fitted the template established by Schlesinger. Others have had some strengths in some areas. While Admiral James Watkins concentrated on DOE's nuclear responsibilities, Bill Richardson energized the department by force of personality and skillful delegation of the minutiae.

The brief tenure of Federico Pena was something of a nadir of leadership at DOE. But there were others who did not really get the hang of the role of the national laboratories, world oil resources, or natural gas reserves. They included a dentist and a Coca-Cola executive. Hazel O'Leary treated the agency as a civil rights forum. John Herrington was obsessed with nuclear waste. He now runs a steakhouse in California. The outgoing secretary of energy, Spencer Abraham, struggled in vain to persuade his former Senate colleagues to pass the Bush energy bill.

Card might mention to the candidates that Department of Energy designs, tests and manufacturers nuclear weapons, verifies compliance with the Nuclear Non-Proliferation Treaty and is, through the national laboratories, at the cutting edge of science as diverse as high-energy physics and global climate change. He might also mention that the secretary of energy must be a diplomat, prepared to cajole Saudi princes, calculate a world economy excluding Iran's oil production, and argue with African oil producers to reinvest their wealth domestically.

The secretary of energy must appear on the Sunday morning talk shows to explain away the price of gasoline, the cost of heating oil and shortages of natural gas. He or she must support Bush's hydrogen car initiative while damping public expectations that the hydrogen economy is just around the corner. Likewise, the secretary must deal with environmental issues, energy production from public lands, and wrangle with Sen. Harry Reid of Nevada over the Yucca Mountain nuclear waste repository.

In the next four years, energy consumption in China and India, instability in the Middle East and mismanagement in Africa could impact the oil supply with devastating effects for the economy.

Few have left the top job at the Department of Energy to forge careers with great success. Only Schlesinger, who has become an elder statesman, Richardson, who is governor of New Mexico, and Hazel O'Leary, who is president of Morehouse College, have not been swallowed up by oblivion.

Given how important energy will be in the years ahead, Card needs to cast his net wide and hope to ensnare a futurist who is also a diplomat, a globalist and a scientist. Best of luck, Andy.

November 17, 2004

TALLYHO! TALLYHO! TALLYHO! . . . NO MORE

Farewell then to nearly five centuries of fox hunting in England and Wales—Scotland has already banned fox hunting. No more will the horn sound, will the hounds yelp, nor will the resplendent men and women on horses, fortified with a stirrup cup, charge across the countryside in pursuit of the elusive fox.

Another emblem of English country life is to be consigned to the dustbin of history. Another symbol of Englishness is to fall to contemporary values. Or, to be more precise, hunting with hounds has become another casualty of Britain's relentless class war.

Didn't class war go out with Margaret Thatcher, its last vestiges eradicated under Tony Blair? Not exactly. A Labor Party politician, Peter Bradley, writing in London's *Sunday Telegraph*, said that Labor's animosity to fox hunting was not about cruelty to animals but about class warfare itself. Bradley claimed that the struggle over the anti-fox hunting bill, which will go into effect in February 2005, was "not just about animal welfare and personal freedom, it was class war." He said: "Ultimately, it's about who governs Britain."

Bradley is not just a vociferous left-winger, he is also secretary to the rural affairs minister in Blair's government. What he has done is to validate the long-espoused conviction of the pro-fox hunting forces that Labor's determination to stop the sport is not about the cruelty to the foxes but about the deep-seated class prejudice that still pervades Britain. To this point, allegations that the real motive of Blair's party was to punish the landed gentry had been denied by the government. Now a junior member of the government has said that is exactly what the controversy is about.

As in America, the British working class is gradually being assimilated into the middle class. It has largely traded the factory floor for the computer, the housing estate for the suburban house. And it has traded the labor strike as its means of expression for the more sophisticated path of legislation.

But even as the working class has taken the middle-class mantle, designer jeans, holidays abroad and wine instead of beer, it has kept alive its ancient hatred for the landed gentry and the bosses.

Incorrectly, the rump of the Labor Party has identified all those who fox hunt as being upper-class, privileged, wealthy and somehow aristocratic. In fact, fox hunting has become as egalitarian as any other sport. Bus drivers, schoolteachers, geeks and journalists all hunt, along with the despised landowners.

The attack on fox hunting is one in a series of assaults on the traditional uses of private land in Britain. First there are the ramblers, who by law are allowed to hike across private property without responsibility, often leaving gates open in fields with livestock, littering and trampling crops. This, they assert, is their right. Then there are the gypsies and hippie travelers who camp where they will.

Bradley leaves no doubt that not only does his party have a vicious antipathy to what they believe the hunting class comprises, but also they favor a backdoor nationalization of open land.

Blair himself has tried to stand aside from this ugly confrontation, leaving its resolution to the House of Commons, and ineffectively to the House of Lords. He was not prepared to use his own prestige to divert the party activists.

Hunting is a tough game. It requires considerable courage, horsemanship and a love of animals, even while it is about pursuing and killing a fox. It is practiced without conflict up and down the East Coast of the United States, and almost throughout the nation. There are differences: The British made a somewhat more gory undertaking of hunting than is the case here. Some of British hunts had been advised to clean up their acts by eliminating the cosmetically offensive practice of "blooding," in which the youngest hunter has his or her face smeared with the blood from the foxtail, and of driving, or beating, the fox toward the hounds.

British hunting enthusiasts are suing in the European Court of Justice and they have promised to defy the ban, possibly landing some otherwise dignified persons in jail.

The real losers are the hounds, maybe as many as 8,000 who will have to be put down. A foxhound has no purpose other than to hunt and cannot be made into a household pet. As the foxes will now have to be shot, trapped or poisoned to keep their numbers in check, the cruelty may increase.

The winners are the petty, the vicious and the envious, who would destroy an ancient tradition to satisfy a sense of class inferiority.

November 24, 2004

STOP THE CRITICS, NOT THE PRESSES

They wear hair shirts, beat their breasts, wring their hands, and seem to have endless funding to keep up their flagellation. I speak of the proliferating institutions that concern themselves with media oversight. They are housed in universities, think tanks and comfortable offices around Washington.

Some think journalism, as we have known it, is dead—a victim of the 24-hour news cycle and the Internet. Others are convinced that there is liberal bias and conspiracy across the length and breadth of the journalistic enterprise, and that they must root it out for the good of the republic.

Still others believe that there is a right-wing conspiracy, evident in broadcasting, to contaminate journalism with conservative theology. Those who are not after bias believe that journalism is a dying art—a victim of short attention spans, entertainment media and other distractions.

Finally there are those who doubt the need for traditional journalism; who believe that critical information can be garnered from source documents on the Internet and all the rest is show business. Wow.

The fact is that journalism has remained constant for 200 years; a simple craft that seeks to tell people what is going on. The changes—and there have been changes aplenty—are dictated by technology, which continues to forge change.

The greatest American journalist, H.L. Mencken, worried about the future of the morning newspaper. He saw it as being totally pushed out of the market by the fatter, richer evening papers that dominated. And, of course, they did. With electric light, greater literacy and very little to do, people read newspapers at night. Television reversed that rend. It killed off the great magazines like *Collier's, Life, Look* and *The Saturday Evening Post*. Journalism was alive and well, but it was appearing elsewhere.

The dirty little secret about journalism is that journalists are enormously conservative about their own craft, which is why newspapers are written much in the same way as they were in the 19th century; why old rules persist that no longer have a rationale, such as the way headlines are written and the attempt to get nine stories on Page 1. When cities had many newspapers, these practices were designed to sell them on the street. Now most newspapers are delivered to homes, but the devices conceived for street sales remain in place.

Universally newspaper readership is down, not because newspapers are facing extinction but because breaking news is now an electronic commodity. Consider the modern newspaper. It is made in a factory in the middle of the night, loaded on a truck to compete with the early traffic, and entrusted to a 10-year-old child for delivery. How can this product compete and deliver a perishable commodity: news?

Even if a newspaper breaks news, radio and television will quote it before it arrives at the consumer's door. The role of the newspaper is changing, but it is not at death's door. It simply fills a different niche—more expansive, more discursive, more analytical and better medium for debate.

The movies did not kill the live theater, they simply curtailed it. But because of the movies, more people were able to see theatrical entertainments than in the theater's golden age. Likewise, there is more news available for more outlets today than has ever been the case—and more journalists are employed to provide it.

The great challenge for newspapers, and the companies that control them, is whether they can adjust to the Internet and devise products appropriate to the new medium. So far, they have failed. So far, they have put newspaper pages down a wire and believe they are participating in the future.

The story of broadcasting does not bear out their expectations. In the early days of radio, most stations were owned by newspapers that did not know what to do with them. It took broadcasting visionaries—David Sarnoff, William Paley and Leonard Goldenson—to develop and exploit the new medium.

If newspapers want a big presence on the Internet, they will have to think beyond putting newspaper stories in cyberspace. New products formulated for the Internet will win the day.

Newspapers have been slow to change with time, lacking the ratings goad that keeps television experimenting. Magazines have been more imaginative, with such extraordinary creative figures as Henry Luce of *Time*, DeWitt Wallace of the *Reader's Digest* and, more recently, Jann Wenner of *Rolling Stone* revitalizing magazines. But *The New York Herald Tribune* stirred things up with horizontal makeup, now the standard. And another creative figure, Al Neuharth, perfected the use of color in *USA Today*.

If the media analysis industry wanted to do something for journalism, it would stop carping and start creating.

December 1, 2004

WHERE'S THE PIG WHEN I NEED HIM?

It is like hunting for truffles without the pig. I have referred to a new place I have arrived at: satellite television.

Although I have worked periodically in television—as a writer, presenter and producer—since the early 1960s, I have not enjoyed the wonders of cable or the charms of satellite television. Now I have it in rural Virginia, and my report from the frontline—an easy chair in my living room—is as follows.

Naively, I thought there would be an Aladdin's cave of things I desperately wanted to watch, such as great history, superb talk and irresistible drama. Not quite. The things I do not want to watch abound: I am offered cheap jewelry, old, old movies, and detective programs that show their age by the dial telephones that are the day's state-of-the-art communication.

The biggest disappointment is the unspeakably bad BBC America Channel. It is without the great dramas that the BBC is famous for; has many of the tired, old comedies with which PBS has been boring us for years; and endless—yes, endless—makeover programs.

The BBC makes over gardens, houses, people and vacations. All of this must be fascinating stuff if you live in the suburbs of London and want to know what it costs to re-plumb the bathroom in pounds sterling. But from the American point of view, it is idiotic.

Then there are programs about people who want to enlarge their houses but must first get through the labyrinth of British planning permission. In some buildings, apparently, you cannot even put in new windows without planning permission, which may explain why everyone goes to the pub so frequently.

What, I wonder, are the great minds of the world's largest broadcasting enterprise thinking when they foist this off on an American audience? Questions should be asked in the House of Commons.

But things are not much better on the Arts & Entertainment network, which is devoid of art and sparsely populated with entertainment.

The vaunted History Channel has a formula, which might be summed up as "pump it out cheap." It consists of all the file footage they can lay their hands on, with commentary from obscure academics—the kind of academics who write for Monarch Notes. This gruel is very thin.

The channels that critics of public broadcasting like to cite as carrying the alternative programming shunned by the networks are a sham.

Then there is the news. Whatever has happened to CNN since the glory days of Ted Turner? But all of them—CNN, CNN Headline News, Fox cable news,

MSNBC and CNBC—have entered the nudge, wink and giggle business. If there is more than one person on the set, they are off and running, larding the news footage with their banalities. Worse, maybe, is the irresistible, twenty-something beauty queen, who giggles and chirps through the news.

Nothing is sacred to Ms. Twenty-Something. If it is a fashion show, where opinions might actually be valid, she is in full voice. Unfortunately, Ms. Twenty-Something is also in full voice after footage of carnage in Iraq, tragedy on a U.S. highway, or the aftermath of a hurricane. Ms. Twenty-Something speaks to us as though she were talking to her best girlfriend on a cell phone. This is news delivery? I feel for the serious correspondents of the networks who are bookended by these inanities.

In fact, these inanities go a long way to explaining the phenomenal success of C-SPAN. Often boring, it is never inane.

The broadcast networks have always defended themselves, and probably rightly, that they are giving the public what it wants. What, I wonder, is the defense of the cable networks, especially those that purport to be an alternative: beacons in the night of television?

The sports networks are better, except that there does not seem to be enough of real sport to go around; so they have enlarged its meaning to include unicycle racing, fire-walking and eating contests.

After two months on my self-imposed television beat, I pray that in the new year I will be saved from my dish. Come back, Dan Rather. All is forgiven.

December 8, 2004

2005

CBS IS IN THE DOGHOUSE, AND BROADCASTING TANKING

Broadcast television is taking a thrashing.

CBS is abject after the investigation it commissioned into the "60 Minutes Wednesday" story about President Bush's service in the National Guard. First CBS believed, and wanted to believe, in the authenticity of forged letters, allegedly written by Bush's commander, and then it vigorously defended its own actions for 12 days. Altogether, this is a stain on what was once called the "Tiffany Network."

CBS, for all of its resources and all of its seasoned professionals, drank deeply from a poisoned chalice that is often passed around in newsrooms: a story so big that you want to believe in it. Big news consumes a news organization, intoxicates it, stimulates it, and puts it into an awkward position. There are as many examples of big stories not being aired or published because of editorial timidity as there are about those that have crossed the line.

London's *Sunday Mirror* failed to publish the story of Christine Keeler, the beautiful party girl who was sleeping both with British War Minister John Profumo and the Soviet Embassy's military attache. It was a scandal of huge proportions that rocked the government and caused the downfall of Profumo and many socialites, including Lord and Lady Astor. *The Sunday Mirror* itself was the victim, castigated for decades, for its timidity. It soon got a new editor. I know something about this because I was there at the time.

More recently Newsweek, showing too much restraint, sat on the Monica Lewinsky story, which was leaked subsequently to Matt Drudge, who has never looked back.

Had *The Washington Post's* Katherine Graham and Ben Bradlee not shown courage and resolution, there might not have been a Watergate scandal.

To journalists, the scoop, the big story, the blockbuster is the Holy Grail. It is what transmutes leaden metal into gold. A newspaper, or a broadcast outlet, is an electrifying place when it known that the big one is coming. So it is possible to understand, but not to excuse, CBS erring,

The perception that mainstream media is liberal, and that CBS is the pink center of liberalism in journalism, seems to be irreducible. In fact, more and more publications are voicing more and more conservative views, as are the networks. Conservative commentators, talk shows, and programming designed to appeal to conservatives has grown exponentially. Even PBS has added conservative programming.

In part, this swing to the right has been to mollify the critics and in part, it is a genuine reflection of the nation's swing to the right. With Republicans in charge of the White House and Congress, the media, the mirror of society, needs must reflect that society.

But CBS's woe is not its alone. Fox, staunchly and unashamedly conservative, is in trouble with its latest reality show, "Who's Your Daddy?" The family-values crowd do not like it. Across the board, this program has been criticized as tasteless. But to the family-values constituency, it is an attack on their core creed.

These difficulties for broadcasters come at a time when broadcasting finds itself at the low end of an unlevel playing field. They have gotten it in the neck for the Janet Jackson episode at the Super Bowl, and for an advertisement in which a woman drops her towel in front of an athlete. Shock jocks are taking a drubbing, and rap music is under scrutiny.

However, it is only broadcasting that faces the wrath and fines of the Federal Communications Commission. No wonder the best TV shows, with real-life profanity and nudity, are headed for cable and the shock jocks for satellite radio. The FCC, with its power over licenses and its ability to affect content, is out to discipline a shrinking industryone that is already much less than it was, and is likely to be even less in the future.

Broadcasters feel it necessary to push the envelope to compete with cable, but they have to face FCC Chairman Michael Powell and his Victorian values.

When the dust has settled on the CBS transgression, the more extraordinary thing is that we still do not know all there is to know about Bush's Guard service. Do not look for any broadcasters to find out. CBS's laxity has drawn another veil of secrecy over the president's past.

January 12, 2005

BUSH, BLAIR AND PUTIN 3 AMIGOS, DIFFERENT HORSES

Meet the Three Amigos: President George W. Bush, British Prime Minister Tony Blair and Russian President Vladimir Putin. They are more than three world leaders who get on: they are three leaders who will play critical roles over the next four years. And they are, in a sense, similar men of similar ideology, though sometimes of differing views.

Their political style is also very similar, as is their view that each of them is essential to his country at this time. Bush believes that he is a man with a mission to reform domestic institutions and to spread American values abroad. Deep religious beliefs anchor and inform his views.

Blair is something of a contradiction in British politics, with his upper-crust education and his working-class following, and his preparedness to support the United States while making the United Kingdom a bridge between Europe and America, and other traditional English-speaking parts of the world. It is a strategy that has kept British political commentators, and his own party, off-balance. Nobody quite knows what Blair thinks, or what his domestic vision for Britain is. They do know that Blair loves to play the internationalist—to circle the globe to mix with other leaders, and even to vacation outside of Britain. He, too, has deep religious convictions, which may play a part in his bond with Bush.

Then there is Putin: worldly wise, multilingual but determined to keep Russia a separate place, as it has been historically. Putin may move easily through the world, but it is not clear that he thinks Russia should. There are things from the tsarist times that tug at Putin. He sees his home town, St. Petersburg, as epitomizing Russia's greatness. And he clearly does not want to see Russia as just another European country. Russia, unique and unfathomable, is just fine with Putin. Bred as a KGB officer and for a while the head of its successor organization, the FSB, he is prepared to sacrifice Russia's economic interests for its imperial legacy. Putin is conspicuous in the congregation of the Russian Orthodox church, crossing himself and kissing icons. Whether he is, in fact, a religious man, no one knows.

All three men derive political strength from skillful political jingoism. Bush's appeal is to American exceptionalism and American values. Blair holds back the jingo card, but is happy to let Rupert Murdoch's powerful newspapers and satellite broadcasting company fan the flames for him. Murdoch gets the concessions he needs from the British government and Blair gets the endorsement of the Murdoch press.

Putin has increased his popularity by appealing to Russians' sense of their history and by making war on Russia's richest, known as the oligarchs. These are men who gained control of Russia's major assets under Boris Yeltsin, who, ironically, was Putin's patron.

All three men have a common body language. They are nice-looking, they convey physical vigor, and they can produce a quick and effective amiability when it is needed.

In reality, the long-term interests of neither the United States, Britain nor Russia are in confluence. But their leaders are and for the time being, it suits them well. The closest they have come to strain was over the Ukraine elections, when Putin dug in for his man, Yanukovich, as Blair and Bush dug in for theirs. Putin will not quickly forget the incident. Meanwhile, he hopes to lasso western Europe by building up its dependence on Russian gas. Likewise, he hopes to influence Japan and China with gas and oil. Russia is the world's third-largest oil exporter.

In the next four years, you can look for the Three Amigos to fall out. It is improbable that Blair will be in a position to endorse all of Bush's actions, or in the case of Palestine, his in action. Likewise, Putin will press his agenda in the Caucasus and eastern Europe. That could lead to trouble.

Meanwhile, Bush and Blair are shoulder to shoulder, and Putin is still a favorite of Bush.

Could it be that when these three men look into each other's eyes, as Bush famously did with Putin, they see each other? They are men supremely certain that they know best.

January 19, 2005

REMEMBERING AUSCHWITZ, THE ULTIMATE PROFANITY

The world has been marking the 60th anniversary of the liberation of Auschwitz, the production line of torture and death that the Nazis set up in southeastern Poland during World War II.

I visited Auschwitz once, 20 years ago, but Auschwitz visits me often. The scale of the barbarity, the consummate cruelty and the killing at this the largest of the death camps is such that you cannot fit it all into your head at one time.

Everything about Auschwitz is upsetting even before you get to the piles of human hair, the little children's shoes, the teeth and the pathetic rags. It does not look like a factory of death. It has the air of a campus; with so many attractive huts, neatly spaced, you could be forgiven for thinking it was designed as a holiday camp. Even the mocking sign over the main gate, "Work Makes One Free," is artfully executed.

In fact, it was a barracks before it was designed as a site for mass murder on a scale, in one place, that the world has never seen.

Some 1.5 million people died at Auschwitz and 7,000 were rescued 60 years ago. An old newspaper friend of mine told me not to go there: it would mess with my head. It has messed with my head, but I am glad I went.

As you walk through Auschwitz, your mind begins to play tricks on you. You wonder whether it was a million people and not 1.5 million. Then you wonder what you were thinking, as though a million deaths were nothing.

Of the panoply of horrors in this fantasy-land of killing, some are most affected by the relics, some by the shower heads—so fiendishly realistic but without plumbing. Yet others will shiver at the building, known as Canada, where gold teeth ripped from cadavers and other looted valuables were stored prior to shipment to Berlin. Some will retch for the first time outside Building #10, where Dr. Josef Mengele turned the healing arts into killing arts.

But for me, three things stood out: First, the gallows that dot the place where Jews, Gypsies, Poles, Russians, homosexuals, socialists, and other deemed enemies of the Third Reich were hanged at the caprice of the guards to maintain discipline and to save ammunition.

Second, the Gestapo wall, also known as the Black Wall, where very young policemen stripped prisoners naked and shot them in the back of the head with pistols, the bullets lodging in 6 inches of cork padding on the wall, thoughtfully provided for the purpose. This was a little bit of a freelance operation where crazed 16- and 17-year-olds killed people they had picked up in their forays outside the camp. There is a photograph there of a naked man being carried by two kids out to the wall to be executed.

Third, the precise engineering of the ovens overwhelmed me. In particular, I was struck by the little dollies designed in great detail to carry the victims to the ovens after they died from the poison gas in the showers. On those dollies, gold teeth were extracted and womens' and children's hair was cut off.

I am interested in engineering, and I wondered what engineers and architects in faraway Germany labored over the blueprints, completed the mechanical drawings, specified the materials, and possibly drew bonuses for work well done.

Auschwitz went into full operation in 1942—three years after I was born, which added to my anguish. This was not some slaughter in the ancient world, nor a medieval horror. It was something that happened in the early years of my life. Realizing these things shattered me: the engineering, the science, the time frame, and the unbridled bestiality.

An individual cannot calculate the suffering because it is incalculable. But an individual can ponder how a society went off the rails so extremely and in so short a space of time; how a nation bought into an ideology of the most naked racism the world has ever seen.

Of course one hopes that Auschwitz was a lesson for the world. But it does not seem to have been well learned: recently, we have had Darfur.

Chroniclers of the Holocaust like to invoke the refrain of Rudyard Kipling's poem "Recessional": "Lest we forget—lest we forget!"

In the final profanity, Auschwitz is being exploited by tour operators selling it as a horror show. That it is.

January 26, 2005

THE PITFALLS OF DRESS ON THE INTERNATIONAL STAGE

While the world is chortling at Vice President Cheney for showing up at the solemn ceremonies marking the 60th anniversary of the liberation of the Auschwitz death camp dressed in college football game attire, I have some sympathy for him.

It is hard enough to know what to wear at international occasions, let alone if you are the focus of global attention. No wonder blue and gray suits dominate international summits. Brown shoes when black are in order bring sniggers. Sometimes the garb of the great changes history.

Everyone knows that Franklin D. Roosevelt and Joseph Stalin got a little too chummy at Yalta for the good of the world. What's not widely known is that the bond they forged wasn't geopolitical but was in the delight they took in criticizing Winston Churchill's clothes. Not, mind you, that Churchill didn't have the right duds; he just didn't care to wear them, favoring instead the bespoke boiler suits he designed for himself during World War II.

Churchill found his unusual garments more comfortable, more practical, and ideal for taking naps. But they set off Roosevelt and Stalin, and the rest, as they say, is history.

An English monarch changed fashion when he appeared in a blue shirt with a white collar. Those were the days of detachable collars, and the Royal One simply put on the wrong collar, in absence of his valet. Now it's the fashion.

Henry Kissinger, on his first secret visit to China for President Nixon, was as concerned with the difficulty of getting a clean shirt as he was with the geopolitical changes he was initiating. Kissinger had to borrow shirts from his aides, many of which were ill-fitting, to his embarrassment in front of his hosts. But his hosts did not notice or know, and history moved ahead. Had he flown back to Washington to secure a better wardrobe, China might not have opened.

I always get it wrong. I went to a formal school where we wore jackets and neckties. To this day, I am more comfortable in a jacket and necktie. California is always a trial to me because people are always trying to peel off my clothes to make me more comfortable, which has twice led me to lose my wallet. The Hollywood thing I don't get. I don't know why actors can't go on a television talk show wearing a suit and necktie. What's the point of being so rich if you can't have a decent suit made?

I was part of the press corps accompanying President Clinton to China. My colleagues ragged me for always wearing a jacket and necktie, and finally I decided to throw caution to the wind and step forth in a polo shirt. Unfortunately, it was the day that Clinton debated Jiang Zemin in the Great Hall of the People on Tiananmen Square. By some telepathy, to which I was not attuned, my colleagues realized that this was a formal occasion and dressed accordingly. I felt somewhat the way Cheney must have felt at the Auschwitz commemoration.

In the world of clothes, it seems to be especially ticklish when Americans meet with the Japanese, who appear on nearly all occasions dressed in dark blue suits. At at a Japanese-American dialog held in Hawaii, the American delegation, of which I was a member, came to the first session dressed casually. Our Japanese counterparts were all in suits. After lunch, the Americans had changed into suits and the Japanese had changed into casual clothes.

Some of our mighty law firms have been experimenting with casual dress. In one, I found the older male lawyers looking extremely uncomfortable, if not chagrined, because they couldn't wear the bespoke suits they had tailored in England, and the young female lawyers feeling cheated. What's the point in climbing the legal ladder if you can't wear a gorgeous designer outfit when you make partner?

Europeans, as arbiters of taste, have taken particular glee in criticizing Cheney's casual outfit. While one feels sorry for the vice president, he might be advised in the future to pack a suit and check with the State Department's protocol office before he steps out. It's a sartorial minefield out there.

February 2, 2005

RETIREMENT: DO NOT GO GENTLE
INTO THAT GOOD EVENING

PHOENIX—It is a good thing that Winston Churchill did not believe that he should retire at age 65. If he had, World War II might have gone to Adolf Hitler. Churchill was 65 when he became Britain's wartime prime minister. The current ghastly and contradictory debate over Social Security throws a light on the vexing question of retirement. Who? At what age? And in what jobs?

Retirement is an unequal thing, depending on health, wealth, but above all on the occupation of the oldster. Like Churchill, many are in their prime at 65 and are cruelly forced out by company policy to be premature has-beens, to hanker for the harness they loved, to busy themselves on the periphery of what was once the central purpose of their lives. This is true of managers, professionals and simply those who love what they do. It is not true of those who do menial and manual work. For them, 65 is a blessed release. Their bodies are often broken, as was my father's, he being a mechanic. But for most of us who sit behind desks, and who suffer nothing more arduous than a long meeting, retirement at 65 is the opening of the door to death's anteroom. For the professional classes, 65 is simply too early to cross the great divide from work to leisure.

The British playwright Noel Coward said: "Work is much more fun than fun." So it is for many of us. Retirement means a new kind of stress: a premature preoccupation with health, finances and finding something to do with the long, empty days.

In this limbo, blessed are the golfers. But if you have run a company, contributed to the national debate, or otherwise thought you were doing something of real consequence, the golf course is poor recompense and like as not, you will hire yourself out as a "consultant"—that uncomfortable place of trying to do what you used to do from a disadvantaged position.

When the good works have failed, the recreations have grown tired and no one wants you to consult, you probably will find something menial to fill in the time. In a retirement community like Phoenix, you can see the oldsters working at restaurants, driving shuttle buses at the airport and even working as bellhops. Some of these lesser second careers may be dictated by financial need, and others help people to escape the grinding boredom that they have inherited with their release from work.

Daily, retired men and women come by my office asking to be involved in some activity without pay, just to be included. The retirees peer through the window and see the party to which they are no longer invited.

It is no accident that the news channels, C-SPAN and PBS, draw their largest stable audiences from the retired. People who used to get the news in a few minutes a day now can spend all day getting it. For them, retirement is not the golden years but the tedium years—years of free-floating anxiety, apprehension and an increasing sense of purposelessness.

Nelson Mandela, Pablo Picasso, Konrad Adenauer and George Bernard Shaw did their most important work after the age of 65. Not for them the *ennui* of cruising the world or the banality of yoga in the community center. Rupert Murdoch, in his mid-seventies, runs the greatest media empire ever assembled. Had he been the chief executive officer of General Electric, he would have been obliged to retire nearly a decade ago. No! No! Let us stop throwing the able-bodied and productive away.

The poet Dylan Thomas wrote, when his father was dying, "Do not go gentle into that good night." For myself, and many like me at age 65, we do not want to go gentle even into that good evening.

February 9, 2005

IF JOURNALISM IS SO EASY, HAVE A GO

Now that the news is the news, through fabrication (Jayson Blair), ineptitude (CBS and Dan Rather), and most recently political bias (James Dale Guckert, aka Jeff Gannon), you may be tempted to try your hand at journalism.

If you think it is a free-for-all, you are right. There is no particular qualification that will make you a journalist, and no indication of who will rise from the pack and enjoy greatness. Sure, there are those who go through journalism school and head for the stars, and appear to do so rung-by-rung without impediment. But those who reach the heights in print and television often get there circuitously. And many who deserve to get there are sidelined in minor publications for all of their productive lives.

It is a little like entering the church: a vow of poverty helps. Even if poverty is not the case, as with a fistful of television reporters and newspaper columnists, the working conditions are appalling. I mean it-appalling: broken chairs, cracked coffee cups, psychotic bullies (Those who can write write. Those who cannot become editors and bully).

The workplace is a thing of horror for many journalists. New York newspapers, until quite recently, did not have air-conditioned newsrooms and appear to have gotten their furniture at Civil War surplus sales. Also, many newspapers are located in tenderloin areas. The most dangerous part of the day may be leaving work at night, fighting your way through the winos, the schizophrenics, and n'er-do-wells who seem to hang around newspaper buildings.

Two of the great plums in journalism are covering Congress and the White House. In both cases, the workspaces are so cramped and so dirty that were they subject to the Occupational Safety and Health Administration standards, they would be closed down. Charles Dickens would have had a thing to write about them.

Then there are the hours. You want to work on NBC's "Today" show? Try getting up at 3 a.m. every day. I have not worked on the "Today" show, but I have had jobs where I had to get up at 3 a.m. every day. You have no social life, and you are always falling asleep at your desk and in buses, trains and taxis. Traveling with the president may seem like fun, but some of the glamor ebbs away when you are fighting the security at Andrews Air Force Base at 4 a.m.

So you have decided to take the plunge. You write quite nicely and you are addicted to current affairs. Well, sorry, there is one qualification that dwarfs all of the others: news judgment. It is an amorphous ability to know what is news. It cannot be taught.

Because most successful reporters are attuned to the same stimuli, they come up with the same stories when competing with each other, causing their critics to say that they conspire. Anyway you have to have news judgment or you cannot perform the work. And you have to be able to get things right, or mostly right, otherwise you will shortly be joining the street people around the newspaper building.

It used to be that you had to have a titanium liver. But drinking has declined in journalism, and now one of cast iron will see you through.

After the physical deprivations of the work come the psychological traumas: rejection by those you are trying to speak to, exclusion from places you want to get into, and a general sense that you belong to a lower order of humanity-that you are reprehensible by nature and generally unfit for the company of the movers and shakers with whom you have to try and mingle.

If you should be so lucky as to find yourself at a great newspaper, such as *The New York Times, The Washington Post, The Los Angeles Times* or *The Chicago Tribune*, you have to begin to plot to get the beat you want. Likewise television. It is the second struggle for a job in the journalistic career. First you try to get hired. That is the easy part. Then you have to convince the people who hired you to let you have a go at something that might make your name. Carl Bernstein and Bob Woodward were not stars at *The Washington Post* when Watergate broke. They were city-side reporters sent to cover a minor break-in, as their assignment editor thought.

So you write like a demon. Cool it. There is a whole section of disgruntled, unhappy people called copy editors who fight an undeclared war against adjectives and adverbs.

When Tom Wolfe, the novelist, was a reporter for *The New York Herald Tribune*, to get into print the kind of writing he knew he could do, he had to do an end-run around his own editors and sell freelance pieces to the newspaper's magazine.

The race goes not necessarily go to the talented. More often, it goes to the obedient and reliable—those in television who can do faultless "standups," or those in newspapers who file "clean" copy.

The ability to ingratiate yourself with people who know things is essential, and ultimately it can be your downfall. Poor Scotty Reston, the storied *New York Times* columnist, got just too close to Vice President Spiro Agnew and was defending him almost until the indictments came down.

There is one more thing: We love this work. And if our families can stand the impoverishment, the hours and the general excesses, most of us would stay in it until we are called to the great newsroom in the sky.

February 16, 2005

VELVET REVOLUTIONS NEED A GOLDEN UNDERPINNING

Freedom is what you do with what's been done to you.

—Jean-Paul Sartre

Velvet revolutions are all the rage in Washington: South Africa, eastern Europe and Ukraine. Now there is something close to euphoria in Washington, and praise for President Bush as the goad to incipient change in Lebanon, Egypt, and even Saudi Arabia.

If democracy is on the march, Bush deserves credit. Even National Public Radio's Daniel Schorr, no fan of the president, has conceded that Bush may be succeeding in his grand plan for a democratic Middle East.

Indeed, if he succeeds beyond Afghanistan and Iraq, Bush, the unlikely internationalist, will have earned his place in history.

But those of us who saw democracy flourish and wither in short order across Africa will withhold our judgment. Democracy without real pluralism and without prosperity is the most fragile of structures.

The Middle Eastern challenge is to bring democracy to lands that have never known it, where there is only one strong alternative institution: Islam. For the Middle East, Islam is always the refuge. It offers a place of assembly for those who have been denied the right of assembly; and being a religion of law, it contains within it a sense of constitutional procedure. The princes of this religion are as defensive, imperial and proselytizing as were the princes of Christianity. Democracy, whether it intends to or not, challenges the concept of divine organization on earth.

Ergo, democracy in Muslim countries must accommodate religion without confronting it. The devout Muslim must either oppose this new order, or bend it to the will of Islam. That is what happened in Algeria, where an election was set aside, and what nearly happened in more secular Turkey. If democracy is seen as a challenge to Islam, it will be doomed to a violent extinction.

The other challenge to democracy in the Middle East is the one created by expectations. In Africa it was assumed that the prosperity of the ruling European colonial class would pass unfettered to the masses. When it did not do so, there was disillusion and collapse. To this day, this is the challenge in South Africa, where 25 million Africans anticipated that with the end of apartheid, they would enjoy automatically the prosperity that the white minority enjoyed under apartheid and continues to exhibit. This makes for a different kind of revolution; not one of street protests, but one of Kalashnikovs, rocket-propelled grenades and bombs.

The West, led by the United States, needs a serious economic plan for the Middle East that will show gains in prosperity after political revolution. In the oil-producing countries of the region, this is achievable. But it is a tough call for the poorest parts of the Middle East—and they are very poor indeed.

What would a democratic Palestinian state have to export? At this point, a trickle of dates and olive oil, not enough to build anything upon. Similarly, Jordan, Syria and even Lebanon are bereft of anything approaching export economies. Handicrafts and agricultural products from the Levant will not fulfill democratic expectations of the people in the streets of Amman, Damascus and Beirut. Tourism could bring an early revival in a few destinations, but the chief beneficiary would be Egypt. And tourism alone will not lift populous countries out of poverty.

Therefore a pervasive economic plan for the Middle East, including widespread educational reform, has to underwrite the first shoots of democracy.

To date, the Bush administration has been weak in dealing with the day after tomorrow. The conquest of Afghanistan has led to a gigantic increase in heroin production and little else by the way of economic activity. Likewise, outside of oil, there seems to be no economic plan for Iraq. And the problem with oil is that it has no value-added component, creates few jobs and has proven to be antithetical to a work ethic.

In Saudi Arabia and Kuwait, oil has led not to prosperity but to welfare; to indolent, frustrated populations. Little Qatar is struggling to avoid the oil trap: enough money and nothing to do.

The administration and its allies need to conceive an economic plan for the Middle East—one that encourages investment, protects exports, and stimulates, along with the ballot box, the bank account.

March 2, 2005

LONDON SWINGS TO A NEW AND DIFFERENT DRUMMER

LONDON—By far and away, this is Americans' favorite overseas destination. Americans love London, or that part of it that most tourists see—the West End, London's version of Manhattan.

The 1960s started for London gray and drab. It was still recovering from the bombing of World War II and it was a place where life was difficult because of the British habit then of shutting things down at appointed hours. Pubs closed variously at 9:30 p.m., 10:30 p.m. and 11 p.m. You could drink around the clock but it took great skill and personal knowledge, as you moved from the flower market to the fish market to the meat market and had a pint with the rough denizens of those places.

But for all visitors, and nearly all Londoners, this was not an option. You went to bed early. The Underground, known as the Tube, stopped running at 11 p.m. And most bus service was suspended. Right around that time, Britain's two television channels signed off.

Things began to change radically in the 1960s, with designer Mary Quant's hot pants and miniskirts and a slew of new clubs, restaurants and wine bars that shook things up. Carnaby Street was the emblem of swinging London, but new vitality sprouted everywhere.

As Britain declined as an imperial power and its manufacturing traditions eroded, it was replaced by a jazzy new consumerism, where hairdressers and designers stole the glamor from the captains of industry, the landed gentry, and even the royal family. Satirists such as David Frost, John Cleese and Spike Milligan were in, and Shakespeare and Swift were out. The new London was about fun, fun, fun. And even the boring old BBC came around and gave a home to the impudence of the time, with programs like "That Was The Week That Was," "The Goon Show" and, later, "Monty Python's Flying Circus."

In an act that would have been heresy in the middle 1950s, the Union Jack appeared on clothing, shopping bags, and ultimately on the tails of airplanes. Retailing loosened too. Particularly thanks to a new generation of shopkeepers from Asia, who did the unheard of: They stayed open late and, goodness gracious me, opened on Sunday.

London had turned into a party city—no invitation necessary, come as you are. And they came. What is more, they are still coming, and in such numbers and variety that the London of yesteryear is still evolving into something even more cosmopolitan, chic and, well, less British. Twenty-seven percent of London's population today was not born in Britain. In inner London, that figure rises to 35 percent.

The first wave of immigrants came from India, Pakistan and the West Indies. Now the floodgates are open to Eastern Europe, Russia, Africa and the Middle East. Immigrants are everywhere and with them their cultures, again changing the fabric if not the face of London.

Bayswater, long a middle-class area of apartments and small hotels, bordering on the northern edge of Hyde Park, is a case in point. I have been staying in a hotel where the staff comes variously from Malaysia, Russia and the Czech Republic. No English people here and not much English spoken. Queensway, a major London thoroughfare that bisects Bayswater, epitomizes the new London. Throngs of energized people move up and down the street, talking in Arabic, Chinese, Czech, French, Japanese, Polish, Russian, Shona, Swahili and, just occasionally, English.

A friend in the hyper-fashionable Knightsbridge area, which houses Harrods department store, tells me that he hears mostly Russian in the shops and restaurants, and even in the building where he lives.

So far, so good, but it is not the London that I knew 40 years ago. It is New York East—as frenetic, expensive and exciting as the Big Apple.

Other English cities have been similarly affected, but none to the extent that London has. And much of the English countryside, in the smaller towns, is untouched by the revolution in population. Of course, all of this has English politicians greatly worried, as many of the new immigrants come in as "asylum seekers" or simple illegals.

If present trends continue, it will not be long before half the people living in London are of foreign extraction or are born elsewhere. So far, London has been a beneficiary of this huge inward migration. But the bugaboos of assimilation, and of an English identity, are being felt. Wales and Scotland have been much less affected than England and, of course, London. Some Brits ask when London will lose its essential English character, which predates the Romans and the enormous swath of history since then.

Samuel Johnson said," When a man is tired of London, he is tired of life." William Wordsworth reflected "Upon Westminster Bridge" at midnight. And Noel Coward buoyed Londoners during the blitz with "London Pride," the key refrain of which is that it is "handed down to us." Now it has been handed to a huge wave of new Londoners. We Americans hope they treasure our favorite offshore city.

March 9, 2005

THE NEW OIL SHOCK: SHOCKING AND PERMANENT

There is bad news from the global oil patch: it is drying up. For 30 years, political forces have been blamed for volatility in the price of oil. But ruthless exploitation, better technology and a global thirst for oil is putting measurable strain on the reserves.

Production in many non-Organization of Petroleum Exporting Countries (OPEC), including the United States, has either peaked or is close to peaking. In the contiguous United States, production peaked in the 1970s. More recently, production in Alaska's North Slope has gone into decline.

Today the 11 OPEC member nations are more important than ever, and not all of their reserves are in good shape. Some analysts believe that Venezuela, and even Iran, are close to their production peak.

At the same time, global demand has surged since 1995, from about 70 million barrels a day to about 83 million barrels a day today—a reflection of new demand from China and India and heavy U.S. consumption.

In the past, many analysts, and the oil companies themselves, believed that the impediments to producing more oil are political. They put the blame on wicked OPEC, environmentalism and government market intervention. Now they are taking stock again, recognizing that the world's oil resources are under pressure and it is unlikely to ameliorate, short of a global recession.

This week the Saudi oil minister, Ali al-Naimi, announced that world oil prices were too high and that Saudi Arabia, the world's largest oil exporter, would push for an immediate lift in OPEC's ceiling of 500,000 barrels a day—a modest amount, suggesting that it is feeling supply constraint. OPEC's president, Sheikh

Ahmad Fahad al-Ahmad al-Sabah of Kuwait, at the oil-exporting group's meeting this week in Isfahan, Iran, responded with a two-step plan to increase its production ceiling by 1 million barrels of oil a day by May.

Last year, oil markets were shattered when Royal Dutch Shell downgraded its reserves. Others followed suit. Suddenly, the world is facing an oil crisis keyed to demand outstripping supply in real terms. Only a fistful of producers can increase their production in the future, and these do not have enough oil to seriously alter the imbalance in supply and demand. They include Chad, Equatorial Guinea, Qatar, Sudan and the United Arab Emirates.

Last week the International Energy Agency (IEA), created by Henry Kissinger after the first oil crisis, took a dismal view of the oil future. For the first time, the agency acknowledged that supply and demand were driving prices not cartel action or geopolitics. In its wordy way, the IEA acknowledged that the crunch is now. London's *Financial Times* splashed the story on Page One, and the price of oil jumped.

The Saudi oil minister, who last week blamed lack of refining capacity, especially in the United States, for high gasoline prices, has since reversed himself by offering to increase output.

The Europeans have been so alarmed by oil prices that they have created a special unit to look at the world supply and demand, and they calculate an absolute reversal of the rate of production by 2010—other analysts are calculating a reversal by 2008.

These grim predictions will not be erased by small local discoveries if demand shows no abatement. The best hope is that high prices will induce conservation by the world's largest oil-consuming nations, led by the United States and followed by western European countries.

Suddenly, Russia becomes an even more critical supplier. It is already the world's second-largest oil producer and can probably increase its production from 6 million barrels a day to 8 million barrels a day, if the Putin administration releases its grasp on the nation's oil industry and encourages Western know-how and technology to both find new oil and to build desperately needed pipelines to bring it to market.

While the Bush administration has been publicly silent on the new oil crisis, it has been privately pressuring OPEC ministers to increase supply. The administration's public silence is partly due to its adherence to the mythology that governments hinder new oil supply, and partly because it is caught on the horns of its own rhetoric opposing conservation.

If oil prices stay high, and the world economy survives them, conservation would appear to be the only smooth transition to the future. Like the depleted fish stocks in the North Sea, the day of reckoning for oil production is at hand.

March 16, 2005

A LETTER FROM 'OLD EUROPE' MON DIEU!
IT IS THE STYLE NOT THE SUBSTANCE

Dear America, indeed America the Beautiful,

I take second place to no one in my admiration of the United States. From sea to shining sea, it is the exemplar of much that will be right in the world. More to the point, it is the laboratory that will produce much that will be right in the world. But I have a caveat: something has happened to your manners.

I did not support the war in Iraq and I may have been wrong in that. But even so, I was not one of those Europeans who thought that President Bush was an itchy-fingered gunslinger. Indeed, his radicalism appealed to the radicalism of my youth—barricades in France, marches in London and demonstrations in Rome. As the British writer Christopher Hitchens has said, there is an appeal in Bush's radicalism for all radicals, even if they have cut their teeth on the left. Big change, and political figures prepared to engineer it, has an undeniable appeal.

So here those of my generation, formed by the 1960s, sit, half appalled, half enchanted by this very different American president. What upsets us and the larger European population is the gratuitously rude way that Bush and his neoconservative radicals go about their business. In particular, they seem committed to giving us Europeans the back of their hands whenever a change, in American policy, or even a change in personnel, is in train.

We are not consulted, and often we are insulted. It began with Bush's unilateral abandonment of the Kyoto Protocol, along with his unilateral withdrawal from the Anti-Ballistic Missile Treaty. Likewise, there is the scorn the administration has poured on the International Criminal Court.

These acts raise hackles in Europe, not because of their substance but because of the style in which they were delivered. Or, more exactly, because of the gratuitously rude way in which we were kept out of the information-forming process until the edicts were handed down from the White House.

Yet all was forgiven when we poured out our hearts to our American friends over 9/11. It was a time of a new beginning, of a slate wiped clean by sorrow.

But it was not to be a new beginning; The back of the hand kept coming, whether it was an insult ("Old Europe") from Defense Secretary Rumsfeld, or the relentless attack of the Bush claque of neoconservatives. Pummeling Europe reached the point of a vindictive sport played by the neconservative intelligensia: people like Richard Perle, Christopher Caldwell and William Kristol. They derided our social structure and our weak defenses. They even attacked our superior surface transportation system.

Every European country, with the exception of the United Kingdom and eastern Europe, was fit for derision, Hell, French fries is an American term for fried potatoes. In France and Belgium, they are frites and in the UK, they are chips. The congressmen who sought to rename fried potatoes were taking back a name they had bestowed on what was originally a New World vegetable.

If the administration and its supporters had chosen to level the same abuse on friends in Egypt, Pakistan, Saudi Arabia and Turkey, Bush's war in Iraq might not have gone so well.

The sad thing about his decision to denigrate America's friends and cultural parents is that it is counterproductive. We have seen the president and Secretary of State Condoleezza Rice come to Europe to try to patch things up. The administration has been forced to abandon its favored proactive posture for a reactive one.

We are, my friends, on the same side in the great schisms of history and culture. We can tolerate divergent policies between Washington and European capitals if the United States stops reaching for the salt every time there is a wound. Style counts for something.

The president is entitled to appoint John Bolton as his ambassador to the United Nations, and to appoint Paul Wolfowitz to lead the World Bank. We have no veto on these appointments, nor should we. But a few phone calls, covering that part of diplomacy that is classified as manners, would have avoided the current storm in the Atlantic.

Europe needs America. And we Europeans have the temerity to believe that America needs Europe, if the democratic project is to prosper.

All the best, Your Cousin

March 23, 2005

QATAR: LAND OF SAND AND MEGA HYDROCARBONS

DOHA, Qatar—Given that the highest accolade that President Bush bestows on foreign leaders is a visit to his Prairie Chapel Ranch in Crawford, Texas, can an invitation to the emir of Qatar, Sheikh Hamad bin Khalifa Al Thani, be far off?

The Qatari emir is just the kind of leader that Bush likes. He hosts one of the United States' largest air bases in the Middle East, which was invaluable during the invasion of Iraq. He advocates free trade and equal rights for women. And he has taken the first tentative steps towards democracy in Qatar. What is more, he has encouraged his subjects to wear their religion lightly.

Qatar, a sandy peninsula that juts into the Arabian Gulf, has something else that should commend it to the president: it has Texas-size ideas about the future—ideas that belie its population of under a million. Qatar is turning itself into the world's leading producer of liquefied natural gas (LNG). Through this resource, it is extending its reach into Europe and Asia, with plans to tap the U.S. market in 2009.

All this makes Qatar geopolitically important. With the third-largest reserves of natural gas in the world, Qatar is rapidly getting into a position where it could buffer dependence on more mercurial suppliers. It is a strategy that is not wasted on the Europeans—and particularly the British—who fear their growing dependence on pipeline gas from Russia.

Qatar is building the world's largest gasification plants, and it has ordered the world's largest LNG tankers. If discussion of oil cannot take place without mentioning Saudi Arabia, very soon discussions of natural gas will have to include a reference to Qatar and its global reach.

In short, Qatar is set to become a superpower in hydrocarbon exports. And along the way, it may also become the world's richest country.

Qatar oil also flows in international commerce. But with production of under a million barrels a day, natural gas will soon dwarf the emirate's oil production as it shoulders its way into world markets.

The Qataris are mindful that huge hydrocarbon wealth is not by itself a guarantee of social stability, and they are aware of what has happened to their neighbor, Saudi Arabia, and other oil-rich nations that have failed to establish an integrated economy.

It remains to be seen whether Qatar can develop supporting industries. The first step planned by Qatar is an expansion of its petrochemical and plastics industries. Indeed, the Qataris talk boldly about becoming a world leader not only in LNG but also in petrochemicals. The challenge, as other oil-rich states have discovered, is whether low-margin chemicals and plastics industris can prosper alongside hydrocarbon wealth.

Twenty-five years ago, I remember being lectured on the coming world domination of a petrochemicals industry in Saudi Arabia. It has not happened. The Saudis over-invested in many industries in the hope that they could diversify their economy, but all they achieved was a series of spectacular white elephants. These included a French-built cement plant that could only operate on sand imported from France.

Qatar has the luxury of looking over its shoulder at the successes and failures of its sibling emirates, Bahrain and Abu Dhabi. Doha would like to rival Dubai as a financial center, and both are locked in hot competition for tourism. A diplomat here told me: "They would both like to be thought of as the Monaco of the Middle East. They have got the beaches, they are liberal about Western ways, and they are building the hotels. But will the people come?"

Historically, Qatar was so irrelevant that hardly anyone noticed when it ceased to be a British protectorate in 1970. Ergo, it cannot be blamed for being intoxicated with its new relevance. The atmosphere here is akin to a grand 21st birthday party. But the 75-billion-dollar question (that is the amount that has been invested in hydrocarbon development) is whether Qatar can keep its Islamic traditions while pushing its liberal agenda. That is something that Bush can ask the emir, if he gets around to inviting him to his Texas ranch.

Amazingly, U.S. anger over Al Jazeera, the Qatar-based satellite television service, is subsiding. It has been showing pro-democracy demonstrations in Jordan and elsewhere in the Middle East, which pleases the administration as much as Al Jazeera's coverage of the war in Iraq has irked it. Score another point for the emir.

April 1, 2005

THE BLESSING OF BREVITY, BRITISH STYLE

In a few short weeks, Britain will elect a new Parliament. On April 5, Prime Minister Tony Blair called the election for May 5. The result is four short weeks of incredibly hectic campaigning, and then the whole thing is over. How merciful, we might say as we contemplate permanent campaigns for House members and campaigns of two and three years for the presidency.

What is more, the average British member of Parliament will spend a pittance in comparison with his or her American counterparts. In fact, individuals have to raise very little money in Britain, largely because they have no way of spending it. Constituencies are small and can be traversed easily by car. The expenses, mostly borne by the local constituency party, are in organizing rallies, and printing posters and direct mail pieces.

British elections are quick but not necessarily clean. The fact is that the British system of democracy is not as open as the American one. In Britain anyone can stand for Parliament, but unless you have the nod of the local party and the imprimatur of the national party, the only way you will get to the House of Commons is as a tourist.

The real constriction on British democracy is the party selection system, which is secretive, often manipulative, and disadvantageous to the individual who does not fit the mold of his party. Each of the three contending British parties—Labor, Conservative and Liberal Democrat—has its own selection criteria. But getting selected is an inside job and can be orchestrated by the national party leadership. For example, Blair's Labor Party wanted to increase the number of women and minorities in the House of Commons and decreed that half the candidates had to fit these criteria.

In Blair's first government, therefore, women were a huge factor and did not reflect the political class in the country. In short, able and ambitious men were passed over in favor of women or minorities.

Likewise, the national parties move their star candidates around safe constituencies. Members of Parliament have been elected from parts of the country they have never visited, although this is not the case today. It works like this: if the party leader wants a particular candidate to be elected, he will simply insist that he is "adopted" by the constituency party in a seat that is safe. In this way the same figures appear routinely in British parliaments, where they have used their national reputation to secure a constituency heavy in core voters.

All parties play this game—and have played it through the long history of the House of Commons. Sometimes, just occasionally, there is a hiccup and the party patrician loses his or her seat. Most notably in recent times, this happened to Michael Portillo, who unexpectedly lost his seat, and with it his chances of becoming the Conservative Party leader. Winston Churchill came close to losing his seat several times and changed his constituency.

If you favor a candidate to be prime minister and you are a British voter, all you can do is vote for the leader's party. The prime minister is chosen not by the people but by the party, and can be removed—as Margaret Thatcher was—without recourse through a general election.

There are other things in the British electoral system calculated to unnerve a U.S. civics class. Even more than the United States, the popular vote is not determining. Most British governments are elected by a minority of the British electorate. At present, there are 646 seats in the House of Commons and three parties in contention. But the majority of the Tory votes will be cast overwhelmingly in rural and country areas, while the urban vote will go to Labor, and the suburban vote will be split among all three. Because of the heavy Conservative vote in the countryside, many of those votes will be wasted.

Polls are showing the Conservatives, under Michael Howard, to be neck and neck with Labor. But the electoral map overwhelmingly favors Labor, with a majority of about 50 seats in the House of Commons.

Think red states, blue states and pink states, and Blair should romp home.

What is to envy about the British electoral system? Just the brevity of the convulsion.

April 13, 2005

WILL THE ZIMBABWE CONTAGION SPREAD?

Winter is setting in South Africa but climatically it is of little consequence. The arid, hot northern areas along the Limopopo River will be bearable and the lush Mediterranean climate of the South toward Cape Town will be a little chilly but not severely so.

It is another winter that worries people in South Africa: a long, terrible winter that might be described as the Zimbabwe effect. South Africans are beginning to wonder how long it will be before the outrages of Zimbabwe's President Robert Mugabe are imported into South Africa. If South Africa begins to fail, and is contaminated by the African diseases of corruption, tribalism and paranoia, the last jewel in the African crown will lose its luster.

And if it happens, it will not be because of Mugabe alone, but because of South Africa's own inscrutable President Thabo Mbeki, who has acted as Mugabe's enabler: a silent partner in the crimes and excesses that Mugabe has inflicted on his people, destroying the once prosperous past and the racial and tribal amity he was handed at the end of white rule in 1980.

It is hard now to remember just how euphoric things in Zimbabwe were when Mugabe took power. A bloody civil war was put out of mind and the country basked in international approval as the model of the New Africa. The honeymoon lasted a decade and a half. Then Mugabe, to all appearances, began to lose it. In the beginning, he was allowed his eccentricities without protest from the majority of Zimbabweans, both white and black, and the international community. Happy prosperous Zimbabwe was the success story of Africa: multi-cultural, multi-ethnic and full of hope.

Then Mugabe began to go seriously mad. That is a strong statement, but what else do you say about a man who would willingly grab defeat from the jaws of victory? A man who would destroy one of the best little economies in the world, run down the infrastructure and evict essential farmers, black and white, in a despotic attempt to re-write history?

Mugabe's story is worthy of Italian opera. As a victorious freedom fighter he acquires more than he had ever dreamed of and is acclaimed around the globe. But then things start going wrong for Mugabe and his paranoia increases. He intervenes in the civil war in the Congo for no apparent reason, and launches a relentless attack on his own commercial farmers, most of whom bought their farms from the Mugabe government.

Many of the extremes of Mugabe's behavior may be attributable to none other than the saintly Nelson Mandela. Mandela usurped Mugabe's role as the poster boy for the New Africa. And then—this is the operatic bit—Mandela married the widow of Mozambique leader Samora Machel whom Mugabe had hoped to marry. After that, there was no stopping Mugabe. He sent thugs, he called war veterans, out to seize white farms, terrorize their African employees, destroy their equipment and kill or drive off the farmers. If his intent was cleansing Zimbabwe of it's small white population, he succeeded. At independence, Zimbabwe had a population of 300,000 whites, many of them third and fourth generation settlers. Now there are 25,000, many of whom were not born in Zimbabwe.

Mandela's successor, Mbeki, might have been expected to restrain his northern neighbor. Instead, he has encouraged him. Zimbabwe cannot function without the cooperation of South Africa. A land-locked country, it depends on road and rail links through South Africa (and one rail line through Mozambique) for its exports and imports. Without South Africa, Zimbabwe, under any government, is not viable. It was the South Africans who enabled Ian Smith to defy the British government and maintain the ill-conceived independence of white-ruled Rhodesia. Nothing has changed.

Rather than curb Mugabe, Mbeki endorses him, refuses any criticism and, as much as Mugabe's own thuggish police, enables the mad dictator of central Africa to continue the destruction of his country, the starvation of his people and its relentless depopulation through AIDS.

What does Mbeki have in mind? Does he share Mugabe's sick delusions? Would he rather see bountiful, beautiful South Africa taken down the Zimbabwe path? One is tempted to say "yes," otherwise, why would Africa's most important ruler of its most industrialized country encourage a man who has brought nothing but death and incalculable suffering to his people?

Maybe Mbeki is as great a racist as Mugabe. The clouds are there. The long winter is an open question.

April 20, 2005

CAN'T SLEEP? TRY A NEWSPAPER

Rupert Murdoch, a master of public vulgarity and an endless seeker of the lowest common denominator, is not much liked in the publishing industry, but he is feared and admired. Not without reason. He is the most successful publisher of all time, with an uncanny sense of the public frustration.

So when he spoke to the American Society of Newspaper Editors, his dry, matter-of-fact tones fell on eager ears. It was not the greatest speech on newspapering ever delivered, but it was voiced by the most successful exponent of the art—and people listened.

He told the editors that they were out of touch with their readers, they were complacent and they were facing a tidal wave of competition, which is robbing them of new readers and cutting down their influence as an advertising medium and source of information. Every editor in the room knew this. And while few would wish to follow the extremes of the Murdoch press, especially in Britain, they were hoping to hear about the silver bullet.

The bullet, if there is one, is people like Murdoch himself: auteur publishers. Murdoch qualifies as an exemplar of that dying breed. He started with a small newspaper company that he inherited in Australia and then bought *The Sun*, a failing, left-wing English tabloid, from its competitor, the mighty *Daily Mirror*. He then did the unthinkable: He turned the newspaper, which at one time had been the voice of the trade unions, into a raging, jingoistic, patriotic and mildly pornographic publication. Within months, *The Sun* was eating into the circulation of its former proprietor, *The Daily Mirror*, and was on its way to becoming Britain's most profitable newspaper.

The Murdoch formula—or magic, if you prefer-did not work on American newspapers. He damaged *The Chicago Sun Times*, made a mess of the paper in San Antonio, Texas, and found no traction in Boston. However, the canny Australian was not through with America, or with his formula. He applied it to Fox broadcasting, where the mixture of conservatism and vulgarity has led on to huge success.

Editors and publishers trying to understand what to do now should realize that as much as they dislike Murdoch's vision, it is a vision and he is a successful publisher in the tradition of the giants of publishing: giant men, not giant corporations.

What Murdoch might have told the editors is that you cannot run a newspaper or a network through focus groups, opinion polling, or other market research. The great publishers who have moved forward the publishing enterprise have been men of single vision: dictatorial, aggressive and prepared to be disliked.

The titans include: Joseph Pulitzer, William Randolph Hearst, DeWitt Wallace, Henry Luce, Roy Howard and, more recently, Al Neuharth. They were the directors of the business and of the content, more akin to filmmakers than publishing executives. They broke the rules, angered the investors, perturbed all manner of civic bodies, and made great fortunes for themselves while leaving indelible imprints on journalism.

If you cross the Atlantic, there are other greats—men like the Harmsworth brothers, the Berrys, Beaverbook and Cudlipp—who invigorated newspaper and magazine publishing. They are not dwarfs next to Murdoch. He is simply larger still: a globalist of all media.

The common trait in all great newspaper proprietors was that they divined a public mood, a vacuum where it was not apparent. No one but Murdoch, for example, understood that the British working class yearned to think of itself as anything but working class. It was genius of Ted Turner to create CNN. But it was up to Murdoch's particular talent to understand that there was an untapped seam of conservatism in the American couch potato.

Newspapers are unlikely to enjoy another golden age as they did in the first half of the 20th century. But they can do something to make themselves more user-friendly, to avoid repeating the news that everyone has heard already on radio and television or read on the Internet. The editors must ask themselves every day: What is compelling in tomorrow's newspaper?

The great publishers have always understood that they must produce organs that are compelling as well as excellent; that entertain as well as inform; and that reflect the frustrations of their readers, not of the newsmakers.

There is no level of creative endeavor that can be forgiven for dullness. And increasingly, newspapers are guilty of being just that: dull.

April 27, 2005

THE BIG NEWS: DOG BITES ITSELF

There is something wrong when the big story in the media is the media (dog bites itself). But that is the way it is in Washington at present.

Front and center is *Newsweek* magazine. It is taking a whipping from the right wing and the White House for a small item that said the Qu'ran, Islam's holy book, was washed down a toilet at the U.S. detention center at Guantanamo Bay. This allegation has been made before in court papers and published in newspapers, but the *Newsweek* Periscope piece lit a fuse that set off rioting and loss of life in Afghanistan and Pakistan.

Newsweek has reacted handsomely by apologizing and casting doubt on the veracity of its source. President Bush's mouthpiece, Scott McClellan, implied, when he joined the attack on the weekly magazine, that it should do more to put things right.

What can it do? It cannot go into the Muslim world and do the job that the U.S. information organizations have failed to do. It cannot go to Guantanamo Bay to find out exactly what is happening with prisoners. The administration has denied the allegation, but has not offered any corroboration of its own denial. It has not offered to let teams of reporters interview the prisoners, interrogate the interrogators. And it is not reassuring to think that the world must accept the word of the Pentagon on its secret treatment of prisoners.

The White House could reassure the Muslim world, but it will not do so unless it opens up its detention facilities to independent observers. In this case, it should open them up to the editors of *Newsweek*.

There would have been no credence given in the Muslim world, or anywhere else, to *Newsweek's* slight report if it had not been for many allegations of mistreatment of prisoners and if the excesses of Abu Ghraib had not been caught on film. If you have seen the photographs of Abu Ghraib, it is not hard to believe that there were equal excesses in Guantanamo Bay. The U.S. government would have been saved considerable embarrassment and advanced its cause around the world if it had not chosen to act by stealth and in secret.

Then we come to what prima facie looks like the muzzling of the Public Broadcasting System by Kenneth Tomlinson, chairman of the Corporation for Public Broadcasting. Described by *The New York Times* as a friend of presidential counselor Karl Rove, Tomlinson, who once edited the conservative *Reader's Digest*, is leveraging program content in the Public Broadcasting System to eliminate what he perceives as liberal bias. Unfortunately, he chose to explain himself on the Fox News network's "O'Reilly Factor" rather than on a PBS talk show.

Under Tomlinson two new programs have appeared on the regular PBS schedule which are unashamedly right wing. One is "Tucker Carlson: Unfiltered" and the other is "The Wall Street Journal Report." Carlson is a professional broadcaster with an interesting mind and a stimulating view of the world. No problem there. But "The Wall Street Journal Report," hosted by Paul Gigot, is bad, boring television. As a TV program it is a shocker—left wing, right wing or in between.

What is more shocking is that CPB is paying $5 million to *The Wall Street Journal* for this nonsense; for this bunch of editorial writers to sit around scratching each others' biases. It is a little like the White House: it is hermetically sealed against other opinions. These guys all work for Gigot, writing editorials. So the program is an infomercial for a set of well-known views.

Finally, Washington reporters have been running out to buy *Vanity Fair* magazine to read about Jeff Gannon, who covered the White House for an organization known as Talon News. It turns out that he had a checkered past, including operating a male escort service, and that Jeff Gannon was not his real name. Like other reporters who cover the White House, I met Gannon and found him likable. Democrats jumped on the Gannon affair as though it were sinister and suggested wrongdoing by the White House. They got this one wrong. There are many lost souls who drift into journalism's big tent—and so it should be.

Assiduous reporting by David Margolick and Richard Gooding turned up nothing new about Gannon. As is so often the case with magazine pieces, they simply assembled the known facts. And the principal fact is that Gannon is a conflicted man, not a right-wing conspirator.

Hopefully next week, the media can get back to reporting the news. It is really a simple undertaking. It is best explained by CBS's Dan Raviv: "I find out what is going on and I tell people."

May 18, 2005

MARIJUANA: THE FOLLY AND THE CRUELTY

It is not the Commerce Clause, it is the marijuana. Maybe the Supreme Court, when it asserted federal jurisdiction over the production and usage of medicinal marijuana in California, was concerned with protecting precedents regarding federal preemption. After all, for over 60 years, the court has shown a special tenderness toward the Commerce Clause at the price of states' rights.

But for the Bush administration, which was joyous about the ruling, it was all about marijuana. Particularly discouraging were the yelps of joy from the federal drug czar, John P. Walters, who belongs to that spectrum of the right that has a pathological paranoia about marijuana. To him, judging by his remarks, and to many in the administration, marijuana is more than a drug favored by young people: it is an incarnation of evil, the emblem of social disintegration and the mother-food of liberals.

To be honest, not all conservatives are as kooky about marijuana as Walters. But fear of the weed affects many of them. The poster boy for tolerance is none other than William F. Buckley Jr., who believes that enormous national resources are wasted in the fight against marijuana. He also believes that the arguments against it, advanced by conservatives, are spurious and out of date. Memorably, Buckley trounced the argument that marijuana is the gateway to serious drug-taking of heroin, cocaine and methamphetamine by saying this argument "is on the order of saying that every rapist began by masturbating."

Alas for many conservatives, Democratic and Republican, marijuana is not a mild drug that governments have failed totally to control, but is the ghost of the 1960s—of campus unrest, profane comics and free love. Psychologically for conservatives, marijuana is the unacceptable face of social degeneration and in its way more frightening than hard drugs.

So rigid is this antipathy that the White House drug czar is prepared to countenance the suffering of cancer patients, and others in extreme pain, rather than allow them the relief prescribed by their doctors. Gone is the nanny state, replaced by the prefect state, where politicians not only feel they know better than the judicial system, the democratically expressed will of the people and the medical profession.

After decades of a failed war on marijuana, Walters might be expected to be looking for another solution: for a truce and an accommodation. The war against marijuana, Buckley has calculated, costs $10 billion to $15 billion a year in direct expenditures.

But the larger issue of marijuana in society is not the issue of the day. The issue is simply that 11 states have democratically sanctioned the use of marijuana as a medicine, and the administration is jubilant at frustrating democracy and injuring the sick. One has to ask if a drug with the same effects had been produced by Merck, Pfizer or Abbott whether the administration would have had anything to say about it whatsoever. That most conservative of senators, Orrin Hatch, favors unregulated health remedies except, of course, the dreaded marijuana.

A ban on medicinal uses of marijuana, like so much else, will adversely affect the poor. They do not have the mobility to go to countries where marijuana is legal and live there for as long as they need the relief from nausea and pain.

Without having any brief for the larger issue of legalizing marijuana, one still has to note that its prevalence grows even as law enforcement continues to be diverted from serious crime. In Toronto recently, the Royal Canadian Mounted Police told me that they are fighting a hopeless battle against modern "grow houses." One officer told me the RCMP believes that there are 10,000 of these in Toronto alone, and thousands in every Canadian city.

How long, one wonders, can the fanatical obsession with marijuana persist? If the gateway argument is valid, then marijuana needs to be unbundled from hard drugs and classified in a category on its own. When absinthe was causing havoc in the French slums, the French did not ban all alcohol but substituted Pernod, which tasted and smelled similar to the toxic absinthe.

After so many years of the failed war on drugs, it is time that some administration had the moral courage to find out how to live legally with the mildest of these. As it is, we live illegally with all of them. And they are available even in the prisons, the most secure environment we have.

June 8, 2005

GOOD INTENTIONS AND BAD CONSEQUENCES

The name Gordon Brown is not well known in the United States. It will be.

Brown is Britain's chancellor of the exchequer, or finance minister, but his influence exceeds his office. He is the great second force in Prime Minister Tony Blair's ruling Labor Party and the next prime-minister-in waiting.

But Brown is not waiting. His views will dominate the G8 summit in his native Scotland next month, although Brown himself will not be on the stage. It is Brown who has forced Blair to put Africa front and center on the agenda. And it is Brown who keeps up a constant drumbeat for Blair to take a harder line with President Bush on global warming and aid to Africa.

Brown has been Blair's chief adversary within the Labor Party, and he has been the prime minister's necessary partner in three elections. A deal was cut between Blair and Brown: Blair would become prime minister if Brown was guaranteed the succession.

Now that Blair has said that he will leave during this Parliament, Brown has been able to push his agenda—particularly debt-forgiveness and increased foreign aid for Africa. For years, Brown has been agitating for the cause of Africa. Now his cause has become Blair's cause.

The importance of Brown to Blair has been that Brown represents the old left in Britain: the left of the trade unions, of the social safety nets, and of the welfare institutions. Although Brown has been an effective finance minister, he has not forgotten what the Labor Party once stood for—and when he becomes prime minister, life could become considerably more difficult for the White House.

Whereas Blair is modern politician—enchanted with business and the American model—Brown is much more committed to the socialist principles of his past. The Blair-Brown accommodation has been turbulent and effective, but Brown's supporters are waiting for their time to come. They despise Blair as an opportunist and a toady, and they wish him gone.

The national enthusiasm for Blair has waned—not enough to really favor the conservatives, but certainly enough that people are ready for a change. Ergo, Brown's peculiar strength at this time, and his ability to shape the British positions on Africa and global warming.

Though Brown is a tough politician, he has some of the naivety of an idealist. He has not really come to terms with the difficulty of delivering aid in Africa and reversing its descent into chaos. A couple of years ago Brown was in the United States, seeking to create a Marshall Plan for Africa. Brushing off questions from reporters about how it could be implemented, he said aid would be given to the right people. But in Africa, the right people become the wrong people as quickly as a summer storm in the Serengeti.

Africa's problem is that it has never developed—in any of its countries—a sense of civic responsibility. African leaders are uniquely without a highly developed sense of cause and effect.

Back when the breakaway colony of Rhodesia was under sanctions, the British government airlifted fuel into neighboring Zambia because the railroad ran through Rhodesia. But rather than Zambia—a front-line state in that struggle—making good use of the precious gasoline and diesel, they happily sold it across the Zambezi River to their enemies in white-ruled Rhodesia.

Now there is the Malawi scandal. Pathetically poor Malawi—it is among the 10 poorest countries in the world—is a favorite for British aid. But a portion of that aid has been used for quite the wrong purpose. The Malawi government did some Enron-style bookkeeping and spent the money buying tear gas, which it is apparently resold to its neighbor Zimbabwe, the former Rhodesia, where the government of Robert Mugabe has used it to devastating effect to clear his shanty towns. Aid groups and civil rights monitors say the tear gas has been responsible for deaths as well as the total devastation of the tens of thousands of people evicted from their shanties.

Throughout the world, people of goodwill would rally to Brown's side in his noble fight for Africa if there was a way to bring about a palpable improvement in the lives of the tens of millions of destitute Africans. Instead, the history of the last half-century in Africa is that aid is either misused or stolen at the source. I asked Brown about this when he was in Washington, but he would not discuss it. True to his British liberal traditions, he still believes that the fault is with the West and with the former colonial rulers of Africa.

Africans, in every country south of the Sahara, also love to blame their troubles on the colonial period. Quite possibly, they are correct, but not in the way that they and Brown believe. The evils that still stalk Africa come not from the colonial example, but from the implementation of chosen Western philosophies. Most African leaders are more than a little devoted to command economies and socialist and communist principles. This suits them well: It concentrates power in the hands of the dictator.

African leaders have interpreted capitalism as corruption and entrepreneurialism as, well, selling gasoline to your enemy and tear gas to a repressive dictator.

Maybe Brown will find time to spend a few months on the ground in Africa before he starts handing over sacks of money.

June 15, 2005

FIXING PBS: BE CAREFUL OF WHAT YOU WISH

Every 10 years, conservatives and their Republican allies launch a major assault on public broadcasting. So far, National Public Radio (NPR) and the Public Broadcasting System (PBS) have beaten back the attacks. But this year the enemies of public broadcasting seem to be more determined and more vindictive than ever.

The House of Representatives has voted to cut $100 million out of public broadcasting's measly budget of less than $400 million. As it happens, this is also less than half of what the United States spends on propaganda broadcasting in Europe, Latin America and the Middle East. No matter. The excuse offered up for the cut is that it will help reduce federal expenditures.

While Congress is seeking to cut the funds, PBS's federal paymaster, Kenneth Tomlinson, president of the Corporation for Public Broadcasting, is seeking to control the content of public radio and television. Here the allegation is that they are too liberal and lack conservative input. It takes a special cast of mind to think that radio in America does not adequately represent the right wing. Ditto television.

The public is in another place, as reflected both in the viewership of PBS and the large and growing audience of NPR. Clearly the public is not to be consulted in the hobbling of public broadcasting.

For all of the complaints, public broadcasting in the United States is held together by the most fragile arrangement. It breaks down to about 15 percent of government money and the rest coming from members, business, foundations and local government. By comparison, the giant British Broadcasting Corporation levies a direct tax—in the form of a license fee—on viewers and listeners that brings it a whopping $5 billion a year. No wonder they employ 5,000 journalists—which enables BBC to establish a gold standard for global reporting.

Public broadcasting is not a healthy institution. It is poorly managed, lacks transparency; and the stations are impenetrable fiefdoms, self-satisfied and self-deceived. Yet they are the flawed jewels in the tarnished crown of American broadcasting.

Rather than examining the whole structure of public broadcasting, its critics are out to weaken and destroy it. They have decided that the patient needs the leeches before the disease has been diagnosed.

The critics' course is a dangerous one. If they succeed in de-funding public broadcasting, it will drift off like an untethered balloon, answerable to no one—an accusation that has been leveled at the BBC for 50 years. If you think that public broadcasting is too liberal now, imagine what it would be if its tether were cut.

My prescription is that PBS should become a membership organization subject to the will of its contributors, who could vote in and out programming and managements as they liked. I believe it should receive some public money for infrastructure and none for programming.

Subsidies to news organizations have always been a ticklish matter, but not beyond intelligent resolution. The British government, for nearly 100 years, subsidized the Reuters news agency, and all other British news undertakings, with a device known as the Commonwealth Cable Rate. This was as elegant a subsidy of news as ever devised. All news organizations benefited from cheap cable transmission, while the government could not be accused of influencing editorial content. Even American publishers and news agencies found ways to avail themselves of the Commonwealth Cable Rate by routing their transmissions through outposts of the British Empire. Time magazine correspondents, for example, filed their stories through Montreal, while United Press used a subsidiary called British United Press.

If you want to see where public broadcasting might go without any government funding, tune into Pacifica Radio: it is the closest thing to socialist broadcasting in the United States. While PBS has carried such conservative voices as William F. Buckley and John McLaughlin, Pacifica is untrammeled by conservative thought.

Those who would de-fund public broadcasting might end up with an alternative they find even more disagreeable. Be careful what you wish for.

June 22, 2005

APOLOGIZE, DAMN YOU, APOLOGIZE!

Apology is in the wind. Everyone is apologizing. And those who are not apologizing are demanding that others apologize.

Apologies run from governments, apologizing for historical injustices, to individuals—particularly politicians—apologizing for what they have said. Even magazines and newspapers are apologizing.

Therefore, as I can avoid it no longer, I must apologize for all the horrid things I have said in recent times. To start, I would like to apologize effusively to Howard Dean for suggesting that he was a loose cannon, loud and embarrassing. After reviewing the evidence, I have concluded that Dean is a gentle soul; a quiet, contemplative man—tranquil in the extreme.

Likewise, after viewing hours of tapes, I have concluded that I was in error in writing about Bill O'Reilly as a rude, ignorant zealot who performs without any regard to the norms of journalism. Now I realize that O'Reilly is a sensitive, erudite and compassionate interlocutor; a man of deep understanding and subtle nuance.

In the same vein, I have misrepresented Tom DeLay. Whereas I have accused him of being a bigot, a perverter of the course of justice and a power-hungry, money-grubbing lobbyist-indulging demagogue, after careful consideration, I see that he is a thoughtful legislator, committed to seeing both sides of every issue. Further, rather than gerrymandering the electoral districts in Texas to the benefit of his party, I now realize that this selfless public servant was only perfecting democracy.

Nancy Pelosi has been hard used by me. I am ashamed that I have said she has no ideas and a delivery that would not distinguish her at a parent-teacher meeting. Through meditation, I have come to realize that Pelosi is an inspired leader with great vision and a speaking style so deft that she could convert a Chamber of Commerce audience to socialism. What a charmer!

Alan Greenspan has unfairly received the sharp end of my pencil. Can you believe that I have said that he is a study in obfuscation, a confused old man who gets his jollies from impenetrable speeches about the economy—speeches that leave the impression that he does not even read The Wall Street Journal? Well, after taking a speed-reading course in economics, I now realize that he is a towering intellect in the field; the greatest central banker who has ever lived; and that if you are attuned, he speaks of economics with clarity and enlightenment. Not only that, as he plays tennis, he clearly is still in his prime and a national treasure.

Speaking of clarity, the Supreme Court has been unfairly tongue-lashed by myself. On re-reading my notes, I find that Clarence Thomas is a strict constructionist, not a dummy operated by ventriloquist Antonin Scalia. My notes clearly reveal that he is a justice of profound depth, few but exquisite words, and his own man. It was without charity or decency that I subscribed to the view that the only construction he understood was payday.

I am ashamed that I have misunderstood Karl Rove and characterized him as a strategic planner of class warfare, bent on demonizing liberals and advancing the agenda of television preachers. Nothing could be further from the truth, I now understand. Rove is revealed to me, after contemplation, as a steadying hand: the self-effacing architect of a kinder, gentler America. Rove reads many books, which reveal that he is not the Rasputin of the right but a wise political philosopher who puts national unity above all else.

When it comes to Grover Norquist, the man is inspired. Who else without office could reveal and entirely new concept for the nation: governance without taxation? I have unfairly accused him of taking corporate dollars and playing to the greed of the moguls. No, no. After counseling, I see plainly that a great nation in debt is a great nation triumphant. It is abysmally low of me to suggest that the United States is becoming a wholly owned subsidiary of Asian financiers because of Norquist's philosophy. It is brilliant that we can leverage the world's lenders to keep ourselves afloat. Right on, Grover!

Ann Coulter is a woman wronged by myself. Rather than being insanely obsessed with liberals, pathologically indignant over former President Clinton, and
a relentless self-promoter, Coulter, I find, is sensitive, feminine, concerned and
anxious to understand other points of view. She is a woman of towering intellectual ability, without meanness or ego. And she does not fire relentless accusations
at those on the left. No, gentle persuasion is her forte.

To all these, I offer the most profound apology for my own snap judgments, preparedness to take them out of context and general awfulness. So sorry.

Next week: Berlusconi apologizes to Chirac for Caesar's invasion of Gaul;
Scandinavians apologize to Britons for the Vikings; and Tony Blair writes an abject letter to the Pope, denouncing Henry VIII. Also: Pfizer apologizes to Elizabeth Dole for Viagra.

June 29, 2005

A LETTER TO LONDON, A GRIEVING FRIEND

Dear London,

A tear rolls down the cheek of the world today. Not you, not you—the mother
city of so much compassion and generosity, of history and aspiration, of invention,
creativity and hospitality.

This act joins those other indecencies of history that have blighted just a few
pages of your glorious manuscript: the Plague, the Great Fire, and the Blitz. Damn
those who would abuse your open heart and arms.

What do the perpetrators—the real infidels—know of your Roman past, your
Norman Conquest, and your Saxon underpinnings? What do they know of 2,000
years of creativity, courage, invention and endless gifts to all the peoples of the
world? Gifts of democracy, law, literature, medicine, navigation, and scholarship.

Do they know you, spread as you are along the River Thames? Have they followed the river from Greenwich to Richmond and seen the finest and worst of
man's works arrayed along this waterway? At Greenwich, whose time they keep,
great voyages of exploration began. West of Greenwich, when they enter the
pool of London, do they know that they are passing through the docks that
brought trade and prosperity to much of the world? Do they shudder at the
Tower of London and the dark deeds that were committed there? Do they marvel at the new London of concert halls and galleries and a giant Ferris wheel?
Do they glance to the right to see Christopher Wren's masterpiece, St. Paul's
Cathedral, paying, as it does, as much homage to the architecture of Islam as to
the traditions of Europe?

Clearly, their breath did not catch when they surveyed the Houses of Parliament—if not the cradle of democracy, certainly its stroller. Maybe they would
glance towards Buckingham Palace and marvel at a city so subtle that it can revere a monarch and abide by the rule of the people.

Did they wonder at the beauty of Kew Gardens, where desert flowers bloom in a northern climate? Did they wonder about the kings and princes who built their palaces along the Thames and rowed up and down in it their grand barges?

Lessons here, maybe, for the absolute monarchs who sit on top of the peoples of Arabia.

What do the terrorists see so differently that they would wish harm on a city that has given birth to much that is best in the world? How different from the reaction of Americans, who revolted against the rule of a British monarch but now hold London dearer than any other foreign city.

Oh, London, Napoleon failed, the Kaiser failed, Hitler failed. And this barbarity will fail.

Great city, the world hurts with you—and is permanently glad that you are there.

Sincerely,
Your American Cousins

July 8, 2005

THE ENEMY WITHIN: EUROPE'S PARTICULAR AGONY

The espionage writer John le Carre nailed it. In his novel "A Perfect Spy," the protagonist explained why he chose to betray Britain to the Soviet Union. He explained the joy of "being well run" and the intoxication that comes with a sense of higher purpose.

Britain's security forces might want to ask Le Carre to explain the phenomenon, in trying to understand why young British Muslims are prepared to give their own lives and inflict suffering on their fellow citizens. The stimuli at work here are alien to Westerners. Incomprehensible.

In Britain, and across the globe, a growing number of young Muslims intoxicated—indeed possessed—by religious fanaticism are prepared to do the unspeakable in the name of Allah. The London bombings, and other acts of terrorism across Europe, have not been perpetrated by the first generation of immigrants from Muslim countries, but by the second and third generations—young people who know nothing of the deplorable conditions in the lands from which their parents and grandparents migrated.

Instead, they know everything about the real and imagined hurts perpetrated on Islam, even while they grow up in Western Europe, succored from cradle to grave by generous welfare systems.

Apologists in Britain—many of them in the Muslim community—are laying the blame on the Arab-Israeli conflict, the war in Iraq and, yes, British society. Britain's Muslims are not bondsmen, transported in chains. They did not arrive in the British isles for any purpose except betterment.

The first generation understood this. But subsequent generations are consumed with a vile ingratitude. They seek to exploit the liberal nature of Europe to redress grievances, which they have not suffered and have only heard of through the distortions of clerics.

Disaffected Muslims in Europe have not sought to return to their ancestral lands, but rather to take up arms against their hosts—a violation of the Muslim tradition of hospitality.

The only justification that you hear from Muslims in Europe for special entitlement is summed up in a sign that often appears in demonstrations there blaming colonialism. This sign reads: "We are here because you were there." It is catchy, but history cannot be redressed. And if it could be, the whole world would be in conflagration over ancient insults.

Europeans will blame themselves more than necessary for their failure to force assimilation—if that can be done—on their immigrant population. If there is fault at all, it is the generous way that Europe allowed its former colonial subjects to move freely to the homeland.

For Britain, the problem was the idealism that swept the country after World War II, coupled with an unreasonable belief in assimilation. The second Churchill government was particularly blind to this gathering storm.

There were other villains, too. British businesses welcomed a laboring class that would do very low-end work, and the middle classes appreciated the proliferation of shops that opened on Sunday and a diversity of new restaurants. Mosques were celebrated along with Pakistani and Indian restaurants. Diversity was going to be neat.

The concerns at that time had to do with social services and education. The first hostility to immigrants was not to those from the Subcontinent and Arabia but to those from the Caribbean, who were accused of bringing with them drugs and crime and taxing the social services. "Asians fit in," people said. "They work hard and keep to themselves." Now it appears that they have indeed kept to themselves and the results have been a beachhead for militant Islam.

Romanticism has always attracted the young. But the romanticism that now spreads throughout Islamic Europe, and which has manifested itself with such terrible horror in London, is not the romanticism of past generations of Utopians. It is the romanticism of a death cult. Its antecedents are not Saladin and Sulaiman the Magnificent but Syria's Assassins and India's Thuggees.

Behind this evil are the calculating men who choose vengeance over progress, who seek for societies not what Churchill called the "sunlit uplands" but an insane cycle of death, violating all known decency and, especially, the tenets of Islam that cherish hospitality and sanctuary.

June 13, 2005

WHERE ARE YOU QUINTUS FABIUS MAXIMUS?

Where is Quintus Fabius Maximus when the Democrats and their allies on the left need him? Fabius was, of course, the Roman general who contributed to the defeat of Hannibal with hit-and-run tactics. Fabius never engaged in a battle he was not sure he could win and left Hannibal, one of the greatest military leaders of all time, confused and impotent.

Since ancient Rome, Fabian tactics have been hugely effective in politics. Without them, there would probably have been no British Labor Party, hence no Tony Blair and no staunch ally.

The British Fabians were a group of left-wing public intellectuals and writers that included Sidney and Beatrice Webb and George Bernard Shaw. They emulated in politics the tactics of the Roman general. Their philosophy was to choose their targets, hit hard and fade away. They also united disparate, late-19th century socialist and left-wing groups into an organization that was to become the Labor Party.

While the British Fabians were pacifistic, they admired the strategies that enabled Fabius to play a critical part in defeating Hannibal. It can all be summed up this way: Pick your fights carefully.

Alas for the Democrats, they have no sense of this nor the discipline that it requires. Particularly, the friends of the Democrats in the women's movement and other foes of President Bush's judicial nominees don't get it.

In Judge John Roberts, Bush has picked as his first nominee to the Supreme Court someone who is prima facie confirmable. But rather than the Democrats and their allies sounding statesmanlike and contemplative, these worthies launched an erratic attack on an impregnable fortress. They are playing the president's game.

The next nominee Bush offers is almost certain to be less acceptable to the defenders of abortion rights. But by then, half of them would have destroyed themselves. Fabius would have been appalled. His central thesis was: Do not enter into a fight that you cannot win; keep your opponents off balance.

Yet various Democratic senators, including Chuck Schumer of New York, Dick Durbin of Illinois, and Ted Kennedy of Massachusetts, are hard at it, laying a futile siege. Likewise, and even more egregiously, the pro-choice groups are attacking blindly. You begin to wonder whether they enjoy the battle more than they savor the victory.

A loyal opposition gains strength and credibility by sometimes lying low. Fabius knew that nothing intimidated the Carthaginians more than his orchestrated lulls in the fighting. It is a strategy that has worked for many military commanders and politicians since the days of Fabius. The most powerful senators in any debate are those who do not declare their positions until late in the battle.

The computer on which I write this is jammed with hysterical e-mails from Democrats raging against Roberts. They have not done their due diligence. They have revealed their hands before the White House has finished dealing the cards. All we know about Roberts is that for a great, legal intellect—which is what the White House says he is—he has been very repressed. Great intellects generally do not do repression very well. Yet, Roberts looks like a solid citizen even if he has not engaged in the maelstrom of ideas.

Clearly, the White House has chosen Roberts with great care. They have found a man who has climbed the legal ladder with little controversy, with few enemies and, apparently, without scandal. They have found confirmable Wonder Bread.

Instead of assessing the situation, a horde of liberal activists has been on the Internet, radio and television attacking Roberts, implying that he is a monster, a stalking horse for the religious right, and a danger to the republic. Do these people talk to each other? Do they ever sit down and have strategy sessions? It seems not.

Fabius picked his targets. The early British Fabians picked their targets. Alas, the irregular forces of the American left fling themselves into battle without strategy or hope of victory.

The issue of Supreme Court justices is many times more important to the future of the country than whether Karl Rove leaked a name to reporters. Nonetheless, the decibel level does not change, but after a while, the robust tones will change into a whine.

When the opposition to Roberts has spent itself, Bush will have a free hand to trot out a real ideological monster for his second shot at the Supreme Court. And no one will be listening.

June 20, 2005

THE OIL PREDICAMENT: SAY IT IS NOT SO

As agriculture in the United States and Europe matured, the need for fertilizer grew exponentially. Guano, or sea bird droppings, was the answer. There were small guano sites in the Carolinas and other Southern states. But the mother lode was concentrated on the islands off the Peruvian coast, where light rainfall and thousands of years of sea bird droppings made for the best fertilizer.

So it was that guano became a world commodity in the 19th century, and hundreds of thousands of tons were stripped from the Peruvian islands. Then it ran out. Luckily for farming, synthetic fertilizers were developed toward the end of the islands' supply of guano.

At one time, North Sea cod was so plentiful that it was said that fishermen had walked on the shoals. Indeed, it was so plentiful that it was ground up as a fertilizer and spread on fields. Today cod supplies are endangered and strict fishing limits have to be enforced.

Likewise, the American plains were once home to millions of buffalo. No need to ask about the buffalo herds today.

The facts about resource depletion are incontrovertible, and yet there are those who are in deep denial about the depletion of the world's oil resources. In fact, it has become a tenet of some conservative thinking that global oil supplies are inexhaustible and not subject to the depletion seen in other natural resources, including copper, gold and silver. It is a heresy in some quarters to suggest that the irrefutable law of depletion applies to oil.

Vice President Cheney has scoffed at the idea. Influential conservative writers, like Irwin Stelzer of the London *Sunday Times* and Tony Blankley of *The Washington Times*, frequently urge people to purchase large, fuel-inefficient SUVs. It is as though the letters S-U-V have been inserted into the Second Amendment of the U.S. Constitution. Maybe the preamble as well. Some conservatives apparently read the latter as "the pursuit of happiness in a sport utility vehicle."

As an energy supply-sider for the last 35 years, it saddens me to see the blind rejection of the obvious, when the intimations of oil peaking are everywhere. It also saddens me because for much of the past 35 years, conservatives have led the intelligent approach to energy supply. But when they substitute ideology for fact, one must part ways with them.

The world is consuming 83 million barrels of oil a day and depletion is everywhere at hand: in the contiguous 48 states, on the North Slope of Alaska, in the North Sea and elsewhere. The world is pumping as much oil as it can to keep up with current demand, which is expected to rise by 3 million barrels a day in a few years, as China and India increase their usage.

Worse. The great treasure trove of oil, Saudi Arabia, may not be in as good shape as we have believed. Matthew R. Simmons, author of "Twilight in the Desert: The Coming Saudi Oil Shock and the World Economy," claims that Saudi Arabia's two most productive fields are in decline and that the country is unable to pump much more oil than at present. Simmons is not a flighty environmentalist. He is a smart, tough Texas oilman who analyzes oil production data from thousands of technical reports.

Those who believe there is no oil problem tend also to be those who believe in market signals, except for this one signal they do not want to see: that $60-a-barrel oil is the market crying out for supply that cannot be met.

Amazingly, the energy bill that has just cleared Congress does nothing about fuel economy standards. And it does nothing about them at a time when there are options offered to automobile manufacturers through hybrid technology. Go figure—and keep a bicycle handy.

August 3, 2005

GIVE THEM DIGNITY, LEAVEN THE PITY

The hurricane that battered the Gulf Coast, and sent New Orleans to a watery grave, also has blown away some cherished illusions about ourselves. It is as though a sodden carpet has been lifted to reveal the social debris of a great, self-confidant nation.

One terrible storm has reintroduced America to its underclass, to the hapless many who live on the fringes. Unseen America is suddenly visible and disturbing. Disturbing not because they are seeking refuge from the storm, but because of the refuge they have always sought on the fringes of society.

Doctors treating hurricane victims have been as appalled by the preexisting conditions in many of the hapless as they have been by their hurricane-related injuries. Uninsured, uncounted and little-regarded, the people of the New Orleans ghettos, the Mississippi bayous, and other places, are reproving in their numbers and their plight.

We knew that the people of Alabama, Louisiana and Mississippi were among the poorest in the nation. And we let it go at that. Now, they are wards of the United States, in the full glare of our consciousness. No longer can we be incurious about their limitations and what have been their survival mechanisms.

Their limitations will become more and more apparent, and the nation has to reinvent their survival mechanisms. We must think anew about social responsibility and devise mechanisms to give the evacuees dignity.

Charity alone becomes a disservice. Charity alone leaves a class of victims whose only tenable asset is their victimhood. I have been to refugee camps all over the world and have seen the phenomenon of victimhood being translated into a belligerent sense of entitlement.

The antidote to victimhood is dignity. Dignity comes first with employment, shelter and then, in time, with hope and ambition.

Whether or not New Orleans is rebuilt, the dispossessed should be offered work immediately in creating new housing and rebuilding the Gulf Coast. This enormous army of the unemployed may not be the workforce with the highest skill levels, but it is the force that needs to work. It behooves us collectively to devise strategies that will stabilize the evacuees and set them on a path to a future at least as appealing as the past that has been taken from them.

The Europeans might describe this arrangement as a social contract. It will need another name in the United States. But if it is not done, defeat and degeneration among the hundreds of thousands of evacuees will set in.

Before huge contracts are let to the likes of Kellogg, Brown & Root, they need to be structured so that they provide the earliest employment to the maximum number of able-bodied hurricane victims. In short, the model of FDR's Works Progress Administration is a good one. The victims must be offered adventure over pity and practicality over ideology.

Some will go to jobs elsewhere, their families will follow. Probably, the majority of the underclass will remain suspended in time and place: a new generation of welfare recipients with an evolving structure of entitlements.

If we do not move with alacrity, compassion and realism, an entirely new class of American will emerge: angry, damaged, demanding and sullen.

September 7, 2005

NO NEWS PLEASE, WE'RE GOVERNING

Let us now do something unlikely: praise the media.

When big news happens, it is awesome how the press swings into action. It does catastrophe, riot and war superbly. Exhibit I and II are Hurricanes Katrina and Rita, and Exhibit III and IV are the wars in Afghanistan and Iraq.

I hear carping, but I see real courage, selflessness, logistical skill and supreme professionalism.

Unfortunately, the Bush administration and others go through periods where they are determined to get along without the benefit of the most reliable intelligence source we have: the media.

Former Federal Emergency Management Agency director Michael Brown appeared to have gone for 28 hours without knowing what was going on during Katrina, deprived of information available to every couch potato in the country. The one thing broadcast and print journalists are good at is getting somewhere fast and showing and telling us what they find. No bureaucracy, intelligence network or military operation comes close. In crisis, the press is superb at what it does.

President Bush has told us that he does not watch television or read the newspapers. Instead, he says he relies on his staff for "unfiltered" information.

Yet Newsweek reported that when the magnitude of Katrina became apparent, his immediate staff caucused to see who would break the bad news to the president. They feared being castigated by Bush. According to *Newsweek*, Bush turns on people who bring him bad news and snarls at them. Hence not only does Bush operate in a bubble, as all presidents do, but in one that is almost hermetically sealed from reality.

In most White Houses, media is a dirty word. And in this one, it is a filthy one.

The White House isolation is encouraged by the small but vociferous commentators on the right: commentators who, one assumes, meet with approval in the White House, and therefore are listened to and read. If you devoutly wish the war in Iraq to go well, you will be encouraged by The *Weekly Standard's* Bill Kristol, who said on Fox News that "we have turned the corner," or *Roll Call's* Morton Kondrake, who just told an audience in Phoenix that things are going better in Iraq than the press allows. He said he got his information from a congressman who visited Iraq and was persuaded by Iraqis who waved at his helicopter.

That may be the kind of nonsense that lifts hearts in the White House, but to believe that the world's media covering Iraq, for proprietors of every persuasion, are inventing carnage defies gravity.

The White House has come to rest in a dangerous place, where it believes that bad news is political; that it is constructed by the messenger to deceive and discomfort; that it is, from the start, invalid.

This requires a massive political bias itself. To view people clinging to rooftops, as New Orleans was swamped, or to see the chaos after a car bomb in Baghdad, and to find political intent in irrefutable truth is scary.

The coverage of the hurricanes and the ongoing attempt to tell the story of the wars is itself a noble tale. Any commendation of the broadcast and print media should include a salute to the unsung camera crews, drivers and translators who also bear the battle.

The media is riddled with folly and vanity, but it lifts itself above its own foibles when the story calls.

September 28, 2005

Index

3M Company, 143

Abraham, Spencer, 146, 239
Abu Ghraib, 267
accountability (lack of), 159–61
Adenauer, Konrad, 76, 252
administration of George W. Bush: culture
  of, 128; disastrous environment policy
  of, 11; efficacy of its policies, 174;
  environmentalism and, 127–29, 162;
  first 100 days of, 10–12; foreign policy
  woes of (2001), 2–4; imperialism and,
  106–07; introspective memo of, 174;
  Iraq, April of 2004 and, 208–10; Iraq,
  erroneous assumptions of, 156–57; Iraq
  quandary and, 174; Iraqi oil and, 102;
  Kashmir crisis and, 68; Kyoto protocol
  and, 10–11; manners of, 193; the media
  and, 281; moral superiority and,
  156–57; partisan politics and, 34–36;
  peacekeeping and, 53–54; philosophy
  toward business, 63; prisoner abuse and
  torture, 217; problems of (2003),
  152–53; relationship with big business,
  60; relationship with the Senate, 128;
  rigidity of, 161–62; secrecy of, 89–90;
  small business and, 60–61; its stance on
  arsenic, 11, 129; word ploy of, 116
Afghanistan: Americans concerned for,
  174; balkanization of, 102; heroin
  production, 255; position of U.S.
  military in (2003), 163

Africa: attributes of the British Empire in,
  210–11; brutality and insanity in,
  207–08, 269–70; democracy and, 197;
  diversity of, 149; George W. Bush's
  visit to (2003), 148–50; Gordon
  Brown's concern for, 269–70; women
  as the salvation of, 83–84
ageism and the media, 51–52
aging: Florida-style, 112–14; money and,
  113–14; realization of, 76–77, 113;
  retirement, 251–52
Ahern, Irish Prime Minister Bertie visit
  with George W. Bush, 47–49, 123–24
AIDS, 83, 84, 149, 264
Aiken, Senator George, 30
Air America Radio, 200, 201
Aircraft Owners and Pilots Association,
  125
Airline Pilots Association, 125
Al Jazeera, 261
Algeria, 92
Allen, Mike on John Kerry, 207
Al-Qaeda, 103, 104, 204
alternative energy concept, 214–15
America, in praise of, 259–60
American conservative movement:
  commercial radio and, 200;
  disappointment in George W. Bush,
  163–64; elements of, 163; Howard
  Dean and, 164; invention of the
  neoconservatives, 216; its hostility
  toward France, 120–21;